LBJ
AND THE
KENNEDY
KILLING

BY ASSASSINATION
EYEWITNESS

James T. Tague

LBJ and the Kennedy Killing – By Assassination Eyewitness
Copyright © 2013 James T. Tague. All Rights Reserved.

Published by:
Trine Day LLC
PO Box 577
Walterville, OR 97489
1-800-556-2012
www.TrineDay.com
publisher@TrineDay.net

Library of Congress Control Number: 2013949711

Tague, James T.
LBJ and the Kennedy Killing–1st ed.
p. cm.
Includes index and references.
Epud (ISBN-13) 978-1-937584-75-7
Mobi (ISBN-13) 978-1-937584-76-4
Print (ISBN-13) 978-1-937584-74-0
1. Kennedy, John F. -- (John Fitzgerald), -- 1917-1963 -- Assassination. 2. Tague, James T. 3. United States. -- Warren Commission. -- Report of the President's Commission on the Assassination of President John F. Kennedy 4. Johnson, Lyndon B. -- (Lyndon Baines), -- 1908-1973. I. Tague, James T. II. Title

First Edition
10 9 8 7 6 5 4 3 2 1

Printed in the USA
Distribution to the Trade by:
Independent Publishers Group (IPG)
814 North Franklin Street
Chicago, Illinois 60610
312.337.0747
www.ipgbook.com

TABLE OF CONTENTS

INTRODUCTION

It has been nearly 50 years since I braked to a halt because of the traffic that was stopped in my lane as I was about to enter Dealey Plaza that day in November 1963. My car was not quite out from under the Triple Underpass, I sat there for a moment wondering why traffic was stopped, and then got out of my car and walked the three or four short steps into the openness of Dealey Plaza to see why traffic had stopped, when I noticed the President's limousine up by the School Book Depository. I then heard the pop of a firecracker.

As I stood there thinking what kind of an idiot would be throwing firecrackers with the President passing by, there was the crack-crack of two high powered rifle shots and I felt something sting me in the face. I did not realize it in that instant, but the sting in the face was caused by debris flying up from a bullet hitting the curb of the street in front of me. That bullet was from a missed shot intended for President John F. Kennedy. It was the start of making my life very interesting.

Over half of all Americans living today had not yet been born in 1963; a boy or girl who was 15 years old when Kennedy was killed is now 65 years old. To bring those of you who are under 65 up to date, I must start with that day, November 22, 1963.

I must tell you that on November 22, 1963, I was a very naïve "country boy" fresh off the farm and fresh out of the Air Force. I was just starting to learn about the big city and getting some "street smarts." I did not know it at the time, but being a naïve country boy was a blessing in disguise.

I have written this book so present and future researchers and historians may understand what I witnessed, and to tell what I have learned over the past 50 years to be the simple truth of what really happened regarding the assassination of President John F. Kennedy.

I am sure I have made an error or two, like a misspelled name or be off a day or two on something. But you must understand I am not a writer, and I will tell you a little secret, when you are writing about something you know – something true – the words come easy, they flow and you do not have to stop and think up something to say. The facts written in this book are waiting for other researchers and historians to expand on and add their own future discoveries.

I hope every word I have written in this book is put under a microscope and each word, each fact, tested for its accuracy. By putting every word, every fact, under a microscope you will have answered every major question hanging around about the Kennedy assassination and by doing this, you will have learned the truth, just as I did, about what really happened. Most important, you will be able to build on these facts and be able to understand how our Nation has been fooled.

Being slightly injured during the shooting that day in Dealey Plaza, and by speaking up – today it is called being a whistle blower – when the Warren Commission was about to tell America a big lie. And by living in and around Dallas for the last 50 years, enjoying a good reputation for honesty and for telling it like it is, has resulted in people with secrets about the Kennedy assassination coming to me and confiding in me. Interesting details and facts have fallen into my lap without my having to go look for them.

Coincidence after coincidence has been part of my life. As an example, when I bought my east Texas retirement acres in 2005, I soon found out that a man many claim is Kennedy's real assassin, Malcolm Wallace, had been killed three-quarters of a mile down the road. Also I had the good fortune of having the granddaddy of all researchers, Harold Weisberg, to be a close friend and mentor for over 35 years until his death in 2002.

The basic facts of this book are not coming from what someone else has written in the over 2,000 books published about the Kennedy assassination, though I must admit I have read some biographies and history books for background information. And thanks to my wife, I have wound up with a huge library full of assassination books that have been amassed over the years. I do not read these books, I have maybe scanned a chapter or two but I have not read entire books. I am proud of the fact that I have not read these books, the reason being that I knew in the back of my mind that I would write this book some day and I did not want my mind to be overly influenced by another's thoughts.

In writing this book I have relied mostly on face-to-face conversations and the other (nearly 600) witnesses' Warren Commission testimonies contained in the complete 26-volume Warren Commission set. The 26-volume set is not to be confused with the Warren Commission's one volume report. The one volume Warren Report has many problems in its conclusions.

More than once during the first 25 years after the assassination of President Kennedy, Lyndon Johnson's name has popped up as being behind the assassination. I could not and would not accept that accusation; President Johnson was a fellow Texan and I was proud of Lyndon Johnson for being a fellow Texan and serving as President. I found it impossible to accept as fact that a man who had attained the Presidency of the United States could be a conspirator to murder. Then over a 25-year period starting in 1988, items I could not dismiss came to my attention. Even my childhood hero, FBI director J. Edgar Hoover was not the person I thought he was.

As I added it up and put the bits and pieces together, I made a startling discovery. I found that when Lyndon Baines Johnson was sworn in as President – the very same afternoon that President John F. Kennedy was killed on a Dallas street on November 22, 1963 – two of the most powerful men in the world, Lyndon Johnson and his buddy J. Edgar Hoover (who handled the cover-up), who were now in control of our country's future.

So, if some poor civilian or Warren Commission lawyer figured out what had really happened in and to America, there was no one to go to, and nothing he or she could do but keep their mouth shut and try to forget what they had learned. It was all over.

The Warren Commission was following the "clues" laid out for them by J. Edgar Hoover. He outlined the "facts" for the Commission to "investigate." Lee Harvey Oswald was the "lone-nut assassin," there were three shots fired, the first shot hit President Kennedy in the back, the second shot hit Governor Connally in the back and the third shot hit President Kennedy in the head killing the President. No conspiracy found, case closed.

In early June 1964 I read in a newspaper that the Warren Commission had finished its investigation, was sending its Commission helpers home, and was going to write its report: three shots fired: first hitting Kennedy, the second Connally, the third Kennedy, and the deed was done by a "lone nut assassin" named Lee Harvey Oswald. The "facts" were just as Hoover had stated 48 hours after the assassination.

It was now over six months after the assassination. I had not been called to testify, even though the FBI had interviewed me on December 14, 1963 about the missed shot.

Something was wrong. I felt the missed shot was important, because to me it indicated there was more than one shooter. I raised my hand and related to a reporter what I knew – the story was printed nationwide, and I was at last called to testify. The Warren Commission's findings were altered and history took a different direction.

Later, when the Warren Report was published I accepted it as being the truth like most Americans did. Then came a flood of books pointing out the flaws in the Warren Report. I saved the books and put them aside. I had a family to raise, a career to follow, and I did not want the Kennedy Assassination to consume my life. It was not until the 1980s that questions started to develop from the bits and pieces of data that had begun to drop into my lap. I have tried to make each chapter a story within itself, so I do repeat myself on occasion, but I think you will find my story interesting, thought-provoking, and relevant. The words come easy when you are telling the truth.

About the Author

I was born at home on a farm near Plainfield, Indiana with the local doctor in attendance and was the youngest of five children. I had three brothers 21, 20, and 19 years older than me as well as a sister 14 years older. Mother was an ex-school teacher and Dad was a farmer. My parents saw to it that I attended church, was a Cub Scout, a Boy Scout (honored by being selected as one of two Boy Scouts to represent central Indiana at the National Boy Scout Jamboree at Valley Forge Pennsylvania), participated in the Soap Box Derby, had a paper route (won a trip to Washington D.C. for most new subscriptions), was a 4-H club member and won many ribbons showing livestock at the county and Indiana State Fairs. My parents made sure that I had a wonderful farm life, and even after years of living in the city, I still think of myself as a "farm boy."

Dad lived a long, honorable life, dying just a couple of months before his 60th wedding anniversary. The family had land, not much money, but we were not poor. My father's word was his bond in our community.

I graduated from Plainfield High School at age 17, enrolled in Purdue University to follow in my brothers' footsteps, but entered the United States Air Force instead. I graduated from the Air Force School of Aviation Medicine, and rapidly rose in rank. I was in Aviation Physiology teaching pilot's survival at high altitude, both in the class room and in the altitude chamber. After spending five great years in the United States Air Force I received an honorable discharge and settled in the Dallas, Texas area.

My old car had seen its last mile when I noticed an ad in the *Dallas Morning News* for a sales job with a new car furnished. I answered the ad and I was hired. The sales manager was a nice guy, but he tried to teach me questionable sales techniques that did not quite agree with my naïve "country boy" up-bringing.

In the first two weeks as a new car salesman, I did not sell a car. The sales manager called me into his office and politely told me he did not think I could make it as an automobile salesman, and that I might want to look for another job, but he would give me two more weeks to try and learn how to sell cars. I walked out of his office mad; my first thought was to just quit.

I did not quit, I started being myself with customers, talking to them in a straight-forward and honest way, and I started selling cars. Soon, I was often leading the dealership in new car sales.

A few short years later I was recognized in *Time* magazine as one of the nation's top salesmen. The *Time* recognition led to my first Sales Manager's position. That led to a General Sales Manager's position, and finally General Manager of one of the largest automobile dealerships in the nation.

My reputation was such that I could choose to work at the most reputable new car dealerships in the Dallas area. The automobile business has been good to me, and I have always taken pride in treating people fair and honestly. I have worked with many very fine people in my career, honest people, and also a few that have sometimes given the automobile business a black eye.

It was simply by accident that I was even in Dealey Plaza at 12:30 P.M. on November 22, 1963. That I was slightly injured by a missed shot during the assassination of President Kennedy was inconsequential, but the subsequent attempt by the Warren Commission and the FBI to leave out of their findings the fact that one shot did miss the President and hit the curb near my feet throwing debris into my face is important in understanding the problems the Warren Commission had in their investigation.

The fact that I was there at the moment of the assassination of President Kennedy did cause me to write down what I had witnessed that very evening – and has held my interest through the years.

Most people, who are knowledgeable about the assassination credit Harold Weisberg as being the person who was most knowledgeable about the cold, hard facts.

Harold Weisberg and I became friends about a year after the Warren Commission findings were published, and our friendship stayed close for over 35 years until Harold's death in 2002. Harold has been a guest in my home in Dallas and I have been a guest in his home in Frederick Maryland. Harold Weisberg was the person who sued the United States Government under the Freedom of Information Act to get the Kennedy and King Assassination documents released from the FBI.

Harold asked me to join him in his FOIA's lawsuit and I did. Besides being an eyewitness and giving key testimony to the Warren Commission, I have done extensive personal research on the assassination.

As well as visiting the National Archives in Washington D.C., I have spent many hours in Harold's basement doing research, where Harold kept over 60 four-drawer filing cabinets full of these FBI documents. Through the years, in my spare time, I have amassed several cubic feet of information.

The information in this book is the best I have found and is backed up by FBI reports, government correspondence, taped interviews, face-to-face conversations with insiders and much other documentation.

I have sat mostly silent for almost 50 years, and have watched as over 2,000 books have been written about the assassination of President John F. Kennedy, some of these books are pure fiction, some have been written with good intentions, and some have touched on the truth, but are lacking in documentation.

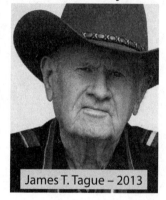

James T. Tague – 2013

For some reason I have had information dropped in my lap without any effort on my part. It all started with my becoming stopped in traffic in Dealey Plaza on November 22, 1963 – a place I had not intended to be.

James T. Tague
August 22, 2013

TAGUE

CHAPTER ONE

NOVEMBER 22, 1963 – THE ASSASSINATION OF PRESIDENT KENNEDY

After nearly fifty years I wrote this chapter from memory as to what I witnessed in Dealey Plaza at 12:30 P.M. on November 22, 1963, the moment that President John F. Kennedy was assassinated in front of my eyes in Dallas, Texas.

When I had finished writing the chapter from memory, I then retrieved from my closet a spiral notebook in which I had written, the very evening of November 22, 1963, everything I could remember about the events of the day.

I then compared the two, what I had written then, and what I had written nearly fifty years later; there was no difference – they were identical.

Today, though, I can put names on the witnesses and others I encountered that day, and know the exact distances that I had guessed at on the evening of November 22, 1963. To me personally it has been a lesson in the reliability of eyewitness testimony: visions that are burned into your mind. There do appear to be collateral influences that have a tendency over time to alter and distort those original visions. One has to have a strong mind-set in order to not allow these outside influences to corrupt what one has originally witnessed.

After I was discharged from the Air Force, I had taken a job as a new car salesman. It was something I enjoyed doing. Selling new cars was quite different 40 years ago than it is today – it was low key, no pressure, you made friends with your customers, and most became repeat customers. On November 22, 1963 I had a luncheon date with a friend at noon in downtown Dallas.

I was about to leave for lunch, when an old customer came in to buy a car. Business came first and I did not get away until after 12:00. As I drove down the Stemmons Freeway toward downtown Dallas, the only thing on my mind was hoping that my friend would not be upset with me for being late.

I exited Stemmons onto Commerce Street, a one-way street going east toward the center of Dallas and swung into the far left lane next to the curb. As I entered the triple underpass I noticed that traffic was stopped ahead of me and I came to a stop just as the nose of my car was about to exit from under the triple underpass.

I could only see straight ahead as there was a man in front of me standing by his car, between his car and car door, looking off to the left. I sat there for a second or two, and then got out of my car to see what was happening that had stopped traffic. I walked the four or five steps it took to be out of the underpass and stopped on the curb at the east edge of the underpass facing Dealey Plaza.

At this location three streets come within three feet of each other to go under the railroad tracks, Elm on the north, Main in the center, and Commerce on the south. I was standing on the narrow curbing between Commerce and Main Streets, a couple of feet or so east of the underpass. Other than the cars that were stopped ahead of me there was no one else close to me, and I had a clear view of Dealey Plaza.

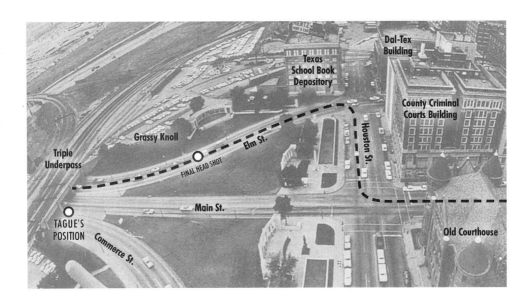

I noticed a crowd up by the School Book Depository on the corners of Houston and Elm Streets; I was wondering what was going on when a limousine with flags on the front fenders emerged from the crowd on Elm Street in front of the School Book Depository. It was only then that I remembered having read in the newspaper that President Kennedy was going to be in Dallas that day and that this must be his motorcade through Dallas.

The President's car had barely cleared the crowd around the intersection of Elm and Houston Streets when I heard the pop of a firecracker going off. I remember thinking what kind of fool would light a firecracker with the President driving by – the police will get him for sure. My line of vision was toward the crowd as the Presidential limousine was curving down Elm Street directly at me. The limousine was between me and the crowd in front of the School Book Depository.

The President's limousine was slowing down when I heard the very distinct crack of a high-powered rifle shot, then, rapidly, the crack of another shot. The limousine was almost upon me with this shot, there was movement inside the limousine, then the limousine accelerated and went under the triple underpass.

Something stung me in the face during the shooting and it took a second or two for all of this to start to register, my mind was racing, somebody had just shot at the President. Something sent a signal to my brain that I was in danger, I ducked back behind the protection of the concrete. I stood there frozen trying to grasp what had just happened – my mind racing.

Later, on television that night I watched a news clip that showed almost immediately after the shooting there was a rush by the crowd and a motorcycle policeman toward the Grassy Knoll and the picket fence. My mind had been so absorbed with trying to grasp what I had just witnessed that I have no memory of this rush of people toward the Grassy Knoll right in front of me.

But back to that afternoon, when my frantic thoughts were broken by a man (I was to later learn this was Deputy Sheriff Buddy Walthers) in a suit standing in front of me asking very excitedly, "What happened down here?"

I replied that I did not know, and as Deputy Sheriff Walthers and I stood there talking, we noticed a policeman had parked his motorcycle across the street on the north curb of Elm Street near the Grassy Knoll and was talking to a couple of men.

We crossed Main and Elm Streets and walked up to the policeman in time to hear one of the men standing there sobbing, "His head exploded, his head exploded." The motorcycle policeman asked him whose head. The man replied, "The President's."

With that statement I remember Deputy Walthers turning to the grass beside the sidewalk and kicking the grass with the toe of his shoe as hard as he could three times, saying, "Damn, damn, damn!" It was at this point that Deputy Walthers said, "You have blood on your face." I reached up and felt my face. There were three or four drops of blood on the palm of my hand.

With the overwhelming intensity of what had just happened, it was only then that I recalled that something had stung me in the face during the shooting. Deputy Walthers asked me where I was standing during the shooting and I pointed to where he had run up to me and had asked me what happened down here. We crossed Elm Street having to wait for the Main Street traffic to clear in order to cross Main.

As we stood there Deputy Walthers said, "Hey, look at that mark on the curb." There were four traffic lanes between us and the curb, but even from that distance there was a very visible gray-whitish mark on a dirty much darker curb. The mark was a few feet in front of where I had been standing.

We both closely examined this small scrape, it was very fresh, not dirty like the curbing around it and was about a half-inch wide by three-quarters of an inch long. It was a no brainer – it was a bullet mark. The bullet had dislodged about an eighth of an inch of concrete and was at the part of the curb where the side rounds into the top. It had obviously glanced off the curb at an angle.

I remember Deputy Walthers taking out his ballpoint pen and trying to draw a large circle around the bullet mark and my telling him he was going to ruin his pen on the concrete. It was obvious to both of us that either concrete debris or bullet fragments from this missed shot was what caused me to be stung in the face during the shooting. We crossed back across Main and Elm Streets to where the motorcycle policeman was still standing near the Grassy Knoll.

There was now a large crowd gathered around the policeman. Deputy Walthers told the policeman what we had discovered, and the policeman radioed in that he had one man there with a slight injury. According to the Dallas police radio logs, it was now 12:37 P.M. I was told that they needed to get a statement from me. With the intensity of this event I had forgotten that my car was still parked on Commerce Street in a traffic lane.

I went back to my car and drove out from under the triple underpass to park my car. It had been 15 or 20 minutes since the shooting and curiosity seekers were now clogging the streets around Dealey Plaza. There was no place to park, so I headed down Commerce towards the Dallas Police headquarters to give the requested statement, my mind still trying to digest what I had just witnessed.

I then remembered my luncheon date, her office was also on Commerce Street on the way to Police Headquarters, and there was a parking place in front of her office building, so I stopped for a minute to run in and tell her what had happened.

She worked at a brokerage firm and the phones were ringing off the wall – I stood by her desk for a minute or two as she answered call after call from people across the country wanting to know what was going on in Dallas. She finally waved me off, so I left.

As I started to leave the building, I noticed a pay phone and called my parents in Indiana. I remember telling Dad that President Kennedy had just been killed in Dallas. Dad told me he was watching TV and that the President was still alive. They were attending to his injuries at the hospital. I told Dad, "No Dad. He is dead. I was there."

At the Dallas Police Headquarters I explained to the officer at the desk why I had been sent there, and he sent me to the homicide office. The police building was a buzz of activity as police officers scurried up and down the hallways. I found the homicide office and there was no one there, so I waited a few minutes. An officer in plain clothes came in (I was to later learn this man was Gus Rose) and I again explained why I had been sent there. We went into his office and the officer took notes on a pad.

While Detective Rose was taking notes there was a commotion at the door to Homicide, and a disheveled young man was brought into the room in handcuffs. Detective Rose, who was taking my statement, asked one of the officers who had brought in the handcuffed man, who he was and the officer replied, "This is the man who just killed a police officer in Oak Cliff." With these words my interview was over, and I was dismissed.

When I stepped out of Dallas Police Headquarters there was a chill in the air that I felt for the first time that day. The most direct route to work took me down Elm Street back through Dealey Plaza. As I approached Dealey Plaza the traffic became heavy and there were now police officers directing traffic. At about the spot where President Kennedy had received the fatal head wound, an officer held up his hand for me to stop and I did. He came to my driver's window and stated that they had just found a piece of the President's skull there by the curb and described the size, about one inch by six inches. Why this officer stopped me and told me this, I do not know to this day.

When I got back to work the manager was closing the business and I went home.

Later that night as I was watching television they showed a picture of the man who had been brought into the office while I was giving my statement – it was Lee Harvey Oswald.

DALLAS RADIO TAPES

22	Get some men up here to cover this school depository building. It's believed the shot came from, as you see it on Elm Street, looking toward the building, it would be upper right hand corner, second window from the end.
Disp	10-4. How many do you have there?
22	I have one guy that was possibly hit by a rickashay from the bullet off the concrete and another one seen the president slump.
Disp	10-4.
137	We have a man here who says he seen him pull the weapon back through the window from Southeast corner of that depository building.
Disp	All right, do you have the building covered off?
137	No, about 3/4 of a block away from there.
Disp	All right, pull on down there.
137	10-4. I'll leave these witnesses here.
257	Do you want us to go back to Mockingbird and Cedar Springs?
290	See if you can contact 125.
125	290, I am at Parkland.
290	125, do you want us to stay on Industrial or where do you want us to go?
125	At your location right now.
2	Can you give us any information as to what happened for these people out here, evidentally they had - seriousness of it - the president involved - one is at Parkland, along with Dallas 1. We have word it is unknown - Texas Depository Store, corner of Elm and Field - officers are now surrounding and searching the building.
2	Where did this happen - at Field and Main?
Disp	At Stemmons and the Triple Underpass - 12:40 p.m.
Disp	2, there's a possibility that 6 or 7 more people may have been shot.
295	I believe the president's head was practically blown off.
303	What hospital did the President go to?
Disp	Parkland Hospital
Disp	303, where are you?

74

COMMISSION EXHIBIT 705—Continued

Copy of the Warren Report, p. 463 of Volume X

CHAPTER TWO

THE MOTORCADE

The President's motorcade consisted of 17 cars and one bus. There was a pilot car that was to travel about a quarter of a mile ahead of the motorcade. The purpose of the pilot car was to alert the motorcade of any accidents, fires, obstructions, or anything that could be detrimental along the motorcade route. Then came the lead car, it would travel about 100 feet in front of the Presidential limousine. Behind the President's limousine would be the Secret Service car and behind it would be various dignitaries and a bus with the White House Press.

The motorcade started at Love Field where the President had landed after spending the night in Fort Worth. The route from Love Field through the streets of Dallas and through downtown Dallas was uneventful, the President was greeted by a pleasant and cheering crowd; the crowds were large and well under control.

When the President's car turned onto Elm Street, in front of the Texas School Book Depository, it only needed to go through Dealey Plaza and then there was a clear path on Stemmons Expressway to Market Hall, where the President was scheduled to speak. Dallas Police Chief Jesse Curry drove the lead car.

In his book *JFK Assassination File,* Chief Curry states he was traveling at a speed of approximately eight to ten miles per hour toward the underpass on Elm street and was about halfway between Houston Street and the triple underpass, when he heard the first shot. Chief Curry remembers someone in the car saying, "Is that a firecracker?" Chief Curry also remembers the shots as being fairly close together, but with a longer pause between the first and second shots.

There were police motorcycle officers riding on each side of the President's limousine slightly to the rear of the limousine. Motorcycle officer Bobby Hargis was riding near the left rear fender of the President's limousine when a bullet hit the President in the head. With the impact of this frontal headshot, a sheet of blood and brain tissue exploded backward and to the left and into the motorcycle's windshield of Officer Hargis. Officer Hargis parked his motorcycle and started running up the Grassy Knoll towards the picket fence.

In the lead car, Chief Curry heard on the police radio channel someone in the President's car say, "Let's get out of here." There was an immediate exchange of messages by Chief Curry and it was quickly determined that the President had been hit and a motorcycle escort was quickly formed to lead the Presidential limousine to Parkland Hospital. In the first minute Chief Curry was on the air saying, "Go to the hospital, officers, Parkland Hospital, have them stand by. Get men on top of the underpass, see what has happened up there, go up on the overpass. Have Parkland stand by … I am sure it's going to take some time to get your men up there. Put every one of my men there.… Notify station five to move all men available out of my department back into the railroad yards and try to determine what happened and hold everything secure until Homicide and other investigators can get in there."

Besides Chief Curry in the lead car, there was FBI SA Winston George "Win" Lawson, Sheriff James Eric "Bill" Decker and FBI SAIC Forrest V. Sorrels. The Secret Service follow-up car had special assistants to the President, Kenneth "Ken" O'Donnell and David F. Powers plus Secret Service Agents Samuel A. "Sam" Kinney, Emory P. Roberts, George W. Hickey Jr., Glen A. Bennett, Clinton L. "Clint" Hill, William "Tim" McIntyre, John D. "Jack" Ready, and Paul E. Landis.

In the car behind the Secret Service car was the Vice President's car with V.P. Lyndon Johnson, his wife Lady Bird, SSA Rufus Wayne Youngblood, Congressman Ralph W. Yarborough, and Texas Department of Public Safety Hurchel D. Jacks. There were ten cars and one bus after the V.P.'s car.

Chapter Three

INSIDE THE PRESIDENT'S LIMOUSINE

The Abraham Zapruder amateur 8mm home movie captured the reaction of the occupants of the President's limousine from a split second after the first shot was fired until the limousine went under the triple underpass. A road sign obscured the limousine at the moment the first shot hit the President.

As the limousine came into view from behind the sign, the President was raising his hands and forearms in a horizontal motion as if he were reacting to a sharp poke in the back, or, as most interpreted this reaction, as if he was reaching for his throat. Zapruder's home movie did capture on film everything else but that first split second.

What the occupants of the limousine remembered months later when they testified before the Warren Commission varies with what was captured on film. And the Warren Commission's final conclusions vary with both the occupant's memory and what was shown in the home movie.

That there were only three shots heard, does not eliminate the possibility of more than three shots due to the possibility of a silencer or simultaneous shots, and all the testimony by the occupants of the car assumed that there were only three shots.

There were six people riding in President Kennedy's limousine when the shots were fired, two secret service agents were in the front seat, Secret Service agent Roy Kellerman was in the passenger seat, and Secret Service agent Bill Greer was the driver. Governor and Mrs. Connally were in the middle jump seats, and the President and Mrs. Kennedy were in the rear seat. Both President Kennedy and Governor Connally were on the right side, the passenger side of the car and seated next to the their wives.

THE FIRST SHOT

Governor Connally testified before the Warren Commission about the first shot as follows: "When I heard what I thought was a shot, I heard the noise which I immediately took to be a rifle shot. I instinctively turned to my right because the sound appeared to come from over my right shoulder, and I saw nothing unusual except just people in the crowd, but I did not catch the President in the corner of my eye, and I was interested, because once I heard the shot in my own mind I identified it as a rifle shot, and I immediately – the only thought that crossed my mind was that this is an assassination attempt. So I looked, failing to see him, I was turning to look back over my left shoulder into the back seat, but I never got that far in my turn. I got about in the position I am in now facing you, looking a little bit to the left of center, and then I felt like someone had hit me in the back."

Mrs. John Connally testified about the first shot as follows: "I heard a noise, and not being an expert rifleman, I was not aware that it was a rifle. It was just a frightening noise, and it came from the right. I turned over my right shoulder and looked back, and saw the President as he had both hands at his neck. It seemed to me there was – he made no utterances, no cry. I saw no blood, no anything. It was just sort of nothing, the expression on his face, and he just sort of slumped down."

Mrs. Kennedy testified before the Commission. Her testimony was short and it was justifiably obvious that her account of the shooting was troubling and that she did not have total recall of the shooting.

What Mrs. Kennedy did say was: "You know, there is always noise in a motorcade and there are always motorcycles beside us, a lot of them backfiring. So I was looking to the left. I guess there was a noise, but it didn't seem like any different noise really because there is so much noise, motorcycles and things.

"But then suddenly Governor Connally was yelling, 'Oh, no, no, no.' I was looking this way, to the left, and I heard these terrible noises. You know. And my husband never made any sound. So I turned to the right. And all I remember is seeing my husband, he had this sort of quizzical look on his face, and his hand was up, it must have been his left hand." (At this point in her testimony Mrs. Kennedy starts talking about later, after the fatal head shot and then reverts back to the first shot).

Then she continues: "I remember thinking he just looked as if he had a slight headache. And then I just remember seeing that. No blood or anything. And then he sort of did this, put his hand to his forehead and fell in my lap. I cried: 'They have killed my husband, I have his brains in my hand.'

"And then I just remembered falling on him and saying, 'Oh, no, no, no, I mean oh my god, they have shot my husband, and I love you Jack.' I remember I was shouting. And just being down in the car with his head in my lap. And it just seemed an eternity.

"And finally I remember a voice behind me, or something, and then I remember the people in the front seat, or somebody, finally knew something was wrong, and a voice yelling, which must have been Mr. Hill, get to the hospital, or maybe it was Mr. Kellerman, in the front seat. But someone yelling, I was just down and holding him.

"I was trying to hold his hair on. But from the front there was nothing, I suppose there must have been, but from the back you could see, you know, you were trying to hold his hair on, and his skull on."

Secret Service agent Roy Kellerman was in the front passenger seat and he testified before the Commission about the first shot as follows: "There is a report like a firecracker, pop. And I turned my head to the right because whatever this noise was I was sure that it came from the right and perhaps into the rear, and as I turned my head to the right to view whatever it was or see whatever it was, I heard a voice from the back seat and I firmly believe it was the President's, 'My god I am hit,' and I turned around and he got his hands up here like this (indicating right hand up toward the neck?). There was enough time to verify the man was hit. So, in the same motion I come right back and grabbed the speaker and said to the driver, 'lets get out of here, we are hit.'"

Secret Service agent Bill Greer was driving the Presidential limousine and he testified about the first shot as follows: "When we were going down Elm Street, I heard a noise that I thought was a backfire of one of the motorcycle policemen. And I didn't – it did not effect me like anything else. I just thought that it is what it was. We had so many motorcycles around us. So I heard this noise. And I thought that is what it was." And later in his testimony Agent Greer states: "The first one didn't sink in to me, didn't give me the thought that it was a shot. I thought it was the backfire of a motorcycle."

THE SECOND AND THIRD SHOTS

Governor Connally's testimony about the second and third shots: "Then I felt like someone had hit me in the back." The Governor was then asked about the time span between the first and second shots and he continued: "A very, very brief span of time. Again my trend of thought just happened to be, I suppose along the line, I immediately thought that this – that I had been shot. I knew it when I just looked down and I was covered with blood, and the thought immediately passed through my mind that there were either two or three people involved or more in this or someone was shooting with an automatic rifle. These were just thoughts that went through my mind because of the rapidity of these two, of the first shot plus the blow that I took, and I knew I had been hit, and I immediately assumed, because of the amount of blood, and in fact, that it had passed through my chest, that I had probably been fatally hit. So I merely doubled up, and then turned to my right again and began to – I just sat there, and Mrs. Connally pulled me over to her lap. She was sitting, of course, on the jump seat, so I reclined with my head on her lap, conscious all the time, and with my eyes open. And then, of course, the third shot sounded, and I heard the shot very clearly. I heard it hit him. I heard the shot hit something, and I assumed again – it never entered my mind that it ever hit anybody but the President. I heard it hit. It was a very loud noise, just that audible, very clear. Immediately I could see on my clothes, my clothing, I could see the interior of the car which, as I recall, was a pale blue, brain tissue, which I immediately recognized, and I recall very well, on my trousers there was one chunk of brain tissue as big as almost my thumb, thumbnail, and again I did not see the President at any time either after the first, second, or third shots, but I assumed always that it was he who was hit and no one else."

During his testimony Governor Connally recalled two statements made by Mrs. Kennedy after the third shot and before he lost consciousness. "They have killed my husband" and "I have his brains in my hand." Also during his testimony Governor Connally is adamant that it was the second shot that hit him, and he states, "It is not conceivable to me that I could have been hit by the first bullet, and then I felt a blow from something which obviously a bullet, which I assumed was a bullet, and I never heard the second shot, didn't hear it, I didn't hear but two shots. I think I heard the first shot and the third shot."

Mrs. Connally's testimony about the second and third shots: "Then there was a second shot, and it hit John (Connally), and as he recoiled to the right, just crumpled like a wounded animal to the right, he said 'My god, they are going to kill us all.'" At that point there is more testimony about Mrs. Connally pulling her husband onto her lap and trying to comfort him. And then she continues: "The third shot that I heard I felt, it felt like spent buckshot falling all over us, and then of course, I too could see that it was matter, a brain tissue, or whatever, just human matter, all over the car and both of us."

Mrs. Kennedy's testimony was very brief out of consideration for the loss of her husband, the President of the United States; she had no distinct memory of a second shot or a third shot. Mrs. Kennedy testified that she had no memory of climbing out of her seat and on to the trunk of the limousine to retrieve a piece of the President's skull, nor did she remember Secret

Service Agent Hill running up to the rear of the Presidential limousine after the third shot and pushing her back into the seat. She also testified that she only heard two shots. Her testimony about the President's head wound was deleted.

Secret Service Agent Roy Kellerman testified that in the seconds he was on the radio talking after the first shot, "a flurry of shells come into the car." His next memory is looking back and seeing Secret Service Agent Hill on the trunk, Agent Kellerman first estimated five seconds between the pop of a firecracker (first shot) and the second shot and then later under intense questioning changed his testimony that there were five seconds between the first and third shots. He also attempted to clarify his statement of a flurry of shells as being two shots coming in rapid succession like bang, bang. Mr. Kellerman also testified that the limousine accelerated immediately after the first shot. Agent Kellerman's testimony left much to be desired.

Secret Service agent Bill Greer's second and third shot testimony: "And then I heard it again (shot). And I glanced over my shoulder. And I saw Governor Connally like he was starting to fall. Then I realized there was something wrong. I tramped on the accelerator, and at the same time Mr. Kellerman said to me 'Get out of here fast.' And I cannot quite remember even the other shots or noises that was. I cannot quite remember any more. I did not see anything happen behind me any more, because I was occupied with getting away." In further questioning, Mr. Greer estimated that there were three or four seconds between the first and second shots and the time between the second and third shots was almost simultaneous, one right behind the other.

The Abraham Zapruder home movie reveals many discrepancies in both of the Secret Service Agent's testimonies. The President's limousine did not immediately accelerate after the first shot, the second shot, or even after the third shot, it was slowing down and almost came to a complete stop after the third shot. The Zapruder movie does seem to back up Governor Connally's version that he was hit by a different shot from the first shot that hit President Kennedy. The Warren Commission initially concluded that the first shot hit Kennedy, the second shot hit Connally and the third shot hit Kennedy. Then after I testified about the missed shot the Commission concluded both the President and the Governor were hit by the same shot, despite the fact that the positions of the men in the limousine at the time of the first shot seemed to indicate that this was an impossibility. That Governor Connally testified that he only heard two shots leaves questions as to his exact recollection of the shooting sequence.

The testimonies of the two Secret Service agents, Roy Kellerman and William Greer coincide with the testimony of myself and Presidential Advisers Ken O'Donnell and Dave Powers, who were riding in the Secret Service car behind the President's car. All five of us directly indicate that there were three to four seconds between the first and second shots we heard and the time between the second and third shot we heard was one right after the other indicating one to one-and-one-half-seconds in my mind between the second and third shots.

Chapter Four

Parkland Hospital

The high speed trip to Parkland Hospital from Dealey Plaza had happened so quickly that, when the President's limousine arrived at the emergency entrance, no one there had any idea what had happened. There were no hospital attendants at the emergency entrance when the President's limousine arrived.

The hospital had been alerted just seconds before the President's car turned into the driveway that the President had been injured and was on his way. Emergency personnel were headed toward the emergency entrance as the President's limousine came to a stop. The hospital's loudspeaker was blaring out, "Dr. Tom Shires, STAT."

Dr. Shires was in charge of surgery at Parkland. He was not in the hospital, but other doctors realized from the tone of voice on the loud speaker that this was no ordinary emergency, and responded.

Six minutes had passed since the shooting. Mrs. Kennedy was in the backseat bowed over her husband covering his head. Blood and gore was everywhere in the limousine, the President looked dead, there was no visible sign of respiration, and his eyes were dilated and fixed. Governor Connally was bleeding profusely, and he had to be removed from the jump seat before anyone could get to the President in the back seat. Governor Connally was quickly put on a stretcher as his wife Nelly looked on. While Governor Connally was being put on a stretcher, Secret Service agent Clint Hill was trying to speak to Mrs. Kennedy.

This scene is described by Dallas Chief of Police Jesse Curry in his book, *JFK Assassination File*: "She just sat there holding the President's head in her lap – somehow hoping to heal it, like a little girl holds a doll. Then slowly she began to bend over the President as if to shield him from the agents and attendants.… Apparently she didn't want anyone to see that the back of the President's head was partially blown off."

Agent Hill finally got through to Mrs. Kennedy and convinced her to let go of the President. Agent Hill gave Mrs. Kennedy his coat and she wrapped the coat around the President's head and neck. Several Secret Service agents then lifted the President out of the limousine and struggled to get his limp body onto a stretcher.

While this was going on outside the emergency room entrance, a full medical staff had assembled and was ready for the Governor and the President as they were rushed into emergency. Several doctors worked in vain trying to revive the President; it was useless, the head wound was massive, and a large part of his brain was missing.

At 1:00 P.M. November 22, 1963, White House Assistant Press Secretary, Malcolm Kilduff, held a press conference at the hospital and announced that President Kennedy had died. Assistant Press Secretary Kilduff told the reporters, who had quickly gathered at the hospital, that the President had died of a gunshot wound to the head, and Kilduff pointed his finger to the right front of his head, near his right temple, to illustrate the point of entry.

After President Kennedy had been pronounced dead, and Governor Connally was still in surgery on the second floor, a Parkland employee, Darrell C. Tomlinson, a senior engineer for the air conditioning services, was in the elevator lobby on the ground floor near the trauma rooms. Mr. Tomlinson had been assigned to manually operate the elevator between the ground floor and the second floor during the emergency.

At one point, Mr. Tomlinson removed a stretcher from the elevator and placed it next to another stretcher near the wall. It was assumed the stretcher he removed from the elevator was the one that had been used to take Governor Connally up to surgery on the second floor. The other stretcher was presumed to be the one that had been used to bring President Kennedy into the emergency room from the limousine.

Later, while standing in the elevator lobby, Mr. Tomlinson observed a doctor or an intern push one of the stretchers away from the wall to gain access to the men's room, and then leave without putting it back. Mr. Tomlinson pushed the stretcher back against the wall, and while doing so, bumped the wall with the stretcher and a bullet rolled out that apparently had been lodged under the edge of the mat.

During his testimony before the Warren Commission, Mr. Tomlinson estimated the time of this event to be at about 1:00 P.M., however, it had to be much later, for both the President's and the Governor's stretchers to be there. Mr. Tomlinson turned the bullet over to Parkland Hospital's head of security, who then handed the bullet over to Secret Service Agent Richard E. Johnson, who put the bullet into his pocket.

This bullet, later Commission exhibit 399, was also known as the "magic bullet," a bullet that the Warren Commission determined had penetrated and gone through the bodies of two men, shattering multiple bones in one of the men, and emerging in pristine condition.

During his testimony before the Warren Commission, the stretcher that was designated stretcher "A" was the one that was removed from the elevator and stretcher "B" was the President's stretcher. When first asked which stretcher the bullet fell from, Mr. Tomlinson replied, "I believe it was "B" (the President's). Mr. Tomlinson was then repeatedly asked which stretcher the bullet had came from and Mr. Tomlinson finally said he could not be positive.

At one point during Mr. Tomlinson's testimony, Warren Commission Assistant Counsel Arlen Specter, states, "Now, just before we started this deposition, before I placed you under oath and before the court reporter started to take down any questions and your answers, you and I had a brief talk, did we not?" Mr. Tomlinson answered, "Yes." And Specter then said, "And we discussed in a general way the information which you have testified about, did we not?" And Mr. Tomlinson answers, "Yes sir." And Specter continues, "And at the time we started our discussion, it was your recollection at that point that the bullet came off stretcher 'A,' was it not?" And Mr. Tomlinson replied, "B."

There were many more questions asked in different ways by Specter, about which stretcher the bullet fell from, with Mr. Tomlinson stating over and over again that he could not remember or be positive about which stretcher the bullet fell from. In reading Mr. Tomlinson's entire testimony before the Warren Commission, it is clear that Mr. Tomlinson wants to say that the bullet fell from the President's stretcher and that Warren Commission Counsel Arlen Specter wanted Mr. Tomlinson to say the bullet fell from Governor Connally's stretcher, causing Mr. Tomlinson to say he could not be positive about which stretcher the bullet came from. It also must be noted that there is no proof that either of the stretchers were the ones that carried the President or the Governor into the emergency rooms.

Miss Margaret Henchcliffe testified before the Warren Commission that after the President's body had been put into a coffin, she had pushed his stretcher across the hall into a vacant room. Henchcliffe's statement beat out Tomlinson's testimony, and the Warren Commission determined that the bullet fell from Governor Connally's stretcher.

In 1963, no federal law covered the assassination of a president. Murder came under Texas law and by Texas law this was murder, and an autopsy should be performed in Texas. Texas authorities invoked that law, but the

Secret Service and Kennedy aides were adamant that they would take the President's body back to Washington D.C. with them. Hot words were exchanged. Witnesses described the debate over control of President Kennedy's body as childish.

A coffin and hearse were ordered from a local mortuary and the body of the President was soon escorted to the presidential plane at Love Field. And once Lyndon Johnson was sworn in on that plane, the new President Johnson, his wife Ladybird, President Kennedy's body, Jackie Kennedy, and the Presidential entourage were flown back to Washington D.C.

A moment after being sworn in as President you see Ladybird Johnson smiling, Jackie Kennedy in shock, and Lyndon Johnson has turned and traded winks with Albert Thomas.

Chapter Five

Trauma Room One

B lood and gore was everywhere in the limousine. The President looked dead, there was no visible sign of respiration, his eyes were dilated and fixed. The witnesses to the removal of President Kennedy from the Presidential Limousine heard Jackie Kennedy's child-like whimpers as she held the President's head in her lap. Mrs. Kennedy did not let go of the President until they reached Trauma Room One.

What the doctors and nurses observed in Trauma Room One about the condition of President Kennedy while they were attending to him should have been crucial to the final findings of the Warren Commission. It was not. These highly experienced doctors and nurses had attended to hundreds of emergencies concerning gunshot wounds. Parkland Hospital was the primary hospital for receiving emergencies in Dallas.

For some peculiar reason the Warren Commission, in its final conclusions, chose to ignore much of the first-hand observations of the attending doctors and nurses at Parkland.

By the time the Parkland doctors testified in late March 1964, before the Warren Commission, they had become aware of the autopsy report and what it contained. They also had made an agreement among themselves not to discuss with the press what they had observed. The Parkland Hospital doctors and nurses who attended to the President were respected professionals, and these professionals were the first ones to see the President's injuries.

It must be noted that Warren Commission Attorney Arlen Specter took the testimony of the Parkland Hospital doctors, and it must be noted that this author suspects and has good reason to believe that Specter had a preconceived idea of how he wanted the facts to be. There will be more examination of Specter's apparent bias in a later chapter.

The doctor's testimony before the Warren Commission should have been taken as an absolute fact as to what they observed, for they had nothing to gain or hide by saying anything but the truth. All the doctors that saw the back of the President's head had seen the same thing and they all testified that there was a large hole in the back of the President's head.

Some spoke in medical terms, referring to the back of the President's head as the occipital area and used other medical terms to describe the President's head wound, but they all testified to a large "exit" wound in the right rear of the President's head extending up to the top of the skull with brain tissue and blood oozing from that wound.

The throat wound was at first believed to be a small "entrance" wound and it was noted that a tracheotomy had been performed through the throat wound. Most of the doctors, given a set of circumstances by Arlen Specter, were made to admit that the throat wound could have been an exit wound. None of the doctors testified that they had seen an entrance wound in the back of the head.

That same evening, the head autopsy doctor, J.J. Humes, did not testify to seeing a large exit wound in the back of President Kennedy's head on his second autopsy report (Dr. Humes admitted he had destroyed his first autopsy report).

RN Diana Bowron was one of the first to respond to the urgency in the voice she heard on the intercom that they needed stretchers at the emergency room entrance. She rushed a stretcher, along with an orderly, down the hallway to be met by what she assumed to be Secret Service Agents. The agents encouraged them to run. When they got to the Presidential limousine they had to wait while Governor Connally was removed from the car so they could get access to the President in the back seat.

When Ms. Bowron testified to the Warren Commission, she was asked, "What she had observed about the President?" Ms. Bowron replied, "He was moribund, he was lying across Mrs. Kennedy's knee and there seemed to be blood everywhere. When I went around to the other side of the car I saw the condition of his head." Ms. Bowron was then asked what about the condition of the President's head and she replied, "The back of his head, well it was very bad you know." Ms. Bowron was then asked how many holes she saw and she replied, "I just saw one large hole." Ms. Bowron was then asked if she saw a small bullet hole below the large hole and she replied, "No."

As soon as Governor Connally was removed from the limousine, Ms. Bowron started to help lift the President's head onto the stretcher, but Mrs. Kennedy pushed her away and lifted the President's head herself onto the stretcher.

Margaret M. Henchcliffe, an RN, was on duty in the Parkland emergency area. She had spent the last seven years as an emergency room nurse and had witnessed hundreds of bullet wounds during that time. When Ms.

Henchcliffe saw the stretcher being rushed through the emergency area, she helped bring it into the Trauma Room. Ms. Henchcliffe did not realize it was the President until after she was sent for blood a couple of minutes later. Ms. Henchcliffe testified to the Warren Commission, "The throat wound was just a little hole and had all the characteristics of an entrance wound, that there was no blood around the little hole and it was not jagged like most of the exit wounds she had seen." Ms. Henchcliffe was not asked about the President's head wound.

Dr. Charles J. Carrico was the first doctor at the Trauma Room to receive the President. Arlen Specter took his testimony. When Dr. Carrico testified before the Commission, he was asked about his initial observation of the President and he replied, "He was lying on a carriage, his respiration was slow, spasmodic, described as agonal." Dr. Carrico was interrupted and asked what he meant by agonal and the doctor replied. "These are respirations seen in one who has lost his normal coordinated central control of respiration, these are spasmodic and usually reflect a terminal patient. His, the President's color, I don't believe I said, he was an ashen, bluish, gray, cyanotic; he was making no spontaneous movements. I mean, no voluntary movements at all."

Dr. Carrico went on to describe the actions taken by himself and other doctors. He described the throat injury as a rather round 4-7 mm wound with no jagged edges or stellate lacerations. Dr. Carrico, under intense questioning, did say that the neck wound could have been either an entry or an exit wound. Dr. Carrico was then asked to describe the President's head wound and the doctor replied, "The wound that I saw was a large gaping wound located in the right occipitoparietal area."

Webster's dictionary defines the occipital bone as the bone that forms the posterior part of the skull. For us who are not doctors, Dr. Carrico was saying there was a large gaping hole in the right backside of the President's head. Dr. Carrico went on to describe the gory details of this injury in medical terms. When asked if he had noticed a bullet hole below the gaping wound, Dr. Carrico replied "No."

Dr. Malcolm O. Perry was having lunch in the main dining room with Chief Parkland Hospital Resident Dr. Ronald Jones when he was alerted by the loudspeaker system to an emergency. Dr. Perry arrived in the Trauma room to find Dr. Carrico at the head of the stretcher attaching the oxygen apparatus to assist in the President's breathing.

Arlen Specter took Dr. Perry's Warren Commission testimony and when Dr. Perry was asked what he had observed about the President's condition he

31

replied, "I noted there was a large wound of the right posterior parietal area in the head exposing the brain." Dr. Perry was asked later in his testimony regarding what he observed about the President's head wound specifically. Dr. Perry answered, "I saw no injuries other that the one which I noted to you, which was a large avulsive injury of the right occipital parietal area." Dr. Perry was then asked if he saw a bullet hole below the large avulsed area and Dr. Perry replied, "No."

Dr. William K. Clark was in the laboratory at Southwestern Medical School right next to Parkland hospital when he got a call to come to the hospital. Dr. Clark immediately rushed to the Trauma Room. When he arrived at the Trauma Room, Dr. Perry was performing a tracheotomy on the President and Dr. Jones and Dr. Carrico were administering fluids and blood intravenously.

Arlen Specter took Dr. Clark's testimony and asked him to describe what he had observed regarding the President's condition. Dr. Clark described the President's general condition, and then testified about the President's head injury, "I then examined the wound in the back of the head, this was a large gaping wound in the right posterior part, with cerebral tissue being damaged and exposed." In layman's terms, the right posterior part is the right rear of the head.

Dr. Clark was also asked if he observed a bullet hole in the back of the President's head and he replied, "No sir I did not, this could have easily been hidden in the blood and hair." It is interesting to note that after Dr. Clark's testimony describing the large gaping hole in the back of the President's head, Dr. Clark was then asked a question that countered what he had previously said. Dr. Clark was asked, "Now you describe the massive wound at the 'top' of the President's head, with the brain protruding, did you observe any other wound on the President's head?"

Dr. Robert N. McClelland was showing a film on surgical techniques to a group of students when he was alerted. When Dr. McClelland arrived in the Trauma Room, several other doctors were already working on the President. Dr. McClelland was soon positioned at the President's head helping Dr. Perry. Arlen Specter took Dr. McClelland's testimony before the Warren Commission and he was asked what he had observed about the President's head injury. Dr. McClelland replied, "I was in such a position that I could very closely examine the head wound and I noted that the right posterior portion of the skull had been extremely blasted, it had been shattered, apparently by the force of the shot so that the parietal bone was protruded up through the scalp and seemed to be fractured almost along its right posterior half, as well as some of the occipital bone being fractured in its lateral half, and this sprung open the bones that I mentioned in such a way that you could actually look down into the skull cavity itself and see probably a third or so, at least, of the brain tissue, posterior cerebral tissue and some of the cerebellar tissue had been blasted out."

Dr. McClelland described the throat wound as less than a quarter of an inch in diameter and he said, "We all thought it was an entrance wound." Dr. McClelland was asked what he meant by "we," to which he replied, "Essentially all the doctors that have been mentioned here." With more questioning, Dr. McClelland said the throat wound could be either an entry or an exit wound, but it would be impossible to determine which.

The Warren Commission made the determination that the throat wound was an exit wound.

I have had the honor of being a co-speaker with Dr. McClelland to a group of students nearly 50 years after the assassination of President Kennedy. Dr. McClelland is still telling the same story of what he witnessed and told the Warren Commission: As an eyewitness to President Kennedy's head wound in the emergency room at Parkland Hospital on November

The author and Dr. McClelland, 2013

22, 1963 – the back of President Kennedy's head had been blown out by a shot from the front.

Dr. Charles R. Baxter was conducting the student health service when he was contacted by the supervisor of the emergency room and alerted that the President was there. Arlen Specter took Dr. Baxter's Warren Commission testimony and he was asked what he had observed about the condition of the President, to which he replied, "He was obviously in extremis, there was a large gaping wound in the skull which was covered at that time with blood and its extent was not immediately determined." Dr. Baxter is then asked questions about the treatment of the neck wound, the tracheotomy, when the priest arrived, time of death, efforts made, what doctors were present, and then asked again about the head wound, being requested to describe in as much detail as he could the nature of the head wound. Dr. Baxter answered, "The only wound I actually saw ... Dr. Clark examined this above the manubrium, the sternum, the sternal notch, this wound was in temporal parietal plate of bone laid outward to the side and there was a large area, oh, I would say six by eight or ten cm of lacerated brain oozing from this wound, part of which was on the table and made a rather massive blood loss mixed with it and around it."

Dr. Baxter's description of the head injury was a little different from the other doctors and nurses and it put the massive head injury at the top of the head, but Dr. Baxter had already said, "Its extent was not immediately determined." Was Dr. Baxter trying to say with this statement that he did not get a good look at the wound?

There were more questions about the neck wound. When asked, Dr. Baxter stated the neck wound was more compatible with an entry wound than an exit wound. Dr. Baxter also stated that he had been at Parkland Hospital for six years and "We admit and treat, I would estimate, around 500 gunshot wounds per year … thereabouts."

He was then asked if he had any formal training in gunshot wounds.

Dr. Marion T. Jenkins had been in the dining room when he heard the Chief of Surgery, Dr. Tom Shires being paged "STAT." Dr. Jenkins knew Dr. Shires was out of town and that "STAT" meant emergency, and something bad had happened. Dr. Ronald Jones was with Dr. Jenkins and Dr. Jones answered the page. Dr. Jones hung up the phone and with an anguished look, the color drained from his face said, "The President has been shot and is on his way to the hospital."

At the same moment, they heard the sirens of the police motorcycles as they turned into the emergency entrance driveway; they knew this must be the President because ambulances always turned off their sirens before entering the driveway. Dr. Jenkins raced upstairs and notified two associates of the situation and then raced to the Trauma Room. Dr. Jenkins was an anesthesiologist, his Warren Commission testimony was given to Arlen Specter and he went into great detail as to what was being done to the President, who was there, who was doing what, and so on.

In reading his testimony, it is obvious that he was too busy with his duties in this emergency to have examined President Kennedy's head wound. Why Dr. Jenkins did not just say that he did not get a look at the President's head wound, I do not know, but it is typical of so many witnesses that when pressed for an answer, and being asked the same question in different ways, they finally answer to please the counsel asking the questions.

The Assistant Counsel for the Warren Commission, Specter, used the "official" autopsy report to invalidate the Parkland doctor's testimonies. When Dr. Jenkins was asked about what he had observed concerning the condition of the President, he described everything in great detail except the head wound. Dr. Jenkins was asked other questions and then once more asked about the head wound. He again skirted a direct description of the injury. Dr. Jenkins was then again, a third time, asked about the head wound and he replied, "I don't know whether this is right or not, but I thought there was a wound on the left temporal area, right in the hairline and right above the zygomatic process." Dr. Jenkins was told by Arlen Specter, "The autopsy report discloses no such development Dr. Jenkins."

Dr. Ronald C. Jones was a resident surgeon at Parkland Hospital. He was eating lunch with Dr. Perry when he heard the "STAT" page for Dr. Shires. Dr. Jones was one of the first doctors to arrive at the Trauma Room. During his tenure at Parkland, Dr. Jones spent many hours in the emergency room, sometimes attending to as many as four or five bullet wounds a night.

When Dr. Jones testified before the Warren Commission, Arlen Specter took his testimony, and he was asked if he had observed any wounds and he replied, "As we saw him for the first time, we noticed that he had a small wound in the midline of the neck, just above the suprasternal notch, and this was probably no greater than a quarter of an inch in greatest diameter, and that he had a large wound in the right posterior side of the head."

Dr. Jones was then asked to describe in detail the head wound and he answered, "There was a large defect in the back side of the head as the President lay on the cart with what appeared to be some brain hanging out of this wound with multiple pieces of skull noted next to the brain and with a tremendous amount of clot and brain."

Dr. Jones then read a report he had made of his activity in the Trauma Room that day. In that report, he noted about the neck wound, "a small hole in the anterior midline of the neck thought to be a bullet entrance wound." Dr. Jones was asked to explain this statement and he replied, "The hole was very small and relatively clean cut, as you would see in a bullet that is entering rather than exiting from a patient. If this were an exit wound, you would think that it exited at a very low velocity to produce no more damage than this had done and if this were a missile of high velocity you would expect more of an explosive type of exit wound, with more tissue destruction than this appeared to have on superficial examination."

Dr. Jones was then asked if he had any experience with a throat wound inflicted by a 6.5 bullet? Dr. Jones replied, "No, not to the throat, but to other parts of the body." Dr. Jones also stated in his testimony that the large hole in the back of the President's head appeared to be an exit wound.

Dr. Gene C. Akin was notified while on duty in the Operating Suite that anesthetic assistance was needed in the emergency room. When Dr. Akin testified before the Warren Commission, Arlen Specter took his testimony and he was asked what he had observed about the head wound and he answered, "the back of the right occipital parietal portion of his head was shattered, with brain substance extruding."

When Dr. Akin was asked if he had an opinion about the direction of the headshot he replied, "I assume that the right occipital parietal was the exit, so to speak, that he had probably been hit on the other side of the head, or at least tangentially in the back of the head, but I do not have any hard and fast opinions about that either."

Dr. Paul C. Peters was preparing lecture material for medical students and went to the Trauma Room to see if he could be of any assistance. Arlen Specter took Dr. Peters testimony before the Warren Commission and when asked about the head wound replied, "and as I remembered, I noticed that there was a large defect in the occiput." Dr. Peters was asked what he noticed in the occiput and he answered, "It seemed to me that in the right occipital parietal area that there was a large defect. There appeared to be brain loss and bone lose in the area." Dr. Peters did say in his testimony that the doctors speculated that the neck wound was an entry wound and the wound in the back of the head was an exit wound.

Arlen Specter took the Warren Commission testimony of *all* the Parkland doctors who worked on President Kennedy. As a group these Trauma Room doctors believed the throat wound was probably an entry wound but possibly could have been an exit wound. They were almost unanimous on the large gaping hole in the right occipital area of President Kennedy's head. In common words, the right rear corner of President Kennedy's head had been blown away. For that to have happened – the rear of Kennedy's head to be blown out – a shot had to have come from the front.

Almost all of the Parkland Hospital Doctors had their Warren Commission testimony taken during the week of March 25, 1964, 4 months after the assassination. It must be noted that all of the Parkland doctors discussed their testimony with Warren Commission Attorney Arlen Specter before they testified. The gaping exit wound in the right rear of President Kennedy's head disappeared before the autopsy was performed at Bethesda Hospital starting at about 8:00 P.M. the evening of the assassination.

It took years for Kennedy researchers and the original Parkland doctors to discover what had happened to the gaping exit hole in the back of President Kennedy's head.

CHAPTER SIX

TRAUMA ROOM TWO

Texas Governor John Connally had to be removed from the Presidential limousine first; he was in the middle jump seat, which prevented access to the President in the rear seat. The Governor was still conscious from his gunshot wounds upon arrival at Parkland Hospital. He was covered with blood but able to assist the hospital aides as they lifted him onto a stretcher and rushed him to Trauma Room Two.

Emergency medical procedures were began immediately, the main concern was a sucking sound coming from his chest wound, he had been hit by a bullet in the back near his right arm pit, the bullet had gone through his chest breaking a rib and exited the front of his chest; he was in great pain and complained bitterly about the pain. Intravenous therapy (IVs) were started and a tube was inserted to expand his collapsed right lung.

Dr. Giesecke was the attending anesthesia doctor. About twelve minutes had elapsed from the time of the shooting until he was rushed from the Trauma Room up to the second floor for surgery. Governor Connally was removed from the stretcher and placed on the operating table; the Governor was now in the hands of two of the most talented surgeons in the United States, both having had extensive military battlefield and civilian gunshot wound experience.

Dr. Robert R. Shaw had been at a conference and was on his way back to the hospital when he stopped for a traffic light near the hospital. As he was stopped at the light the President's car came speeding by with a police escort headed to the hospital. At about that moment Dr. Shaw heard on his car radio that the President had been shot. Dr. Shaw stopped at the Children's Hospital next to Parkland Hospital where he learned that Governor Connally had also been wounded.

Dr. Shaw walked the 150 yards from the Children's Hospital to Parkland Hospital and went directly to Trauma Room Two where Governor Connally was being attended. Dr. Shaw was a certified thoracic (chest) surgeon. During and after WWII, Dr. Shaw had served as chief of the Thoracic Surgery Center in Paris, France.

Dr. Shaw testified to the Warren Commission that at the center he had attended to over 900 chest wounds, many of them bullet wounds. He also testified that he had experience with over 1,000 bullet wounds to the chest. Warren Commission attorney Arlen Specter took his testimony on March 23, 1964, and the questions and answers about Governor Connally's chest wound got sidetracked with questions and answers about the wrist wound and which side of the wrist was the entry or exit. There were many off-the-record conferences. Dr. Shaw did state in his testimony that there were no bullet fragments found in Governor Connally's chest.

Dr. Shaw was recalled to testify again on April 21, 1964. Dr. Shaw had recognized the wound below the right nipple as the exit wound owing to its size and jagged edges. Once fully anesthetized, Governor Connally was rolled over and the back wound was examined: it was a small wound, it had clean cut edges, it was an entrance wound, was roughly elliptical, was located even with the right armpit on the far right side of the back, and the bullet had missed the shoulder blade.

Dr. Shaw had not yet discovered the thigh wound and he assigned the treatment of the wrist wound to Dr. Gregory. During the chest operation, Dr. Shaw discovered that the fifth rib had been hit by a bullet and was shattered and that fragments of bone had to be removed. Dr. Shaw testified that the rib at this point was not of great density but could cause a slight deflection of the bullet. In his testimony Dr. Shaw goes into great detail in medical terminology to describe the damage to the lung tissue and muscle tissues that the bullet had caused and the required repairs needed.

Dr. Shaw was then shown the nearly pristine bullet that was recovered from a stretcher on the first floor of Parkland Hospital on November 22, 1963, and now labeled Commission Exhibit 399. Dr. Shaw was asked if this near pristine bullet could have caused all three of Governor Connally's wounds, wounds to the chest, wrist, and thigh. Dr. Shaw answered, "I feel there would be some difficulty in explaining all of the wounds as being inflicted by bullet exhibit 399 without causing more in the way of loss of substance to the bullet or deformation of the bullet."

The Commission hearing then goes off the record. When the hearing resumes, Dr. Shaw is shown the Zapruder movie and asked if he can pinpoint the frame that the Governor is hit in relation to his injuries. Dr. Shaw states, "Frame 236, give or take 1 or 2 frames." Dr. Shaw is then asked if he has an "opinion" about the possibility that one bullet hit both the President and the Governor. Dr. Shaw replied, "Yes, from the pictures, from the conversation with Governor Connally and Mrs. Connally, it seems the first bullet hit the President in the shoulder and perforated the neck, but this was not the bullet that Governor Connally feels hit him and in the sequence of films, I think it is hard to say that the first bullet hit both of these men almost simultaneously." Dr. Shaw was then asked if a person could have a delayed reaction to

sensing that they have been hit by a bullet and the doctor responded, "Yes, but when a bullet strikes bone, the reaction is usually quite prompt."

Dr. Charles F. Gregory was an orthopedic surgeon who served in the Navy during WW II, and in the Korean War in support of the First Marine Corps Division. Arlen Specter also took Dr. Gregory's Warren Commission testimony and was asked how many bullet wounds he had treated; he estimated he had dealt directly with 500 such wounds. Dr. Gregory was seeing patients at the hospital at the time the President and the Governor were admitted. Dr. Gregory first checked emergency to see if his services were needed with the President and was told they were not; he then prepared to leave the hospital but stopped by the surgical suite on the way out and encountered Dr. Shaw. Dr. Shaw retained Dr. Gregory to treat Governor Connally's wrist wound.

Dr. Gregory examined the Governor's wrist and thigh wounds and found an entry wound on the top of the wrist and an exit wound on the palm side of the wrist about an inch above the fold of the wrist. The entry wound was about half a centimeter by two and one half centimeters and the exit wound was about half a centimeter by two centimeters. The entry wound was larger than the exit wound and in Dr. Gregory's opinion, an irregular object caused the entry wound. Dr. Gregory testified about the shattered bones above the wrist and that the x-rays showed at least seven bullet fragments, which the doctor pointed out to attorney Specter.

The three largest metallic fragments varied from five-tenths of a millimeter in diameter to approximately two millimeters in diameter and no more than a half-millimeter in thickness, these were metal flakes. Dr. Gregory also found cloth fragments in the wound similar to Governor

Connally's coat fabric. Two of the bullet fragments were removed and given to a nurse, who in turn gave them to a Texas Ranger.

During Dr. Gregory's testimony he was shown Commission exhibit 399, the bullet found on a stretcher on November 22, 1963 at the hospital and asked if that bullet could have caused the wounds to Governor Connally's wrist. Dr. Gregory examined the near pristine bullet and answered, "I find a small flake has been either knocked off or removed from the rounded end of the missile, I was told this was removed for analysis, the only other deformity which I find is at the base of the missile at the point where it joined the cartridge carrying the powder, I presume, and this is somewhat flattened and deflected, distorted. There is some irregularity of the darker metal within which I presume to represent lead. The only way this missile could have produced this wound, in my view, was to enter the wrist backward."

Dr. Gregory was then asked if this nearly pristine bullet had enough lead missing to account for the lead found in Governor Connally's wrist and Dr. Gregory replied that he did not know enough about this particular bullet to know what was normal.

LATER THAT DAY

Senator Russell asked Dr. Gregory when he had first seen Commission Exhibit 399, and the doctor replied, "This morning." Dr. Gregory was then asked about the thigh wound and the doctor described the wound as being about a third up from the knee and on the inside of the leg and that it was a puncture wound about the size of an eraser. Dr. Gregory was asked if one bullet could have caused all three of Governor Connally's wounds. The doctor answered that the three wounds to the Governor could have occurred from one bullet. Dr. Gregory was then asked if one bullet could have caused all the wounds to both President Kennedy and Governor Connally, and Dr. Gregory replied, "I believe one would have to concede the possibility, but I believe firmly that the possibility is much diminished."

The doctor was then asked why he said that and the doctor replied, "I think that to pass through the soft tissues of the President would certainly decelerated the missile to some extent, having then struck the Governor and shattered a rib, it is further decelerated, yet it has presumably retained sufficient energy to smash the radius, moreover it escaped the forearm to penetrate at least the skin and fascia of the thigh, I am not persuaded that this is very probable. I would have to yield to the possibility."

CHAPTER SEVEN

THE PRESIDENT IS DEAD

At 1:00 P.M. November 22, 1963, White House Assistant Press Secretary, Malcolm Kilduff, held a press conference at Parkland hospital and announced that President Kennedy had died.

Assistant Press Secretary Kilduff told the reporters, who had quickly gathered at the hospital, that the President had died of a gunshot wound to the head and Kilduff pointed his finger to the right front of his head, near his right temple, to illustrate the point of entry.

CHAPTER EIGHT

THE TEXAS SCHOOL BOOK DEPOSITORY

The Texas School Book Depository was just that, a storage warehouse for school textbooks. The building was seven floors tall and located on the northwest corner of Elm and Houston Streets at the very west end of downtown Dallas.

On November 22, 1963, Roy Truly was the Depository Superintendent, on October 15, 1963, five weeks before the assassination of President John F. Kennedy, Truly received a phone call from a woman named Ruth Paine who lived in the Dallas suburb of Irving.

Mrs. Paine was inquiring about employment for the husband of a Russian lady she had befriended named Lee Oswald. After a brief conversation, Truly told Mrs. Paine to send Mr. Oswald in to fill out an employment application. Lee Oswald did come in and he did fill out an application for employment, was hired, and went to work the very next day as schoolbook order filler. Lee seemed pleased to be hired and quickly learned his job, mostly working on the first and sixth floors. Truly would greet Lee in the morning with: "Good morning Lee," and Lee would reply, "Good morning sir."

If Truly would ask Lee about his new baby, Lee would always give Truly a big smile. On November 22, 1963, Truly was going to lunch at about 12:15 P.M. with O.V. Campbell, who was Vice President of the Depository. As they went out the front door they noticed the crowd that had gathered in front of the building to watch President Kennedy's motorcade, they decided to wait and watch the motorcade also.

When the President's limousine made the turn in front of them off Houston Street onto Elm Street, the limousine made too wide of a turn and almost ran over the curb where they were standing. When the first shot rang out, like the pop of a firecracker, the crowd was stunned.

After the crack, crack of two more shots, the crowd surged back from the street in terror and panic, forcing Truly and Campbell back to the steps of the TSBD building. At that moment Truly saw a young motorcycle policeman run right by him rushing through the crowd and pushing people aside as he ran up to the front entrance of the Depository.

The motorcycle policeman was Marrion L. Baker who had been riding beside one of the press cars, four of five cars behind the President's car. At this position in the motorcade Officer Baker had not yet turned off Houston Street onto Elm Street, and was facing the Texas School Book Depository when he heard the first shot. Baker saw a group of pigeons fly off the roof of the Depository, and his instant thought was that someone was shooting from the rooftop.

When Truly saw Officer Baker run through the crowd, he turned and ran into the depository to catch up to the officer. Truly caught up with him in the lobby of the Depository, and Baker blurted out that he wanted to get to the roof. With Truly leading the way they ran to the elevators only to find that the elevators were stuck on the fifth floor, they then rushed to the stairway and started up the stairs with Truly in front.

On the second floor Officer Baker, out of the corner of his eye as he was running by, saw a man through the window in the door to the lunchroom. Baker drew his gun and entered the lunch room. Truly, who had been three or four steps ahead, turned around and entered the lunch room to find Officer Baker with his gun drawn and aimed at a man. Baker asked Truly if he knew who this man was and Truly replied, "He is Lee Oswald and he works here." Baker put his gun back in its holster and Oswald casually walked back over to the soft-drink machine and bought a bottle of soda.

Roy Truly and Officer Baker then continued up the stairs. In his testimony to the Warren Commission, Baker stated that when he encountered Oswald in the lunch room, just seconds after the shooting, Oswald did not seem to be out of breath and appeared normal, calm, and collected.

Two trial runs were performed to reenact Officer Baker's movements from the time of the first shot until he encountered Oswald in the lunch room on the second floor of the Depository. The time of the first trial run was one minute and thirty seconds and the second trial was one minute and fifteen seconds.

Officer Baker also participated with Secret Service Agent John Howlett in timing how long it would take to go from the sniper's nest on the sixth floor window, where the shots were fired, to the second floor lunch room where Officer Baker encountered Oswald buying a bottle of soda no more than 75 seconds after the first shot. At a normal walk the time was 78 seconds, at a fast walk the time was 74 seconds.

In the Warren Commission's summary after the first shot: Oswald fired two more shots, crossed the length of the sixth floor to the stairwell, hid a rifle in some boxes, went down four flights of stairs and was calmly buying a bottle of soda in the lunch room, appeared normal to a policeman, was not out of breath, all in under 75 seconds at most.

You be the judge if a man could kill the President, act normal, be calm, not be out of breath after coming down four flights of stairs, and do it all in less than 75 seconds. Roy Truly had testified to the Warren Commission that after Mrs. Paine had called him on October 15, 1963 about Lee Harvey Oswald needing a job, he told Mrs. Paine he did not need any full time help, but have Oswald come in, and he would talk to him.

Lee Oswald came in that same day, and filled out an employment application while sitting across the desk from Truly. In questioning Oswald, he said that he had just got out of the Marines with an honorable discharge – which was not quite true.

According to his Warren Commission testimony, Truly was impressed with Lee's good manners and calling Mr. Truly, "Sir." Oswald was hired on the spot and went to work the next day, October 16, 1963. In his testimony to the Warren Commission, Truly stated that Oswald was a quick learner, a hard working above-average employee, and had never missed a day's work.

Roy Truly was highly respected for his management skills, and well thought of in the Dallas Community; he had worked at the Texas School Book Depository since July of 1934, nearly 30 years. But he did something that day, November 22, 1963, that I have not understood. For years people have asked, "How and why was a description of Lee Harvey Oswald put out as a possible suspect within minutes of the assassination of President John F. Kennedy?"

Truly had seen Oswald in the lunch room buying that bottle of soda, where Oswald was calm, and not out of breath. When Truly testified before the Warren Commission he stated: "A few minutes later while Police Officers were all over the Depository building taking names of employees."

They had not yet taken a roll -all of employees, and Truly picked up the phone and called Mr. Aikman at the other Texas School Book Depository warehouse where all the employee records were kept and got the information on Lee Harvey Oswald: address where he lived in Irving, telephone number, general description etc.

It had just been a few minutes since Truly had seen Oswald in the lunchroom, and Truly admitted under oath that he had one or two other employees that were missing, but he did not ask for information from their files.

Truly, standing a few feet from Chief George Lumpkin of the Dallas Police Department, walked over to the Chief and told him he had *one* man missing. Chief Lumpkin then took Truly up to the sixth floor to tell Homicide Captain Will Fritz that Truly had one man missing.

The President had not even been pronounced dead when a description of Lee Harvey Oswald was put out on the Dallas Police Department airways. It would be nice to know the real reason Truly looked up Oswald's and only Oswald's personnel file after seeing a normal and calm Oswald in the lunch room a few minutes earlier.

Bonnie Ray Williams was helping to put a new floor on the upper floors of the TSBD when on November 22, 1963, he had taken a position on the fifth floor to watch the President's motorcade. The position he took on the fifth floor was almost directly under the sixth floor window from where the shots were allegedly fired. Williams testified that the shots shook the building so hard that dirt and debris fell from the ceiling. He stated that the shots came from over his head, from the floor above him.

James Jarman Jr. was an order checker for the TSBD. On November 22, 1963, Mr. Jarman had taken a position near Bonnie Ray Williams on the fifth floor to watch the motorcade, he had raised a window to get a better view and was on his knees watching the motorcade when the shots were fired. He too thought the shots came from inside the Depository, he also noticed white dust, like plaster, in Mr. Williams hair after the shooting.

Mr. Jarman made a statement in his sworn testimony to the Warren Commission that makes one pause for thought. Mr. Jarman testified that earlier he had been on the first floor talking to Lee Harvey Oswald, and I quote: "Well, he (Oswald) was standing up in the window and I went to the window also, and he asked me what were the people gathering around on the corner for, and I told him that the President was supposed to pass by that morning. He asked me did I know which way he was coming and I told him yes, he would probably come down Main and turn on Houston and then back again on Elm." Oswald replied, "Oh, I see," and that was all.

There was no follow-up to be found of any other possible witnesses to James Jarman's statement about Oswald asking about why a crowd was gathering in front of the Depository that morning.

Harold Norman was Order Filler at the Depository on November 22, 1963. Norman was on the fifth floor near Williams and Jarman, and had also raised a window to watch the motorcade. He testified to the Warren Commission that he heard the shell casings hitting the floor above him and the ejecting of the rifle when the shots were fired. He also noticed dust in Bonnie Ray Williams' hair after the shooting.

Charles Givens, also a book handler at the Depository on the afternoon of the assassination, gave a sworn statement to the FBI that he had seen Lee Harvey Oswald in the "domino" room (lounge) on the first floor reading a newspaper at 11:50 A.M. Three other Depository employees also saw Oswald in the domino room at this time.

Givens would later change his statement when Attorney David Belin of the Warren Commission took his testimony in secret. However his testimony can be found in Volume VI, pages 345-356. It is interesting to note that he was blocked out of the TSBD by the Dallas Police and was not present when the police call the roll of the employees.

David Belin took Victoria Adams' Warren Commission testimony. She was one of the few witnesses who mentioned that the power was shut off to the Texas School Book Depository during the shooting of President Kennedy and for a short time afterward. Ms. Adams stated, "I pushed the button for the passenger elevator, but the power had been cut off for the passenger elevator, so I took the stairs." (Volume VI page 361.)

Carolyn Arnold, secretary to the vice president of the Texas School Book Depository, did not testify before the Warren Commission, but did give a statement to the FBI that she went to the Depository lunchroom for a drink of water at approximately 12:15 P.M. on November 22, 1963. She saw Oswald seated at a booth eating his lunch and had absolutely no doubt that it was Lee Oswald she had seen.

Could Oswald have raced up four flights of stairs to the sixth floor, assassinated the President, raced back down to the second floor lunchroom and be buying a soda, and calm, cool, not out of breath, 75 seconds after the first shot as officer Baker has testified?

CHAPTER NINE

DEAD PHONES
& NO ELECTRICAL POWER

Was it planned or was it a coincidence that both the telephone and electricity went off in the Texas School Book Depository building at the exact moment of the assassination 12:30 P.M. November 22, 1963? The telephone and electric systems are independent of each other. What are the odds that both would go off at the same time, then come back on three or four minutes later at the same time? And to also have happened at the same moment the President of the United States was executed in front of that building? The odds are millions to one.

The most glaring evidence of the electrical power being cut off was of the two elevators not working. They were stuck on upper floors. At approximately 45 seconds after the shooting, the Depository manager Roy Truly and Dallas policeman Marrion L. Baker tried to use the elevators and could not and had to use the stairs.

At least two of the women who worked in the building also mentioned that the electricity was off at the time of the shooting in their Warren Commission testimony. Victoria Adams was one of those women and in Volume VI page 391 of the Warren Report she states "Following that, I pushed the button for the passenger elevator, but the power had been cut off on the elevator, so I took the stairs to the second floor."

Geneva Hine was asked in her Warren Commission testimony: "Were you alone then at this time?" Hine stated, "Yes sir, I was alone until the lights all went out and the phones went dead because the motorcade was coming." Geneva L. Hine's Warren Commission testimony is in Volume VI pages 393 to 397.

Ms. Hine volunteered to answer the phones while the other office workers went outside to watch the motorcade. There was no switchboard but the Depository had three incoming lines, a warehouse line, and an intercom system. Ms. Hine states in her testimony on page 395: "And the phones went dead because the motorcade was coming near us and no one was calling, so I got up and thought I could see it from the east window in our office."

Moments later, according to her testimony on page 396, after talking about hearing the shots she states she goes back to her desk, and: "I went straight up to the desk because the telephones were beginning to wink, outside calls were beginning to come in."

It is not clear whether the Depository offices were the only offices in the building that had their phone lines go dead. There were several other businesses that had offices in the School Book Depository with their own independent phone lines.

CHAPTER TEN

BEHIND THE FENCE

The Abraham Zapruder home movie clearly shows President Kennedy's head being violently thrown back so hard, that the momentum also throws the President's shoulders and body violently into the back of the seat.

The Zapruder film clearly shows that at least one shot came from the front. Also the Parkland Hospital doctors who worked on John Kennedy in the emergency room said to a man that the right rear of the President's head had been blown out. This gaping hole in the rear of President's head clearly indicated that at least one shot came from the front. A shot from the front would mean at least two shooters, and that would mean the assassination was more than the work of one "lone nut assassin." It would then be a conspiracy executed by "unknown conspirators."

In spite of hard evidence that at least one shot came from in front of President Kennedy, the Warren Commission declared that the fatal headshot came from the Texas School Book Depository, which would mean from the rear of the President.

Through the years there have been many theories advanced as to why his head would react opposite and contrary to all laws of physics. Two of these theories are a "neuro-reaction" and a "jet effect." These theories have yet to be proven by experts on physics.

When you hit something with any object, the energy expended causes the object to go away from the impact of the hit. I have yet to meet a hunter that has had an animal react toward the shooter after being shot. The power and energy of the bullet hitting an animal knocks the animal away from the shooter. Thus, with the President's head and shoulders being violently thrown backwards into the seat, there is a high probability that at least one shot came from in front of the President.

And there are credible witnesses on the triple underpass and elsewhere whose statements and testimony suggest that a source of a frontal shot was from behind and over the picket fence at the rear of the Grassy Knoll.

51

Motorcycle policeman Bobby Hargis riding his motorcycle at the left rear of the President's car states in his Warren Commission testimony: "It seemed like his head exploded, and I was splattered with blood and brain, and kind of a bloody water." Hargis' testimony is consistent with a shot coming from in front of the President's limousine. Hargis quickly parked his motorcycle and ran up the Grassy Knoll to the picket fence and the railroad yard. Hargis remembers seeing only one man in the yard, who he assumed was a railroad detective. Hargis also assumed that the "detective" had just come into the area. Hargis then returned to his motorcycle and started talking to witnesses.

Lee Bowers Jr. was a railroad tower man for the Union Terminal Company. Mr. Bowers' testimony can be found in Volume VI, page 284 of the 26-volume Warren Report. From his 14-foot tower he had a clear view of the area behind the fence that separated the railroad and parking area from the Grassy Knoll. Mr. Bowers testified that three cars came into the area from around noon until the time of the shooting at 12:30 P.M.

The first was a 1959 blue and white Oldsmobile station wagon with out-of-state plates and a Goldwater sticker. The second was a black Ford with one man in it, holding something to his face such as a telephone or mike and had Texas license plates. The third was a 1961 or 1962 Chevrolet four-door Impala occupied by one white male; it entered just a few minutes before the shooting, it had out of state license plates, a Goldwater sticker, and was covered with red mud up to the windows. This car cruised the area for a few minutes and then slowly drove back toward the School Book Depository.

Bowers said, "The last time I saw him, he was pausing just about in, just about above the assassination site." Bowers also testified that he saw two men standing behind the fence just before the shots were fired, they were standing 10 or 15 feet apart and looking over the fence toward the Presidential motorcade as it approached.

Mr. Bowers, in his testimony before the Warren Commission, stated that he heard three shots, the first shot, a pause, then two shots in rapid succession. He was then asked about a commotion that had caught his eye during the shooting for some reason. Mr. Bowers: "Nothing that I could pinpoint as having happened that—."

Mr. Bowers was cut off by an unrelated question about a different subject. A short time later Mr. Bowers was excused as a witness without ever explaining what had caught his eye.

Mark Lane taped and filmed an interview with Mr. Bowers in 1966, and in Mark Lane's book, *Rush To Judgment*, Mark Lane writes:

Bowers: At the time of the shooting in the vicinity of where the two men I described were, there was a flash of light or, as far as I am concerned, something I could not identify, but there was something which occurred which caught my eye in this immediate area on the embankment. Now, what this was, I could not state at that time and at this time I could not identify it, other than there was some unusual occurrence ... a flash of light or smoke or something out of the ordinary had occurred there.

S. M. Holland was the Signal Supervisor for the Union Terminal Railroad; he had been employed by the railroad for 25 years and was standing on the triple underpass when the shooting occurred. In his testimony before the Warren Commission, Mr. Holland gave an excellent recollection of what was happening in the Presidential limousine at the time of the first two shots.

Mr. Holland thought he had heard three or four shots. I will quote Mr. Holland, "There was a shot, a report, I don't know if it was a shot. I can't say that. And a puff of smoke came out about six or eight feet above the ground right out from under those trees. And at just about this location from where I was standing you could see that puff of smoke, like someone had thrown a firecracker, or something out, and that is just about the way it sounded. It wasn't as loud as the previous reports or shots."

Mr. Holland was talking about the trees just beside the picket fence at the top of the Grassy Knoll. When asked about which shot, he replied, "the third or fourth." Mr. Holland was then asked if he had any doubt about that and he replied, "I have no doubt about seeing that puff of smoke come out from under those trees." Mr. Holland had also made a statement in the Dallas County Sheriff's office immediately after the assassination of President Kennedy on November 22, 1963. In that statement he said, "I looked over toward the arcade and trees and saw a puff of smoke come from under the trees."

Austin L. Miller worked for the Louisiana Freight Bureau and was also on the triple underpass at the time of the assassination of President Kennedy. After the shooting, Mr. Miller was immediately taken to the Sheriff's office to make a statement about what he had witnessed.

In his statement made that day, November 22, 1963, Mr. Miller states, "I saw something which I thought was smoke or steam coming from a group of trees north of Elm" Mr. Miller also testified before the Warren Commission. Assistant Counsel David Belin took his deposition. The smoke or steam, coming from the trees, that Mr. Miller had witnessed during the shooting, was never brought up.

Gordon Arnold was on leave from the Army and had brought a camera to film the President's motorcade. Mr. Arnold was in his Army uniform and he wanted to film from on top of the triple underpass. A well-dressed man with a badge prevented him from doing so. Mr. Arnold then found a spot at the top of the Grassy Knoll, a few feet in front of the picket fence, to shoot his movie film. During the shooting he felt a shot whiz by his left ear and threw himself to the ground. He was questioned by a uniformed officer a few moments later and insisted to the officer that the shots came from behind him. The officer confiscated his movie film. The next day Gordon Arnold shipped out for a tour of duty in the Army. Mr. Arnold never testified before the Warren Commission.

In 1978, the *Dallas Morning News* interviewed Gordon Arnold, and at the time there were some who doubted his story. But it was soon corroborated by U.S. Senator Ralph Yarborough who was riding two cars behind the President's car with Vice President Lyndon Johnson, and had read the *Morning News* article about Gordon Arnold.

Senator Yarborough wrote the *Morning News* that he recalled that during the shooting, "He saw a uniformed man immediately hit the dirt at the spot where Arnold said he was filming." Senator Yarborough remembers thinking to himself, at the time, that the soldier's quick reaction suggested he must be a real combat veteran. What happened to the confiscated film and who took it are still unknown.

In growing up with a rifle in my hand, I had never seen a puff of smoke come out of a rifle barrel when it was fired. But in asking around, I was told that a well-oiled rifle barrel would cause a puff of smoke to come out of the barrel when it was fired. Then, later, when the gulf war broke out I was watching a film clip of Saddam Hussein on television and Hussein fired a rifle into the air. A large puff of smoke came out of the barrel.

CHAPTER ELEVEN

MORE PUFF OF SMOKE

B esides the railroad men who were standing on the Triple Underpass at the time of the assassination, and then made signed statements in the Dallas County Sheriff's office immediately after the shooting about seeing a puff of smoke come from the area of the picket fence during the shooting, NBC photographer David Wiegman captured the puff of smoke on film.

The sixth car behind the President's car was camera car #1, a yellow 1964 Chevrolet Impala SS Super Sport convertible provided by a local Chevrolet dealer. At the sound of the first shot the car is about to turn onto Elm street and three cameramen jump out, David Wiegman of NBC, Thomas Atkins of White House movies, and Thomas Craven Jr. of CBS.

David Wiegman had his 16mm camera rolling on the assassination scene as he ran toward the Grassy Knoll. A frame by frame examination of Wiegman's herky-jerky film by experts clearly shows a puff of smoke coming from the bushes at the top of the knoll. David Wiegman was never called to testify nor was his 16mm film, clearly showing a puff of smoke coming from the picket fence area during the assassination of President Kennedy, ever shown to the Warren Commission. This film of the puff of smoke was further proof that at least one shot had come from in front of the President.

Hoffman

Book depository

Elm

Ed Hoffman relating where h
saw the president's head wound

CHAPTER TWELVE

ED HOFFMAN – A SILENT WITNESS

Ed Hoffman was a deaf mute, back in 1963 deaf mutes were referred to as "deaf and dumb," but Ed Hoffman was not dumb. Ed was a married man with wife and children to support. He had a good job at Texas Instruments.

On November 22, 1963 Hoffman had a dental problem and took off work to see his dentist in Grande Prairie Texas, a suburb of Dallas. The trip took him through downtown Dallas on Main Street. While Ed was driving through downtown Dallas on Main Street he saw the crowd gathering for President Kennedy's motorcade and decided to park just past Dealey Plaza on Stemmons to see if he could catch sight of the President.

After parking his car near the Stemmons on-ramp he climbed to the raised railroad track over looking where Elm Street turns into Stemmons below and overlooks Dealey Plaza to the East. This point where Ed was standing also gave Ed a good view of the rail yard and the rear of the picket fence where Hoffman observed 2 white males standing behind the fence looking into Dealey Plaza and clutching something to their chest. One of the men was dressed in a business suit and the other was dressed in work clothes (train man, overalls).

As the motorcade came into view in Dealey Plaza, one of these men aimed a rifle over the fence, because Ed was deaf he did not hear any shots but thought he saw a puff of fluffy white smoke come from the area of the raised rifle. He watched as the men disassembled the rifle and then the man in work clothes ran and disappeared into the rail yard. The man in a suit assumed a casual composure and was soon confronted by a policeman with a drawn gun. The man in the suit reached inside his coat pocket and apparently showed the policeman some identification. Dallas Police Officer Joe Marshall Smith corroborated this observation by Hoffman when Smith testified before the Warren Commission about a man in a suit behind the picket fence producing Secret Service identification.

And as mentioned before, Lee Bowers Jr. was in the railroad tower that was elevated 14 feet above the rail yard on the west side of the School Book Depository. Mr. Bowers had a clear view of the back side of the picket fence and he testified before the Warren Commission that he observed the two men Ed Hoffman had seen standing behind the picket fence. He testified that something from the area of where these two were standing caught his eye during the shooting. When Lee Bowers started to explain what had caught his eye, he was cut off by being asked an unrelated question. A few moments later Mr. Bowers was excused as a witness without ever explaining what had caught his eye. Lee Bowers Jr.'s Warren Commission testimony can be found in Volume VI, starting on page 284.

When Ed Hoffman used sign language to try and tell his parents what happened, they did not believe him. When Hoffman tried to use sign language to tell the FBI what he had seen, the FBI laughed at him. As the years passed, Hoffman told his story over and over again in sign language with different interpreters, it was sometimes interpreted slightly different causing problems of believability.

I was also in Dealey Plaza when President Kennedy was assassinated. I am not a deaf mute, I speak good English, and I have a good reputation. I understand the problem of people not believing that one was an eyewitness to the assassination of President John F. Kennedy. My own parents had a hard time believing that I had seen the assassination, when I first tried to tell them what I had witnessed.

Brian Edwards, author of *Beyond the Fence Line: The Eyewitness Account of Ed Hoffman and the Murder of President Kennedy*, found Ed Hoffman to be an honest and truthful witness. Brian Edwards was a police officer for 22 years, and had been a lead Fraud & Forgery investigator when he interviewed Ed Hoffman over 25 times with a level-5-5 ASL interpreter. Edwards' book tells the agony that a deaf mute went through in trying to tell about witnessing the fatal shot that killed President John F. Kennedy.

CHAPTER THIRTEEN

THE PSEUDO-SECRET SERVICE AGENTS

A s mentioned earlier, Gordon Arnold was on leave from the Army and
he planned to take motion pictures of the Presidential motorcade
from the railroad tracks on top of the triple underpass. Arnold,
wearing his Army uniform, proceeded behind the picket fence toward
railroad tracks on top of the triple overpass. He was soon approached by a
man in civilian clothes wearing a sidearm and the man told Arnold he was
not allowed up there.

Arnold challenged the man's authority, the man then pulled out a badge,
said he was with the Secret Service and did not want anyone up there.
Arnold then took up another position in Dealey Plaza.

Joe Marshall Smith was a 7-year Dallas Police veteran. On November
22, 1963 he was assigned to the Corner of Elm and Houston Streets. One
of his assignments was to stop traffic on Elm Street when the President's
motorcade arrived at that intersection. When the first shot rang out Officer
Smith was in the middle of Elm Street on the East edge of Houston Street
holding up traffic.

Officer Smith testified before the Warren Commission on July 23, 1964.
He testified, "This woman came up to me and she was in hysterics. She
told me, 'They are shooting the President from the bushes.' Officer Smith
ran to the area immediately behind the concrete structure at the top of the
Grassy Knoll and started checking the bushes and the cars in the parking
lot. Officer Smith encountered a man behind the picket fence and this man
upon seeing Smith and without being asked, produced Secrete Service
credentials. Officer Smith allowed this man to go on his way. *The Secret
Service has denied they had an agent in that area at that time.*

Sergeant D.V. Harkness was a 17-year Dallas Police veteran. On
November 22, 1963, he was the officer in charge of the traffic officers
along the parade route. He was at the corner of Main and Houston Streets

when the shots rang out. Sergeant Harkness testified before the Warren Commission on April 9, 1964.

His testimony shows that when he observed the President's car almost come to a stop, he got on his motorcycle and went west on Main Street to between the triple underpass and the industrial Avenue to see if anyone was fleeing that area. When he saw no one, he then went to the area behind the picket fence where he ran into Amos Euins who told him the shots came from the School Book Depository. He took Amos Euins to Inspector Sawyer's car in front of the depository, and then went to the back of the depository to seal the back of the depository off.

At the rear of the building Sergeant Harkness encountered "some Secret Service Agents there. I didn't get them identified. They told me they were Secret Service." In separate testimony from the Secret Service it was firmly established that of the 28 Secret Service Agents in Dallas that day, *not one agent was in the Grassy Knoll area or the parking lot behind the Grassy Knoll and no agent was on foot in the area before or after the shooting.*

Later that afternoon one lone agent did go into the School Book Depository. The Dallas Police radio communication tapes show that Sergeant Harkness radioed in about Euins being a witness six minutes after the shooting. For Sergeant Harkness to run across the so-called "Secret Service Agents" and seal off the building, it had to be at least two or three minutes later, eight or nine minutes after the shooting.

Dallas County Deputy Constable Seymour Weitzman ran toward the top of the Grassy Knoll and also encountered a man carrying Secret Service identification. Weitzman later identified the man as Bernard Barker. Barker, at the time, was a part-time real estate agent in Key Biscayne Florida – he also was a CIA asset.

Later he led the 4-man group of (Nixon's) Watergate burglars from the Miami area. If Weitzman is correct in identifying Barker, then Barker as a CIA operative would have had no trouble obtaining Secret Service credentials.

Barker was not the only future Watergate conspirator reported to be in Dallas on November 22, 1963. CIA operative Marita Lorenz, under oath, swore that CIA agents Howard Hunt and Frank Sturgis were also at the assassination scene in Dallas on November 22, 1963.

Separately and unaware of the other's testimony, you have at least four men – three of them, law enforcement officers – who encountered fake Secret Service agents moments after the shooting that killed President Kennedy. It is safe to say that these fake Secret Service agents were part of an over-all assassination plan. And as I have noted before, the real Secret Service has gone on record and stated they had *no men* on the ground in Dealey Plaza at the time of the assassination.

The testimony of Officer Joe Smith was taken the same afternoon that I testified. Both of our testimonies was taken by Wesley J. Liebeler on July 23, 1964 in the office of the U.S. attorney in Dallas. Officer Smith's testimony can be found in Volume VII pages 531-539 of the WC.

Officer Smith's police assignment that day was to stop traffic on west-bound Elm at Houston Street. After the gun shots officer Smith testified he went to the parking lot behind the Grassy Knoll area by the School Book Depository and was checking cars when he encountered a man who pulled a Secret Service Agent's identification out of his pocket and identified himself as a Secret Service Agent. The credentials looked authentic and satisfied Officer Smith and the Deputy Sheriff with him. In thinking back Officer Smith said the man looked more like a mechanic with dirty finger nails that a Secret Service Agent. After about 20 minutes of searching cars, Officer Smith was assigned to guard the front door of the School Book Depository.

Amos Euins in back seat of patrol car on November 22, 1963.

CHAPTER FOURTEEN

SOMEBODY RAN OUT THE BACK

James Richard Worrell Jr., age 20, was standing about five feet in front of the School Book Depository. He watched the President's limo pass in front of him, and then the first shot rang out. He looked straight up to see a few inches of a gun barrel sticking out of a window on the fifth or sixth floor window in the far right corner of the Depository, and just in time to see a small flash of fire and smoke come from the barrel as a second shot was fired. Worrell then glanced back at the motorcade and saw the President slumping in his seat.

The shooting scared Worrell, he pivoted to his left and ran toward Houston street, a third shot rang out as he turned the corner of Elm and Houston streets, and he thought he heard a fourth shot. Worrell ran about 100 yards north on Houston and stopped to catch his breath; he turned and faced the back of the School Book Depository. Worrell was there for about three minutes when a man tore out of the back door.

The next morning was Saturday morning and James Worrell heard a plea on television by Dallas Police Chief Jesse Curry for anyone who had seen anything concerning the assassination to call the Dallas Police Department. When Worrell heard this plea, he called his local police department in Farmers Branch, Texas, a suburb of Dallas.

A Farmers Branch officer picked Worrell up at his house and took him to the Farmers Branch police station where Worrell told what he had seen. The Farmers Branch police then called the Dallas PD and a Dallas police officer came and picked up Worrell, and took Worrell to the Dallas Police station where Worrell made a signed statement about what he had seen when President Kennedy was assassinated.

Worrell was also interviewed by two reporters that Saturday, November 23, 1963, and told the reporters the same story. Worrell was notified in late February 1964 that he would be flown to Washington, D.C. and give testimony to the Warren Commission on March 10, 1964. James Worrell was to be one of the first witnesses to testify before the Warren

Commission and a *Dallas Morning News* reporter interviewed Worrell before he went to Washington, and again, James Worrell told the same story. You can find his testimony in Volume II starting on page 190. His Warren Commission exhibits 359, 360, 361, 362, 363, are in Volume XVI, exhibit 363 was the signed statement made at the Dallas Police Department on 11/23/63. Worrell's recall never varied, his recall was the same for the Farmers Branch Police Department, Dallas Police Department, three reporters, FBI, Secret Service, and the Warren Commission, a total of at least eight times that we know of

James Worrell

that James Worrell told the same story about seeing someone run out the back door of the School Book Depository about three minutes after the assassination of President Kennedy. James Worrell testified that he did not see this man's face, that he saw only his back. He stated he was a white man, and guessed he was 5'7" to 5'10" and weighed 165 pounds or so.

ONE MORE EYEWITNESS

Amos Lee Euins, age 16, was excused from school to see the motorcade. Euins was standing across Elm Street facing the School Book Depository. As the President's limo turned onto Elm Euins waved at the President and the President waved back at Euins. Euins then looked up and saw a "pipe," he could see a hand on the trigger and a bald spot on his head.

After the second shot, Euins knelt behind a fountain for protection; Euins thought he had heard four shots. Euins then ran with the crowd to the railyard by the west side of the depository, when he told a police officer he had seen the shooter.

The officer put Euins on the back of his three-wheeled motorcycle and rode around to the front of the TSBD to turn Euins over to an officer to get a statement. As the motorcycle policeman parked, a man who was one of the construction workers working on Houston Street ran up and said he saw a man run out the back door of the School Book Depository. Euins' Warren Commission testimony is in Volume II starting on page 201 and you can find the "man run out the back of the Depository," at the bottom of page 205.

ANOTHER

Sam Pate was a radio station reporter and was in his car on Stemmons Freeway, not far from the triple underpass when he heard on the radio that there had been shots fired at the President's motorcade. In an informal conversation with me, Sam told me he tore off Stemmons Freeway and came around to Houston Street from the north at the rear of the Depository. Houston Street was being worked on and in the excitement of the moment he hit one of the wooden "saw horses" blocking off Huston Street and hit the curb bouncing up on the sidewalk.

Sam remembers James Worrell, the construction workers, and that there was no one guarding the rear door of the TSBD. In summary, there were three people to say that at about two-and-a-half to three minutes after the shooting there was no one guarding the back door of the Texas School Book Depository, and two people saw someone run out the door. It is right there to read in the Warren Commission's own 26 volumes. Sam Pate was never called to testify.

The backdoor and loading dock of the Texas School Book Depository

CHAPTER FIFTEEN

MANIPULATED TESTIMONY

I n March 1964, James Elbert Romack read in the newspaper about James Worrell going to Washington D.C. to testify to the Warren Commission about seeing a man run out the back door of the School Book Depository moments after the assassination. After reading the article James Romack called the FBI and said that James Worrell was not telling the truth, because he and his friend George W. Rackley Sr. were guarding the rear door of the School Book Depository for the first five minutes after the assassination.

Both of these men testified to Warren Commission Counsel David Belin on April 8, 1964. Romack's testimony can be found in Volume VI pages 277-284. Mr. Romack stated he was 39 years old, had been in WW II, a service station attendant and was now a truck driver for the last few months. He stated that he and his friend George "Pop" Rackley were piddling around near Ross and Houston Streets about 100 to 125 yards from the Depository when he heard three shots from the Depository. He said he saw a policeman come to the rear of the Depository and leave. Mr. Romack decided he needed to go down to the Depository and guard the rear door of the building. He testified he guarded the rear door of the Depository for the first 5 minutes after the shooting, and that no one came out the door.

Mr. Romack's friend George "Pop" Rackley's testimony is in Volume VI pages 273-277. Mr. Rackley said he was 60 years old, had been a farmer until three years before, was now working unloading trucks and had dropped out of school in the fifth grade. He testified that he did not see or hear anything.

That James Romack did not speak up for three and a half months after the assassination raises questions. However his testimony was used by the Warren Commission to void James Worrell's statement about seeing a man bolt out the rear door of the Depository about three minutes after the assassination of JFK, and voided Amos Euins' testimony, recounting that a construction worker had run up to a motorcycle policeman and yelled that he, the construction worker had just seen a man run out the rear door of the Depository.

Several of the TSBD employees further discounted James Romack's claim of guarding the rear door of the building during the first few minutes. Many Depository employees stated they had been watching the motorcade through a window from inside the building and curiosity got the best of them about the crowd racing to the railyard on the west side of the Depository. These curious employees stated one by one that they went out the rear door to see what was going on in the rail yard and then reentered the building the same way.

The evidence is overwhelming that someone did run out the back door of the Depository about three minutes after the assassination, and also that many employees also went out the back door out of curiosity. It is sad that the Warren Commission gave credence to James Romack's unlikely story of guarding the rear door of the TSBD for the first few minutes after the assassination, when there was credible evidence that, in fact, a man had run out the back door, and testimony showing that more than one Depository employee had also gone out that same, and *only*, back door.

CHAPTER SIXTEEN

DEALEY PLAZA WITNESSES

Howard I. Brennan was standing across the street from the Texas School Book Depository and heard the first shot, looked up and saw a sniper fire a second shot from a Depository window. That evening, November 22, 1963, Howard Brennan watched a police lineup with Lee Harvey Oswald being one of the men in the lineup.

Mr. Brennan could not positively identify Oswald as the shooter he saw in the window. Mr. Brennan's statements to the FBI varied from month to month after the assassination, and by the time he testified before the Warren Commission, he positively identified Lee Harvey Oswald as the man he saw in the window of the Texas School Book Depository from 150 feet away.

I was standing by the triple underpass on the narrow divider between Commerce and Main Streets about 5-10 feet out from the underpass and over 350 feet from the Texas School Book Depository. A bullet hit the round top of the curb 23 feet out from the underpass and debris from that shot hit me in my face. The debris from the bullet hitting the curb stung me in the right cheek breaking the skin in three or four places drawing three or four drops of blood.

In the excitement of gunshots being fired, my attention was diverted from the sting on my face until it was pointed out to me a couple of minutes later that I had blood on my face.

When I testified to the Warren Commission, and was asked which shot was the missed shot, I only knew for sure that it was not the first shot and answered, "I would guess it was either the second or third." With further questioning I answered, "I believe that it was the second shot," because I had heard the third shot afterwards.

My Warren Commission testimony was given on July 23, 1964 and since that time I have acquired the full 26-volume set of the Warren Report and in reading the testimony of many other witnesses that saw the debris fly up from the curb, I can now state without any reservation that a third shot was the shot that missed and hit the curb in front of me.

There were a couple of pictures of me taken that day. These photos showed the left side of my face, where I had a small scratch that was almost healed. That scratch had nothing to do with the assassination and the debris that had hit me in the right cheek.

I know of only two authors that actually interviewed me in the early years and got it right in their books, Jim Bishop and Harold Weisberg. One thing I need to clear up is: while answering a question years ago in a filmed interview about my minor injury to my right cheek, I reached up and touched my left cheek without thinking, it was an innocent gesture that had no meaning other than I had been stung in the face and was not thinking about which cheek. Newer and more complete information on the curb bullet is presented in a later chapter.

Mr. and Mrs. Arnold Rowland were standing across the street from the Texas School Book Depository a few minutes before the motorcade arrived. Arnold Rowland, while looking at the Depository, before the motorcade arrived in Dealey Plaza, saw two men on the sixth floor, one was a man standing in the west sixth floor corner window of the depository holding a rifle. Mr. Rowland assumed he was an agent assigned to protect the President. At the same time Mr. Rowland also saw a second man "hanging out the window" of the east sixth floor corner window (what was later determined to be the sniper's nest window).

In reading Arnold Rowland's entire Warren Commission testimony about the number of open windows on other floors of the depository and the people in those windows, he was very accurate on the known facts. The Warren Commission *did not want* Arnold Rowland's accurate testimony, and it shows in how they questioned Rowland, and how they worked to discredit his testimony. The Warren Commission did not call any other witnesses to testify that had also seen two men in the windows. The Warren Commission could have called Carolyn Walthers to testify.

Carolyn Walthers worked in the Dal-Tex building, which was the building directly across Houston Street from the Texas School Book Depository. She and another worker had gone outside to watch the President's motorcade.

A couple of minutes before the President's limousine turned onto Elm Street, Walthers noticed two men in an upper floor window of the Depository, one man, a brown-coated man, was holding a rifle that he had pointed out the window toward the street. Walthers also assumed the men were stationed there to protect the President. Ms. Walthers was not called to testify before the Warren Commission.

Richard R. Carr was a construction worker who had been working on the new County Courthouse overlooking Dealey Plaza. Mr. Carr reported to police that he had seen a heavyset man wearing a tan jacket, and horn-rimmed glasses at a window on the sixth floor of the Texas School Book Depository *just before* the shots were fired at President Kennedy.

After the shooting, Carr saw the same heavyset man who had been on the sixth floor hurrying away from the School Book Depository being escorted by two other men. They walked very fast to a Rambler station wagon parked on Commerce Street and the heavyset man got into the Rambler without the other two men. The Rambler made a left turn onto Record Street going north. Record Street dead-ended onto Elm Street and you had to make a left turn into Elm and go back through Dealey Plaza to get out of Dallas.

There are pictures of this Rambler with the passenger door partly open as it makes a stop at the right curb in Dealey Plaza; one witness stated he almost rear-ended the Rambler when it stopped. There are other witnesses who saw it stopping to pick up someone. Richard R. Carr was not called to testify before the Warren Commission.

Charles Brehm was off work that day, and brought his 5-year-old son with him to see President Kennedy. Mr. Brehm positioned himself and his son across from the TSBD a few feet further down Elm Street from the crowd at Houston and Elm Streets. Larry Sneed interviewed Mr. Brehm for Sneed's book, *No More Silence* in the summer of 1988.

Brehm described the first shot as a surprising noise. Brehm was close enough to the President's limousine to see when the shot hit the President in the back. He stated that he saw the President stiffen and raise his hands toward his throat, as the limousine passed in front of him. Mr. Brehm also saw the second shot hit the President in the head, and being a WW II veteran knew instantly it was a fatal shot.

Mr. Brehm then heard the third shot. The third shot scared Mr. Brehm as he heard the "crack" of the shot as it went over his head and guessed correctly that it was a wild shot. Mr. Brehm, like most of us, reacted after the shooting was over by going to the ground and covering his son. It must be noted that Charles Brehm was seriously wounded in the D-day landing in Normandy in World War II. President Reagan honored him on the 40th anniversary of that landing and then he was honored again by President Clinton on the 50th anniversary.

Charles Brehm did not testify to the Warren Commission.

Emmett J. Hudson was sitting on the steps in the "Grassy Knoll area" on the north side of Elm Street. Mr. Hudson was a key witness to the fatal headshot, it happened in front of him as he was looking directly at the President. Hudson testified that he saw the second shot hit the President, and heard the third shot after the President had been hit by the second shot. When asked, "You say that it was the second shot that hit him in the head, is that right?" Hudson replied, "Yes, I do believe that, I know it was."

Warren Commission questioner, Wesley J. Liebeler, continued to question Hudson whether he was sure it was the second shot that hit the President in the head, and he then heard a third shot. Emmett Hudson did not waver in his statement that he had heard the third shot, but did not see it hit anything after he saw the President hit in the head by the second shot.

Up to this point in his testimony, the only thing Mr. Hudson had said about the first shot was: "The first shot rung out, of course I didn't realize it was a shot." Nevertheless, Liebeler did not give up trying to put words in Hudson's mouth, and he continued with a series of questions that were obviously asked to confuse Mr. Hudson.

It did not work, for at the end of Emmett Hudson's testimony, Hudson comes back to his original statement, that he heard another shot after seeing a second shot hit President Kennedy in the head.

Clemon Earl Johnson worked for Union Terminal Railroad, and because he worked for the railroad right near the Texas School Book Depository he was allowed by the Dallas Police to watch the motorcade from the top of the triple underpass. He was just one of about eleven railroad and two post office employees that were allowed to be up there that day. Larry Sneed also interviewed C.E. Johnson for the book, *No More Silence*.

Like most of us Johnson thought the first shot was a firecracker going off, then two rifle shots. As the President's limousine passed under him on Elm Street he could tell: "The whole top of his head was missing," and you could see blood, brains, and bone. Mr. Johnson stated a man named Dodd and our boss, Holland, kept pointing to and saying the shots came from out of those bushes.

Mr. Johnson also stated that Dodd and Holland swore they saw: "smoke come out of those bushes," but Mr. Johnson said the puffs of smoke he saw he attributed to the motorcycles. He did mention about where a woman and child had been sitting, and that the woman had said, "a bullet went into the ground right there" and they kept digging until they finally found the bullet. Mr. Johnson was 81 years old when Larry Sneed interviewed him. He never testified for the Warren Commission.

James Richard Worrell Jr., whose testimony we have explored earlier, was one of the first witnesses called by the Warren Commission. Arlen Specter did the questioning of James Worrell for the Warren Commission. James Worrell had gone to Love Field to see the President and was unable to get close enough to get a good view, so he caught a bus part of the way and walked the rest of the way to get to Dealey Plaza ahead of the motorcade.

He was standing directly in front of the Texas School Book Depository when the motorcade rolled by. When he heard the first shot, he looked up over his head and saw a few inches of a rifle barrel sticking out of a sixth-floor window. He glanced back at the President's car to see the President slumping and when he looked back up he saw the second and third shots being fired from the rifle. He thought he heard a fourth shot as he started to run.

At this point James Worrell describes taking off running around the corner, north on Houston Street along side of the Texas School Book Depository, crossing the street and stopping, to catch his breath, but with a clear view of the rear of the Depository building. He then describes seeing a man run out the door as, "I saw this man come busting out of this door." The door he was describing was the rear door of the Depository, and he never varied in his telling of what he saw that day.

The Warren Commission, in its findings about James Worrell states: "Two other civilian witnesses claimed they guarded the building during the first five minutes after the shooting and saw no one leave the building." James Worrell was killed in a motorcycle accident two years later. It was an accident about which James' mother could never get a straight answer.

At 12:36 P.M., six minutes after the shooting, Sergeant D.V. Harkness radioed in that he had a witness who said the shots came from the fifth floor of the Texas School Book Depository. The witness, whom I have spoken of before, was 15-year-old Amos Lee Euins, who recalled that just before the shots were fired he saw: "This pipe thing sticking out of the window." After the first shot he looked up and saw a rifle with a hand on the barrel and another hand on the trigger sticking out of the open window. Euins identified the fifth floor as the floor under the ledge, when actually he was identifying the sixth floor.

Euins was standing across the street from the TSBD and his testimony, when asked by Specter, "What did you see in the building?" Euins answered, "I seen a bald spot on his head, trying to look out the window. He had a bald spot on his head. I was looking at the bald spot, I could see his hand, you know the rifle laying across in his hand."

Further on in his testimony, Euins discusses the police surrounding the building and states, "Another man told him he seen a man run out the back." Arlen Specter then asks Euins, "Do you know who that man was who said somebody ran out the back?" And Euins replies, "No sir. He was a construction man working back there."

The man Amos Euins was talking about was a Dallas street worker who had ran up to the policeman while Amos was talking to him. Arlen Specter then makes a small attempt to discredit Euins, but that goes nowhere.

The last time I saw Ed Hoffman was about 2006 or 2007, and he was in a wheel chair. As mentioned before, Ed had been deaf since birth, and on November 22, 1963, he was waiting for President Kennedy's car to exit Dealey Plaza so he could view the President. While waiting, he became impatient and was making his way to the Plaza to get a better view, when he saw a man in a suit, clutching a rifle, running behind the picket fence.

The man in the suit tossed the rifle to another man who dismantled the rifle and put it in a bag. Then Ed saw the men go off in different directions. Because Ed Hoffman was deaf, he had not heard the shooting and he could not tell police officers on the scene what he had just witnessed.

Ed Hoffman tried many times to tell what he had witnessed that day, the FBI laughed at him and never took him seriously. In the over 40 years that followed, Ed Hoffman never wavered from what he had witnessed on that day.

Ed died never learning to speak anything but sign language, which he was adept at. In 1963, many he came in contact with thought he was "deaf and dumb," but there was nothing *dumb* about Ed Hoffman, he worked at Texas Instruments, where he was considered a valued employee. Ed Hoffman *was never called to testify* to the Warren Commission.

Ms. Virgie Rachley was married on February 1, 1964 to Donald Baker and testified to the Warren Commission as Mrs. Donald Baker. Mrs. Baker testified that she had been standing in front of the Texas School Book Depository and after the President's limousine passed in front of her, she and others moved out into Elm Street, and that she saw the first shot hit the street behind the President's limousine. It is important to note Mrs. Baker's testimony about the first shot hitting the street was contrary to other eyewitness testimony. Mrs. Baker stated, "Well, after he passed us, then we heard a noise and I thought it was firecrackers, because I saw a shot or something hit the pavement."

Warren Commission Lawyer Liebeler then asks her if she had any idea where the noise came from. And Mrs. Baker states, "No, I thought there were some boys standing down there where he was, where the President's car was." Liebler then asks, "Down farther on the street, you mean?"

Mrs. Baker replies, "Yes; close to the underpass." Mrs. Baker in the next six pages of testimony uses words like, "I don't know exactly," or "this is confusing," several times in her testimony.

Near the end of her testimony Mrs. Baker was asked once again if she did see something hit the street, and if in fact it was a bullet, it would have been the first shot. She says, yes. It must be noted that other witnesses heard another shot after the headshot (after a second shot).

Gerald Posner in his book *Case Closed* and others have used only Mrs. Baker's testimony that it was the first shot that hit the street and have ignored other witness testimony to the contrary.

CHAPTER SEVENTEEN

THE FIRST SHOT

The Warren Commission was going to conclude that the first shot, a shot that sounded like the pop of a firecracker or the sound of a motorcycle backfire, hit President Kennedy in the back four and a half inches below the collar line, slightly to the right of the spine.

President Kennedy's shirt and coat both had bullet holes in them four and a half inches below the collar line supporting that conclusion. Dr. Humes also noted on an autopsy drawing that a bullet had struck the President in the back, four and a half inches below the collar line. This original conclusion by the Warren Commission was a no-brainer as all the evidence supported the conclusion that one bullet had hit the President in the back four and a half inches below the collar line and slightly to the right of the spine.

However, this original conclusion of the Warren Commission was dropped after I testified on July 23, 1964 to the Warren Commission about one shot missing the President's car completely and hitting the south curb of Main Street near the triple underpass. The impact of this bullet hitting the curb threw debris into my face breaking the skin. Dallas Police tapes documented this missed shot and my minor injury fifteen minutes after the assassination of President Kennedy.

Before I testified, the Warren Commission had already started to break up and send people home. But now with evidence of a missed shot, this left the Commission with the problem of only two bullets to cause three and possibly four or more separate injuries, the evidence had been that there were at least two shots to the President, one to his back and at least one (probably two) to his head, and then on top of all of President Kennedy's injuries, there were all of Governor Connally's injuries to his chest, wrist, and leg. When you add one missed shot, plus two shots to Kennedy and at least one shot to Connally, you have a minimum of four shots to account for all the injuries, but as we know most everyone heard only three shots.

The problem did not come to light until late summer of 1964. Warren Commission lawyer Arlen Specter had been wrestling with the problem of too many multiple-injuries by only two bullets and presented an idea he had been toying with for some time: that one bullet had gone through both Kennedy and Connally, causing Kennedy's back injury and throat injury (exit) and all of Governor Connally injuries. The Zapruder movie indicated Governor Connally was hit one to one and a half seconds after the first shot hit President Kennedy, but Specter found that easy to ignore.

The problem Arlen Specter *was having* was trying to line up the shot hitting Kennedy in the back, then coming out Kennedy's throat, and hitting Connally in the back and going through the Governor's chest and wrist before winding up in Connally's leg, and leaving broken bones in the Governor's chest and wrist.

It would not work with a shot coming at a downward angle from the sixth floor. The President's back injury was four and a half inches below the collar line, and was lower than the alleged frontal neck injury. In other words, a bullet coming downward from the sixth floor would, after hitting the President in the back, have to turn upward to be able to exit his throat. Arlen Specter made his normal daily report detailing the problem of lining up one shot passing through both men and turned in his report to Chief Council J. Lee Rankin who forwarded Specter's report to each of the seven Warren Commission appointees.

The seven Commission appointees bought Arlen Specter's idea of one bullet going through both Kennedy and Connally, and it became a main tenet in the Warren Report: one bullet had penetrated both men. The public did not buy this conclusion.

The major problem with this Warren Report assumption is that the "magic" bullet caused too many injuries, broke too many bones, and then emerged in near-pristine condition. The Warren Commission could not duplicate doing all that damage with one bullet, especially in having that bullet end up in nearly new condition afterward.

Also for a bullet to go through both men it would have to turn up, down, and sideways, as it is penetrating both men, something that is impossible for a speeding bullet to do.

It was not until the early 1990s that we found out the full story of how Arlen Specter was able to make his single bullet theory halfway work and get adopted by the Warren Commission.

An Assassinations Records Review Board was established by President Clinton to gather all of the Kennedy assassination information lying around and to get this information into our National Archives. J. Lee Rankin, who had been Chief Counsel for the Warren Commission, still had some of his old notes in his possession and turned these old notes over to the ARRB.

The ARRB staff in sorting through Rankin's notes discovered Arlen Specter's old report and upon close examination found that Specter's report had been altered by Gerald Ford to move President Kennedy's back injury up a few inches into Kennedy's neck so a bullet would come closer to lining up for a single bullet to go through both Kennedy and Connally.

Yes, this is the same Gerald Ford who was later to become President Ford. When this altering of evidence was discovered, Ford was retired from the Presidency, but reporters did ask the ex-president why he had altered key evidence in the Kennedy assassination. Ford's reply to the reporters was: "For the sake of accuracy." There were a few articles in a some newspapers about this alteration of evidence by Ford, but it was soon forgotten.

One thing that I must stress about the first shot is that it did not sound like a rifle shot, it sounded like the pop of a firecracker or a motorcycle backfire – over 90% of the other witness in Dealey Plaza agreed with me. Of the four people unhurt in the President's limousine, Mrs. Connally thought it was a firecracker and Mrs. Kennedy thought it was motorcycle backfire; the two Secret Service Agents were split the same way.

I do not claim to be an expert on rifle shots, but I did grow up on a farm shooting a rifle often as a boy. And firecrackers were very much a part of my Fourth of July. With the autopsy evidence determining that the back injury only penetrated Kennedy's back one and a half inches and with the first shot not sounding like a rifle shot, I am of the opinion that the first shot was from a dud, a faulty bullet, a bullet taken from ammunition that was faulty.

This could also explain that in all probability the near perfect bullet (CE 399) found on a stretcher at Parkland was a bullet that had penetrated Kennedy's back only one and a half inches and then worked its way out, while the doctors worked on the President in the emergency room. This was the bullet from the first shot that sounded like the pop of a firecracker, and this nearly pristine bullet (CE 399) was not the same bullet that had penetrated Governor Connally's chest, wrist, and leg, while breaking the Governor's rib and wrist bones as the Warren Commission had mistakenly concluded.

CHAPTER EIGHTEEN

THE SECOND AND THIRD SHOTS

A second and a third shot hit the President in the head, blowing brain tissue, blood, and skull fragments in all directions. If one studies the Zapruder film closely, at frame 312 the President's head starts to go forward from a shot from the rear, at frame 313 the President's head slams backward from a shot from the front.

These two shots are almost simultaneous, a microsecond apart and heard as one shot. These two headshots are self-documented by the evidence. The President had a bullet hole in the center of the back of his head from an entrance wound. And the President had the lower left rear corner of his skull blown out by a shot from the front.

The Warren Commission's findings on these shots were just as controversial, if not more so than their findings on the first shot. The Warren Commission merges these two shots into one shot – one shot that does all the damage to the President's head. The Warren Commission determined this shot hit the back of the President's head and came from the sixth floor window.

The Zapruder amateur movie captured the President's head exploding on film. The fatal headshot came at frame 313 in the Zapruder movie, and this frame is clear and graphic. According to the FBI reenactment of the shooting, the President was 231 feet from the west curb of Houston Street, 265 feet from the sixth floor window, and 260 feet from the triple underpass. The angle of the rifle shooting down on the President was 15.21 degrees. The President's limousine was directly in front of Abraham Zapruder when this shot occurred. A copy of this frame can be found in Volume XVIII, page 94 of the 26-volume report.

All the evidence clearly indicates that there was a shot from the rear that hit the President in the back of the head. The autopsy doctors found a bullet hole in the rear upper part of the President's head and over 40 minute bullet fragments in the frontal part of his head indicating a shot from the rear.

There was a crack on the inside of the windshield of the limousine from this rear shot or an unknown shot. A piece of chrome molding over the windshield had a large dent from the rear shot or an unknown shot. And it is my personal opinion that a fragment from this rear shot exited the throat causing the throat wound. I hope some expert will in the future study the evidence and verify my opinion.

What the Warren Commission omitted from their report was frames 314, 315, and 316. These frames showed the head being snapped back so violently after being hit by a bullet that the momentum of the head movement slams the President's body and shoulders into the back of the seat.

The Warren Commission did not address this contradiction, that the impact of a bullet would cause the object that was hit to react toward where the bullet came from in such a violent way. Through the years I have asked scores of hunters if they had ever seen an animal they had fatally shot react toward them. Not one hunter could even imagine such a reaction; they all said that the impact of a bullet blows the object away from the source of the shot.

The best witnesses were the railroad men who had gathered at the top of the triple underpass to watch the Presidential motorcade. They had a panoramic view of Dealey Plaza. As mentioned before, two of those railroad men testified that they saw a puff of smoke during the shooting arise from behind the Grassy Knoll near the trees and picket fence. A couple more of the railroad men who were not called to testify made separate statements that they saw that puff of smoke.

The Warren Commission ignored what was on the Zapruder film, that the President's head starts forward a split second before his head snaps backward so violently it slams his shoulders and upper body into the seat back. President John F. Kennedy had been hit in the head from the rear and the front at the same time. The shots were a microsecond apart and the witnesses in Dealey Plaza heard them as one shot. These two shots are in the Zapruder film for everyone to see.

The attending Parkland physicians, to a man, stated the back of the President's head had been blown out from a frontal shot.

One thing that I do not think has ever been properly addressed is the timing between the shots. When I rehearsed in my mind the thoughts I had between the first and second shots and timed it, I came up with 4 seconds.

I kept that to myself until I came across what Ken O'Donnell and Dave Powers had to say. Both O'Donnell and Powers were assistants to President

Kennedy and were riding in the Presidential Secret Service follow-up car. They did the same thing I did later after the assassination, they rehearsed their conversation from hearing the first shot "was that a firecracker, or was that a motorcycle backfire etc.," and they came up with 3 seconds until the second shot. This agrees with most witnesses in Dealey Plaza who stated there was a pause between the first and second shots.

John Dolan

James Tague

HERTZ RENT A CAR 66 CHEVROLETS

TEXAS SCHOOL BOOK DEPOSITORY

James Tague pointing out to a police officer where he was standing

Chapter Nineteen

The Shot That Missed

First off, let me try to clear the record for the umpteenth time. The picture of me taken in Dealey Plaza minutes after the assassination of President Kennedy on 11/22/1963 shows a mark on the left side of my face. That mark is from a days-old scratch, almost healed, a normal protective scab. The fact is I was peppered by debris on the right side of my face hard enough to break the skin and cause three or four drops of blood. I did not seek nor did I need any medical treatment.

One of the two writers to get it right was Jim Bishop who wrote *The Day Kennedy Was Shot*, he interviewed me in the mid 1960s and on page 133 he said: "The spent grains peppered James Tague on the cheek." Harold Weisberg who wrote the Whitewash books also interviewed me and also got it right.

For years, when someone would ask me which shot missed I would reply, "I do not know which shot missed – I just know it was not the first shot that missed and hit the curb near me." Gerald Posner broke me from making that statement. In his book, *Case Closed* he quotes me as saying, "I do not know which shot missed," and he conveniently omits, "I just know it was not the first shot that missed and hit the curb near me."

I do not recall ever talking to Gerald Posner, but it is possible that I did if he telephoned me and pretended to be a student. I never turned down a student. And to this day, almost fifty years after the assassination of President Kennedy, I still get calls from people asking me questions.

Posner might have been one of those people. Posner bases his book on the first shot missing the President. That is a fantasy based on misinformation from J. Edgar Hoover.

From where I was standing I heard the pop of a firecracker and then the crack, crack of two rifle shots, no echo's, and only a slight reverberation from the second and third gunshots. That I only heard three shots had left me puzzled for years; I could not account to myself for all the things that only three shots did that day. I will cover that some more in another chapter.

One thing that I have always been positive of is that the first shot was not the shot that hit the curb near me.

When I testified before the Warren Commission in July 1964, I had not given much thought to the shots and was halfway guessing when I was asked about the missed shot and I testified that, it was either the second or third shot that missed, and I did state that if I had to make a guess, it was probably the second shot that missed.

Today, with the advantage of time to thoroughly study the testimony of other witnesses and compare to my first hand knowledge, I can now safely say with confidence, it was the last shot that missed.

When the first shot, "firecracker" went off, my mind was fully focused, clear, and thinking who is the idiot setting off a firecracker with the President going by. The second and third shots I heard were not that clear. Now, by carefully studying the Zapruder movie, and other witnesses' testimony, the first and second shots heard can be totally eliminated as the shots that missed.

The second shot that I heard was probably two simultaneous shots. The Zapruder film shows Kennedy's head start to go forward from a shot that hit the President square in the back of the head and a microsecond later President Kennedy's head is thrown violently back from a shot from the front. The second shot we all "heard" is actually two shots hitting the President front and rear at the same time and sounding like one shot.

If you count the two simultaneous shots as one, then that would eliminate the first two (three) shots as the shots that missed and hit the curb in front of me. That would leave the last shot we "heard" as the missed shot that hit the curb 23 feet out from the Triple Underpass on the south side of Main Street, throwing debris into my face.

With my own eyewitness knowledge, and by comparing the statements of other eye witnesses to the facts I am personally aware of, I can state with authority and without hesitation, that it was the third shot that I heard that missed. There were many witnesses who saw the debris fly up when the third/last shot hit the curb. I have been able to identify at least 12 credible witnesses who testified before the Warren Commission or gave separate statements that they saw the resulting debris from a bullet hitting the curb in front of me.

I am sure that there were many more witnesses that saw the bullet hit the curb and never testified. After careful study of the known witnesses testimony and statements, along with my personal knowledge, there can be only one conclusion. It was the third shot I heard that went wild and hit the curb near where I was standing. It must be noted that the second and third shots I heard were fired within one and a half to two seconds of each other and many of the witnesses in Dealey Plaza indicated the same timing as I do.

In summary, the first shot sounded like a firecracker and only penetrated President Kennedy's back one and a half inches. There was a pause of at least three seconds and then two shots were fired at the same time, sounding like only one shot, and with both shots hitting Kennedy in the head front and back. The third and fourth shots were spaced close together, had the normal crack, crack sound a rifle makes and then a fourth/last shot went wild and hit the curb on the south side on Main Street in front of where I was standing.

CHAPTER TWENTY

THE FATAL HEAD SHOT

T he fatal head shot, the shot that blew blood, brain tissue and pieces of bone (skull) out the back of President Kennedy's head, has caused much of the distrust of the Warren Report because the Warren Commission in their final report determined that the fatal head shot came from the rear of the President, and not from the front as the evidence indicates. Various scientific studies, the Parkland doctors, Dealey Plaza witnesses, blood-splatter evidence, and a study of the Abraham Zapruder movie contradict the Warren Commission's conclusion.

If you apply the laws of physics, the violent snap of the President's head backward accompanied by the violent slamming of his body backwards into the seat as shown in the Zapruder home movie, it shows the results of a shot from the front. And there are *a couple of frames missing from the Zapruder film* for some reason.

During the Clay Shaw trial in New Orleans, Secret Service Agent Robert Frasier testified that he examined the limousine at 1:00 A.M. that night and that there was blood and brain tissue from the hood to the trunk of the car, on both the inside and outside of the windshield, on the side rails, and inside the limousine, with most of the blood and brain tissue being on the inside of the limousine and on the trunk. In the Zapruder film you see Jackie Kennedy climbing onto the trunk to retrieve a piece of the President's skull.

As mentioned earlier, Bobby Hargis, the motorcycle policeman riding to the left and to the rear of the President, has stated it was: "Like a bucket of blood thrown from the back of the President's head." His motorcycle windshield and helmet were covered with gore. James Chaney, the motorcycle policeman riding at the right rear of the limousine, had some of the gore also hit his windshield. Samuel Kinney, the driver of the car directly behind the President's limousine, had brain tissue on his arm and also on the windshield of the car he was driving. And a large piece of the President's skull was later found next to the south curb of Elm Street later.

The doctors at Parkland Hospital, who worked on the President in the emergency room, almost unanimously said the back right corner of the President's skull was blown out, showing without any doubt that a bullet had exited the President's head in the rear from a frontal shot. An exit wound in the rear of the President's head indicates only one thing; he was shot from the front by at least one shot.

When one takes all of the evidence into consideration, it seems like a bullet hit Kennedy in the right temple and then traveled inside his skull on the right side of his head and exited leaving a large hole in the lower right rear of his head. The Zapruder film shows that this bullet, causes a large piece of skull on the right side of his head to break loose at the top and with the scalp holding the piece of skull bone at the bottom, acting like a hinge, allows this large piece of skull bone to flap over President Kennedy's right ear two or three times. This large piece of skull bone flapping up and down over John Kennedy's right ear is visible to the naked eye in the Zapruder film.

Blood spatter has long been used as a method of solving gunshot homicides. I do not pretend to be an expert on blood spatter, but from what I have read, blood spatter can come from both the entrance and exit wounds and the majority of the spatter will come from the exit wound. Most experts who have studied the above have determined that the headshot came from the front, not the rear as was determined by the Warren Commission.

CHAPTER TWENTY-ONE

GOVERNOR CONNALLY'S WOUNDS

The wounds, that Governor John Connally received during the shooting, is one of the main centers for controversy in the Warren Report. The Governor was hit in the back by a bullet near his right armpit. That bullet struck a rib, shattering the rib, and exited just below his right nipple. This bullet or another bullet then shattered his right wrist and eventually penetrated his thigh, leaving a fragment near the bone.

The Warren Commission determined in error that Governor Connally was hit by the same bullet that hit President Kennedy in the back. The main cause of the Warren Commission's staff making this faulty conclusion was that they did not see any of the photographs that were taken during the autopsy. The Warren Commission used an artist's drawing that falsely placed the President's back wound up into the President's neck, which was about

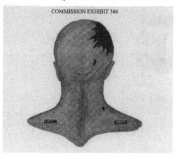

COMMISSION EXHIBIT 386

seven or eight inches higher than Kennedy's actual back wound that was about five inches below the collar line. The autopsy photographs became public years later and verified that Kennedy's back wound was in fact in the back about five inches below the collar line and not in the neck as in the artist drawing used by the Warren Commission showed.

From what Commission Lawyer David Belin told me during our brief meeting in November of 1988, the Warren Commission had been aware of my December 14, 1963 interview and the FBI report dated December 16, 1963, where I had stated there was a missed shot that had hit the street in front of me. But the Commission in secret discussions had decided to dismiss my FBI statement, and to not call me to testify before the Commission. And that as of June 5, 1964 the Warren Commission had all but wound up their investigation: three shots were fired – the first shot hit President Kennedy in the back, the second shot hit Governor Connally in the back, and the third shot hit Kennedy in the head killing him, and that *all the shots came from the south east corner of the sixth floor of the Texas School Book Depository.* Lee Harvey Oswald fired all the shots and was a "lone nut assassin," case closed.

With Kennedy and Connally apparently being hit by two shots so close together, perhaps maybe as much as a second and a half apart, the Commission had secretly discussed the possibility that maybe both men could have been hit by the same bullet. But the Commission attorneys could not make the angles fit. A bullet coming at a downward angle from the sixth floor and hitting President Kennedy in the back five inches below the collar line would have had to then turn upward in his body to come out his throat, and then when it came out of the throat it would have had to turn downward again to hit Connally in the back near the armpit. This scenario was entirely impossible.

Arlen Specter was the Commission lawyer who had been working on this possibility, and he had found that the Governor was also seated too far to the right in the limousine for the trajectory to line up with the President's so-called throat exit wound to have been hit near the right armpit. And then there was the nearly pristine bullet found at Parkland Hospital on a stretcher that was attributed by the Commission lawyers to be the bullet that caused Governor Connally's wounds.

It must be noted that still pictures and movie films taken that day by various witnesses show Governor Connally reacting to being hit about one and a half seconds after the President was hit in the back by a bullet. The Governor swore until the day he died that he was not hit by the same bullet as President Kennedy. The bullet found on a stretcher at Parkland Hospital had virtually no fragments missing. Every test attempting to duplicate the Governor's wounds resulted in a mutilated bullet.

The Zapruder film shows that the Governor did not react to being hit until a second or two after the President was hit in the back. Governor Connally testified before the Warren Commission that he was hit by a different bullet than the one that hit the President. He remembers hearing a first shot, turning to his right to try to see the President behind him, but not being able to do that, and finally turning back to his left when he was hit.

The Governor's wife, Nellie, testified the same thing. The Zapruder movie confirms the Governor's and his wife's testimony. Governor Connally never changed his testimony as long as he lived.

It was the first of June 1964 and the Warren Commission had done its job: Lee Harvey Oswald was the lone assassin, there were three shots fired, the first hitting Kennedy, the second shot Connally, and the third shot Kennedy. There was no conspiracy. The Warren Commission findings were just as FBI Director J. Edgar Hoover had said they would be 48 hours after the assassination of President Kennedy. The Commission was being disbanded except for a skeleton crew to finish up and write the report.

Then a surprise: on June 5, 1964 Jim Lehrer wrote a news story about me and the shot that missed.

Dallas Police Officer J. D. Tippit

CHAPTER TWENTY-TWO

THE SECOND MURDER

After Oswald was confronted in the Texas School Book Depository lunchroom by Officer Baker and identified as an employee by Roy Truly, Oswald bought a bottle of soda from the soft-drink machine in the lunchroom and casually walked out the front door of the depository. Oswald then walked down Elm Street and caught a bus, but the bus became stalled in traffic. Oswald asked the bus driver for a transfer, and that transfer was on Oswald when he was arrested.

The transfer was stamped at 12:40 P.M. Oswald then walked to near the Greyhound bus station and caught a taxi to the 500 block of North Beckley in the Oak Cliff section of Dallas, which was about five blocks from where he had rented a room from Earlene Roberts at 1026 North Beckley, for $8 a week, a month earlier.

At the time he rented the room, Oswald told Mrs. Roberts his name was O. H. Lee. Oswald was separated from his wife Marina at the time, but did spend weekends with Marina and the children at the Paine residence in Irving. Oswald rushed into Mrs. Robert's house at about one o'clock on November 22, 1963, and went straight to his room. Mrs. Roberts remembers that Oswald was in shirtsleeves when he came in, but, when he emerged from his room he had on a jacket. As Oswald rushed out of the house, Mrs. Roberts commented, "My, you're sure in a hurry." Oswald did not answer her.

At 12:54 P.M. Dallas Police Officer J.D. Tippit called in his location as he cruised the Oak Cliff area. Tippit was told to remain at large in that area, and was given a rough description of Oswald as it was known at that time. At 1:18 P.M. a citizen came on Tippit's police radio and said, "Hello police operator." The citizen was told to go ahead and the citizen reported the shooting of Officer Tippit and gave the address.

An eyewitness to the shooting said that Officer Tippit had stopped a man walking down the street and the man then casually stepped over to the police car and asked, "What was up." Officer Tippit opened his door and stepped out of the police car, they stood there for a moment face-to-face and then the man pulled out a gun and shot Officer Tippit for no apparent reason.

The man pumped four shots into Tippit at point blank range. Officer Tippit was already dead when the man then ran down the street with the pistol in his hand. Witnesses gave a description of the man and Dallas Police converged on the area and began a systematic search. A few minutes later a theater cashier called police and reported a suspicious "wild-looking" man had just entered the Texas Theatre on West Jefferson Street.

Several squad cars converged at the theater. Several officers entered the front and Officer N.N. McDonald went in the rear exit door. The movie *War is Hell* was showing. Officer McDonald walked up the aisle and as he was questioning a movie patron he noticed Lee Harvey Oswald sitting three rows away. As Officer McDonald approached Oswald, Oswald jumped up and said, "This is it. It's all over now," and slammed his fist into Officer McDonald's face.

Oswald reached for his pistol under his shirt and Oswald and McDonald grappled for control of the gun. Oswald had his hand on the trigger and the barrel was pointed straight at McDonald. Oswald squeezed the trigger and the gun went click, a misfire. Other officers came running and after a violent struggle Oswald was disarmed. Officers rushed Oswald into a police car and he was taken to the Dallas city jail.

Three bullets were removed from Officer Tippit's body, and along with Oswald's .38 special Smith and Wesson revolver, they were sent to the FBI laboratory for testing. Test bullets were fired from the .38 special and compared to the bullets removed from Tippit. In a letter from FBI Director J. Edgar Hoover to Dallas Chief of Police Jesse Curry, the letter read in part: "A portion of the surface of each bullet is mutilated, however, microscopic marks remain on these bullets for comparison purposes. The bullets were compared with each other and with test bullets obtained from Oswald's revolver." FBI Director Hoover then wrote in his letter to Dallas Police Chief Jesse Curry, *"No conclusion could be reached as to whether or not the bullets removed from Officer Tippit were fired from the same weapon or whether or not they were fired from Oswald's revolver."*

A minute and 15 seconds after the shooting Oswald is seen on the second floor of the building, calm, not out of breath, normal, and in the act of buying a soft drink. He is then seen calmly walking through the front office area and out the front door of the School Book Depository. Oswald then gets on a bus, but when he sees the bus is caught in traffic, he calmly asks the bus driver for a transfer and waits a moment for the bus driver to make a transfer – at 12:40, 10 minutes after the assassination!

Oswald then walks three blocks until he catches a taxi to the Oak Cliff Section of Dallas where he lives. There is absolutely nothing in Oswald's actions or demeanor at this point to suggest he had anything to do with the murder of John F. Kennedy. Would a man who had just committed a murder and was running from that murder take the time to get a bus transfer? *No.*

It is evident to me that the taxi ride to Oak Cliff gave Oswald a moment to think, and he panicked. I still have many unanswered questions. I think Oswald knew he had been put at the TSBD for a certain reason, but he had never been given the true reason; now in the taxi, he was starting to figure things out.

At that time, I lived in Dallas and knew a lot of people including a couple of police officers. Among the Dallas Police Force, Officer J.D. Tippit was thought to be a womanizer and the rumor among Dallas police officers was that a jealous husband had killed J.D. Tippit.

Tippit's murder was never investigated other than "Lee Harvey Oswald did it." A pistol that will not fire when you pull the trigger, and bullets taken from a dead police officer that cannot be matched to Oswald's gun, do not make convincing evidence. Of course, it was natural under the circumstances to assume Oswald killed Tippit, but there should have been a complete investigation.

Chapter Twenty-Three

Dallas Police Headquarters

A t about 2:30 p.m. November 22, 1963, I was sitting in the homicide office at Dallas Police Headquarters giving a statement to Detective Gus Rose concerning what I had witnessed in Dealey Plaza that day. Detective Rose was taking notes on his pad. And as I related earlier there was a sudden commotion and a disheveled young man was brought into the homicide office, handcuffed, and Gus Rose asked one of the officers: "Who is he," and the officer replied, "He is the man who just killed a policeman in Oak Cliff." I was immediately dismissed. I later learned that evening on television that this man was Lee Harvey Oswald.

Soon after the arresting officers brought Oswald into the Homicide office, a group of investigators started assembling in the office. They included a Secret Service Agent, an FBI Agent, a Texas Ranger, and Captain Will Fritz, the head of the Dallas Homicide Bureau, plus others. Oswald was interrogated for most of the rest of the afternoon.

The interrogation of Oswald was a three-ring circus: officers and agents from all branches of Government wanted to be part of the investigation. Captain Fritz felt he should be in charge of the interrogation and should be able to talk to Oswald alone, as was proper and considered good procedure.

Due to pressure from the FBI and the Secret Service, Fritz or anyone else never had a chance to interrogate Oswald in a one-on-one situation. Oswald vehemently denied any involvement in the assassination of President Kennedy or anything else. Those present during the interrogation said Oswald was arrogant, noncommittal, and tight-lipped.

No taped or written records were made of these interrogations, however in November of 1997 the Assassination Records Review Board did acquire Dallas Homicide Chief, Captain J. W. "Will" Fritz's handwritten notes on Oswald's interrogation. Captain Fritz told the Warren Commission in 1964 that he took no notes during the interrogation, but indicated that he later typed a report based on rough notes that were made several days later.

Oswald was allowed to smoke, offered cold drinks, given breaks, and taken to the rest room. Oswald was not pressured, coerced, or harassed, and the interrogators went out of their way not to place Oswald under duress.

At about 4 o'clock Oswald asked if he could make a phone call and it was arranged. Oswald tried to make the call, but could not reach the party he was trying to call; he did complete a call later in the day and talked for about 30 minutes. After about 4 hours the officers and agents present felt their interrogation was going nowhere. Oswald still denied any knowledge of the assassination of President Kennedy and the murder of Officer Tippit.

At about 7:00 P.M. that day, the Dallas Police filed charges against Lee Harvey Oswald for the murder of Dallas Police Officer J. D. Tippit. Shortly after the murder charge was filed, Oswald was transferred from the third floor Homicide office up to the city jail on the fifth floor. As Oswald came down the hall to the elevator to go up to the jail, reporters took photographs and when Oswald was asked about the assassination by a reporter. Oswald replied, "I don't know where you people get your information. I haven't committed any acts of violence."

When Oswald reached the jail he was stripped and searched. Any item ,such as his belt, that might be used to harm himself, was taken from him. He was placed in a maximum-security cell and all other prisoners in adjacent cells were moved. A guard was placed outside his cell.

Later that evening the President of the Dallas Bar Association, Louis Nichols, was escorted to Oswald's cell to confer with Oswald. Oswald spurned any assistance by the Dallas bar, but Nichols was able to advise Oswald of his legal rights. Oswald indicated to Nichols that he wanted a New York Attorney named John Abt to defend him, and, if he was not available, someone with the American Civil Liberties Union.

During the evening, FBI agents repeatedly asked Dallas Chief of Police Jesse Curry to turn over all the evidence on Oswald to them. By midnight, Chief Curry began to waver, with the condition that once the evidence was tested in the FBI laboratory, it would be returned to the Dallas Police Department.

Around midnight, rumors among the throng of reporters who had gathered in Dallas were that Oswald was being badly mistreated by the Dallas Police. The Dallas Police were well aware of the image they must maintain to the world, and a press conference was hastily arranged shortly after midnight to let the press see Oswald's physical condition, take pictures of Oswald.

The reporters were told, and they agreed, to only take pictures and observe Oswald's physical condition. Oswald was then brought down to where the press had assembled and when Oswald entered the room, he was hit by a barrage of questions from the reporters trying to get statements from him. It was pandemonium and Oswald was soon taken back to his jail cell.

Oswald was then taken to the Identification section to be fingerprinted and have his photograph taken for police files. It was now 1:10 A.M., November 23, 1963. At about 1:30 A.M., Oswald was taken to the fourth floor and arraigned for the murder of President John F. Kennedy by Justice of the Peace, David Johnson. Oswald responded to the arraignment with "I don't know what you are talking about. What's the idea of this? What are you doing this for?" Oswald was once again returned to his cell. This time Oswald was left alone for the rest of the night.

The *Dallas Morning News*, Sunday November 24, 1963 had a small picture of the curb that was hit in front of me. It was misidentified as being on Houston Street instead of Main Street.

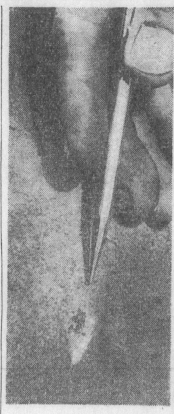

—Dallas News Staff Photo.

CONCRETE SCAR

A detective points to a chip in the curb on Houston Street opposite the Texas School Book Depository. A bullet from the rifle that took President Kennedy's life apparently caused the hole.

Photographer Sells Pict Of Assassination for $25.

President Kennedy flinches as the first shot strikes him.

Mrs. Kennedy takes her husband in her arms.

The second shot strikes the President in the side of his head, toward the back. His head becomes a blur.

Mrs. Kennedy crawls out over the trunk compartment in the rear of the car trying to escape the line of fire. Her husband slumps to the floor. A Secret Service agent runs to aid Mrs. Kennedy.

This historic picture of the assassination of President Kennedy is recorded on 8-millimeter color movie film shot by Abraham Zapruder, dress manufacturer of 3909 Marquette.

Perched on a concret a plaza a few feet awa der took perfect picture rible tragedy.

Saturday, Dick Strob Associated Press, Los Jack Klinge of United ternational, Dallas, Strolle, Los Angeles r tive of Life Magazine,

Mayors Get Request to Attend Rites

SAN ANTONIO, Texas (AP)—Mayor W. W. McAllister asked the mayors from major Texas cities Saturday to join him in a solemn pilgrimage to Washington,

execu-
s State
ro).
s fre-
ed and
in his

en ac-
ational,
achieve
hrough
st visit
is mis-

dy I'd
(where
fund-
im we
et."

exists
the ra-
Daniel

nedy's
think
assas-

"You
caus-
char-
act is

r, Mc-
have
g this

nistra-
er the
Just
critics

CHAPTER TWENTY-FOUR

THE NEXT THREE DAYS

The next day Saturday, 11/23/63, had only the news of the assassination of President Kennedy on television and the newspapers the same. I watched TV all day and read every word of both Dallas newspapers. There was nothing anywhere in the news about the missed shot that hit near me.

Early Saturday morning 11/23/63 Lee Harvey Oswald had been charged with the murder of Officer J.D. Tippit, but had not been charged with the murder of President Kennedy. The Friday evening's premature and ill advised remarks, untrue at the time, made on TV that Oswald had been charged with shooting President Kennedy took its toll as reporters filed their stories that Lee Harvey Oswald was the killer of President John F. Kennedy.

In less than 24 hours, the media as a group, because of the remark on television, had tried and convicted Lee Oswald of President Kennedy's death. In fact, at this time, Oswald had not been charged with the murder of President Kennedy.

Of course Oswald was officially charged with the President's murder later in the day, but the damage had already been done. Oswald was to never have his day in court, he had been tried and convicted by the media before any hard evidence had been put together against him. Oswald was instantly the object of hate the world over.

According to Dallas Chief of Police Jesse Curry, the Dallas Police Department on Saturday afternoon did not assume that Oswald was guilty of killing President Kennedy, although the superficial evidence pointed toward Oswald. The Dallas Police had not really started an investigation.

Other suspects were being sought, people that knew Oswald were being questioned to determine if there was a conspiracy behind the assassination. Dealey Plaza witnesses were being questioned; there were puzzles and unanswered questions from the investigation that are still unanswered nearly 50 years later.

One unsolved mystery was that the witnesses in front of the Texas School Book Depository thought the shots came from the Depository while the witnesses that were in front of the President's limousine told a different story, that the shots came from in front and to the right of JFK's car, from the triple underpass or the parking area behind the Grassy Knoll.

The Dallas Police Department had no doubt that Lee Harvey Oswald killed Officer J.D. Tippit, but the killing of President Kennedy was a different story.

Behind the scenes and with hardly any press the Director of the FBI, J. Edgar Hoover and others began to put tremendous pressure on Dallas Chief of Police Jesse Curry to turn the Dallas Police Department's investigation into President Kennedy's killing over to the FBI.

And it has been reported from reliable sources that the White House sent Dallas Police Chief Curry a message that fateful weekend stating: "It is important to quell any speculation about a conspiracy behind the assassination."

That Saturday evening, Chief Curry caved in and the investigation was turned over to the FBI. Oswald was due to be transferred from the City Jail to the County Jail at 10 A.M. Sunday morning. The time of transfer was kept from reporters and the public. The questioning of Oswald dragged on past the planned 10 A.M. transfer time until after 11:30 A.M.

There had been many threats of harm to Lee Oswald and the police had a well-planned transfer of Oswald to the County jail. Jack Ruby gained access to the basement of the police station and mingled with the reporters, and when they brought Oswald out into the basement to start the transfer to the County jail, Jack Ruby shot Oswald as millions watched on television. Lee Harvey Oswald was pronounced dead soon after arriving at Parkland Hospital.

The Sunday *Dallas Morning News* had a small picture of the bullet mark on the curb on page 8, section 1. The picture was titled "CONCRETE SCAR?" While the picture was accurate, the location of the mark on the curb was in error, the article read: "A detective points to a chip in the curb on Houston Street opposite the Texas School Book Depository. A bullet from the rifle that took President Kennedy's life apparently caused the hole."

President Kennedy's funeral was Monday November 25, 1963 and everything in Dallas was still shut down.

CHAPTER TWENTY-FIVE

THE AFTERMATH

When I left the police station after giving my statement, I headed back to work to find that almost everyone had gone home and the manager was closing the business. I went home, turned on the television, wrote down the events of the day and finally went to bed well after midnight.

Saturday morning, November 23, 1963, I went to work only to find a sign on the door that we were closed for the day. I drove around the local neighborhood for a short while, the streets were deserted, and I did not see one business open – it was as if Dallas had died too. I went back home and spent the day reading the papers and watching television.

The only thing on television, and on every station, was about the assassination of Kennedy and the wounding of Connally. On television, they ran the same stories over and over again, but it did not get old. I watched in amazement, trying to digest the events of the day before. The newspapers were the same, article after article about the assassination. I read through both newspapers twice, just knowing there would be an article about the missed shot that hit the curb near me during the shooting – there was nothing.

On Sunday morning, November 24,1963, when I awoke, my television was still on and there was one story after another about the assassination on all channels. I got my paper and read every article and there on page 8, section 1, of the *Dallas Morning News*, was a small article with a small picture of the exact bullet mark that I had seen Friday after the shooting.

The heading of the article read "CONCRETE SCAR" and the short article read: "A detective points to a chip in the curb on Houston Street opposite the School Book Depository. A bullet from the rifle that took President Kennedy's life apparently caused the hole." The picture was an actual photograph of the scar on the curb on Main Street, which Deputy Sheriff Buddy Walthers and I had located moments after the shots had been fired. But, for some unknown reason the article had placed the location of the curb on Houston Street, not Main Street.

That Sunday morning around 11 A.M., I decided to go downtown to a newsstand on Main Street and buy a couple of out of town newspapers to see what the rest of the country was saying about the assassination. I had my car radio on, and as I was driving downtown, I heard the announcer exclaim "He has been shot, somebody just jumped out of the crowd and shot Lee Harvey Oswald."

Monday, November 25, 1963, was to be President John F. Kennedy's funeral. I was watching television when a friend knocked on the door. He was a local car dealer with whom I had spent many an after work hour, drinking beer and swapping old stories. He asked me if I had anything to drink in the house, and I told him that I did not. He asked me to go with him to get something to drink, and I did. We drove all over Dallas in search of a beer or liquor store that was open, and there was not a business in Dallas that was open that we could find.

On Tuesday, November 26, 1963, Dallas and the country went back to work. The only topic of conversation in the workplace was the assassination of President Kennedy, and the killing of Oswald by Jack Ruby. I told my friends and co-workers about being in Dealey Plaza, the bullet hitting the curb near me, debris hitting me in the face, and being in the Dallas Police homicide office when they brought in Lee Harvey Oswald.

Most were attentive to what I was saying, and one or two said that they had not heard anything in the news about a missed shot. The days ran on into December, The front pages of the newspapers always had a new article about the assassination and television news did the same, but nothing about a missed shot.

Then came an article on Friday December 13, 1963 in section 1, page 22 of the *Dallas Morning News*. The article's heading: QUESTIONS RAISED ON MURDER BULLETS. The article went on to say: "Did a bullet from Lee Harvey Oswald's rifle chip the curb of Main Street near the triple underpass? That question remained unanswered Thursday. And it raised other questions: If one of the three shots from Oswald's mail order rifle struck the curb, is it possible that another bullet ranged through President Kennedy's body and then hit Gov. Connally? If the chip did not result from a bullet, how did it get there?

"Buddy Walthers, an investigator for Sheriff Bill Decker, found the chipped spot less than an hour after a sniper shot President Kennedy and the governor as their car moved slowly over Elm Street toward the triple underpass. 'A man came up to me and asked if I was hunting for bullets fired at President Kennedy.' Walthers related. 'He said he had stopped his car on Main Street and was standing beside it watching the motorcade, when the shooting started. He said something hit him on the cheek hard enough to sting. I checked the area where the man said he had been standing and found the chip in the curb. It was on the south side of the street.

"Main runs parallel to Elm on the south. Walthers and Investigator Allan Sweatt searched the area for about 20 minutes without finding a bullet. They concluded that if a bullet had struck the curb, the slug had ricocheted or disintegrated. The motorist could have been hit by a sliver from the bullet or a particle of concrete from the curb they concluded.

"The chip appeared freshly made. It was in line with the path a bullet would have taken if fired from the sixth floor of the School Book Depository Building toward the Kennedy motorcade. The trajectory, however, would have carried it above the heads of President Kennedy and the governor. Walthers and Sweatt were within a block of the slaying site when the sniper opened fire.

"They agreed with other witnesses that the assassin fired only three shots. Gov. Connally said that the first shot struck President Kennedy and the second shot entered his body. Then, the governor related, another bullet struck President Kennedy. That would account for the three shots. It would not, however, account for the chipped spot.

"Various theories have been advanced. Was Governor Connally mistaken about what happened during the 10-second period in which the sniper shot him and the President? Did the rifleman fire two bullets into the car, with one striking both President Kennedy and Governor Connally, and then hurriedly fire a third that passed over their auto? Or did the chipped spot have no connection with the shooting? Couldn't the motorist have been struck by a speck of gravel thrown up by a car? Couldn't other gravel have caused the chip? FBI and Secret Service agents may have the answer. But they haven't revealed what they learned during their intensive investigation of the murder of President Kennedy."

I read this article with great interest, my friends and co-workers had started to wonder if I had been making up the missed shot that hit the curb during the shooting. I felt vindicated by the article, at last it was coming out now, three weeks later, about a missed shot. The article was generally factual, but not entirely accurate. After reading the article, I had a nagging question in my mind, should I call the FBI so they could get the facts straight, or should I stay out of it?

Deputy Sheriff Walthers had run up to me and asked what happened, not me to him. Once we had located the scar on the curb, we had both agreed it was a fresh bullet mark. What was this about a piece of gravel doing to the curb what a bullet had done?

I wrestled with the question of calling the FBI for the rest of the day. Should I call the FBI or not, I kept asking myself. The next morning I woke up thinking that maybe I should go ahead. I went to work determined to call the FBI. I started to call them 3 or 4 times and backed out each time.

Would the FBI even want to talk to someone like me? They only talk to people with authority and I am just a country boy, new to the big city, and just a car salesman. But the newspaper article was wrong, the bullet had hit the curb on Main Street, not on Houston Street and the Deputy Sheriff had come running up to me asking what happened, not me running up to him, and besides, it was impossible for gravel to do the damage to the curb that the bullet had done. The newspaper article was just not an accurate account of what really happened concerning the scar on the curb.

With knots in my stomach, I finally did pick up the phone and called the FBI. Two FBI agents were in my office within an hour.

FEDERAL BUREAU OF INVESTIGA .)N

1   Date ___12/16/63___

     Mr. JIM TAGUE, 2424 Inwood, Apartment 253, employed
as a salesman, Chuck Hutton Company, 5431 Lemmon Avenue, Dallas,
Texas, advised that he was driving a car on November 22, 1963,
and was stopped in traffic at the Triple Underpass located below
the Texas School Book Depository (TSBD) Building. While stopped,
he saw that the Presidential Motorcade was going to pass nearby,
and he got out of his car and stood near the Triple Underpass
between Commerce and Main Streets. He stood near the curb of
Main Street waiting for the motorcade to come to where he was
standing. When the motorcade was approximately 100 feet from
him he heard a loud noise, and at that time he looked around
as he thought someone had shot a firecracker. He then heard two
more loud noises in quick succession. Other persons in the area
then started scrambling around, and he realized that the noises
must have been gun shots, so he got behind one of the pillars of
the underpass. During the time of the shooting, he felt something
hit him on his right cheek. Whatever it was that hit him broke
the skin and caused about two drops of blood to flow. He thought
possibly that one of the bullets had hit the curb near his feet
and possibly a piece of the curbing had hit him in the cheek.
He did look around the curb and near where he was standing there
was a chip missing, which he stated looked fresh. He stated he
did not see anyone with a rifle and did not look at the TSBD
Building. He did not see the shots take effect and stated he
could not furnish any information as to where the shots actually
came from. He stated he is not acquainted with OSWALD and had
never heard of him prior to the shooting of President KENNEDY

     He has been in JACK RUBY's club on a few occasi
but he actually knows nothing about RUBY, his associatio
his background. He does know RUBY, however, by sight, an
has seen him in his club on a few occasions. TAGUE stat
did not know of any connection or associations between OS
and RUBY.

12/14/63 __ at __Dallas, Texas_____   File # __DL 100-10461__
    HENRY J. OLIVER AND
Special Agent   LOUIS M. KELLEY: mam   31 ____   Date dictated ___12/16/63___

President Kennedy's casket being loaded in Dallas for the trip to Washington.

CHAPTER TWENTY-SIX

NO TEXAS AUTOPSY

In 1963, no federal law covered the assassination of a U.S. President. Murder was a capital crime in Texas and this murder *was* perpetrated in Texas, and by law the autopsy should be performed in Texas.

Texas authorities began to take control of President Kennedy's body at Parkland Hospital for the purpose of an autopsy, but the Secret Service and Kennedy aides stopped them. The Secret Service and the Kennedy aides were adamant that they were taking the President's body back to Washington D.C. with them.

Hot words were exchanged and witnesses described the scene at Parkland Hospital over control of the President's body as childlike: "He is mine, no he is mine."

An expensive casket was ordered from a Dallas mortuary and the body of President Kennedy was soon escorted to the Presidential plane at Love Field. Before the plane took off for Washington a Federal Judge, Sara Hughes, was summoned to the plane and Vice President Lyndon Johnson was sworn in as the new President of the United States.

The plane carried President Kennedy's body, President and Ladybird Johnson, Jackie Kennedy, and the Kennedy entourage back to the nation's Capital. There is disputed and undisputed evidence that the President's body was transferred to a body bag for some reason on the plane while the President's plane was in the air and being flown back to Washington D.C.

David Lifton has spent years researching his evidence on this switch in his book, *Best Evidence*. Doug Horne, using new evidence now available, also makes a strong case of body-tampering. Paul O'Conner who was in the autopsy room while the autopsy was performed states that President Kennedy's body arrived at the autopsy in a body bag in a cheap shipping casket.

There is strong evidence that President Kennedy's body disappeared for a little over an hour between being unloaded from Air Force One and the official autopsy was performed at the Bethesda Naval Hospital.

AUTOPSY

NMS # A 63-272 DATE 11-22-63 HR. STARTED _____ HR. COMPLETED _____

NAME: _____ RANK/RATE _____

DATE/HOUR EXPIRED: _____ WARD _____ DIAGNOSIS _____

PHYSICAL DESCRIPTION: RACE: _____ Obtain following on babies only:

                          Color

Height _____ in. Weight _____ lb. Hair _____   Crown-rump _____ in.

Color eyes _____ Pupils:Rt _____ mm, Lt. _____ mm   Crown-heel _____ in.

                                         Circumference:

WEIGHTS: (Grams, unless otherwise specified)   Head _____ in. Chest _____ in.

                                         Abd. _____ in.

LUNG, RT. ~~350~~ 320   KIDNEY, RT. 135   ADRENALS, RT. _____

LUNG, LT. ~~290~~ 290   KIDNEY, LT. 140   ADRENALS, LT. _____

BRAIN _____   LIVER 650   PANCREAS _____

SPLEEN 90   HEART 350   THYROID _____

THYMUS _____   TESTIS _____   OVARY _____

HEART MEASUREMENTS: A 7.5 cm. P 7 cm. T 12 cm. M 10 cm.

                    LVM 1.5 cm. RVM .4 cm.

NOTES:

Pathologist _____

CHAPTER TWENTY-SEVEN

THE AUTOPSY

The autopsy of President John F. Kennedy is at the center of much of the controversy about what really happened in Dealey Plaza at 12:30 P.M. on November 22, 1963. The official autopsy results do not agree with what the nurses and doctors at Parkland Hospital had observed concerning President Kennedy's head injuries when he was brought into the emergency room and attended to at Parkland.

Through the last fifty years, the more that researchers and medical experts delve into the official autopsy results, the more problems they find with it. First of all, the doctor put in charge of the autopsy, Naval Commander Dr. James J. Humes only real qualification for doing the autopsy was his high rank in the Navy.

Dr. Humes had taken a course in forensic pathology in medical school, but had never practiced forensic pathology. Dr. Humes' position with the Navy was Director of Laboratories at the Bethesda Naval Hospital. Dr. Humes had never performed an autopsy involving gun shot wounds.

I do not want to take anything away from Dr. Humes, by all accounts he was a fine man, a competent man, but autopsies were not an every day occurrence for Dr. Humes. Secondly, there was no attempt by the Warren Commission to reconcile the differences in what the doctors and nurses at Parkland had observed, and what was on the autopsy report. In fact, the Warren Commission in its final conclusion ignored the doctors, nurses, and other witness's observations, that the back of the President's head had been blown out. It must be noted that the Kennedy family had asked that the autopsy be limited to the head.

In closely studying the documents, and other facts concerning the autopsy, there is evidence that the *preliminary autopsy findings did agree* with the doctors, nurses, and other witness' view that the right rear of the President's head had been blown out.

Why did Doctor Humes destroyed his initial autopsy report and why did he not make his final report until December 6, 1963? Later chapters will help you understand why I ask these questions. We do know that the military personnel present were ordered to never discuss what they had witnessed during the autopsy of the President – under threat of court marshal. Now, years later, many of the military personnel who were present during the Kennedy autopsy have finally spoken about what they witnessed and their statements have created more doubt about the truth of the autopsy.

The President's body was flown back to Washington D.C. on Air Force One shortly after being pronounced dead on November 22, 1963. Upon arrival in Washington his corpse was reportedly taken to Bethesda Naval Hospital for an autopsy. The autopsy started at about 8 P.M. EST, November 22, 1963. Naval Commander James J. Humes of the Medical Corps, United States Navy, was in charge of the autopsy. Naval Commander Dr. J. Thornton Boswell and Marine Lt. Col. Pierre A. Finck were Dr. Humes' main assistants. There was an x-ray technician, various medical technicians, photographers, FBI agents, Secret Service agents, and other military personnel present. There were no civilians present. What should have been one of the most thorough and complete autopsies ever performed was not close to being thorough and/or complete, even by military standards, when one views the "official" autopsy report.

The autopsy report concerning the head injury moved the gaping hole in the back of the President's head up somewhat. It does acknowledges that part of the back of the head is missing and I will quote, "There is a large irregular defect of the scalp and skull on the right involving chiefly the parietal bone but extending somewhat into the temporal and occipital regions. In this region there is an actual absence of scalp and bone producing a defect which measures approximately 13cm in greatest diameter."

In laymans terms it reads, "There is a large hole in the scalp and skull on the right involving chiefly the top of the head but extending into the side and back of the head. The scalp and skull are actually missing and the hole measures five and one quarter inches across."

What has confused many experts and medical personnel who have studied the autopsy report is that the undeveloped photo negatives and X-rays taken during the autopsy were turned over to the FBI and replaced with drawings made days later by an artist who had never seen the President's head or the undeveloped photos. These drawings do not depict what the doctors, nurses, and other witnesses observed. To further complicate the matter, the Warren Commission only used the artist drawings to come to their final conclusions. Dr. Humes, in his testimony before the Warren Commission, admitted the drawings were not to scale.

114

What was left of the President's brain was a vital piece of evidence. The brain was removed during the autopsy and was put into a formalin solution, so that it could be sectioned to trace the path of the bullet or bullets through the brain. It is acknowledged in the autopsy report that there were some small brain specimens removed from the brain for analysis, but regarding sectioning the brain to trace the path of a bullet or bullets, there is the notation: "In the interest of preserving the specimen, coronal sections are not made." The preserved brain of the President then disappeared and has never been found.

This raises serious questions. Did someone actually lose the brain of the President of the United States without a trace, or was it dissected as scheduled in accordance with correct autopsy procedure and the dissection of the brain revealed that the fatal head shot had in fact hit the President from the front, which would confirm a conspiracy, or did the dissection of the brain reveal that the President's head had been hit by two bullets, which would also confirm a conspiracy?

Was the brain destroyed deliberately upon learning from the dissection that it pointed to a conspiracy? Will we ever know the truth about the fate of this most vital piece of evidence? Dr. Humes, in his testimony before the Warren Commission admitted that he *had purposely burned* his original autopsy notes and then rewrote the "official" notes two days later.

His excuse was "the original notes, which were stained with the blood of our late President, I felt were inappropriate to retain," and that the President's personal physician, Dr. Burkley, had authorized Dr. Humes to destroy his original notes.

We also know that the military autopsy findings surrounding the throat wound were at odds with what the attending physicians and nurses at Dallas Parkland Hospital had observed. When the President was rushed into the emergency room at Parkland one of the first things noticed was a small round "entrance" wound to the throat. This throat "entrance" wound was promptly widened with a scalpel to do a tracheotomy on the President.

When Dr. Humes performed the autopsy on the President later that evening, the throat wound went unnoticed. It was not until the next morning, when Dr. Humes called Dr. Perry, one of the attending physicians at Parkland, that Dr. Humes learned of the throat wound. Yet this unobserved throat wound during the autopsy was deemed an exit wound in the autopsy report by Dr. Humes.

That Dr. Humes declared the throat wound an exit wound, a wound he admittedly had not even observed, and despite what Dr. Perry had told him, raises more questions about the accuracy in the autopsy report.

When Dr. Malcolm Perry was interviewed again in 1979, he was still adamant that the throat wound was an entrance wound. An entry wound is small and an exit wound is large. For example, when emergency room nurse Margaret Henchcliffe, who had witnessed numerous gunshot wounds in Parkland's emergency room, testified before the Warren Commission, she was asked by Assistant Council Arlen Specter if the throat wound was an exit wound and she replied without hesitation: "I have never seen an exit hole look like that."

The President's back wound was crucial in determining if it was one bullet that had penetrated both the President and the Governor. The official autopsy report diagram showed that the bullet that had hit the President in the back was about four and a half inches below the collar in the shoulder and not the neck. The President's shirt and coat had bullet holes in them about four and a half inches below the collar and none in the neck. The death certificate signed by the President's personal physician, Dr. George Burkley states that the non-fatal back wound was: "In the back at about at about the level of the third thoracic vertebra."

The artist drawing, however, placed the back injury in the President's neck above collar level. The Warren Commission then used the artist drawing to determine the path of the bullet in determining that one bullet penetrated both men. The bullet that hit the President in the back was reportedly fired from six stories up, the fact that the back wound was about four and a half inches below the collar puts the back wound below the front neck wound. A downward moving bullet does not alter its trajectory in soft flesh and suddenly start going up.

With the back wound four and a half inches below the collar and below the front neck wound, it makes it impossible for that shot to have hit both the President and Governor Connally. That the back wound could only be probed about an inch raising more questions. Was the back wound the result of a dud, and that is why the first shot sounded like a firecracker or an engine backfire? Was the pristine bullet found on the gurney at Parkland the bullet that had worked its way out of the President's back, not Governor Connally's leg as the Warren Commission claimed?

There was a large piece of the President's skull found in Dealey Plaza shortly after the shooting, it was laying near the curb where the fatal headshot had occurred. It was a piece of occipital bone, the bone at the back of the skull. The artist drawing that the Warren Commission used, did not show any of the occipital bone missing.

The artist drawing shows the back of the head intact. *This one piece of bone from the rear of the President's head was hard factual physical evidence that the back of the President had been blown out from a frontal shot. This piece of skull was preserved in the National Archives after the Warren Commission made its final report. It has now disappeared from the National Archives and cannot be found.* Fortunately it was photographed and the photograph is still available.

We also know that small bullet fragments were removed from President Kennedy's head during the autopsy, and we also know that a "missile" not a fragment, was removed from the President's body during the autopsy. This "missile" was signed for by FBI agents James Sibert and Frank O'Neil, *and this bullet has never again surfaced in the investigation.*

Admiral Calvin Galloway, who was present at the autopsy, confirmed that this missile was a whole bullet. We also know that when White House Assistant Press Secretary, Malcolm Kilduff announced to the press and the world at Parkland Hospital shortly after 1 P.M. on November 22, 1963, that the President was dead, pointed to his right temple as the point of entrance of the fatal shot that killed the President.

We learned in 1976, when the House on Assassination's Committee was formed to re-investigate the assassination of President Kennedy, that many of the items listed in the official inventory of the autopsy materials were missing. That Floyd Riebe, a medical photographic technician, who took the pictures at the autopsy, said that the President's head had a gaping hole in the back. When Riebe was shown two pictures from the autopsy, he replied, "The two pictures you showed me are not what I saw that night, it's being phonied someplace."

Jerrol Custer, the x-ray technician who took x-rays at the autopsy, and when shown a supposedly official autopsy x-ray, was asked, "Is this an x-ray you took?" Mr. Custer replied by placing his hand at the back of his head and said, "No, this area was gone, there was no scalp there."

It is a fact that the x-rays and photographs shown in 1976 do not relate to each other. Dr. Robert McClelland, one of the attending physicians at Parkland Hospital, also denied the authenticity of these so called "official autopsy x-rays."

The Warren Commission members had lively debates about many of the above issues, and closely studied the admittedly hastily made drawings, but still, in the end, determined that all of President Kennedy's wounds resulted from gunshots from the rear and not the front.

Dr. Humes, in his testimony to the Warren Commission, concerning the autopsy on the President, spoke in medical terminology, but not one member of the Warren Commission had any medical training.

I am not even going to try to go into the detailed problems surrounding the autopsy; I am going to leave that to other researchers and future historians. But one thing that has come to my attention that I will discuss is that a couple of the autopsy witnesses have stated that the President's body arrived in a body bag and was not in the fancy casket he had been placed in at Parkland Hospital.

Also I have been told by reliable sources that when Air Force One landed at Andrews Air Force Base, TV cameras were on the people getting off the plane from the plane's open door and in the background coming from the other side of the plane and unnoticed because the TV camera's were on Jackie Kennedy and other dignitaries, two men were carrying someone in a body bag to a waiting helicopter.

If any of the major TV networks still have their TV footage of Air Force One after the assassination, I urge them to examine the tapes for evidence to verify what I have been told about two men carrying a body bag to a waiting helicopter.

There is strong evidence that something happened to the President's body on the flight from Dallas and in the time before the autopsy later that evening. I recommend you read David Lipton's book, *Best Evidence*. David spent several years in researching this book and his findings cannot be dismissed about the handling of the President's body from the time it left Parkland until the time of the autopsy at Bethesda.

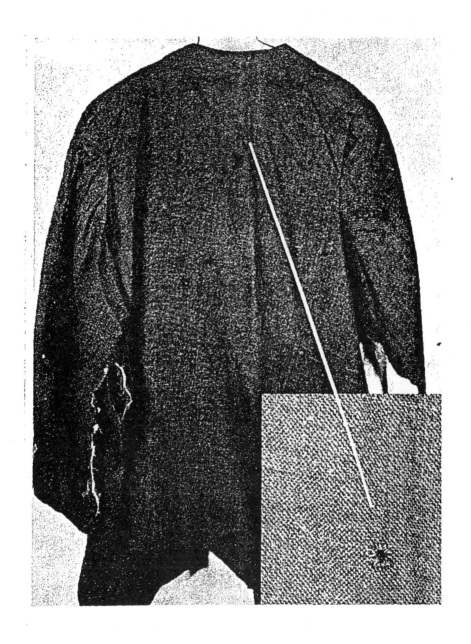

22 November 1963

From: Francis X. O'NEILL, Jr., Agent FBI
       James W. SIBERT, Agent FBI

To: Captain J. H. STOVER, Jr., Commanding Officer, U. S. Naval Medical
       School, National Naval Medical Center, Bethesda, Maryland.

1. We hereby acknowledge receipt of a missle removed by Commander James
    J. HUMES, MC, USN on this date.

Francis X. O'NEILL, Jr.

James W. SIBERT

Autopsy Missile Receipt

This is a copy of the receipt for a bullet removed from President Kennedy's body
by Dr. James J. Humes during the Presidents autopsy the evening of November 22,
1963. It was given to FBI agents Francis X. O'Neill Jr. and James W. Sibert by
Naval Captain J. W. Stovar, Commanding Officer, U.S. Naval Medical School,
National Medical Center, Bethesda, Maryland, who was in attendance at the
autopsy. When this receipt was found among the thousands of FBI documents that
the FBI was forced to turn over under the Freedom of Information Act concerning
the assassination of President John F. Kennedy, Admiral Calvin Galloway, who was
also in attendance at the autopsy, confirmed that the missile was a whole bullet and
not a fragment of a bullet. This bullet never surfaced again in the investigation of
the President's assassination and the members of the Warren Commission and its
staff, were unaware that there had in fact been a whole bullet removed from the
President's body during the autopsy. Although the word missile is misspelled as
missle, this receipt for a bullet is critical to the fact that the evidence concerning the
Presidents Assassination was tampered with and proves without any doubt that
there was a minimum of four shots fired during the assassination.

22 November 1963

From: Francis X. O'NEILL, Jr., Agent FBI
       James W. SIBERT, Agent FBI

To: Captain J. H. STOVER, Jr., Commanding Officer, U. S. Naval Medical
       School, National Naval Medical Center, Bethesda, Maryland

1. We hereby acknowledge receipt of a missle removed by Commander James
    J. HUMES, MC, USN on this date.

Francis X. O'NEILL, Jr

James W. SIBERT

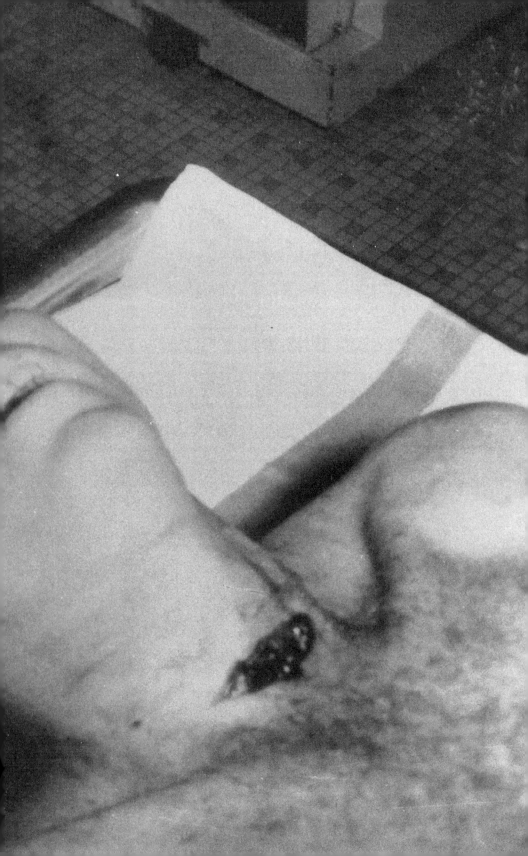

CHAPTER TWENTY-EIGHT

THE THROAT INJURY

The autopsy facts confirms my beliefs that the first shot, the shot that sounded like the pop of a firecracker, only penetrated Kennedy's back one and a half inches. The autopsy doctors could only stick their fingers into President Kennedy's back injury an inch and a half, so the doctors then used a steel rod meant for showing the path of a bullet, and this steel rod would also only go into the President's back injury the same one and a half inches.

Abraham Zapruder had his camera on President Kennedy as the limousine turned onto Elm Street but immediately the President's image disappeared behind a sign. When the President emerged from behind the sign, the Zapruder movie shows the President has both hands raised, like he is reaching for his throat. This image on film makes it evident that the President has been hit by the first shot and is in pain.

The Warren Commission dismissed solid evidence that the first shot only penetrated Kennedy's back one and one half inches, and concluded that the first shot that hit Kennedy from the rear, also penetrated Kennedy's neck coming out the throat. First of all, this conclusion is in error when you take into consideration, the fact that the first shot hit the President in the back four and a half inches below the collar line – the bullet *did not* hit the President in the back of the neck. But by using Gerald Ford's, now admitted, altered evidence of raising the back injury up to the neck – it became possible that a bullet could hit the President in the back of the neck, and would now have a correct angle to exit the front of the neck.

As to the President's throat injury, it is my deeply studied opinion from careful study of all the evidence and discussions with experts that the throat injury was caused by a fragment from the shot that hit the President square in the middle of the back of his head, fragmented and one fragment exited the throat.

Experts have also told me that a very low-speed bullet injury (fragment) and a high velocity bullet injury will sometimes look the same, that both might look like an entrance wound. There have been many who have claimed the throat wound was an entrance wound, but there is not one shred of evidence as to where a bullet might have gone after entering the throat from the front.

As for President Kennedy apparently raising his hands to his throat after the first shot, he is only reacting to the bullet hitting him in the back; he is not reacting to a bullet coming out his throat.

To duplicate this reaction, use a friend and do this, walk up behind the friend, unbeknown to the friend, and punch the friend in the back hard with your finger or the blunt end of a pen. Your friend's hands and arms will fly up exactly like Kennedy's hands and arms did when he was hit in the back by the first shot. You will find that this easy test has the same reaction almost every time.

CHAPTER TWENTY-NINE

THE MAGIC BULLET
ONE BULLET, SEVEN WOUNDS

The Warren Commission concluded that one bullet penetrated the bodies of both President Kennedy and Governor Connally. That one bullet hit President Kennedy in the neck, exited his throat, then hit Governor Connally in the back near his right armpit shattered a rib, exited his chest below his right nipple, then hit the backside of his wrist shattering the wrist bones, exited the palm side of his wrist, and then lodged in his left thigh. There is overwhelming and positive evidence that this conclusion by the Warren Commission was in error.

The main problem causing the Warren Commission to make this conclusion was an artist drawing of the President's back injury. The artist drawing placed the entrance wound 6 inches higher, in the neck, than where the bullet actually hit the President in the back. The Warren Commission did not at any time view any of the autopsy photographs or x-rays. Instead they relied on an artist drawings made by an artist who was not at the autopsy and had not seen the autopsy photographs or x-rays.

The artist made the drawings from a verbal description given to him by Dr. Humes two days after the autopsy. Later, the undeveloped photographs and x-rays would be turned over to the FBI

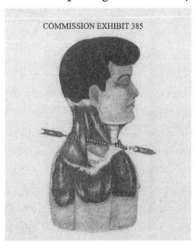

COMMISSION EXHIBIT 385

When Dr. Humes testified before the Warren Commission, he was asked if the drawings were made to scale, and he replied, "It would be virtually impossible for the artist to do this without the photographs." And then he said, "I cannot, did not, transmit completely to the illustrator where they were situated."

Unknown to the Warren Commission, the artist's drawing that the Commission viewed of the President's back wound had moved the President's back injury up seven inches and into the neck, and at the collar line, and not in the back, four and a half inches below the collar line where the actual wound was. Witness after witness who were present at the autopsy, stated the back injury was four and a half inches below the collar.

Dr. Humes autopsy work sheet places the back entrance wound six inches below the collar line. President Kennedy's shirt has a bullet hole in the back six inches below the collar line. President Kennedy's coat also has a hole in the back six inches below the collar line.

A back wound six inches below the collar line would place that wound below the throat wound. A shot from six stories up would have a downward path and its energy will cause it to continue downward in soft flesh. Every law of physics says that a bullet can not mysteriously change direction at 2000 feet per second and suddenly start up and exit through a wound above where it entered the body from a downward shot.

The second problem, as photographs taken at the time show, was that the two men were not in alignment for one bullet to penetrate both men. Governor Connally was seated in front of the President, and was positioned somewhat to the right of President Kennedy. The evidence is overwhelming that the President and the Governor were hit by separate bullets. When the autopsy doctors tried to probe the President's back wound, they could only probe about an inch and a half, in an attempt to follow the bullet's path.

THE PRISTINE BULLET FOUND AT PARKLAND

The pristine bullet, Commission exhibit 399, that supposedly rolled off a stretcher and was found at Parkland Hospital, is just that, a pristine bullet, or it was until a small flake was sliced off the nose for analysis by the FBI laboratory.

Commission exhibit 399 is *the bullet* that is said to have penetrated both the bodies of President Kennedy and Governor Connally. And Governor Connally had bullet fragments in his wrist and a small fragment in his thigh. *This bullet*, Commission exhibit 399, has no fragments missing other than the small flake that was deliberately sliced off for analysis.

When autopsy Navy Commander Dr. Humes testified before the Warren Commission, he was shown Commission exhibit 399, and asked if that bullet could have caused the injuries to Governor Connally's wrist, and Dr. Humes replied, "I think that is most unlikely, was basically intact, its jacket appears to me to be intact, and I do not understand how it could possibly have left fragments in the wrist."

Navy Commander Dr. J. Thornton Boswell who assisted Dr. Humes in President Kennedy's autopsy was asked the same question, and he replied, "Dr. Humes spoke for him as well."

Marine Lt Col. Dr. Pierre Finck, Chief of the Wound Ballistics Branch of the Armed Forces, and who also assisted Dr. Humes in President Kennedy's autopsy was also asked the same question, and he replied, "No, for the reason there are too many fragments described in the wrist."

Dr. Shaw, who had attended to Governor Connally at Parkland, agreed with the autopsy doctors. The Warren Commission was not satisfied with these doctors' conclusion, that Commission exhibit 399, a pristine bullet, was not the bullet that caused Governor Connally's wrist wound and called upon an "expert," veterinarian Dr. Alfred G. Oliver, to do scientific medical experiments for the Commission.

Dr. Oliver reportedly had spent seven years in wounds ballistic research for the U.S. Army. Dr. Oliver had a bullet fired through the carcass of a goat to simulate Governor Connally's injuries: the bullet was "quite flattened."

Dr. Oliver had a bullet fired through a cadaver's wrist: "This bullet was quite flattened." The Commission had Dr. Oliver fire bullets through several different substances to simulate the bullet that went through President Kennedy's neck. Every substance that a bullet was fired through "distorted" it.

All of Dr. Oliver's experiments were done separately. One to simulate the wrist wound, one to simulate Governor Connally's chest wound, and one to simulate President Kennedy's "neck" wound. All of these test firings by Dr. Oliver resulted in flattened or mutilated bullets. None of Dr. Oliver's tests was set up to simulate one single bullet passing through two bodies, shattering a rib, a wrist, shattering the wrist, and then penetrating a thigh.

That the Warren Commission ignored these facts testified to by three of the autopsy doctors, Governor Connally's attending physician, plus their own expert, to conclude that one bullet penetrated both men, caused all of their injuries, and was still in pristine condition – is beyond my comprehension.

Facts about Commission exhibit 399 are at the center of a controversy over the Warren report that has gone on since the report was released. When I decided to write this book, I made up my mind that there would be no speculation, just facts. But I will pass on a thought I have had for years. What if that first shot was a dud?

With few exceptions, the witnesses in Dealey Plaza, including myself, described the first shot as having the sound of a firecracker or of a backfire and not the sound or crack of a rifle shot as was heard with the second and third shots. What if this dud shot only penetrated the President's back an inch or two?

The autopsy doctors stated they could not probe the President's back injury but an inch or two. And if this dud shot, that had barely penetrated the President's back, worked its way out of the President's back at Parkland Hospital, and was in fact the bullet found on the stretcher at Parkland Hospital, Commission exhibit 399, a pristine bullet. Then what happened to the bullet that was lodged in Governor Connally's thigh?

Chapter Thirty

Make the Evidence Fit

There is example after example of how evidence was altered or changed to make it fit a predetermined outcome. There could be hundreds of pages written about all the examples of this in the investigation of the assassination of President Kennedy.

The autopsy was one example of making the evidence fit. I touched on the autopsy in an earlier chapter. But let us take a look at just one portion of the autopsy, how it was determined that the throat wound was found to be an exit wound.

The autopsy doctors completely missed the throat wound during the autopsy. The autopsy doctors were well into the autopsy when they turned the President's body over to examine the President's back, which is when they discovered a bullet hole in the back about five inches below the collar line. Dr. Humes probed this wound with his finger and determined that the wound had a downward trajectory of 45 to 60 degrees. This downward trajectory of 45 to 60 degrees would match a shot being fired down from the sixth floor of the School Book Depository into the President.

Dr. Humes also found that he could only probe this wound an inch or so and his finger could touch the end of the opening. Drs. Boswell and Finck were assisting Dr. Humes and they also probed the back wound and found that they could only probe the wound an inch or so to feel the end of the opening. They then probed the opening with a metal probe, a thin piece of stiff metal with a small ball on the end some eight inches long. The metal probe also could only go into the wound an inch or so.

There were Naval Brass, medical technicians, FBI agents, and Secret Service Agents watching the doctors probe this wound. Secret Service Agent Roy Kellerman testified to the Warren Commission that he finally spoke up and asked of Dr. Finck, "Colonel, where did it go?" The doctor replied, "There are no lanes for outlet of this entry."

Dr. Humes later told the Warren Commission: "Attempts to probe the wound were unsuccessful without fear of making a false passage." According to other witnesses at the autopsy the doctors were confused because there was no exit for this wound and no bullet to be found.

At about 11 P.M. the autopsy was over and the doctors concluded: one missile entered the back of the President and was apparently dislodged during cardiac massage at Parkland Hospital. There are several solid conclusions that can be made from the discovery that one bullet penetrated President Kennedy's back an inch or so and that it hit him in the back five inches below the collar line and not in the neck.

1. The first shot hit President Kennedy in the back 5 inches below the collar line and only penetrated his back an inch or so.

2. This bullet worked its way out of the President's back while the doctors attended to the President in the emergency room at Parkland Hospital.

3. This bullet that worked its way out of the President's back at Parkland is in actuality Commission exhibit number 399, the nearly pristine bullet found on a stretcher at Parkland.

4. This first shot that hit the President in the back was a dud, faulty ammunition that did not have full power, it only penetrated the President's back an inch or so and to most of us in Dealey Plaza sounded like the pop of a firecracker or the backfire of a motorcycle. It did not have the sound like the crack of a rifle shot.

5. The picture taken of President Kennedy apparently reaching up for a throat injury is misleading. If you punch someone in the back hard with a semi-sharp object, their arms will fly up like President Kennedy's arms did in the picture, he was not reacting to a throat injury, but reacting to the sharp pain and impact of the bullet that hit him in the back. Try this experiment with a friend, without the friend knowing it, punch him in the back with a semi-sharp object and watch his arms fly up just like President Kennedy's arms did after being hit by the "dud" shot in the back.

There was one documented shot that hit President Kennedy square in the upper rear and the middle of the back of the President's head. This bullet fragmented all over the front of the interior of his brain, and it may be that it was a fragment from this bullet that caused the small injury to Kennedy's throat. Experts have told me that a low-speed exit wound will sometimes look like a high-speed entrance wound. *There was not one shot that took a zig-zag course and penetrated both men with one bullet.*

On June 5, 1964, more than six months after the assassination of President Kennedy, I read in the paper that the Warren Commission was all but done with their investigation, concluding there were three shots, with the first shot hitting Kennedy, the second shot hitting Connally, and the third shot hitting Kennedy.

I raised my hand and asked what about the missed shot. *Dallas Times Herald* reporter Jim Lehrer wrote the story about a stray bullet hitting the street in front of me and throwing debris into my face, and history was to change.

Under pressure to keep their three-shot, no conspiracy, one lone nut shooter story together, the Warren Commission, by using Gerald Ford's altered evidence, came up with the "single bullet theory" that one bullet went through both Kennedy and Connally and published a report that they expected the dumb American public to believe. *Again and I will repeat, one shot did not take a zig-zag course and penetrate both men with one bullet.*

Back to Dr. Humes and the autopsy: on Saturday morning Dr. Humes talked to Dr. Perry at Parkland Hospital, who had attended to the President the day before. In the course of that conversation, Dr. Humes learned from Dr. Perry that there had been a bullet wound in the President's throat and that the Parkland Doctors had performed a tracheotomy at that spot.

Commander Humes left Bethesda Naval Hospital carrying the autopsy notes from the night before and went home. At home he rewrote the official autopsy report, which included the finding of a wound in the President's throat. Dr. Humes then burned the original autopsy report. As Dr. Humes rewrote the autopsy report about finding the throat wound, the President's body was lying in state at the White House.

More than a decade later, Dr. Humes was called to testify before the House Select Committee. Dr. Humes testified that when Dr. Perry told him about the throat wound: "Lights went on, and we said, ah, we have some place for our missile to have gone."

The entrance wound in the President's throat that the Parkland doctors had observed was now officially an exit wound. A back entrance wound four and a half inches below the collar was now in the shoulder near the collar line. A back wound that earlier had a downward slant of 45 to 60 degrees was now more horizontal so that the bullet could come out the throat. Two days later Dr. Humes orally instructed an artist how to draw the back wound for the Warren Commission in the neck so it would be higher than the throat "exit" wound.

Dr. Humes evidently forgot to put the back wound up in the shoulder on the autopsy report. And he evidently did not realize that the President's coat and shirt with bullet holes four and a half inches below the collar would also be evidence. As you can see, it was not at all hard to make the evidence fit. Just an example of why we will never know the truth about the assassination.

CHAPTER THIRTY-ONE

THE SUSPECT

When Mrs. Robert Reid, a clerical supervisor who had been standing outside the front door of the School Book Depository, heard the shots, she ran back inside the Texas School Book Depository to her office on the second floor. As she walked to her desk she noticed Lee Harvey Oswald slowly walking through the office. In her testimony to the Warren Commission Mrs. Reid stated Oswald was "Calm and walking at a very slow pace."

Lee Oswald left the building, walked two blocks and boarded a bus. The bus became stalled in traffic, Oswald got off the bus and then took a taxi to his room, changed clothes and left hurriedly, 45 minutes after the President was murdered. Dallas Police Officer J.D. Tippit was murdered near where Oswald lived. Oswald was traced to a nearby theater. Dallas police officer M.N. McDonald was the first to confront Oswald in the theater and there was a struggle with Oswald reaching for his gun under his shirt.

It has been reported that Oswald pointed his gun directly at Officer McDonald's head and pulled the trigger, there was a click, and the gun misfired. Oswald was subdued and arrested for the murder of Dallas officer J.D. Tippit.

Oswald was soon brought up to the Homicide Office where I witnessed him being placed in the cubicle next to me. It had been only a little more than an hour after President John F. Kennedy had been assassinated.

Normal booking procedures were bypassed and Oswald had been taken directly to Homicide in room 317 under the control of Captain J.W. "Will" Fritz head of Dallas Homicide.

Oswald was interrogated for the next three or four hours by a Secret Service agent, an FBI agent, a Texas Ranger, and Captain Fritz. Because of the pressure from the other investigative agencies Captain Fritz was unable to conduct an orderly private interview with Oswald.

The interrogation was a three-ring circus according to Dallas Chief of Police Jesse Curry. Oswald claimed to be indignant and claimed he knew nothing about anything.

By 7:00 P.M. on that day, November 22, 1963, the Dallas police believed they had enough evidence to file a charge of murder against Lee Harvey Oswald for the death of officer J.D. Tippit.

Throughout the evening the FBI continually asked the Dallas Police Department for the FBI to take over the Tippit murder case against Oswald from the Dallas Police Department, and asked Dallas PD to give the FBI all the evidence.

By midnight that same day, Friday November 22, 1963, Chief Curry caved in to the FBI and released the evidence in the Tippit murder case to the FBI. It was understood that the physical evidence would be returned to the Dallas Police Department later.

At about 11 P.M. reporters started showing pictures of Lee Harvey Oswald on television and stating: "This is what the man who is charged with shooting President Kennedy looks like. We don't know what he looks like now after being in custody of the Dallas Police Department."

The pressure put on the Dallas Police force was unlike any murder case ever experience by any American city. Dallas had pride and because of the continued suggestion by newsmen that Oswald was being mistreated by the Dallas police, an ill-conceived press conference was arranged for shortly after midnight for newsmen to take pictures of Lee Harvey Oswald face to face with reporters.

CHAPTER THIRTY-TWO

OSWALD'S MOVEMENTS

Bonnie Ray Williams' testimony to the Warren Commission is found in Volume III pages 161 to 184. On November 22, 1963 he was working on the sixth floor of the School Book Depository helping to lay a new floor with about five other men.

They did the floor-laying job by moving the school book cartons from the west side of the sixth floor and stacking then head high on the east side and then laying new flooring the area on the cleared west side.

Bonnie Ray had noticed Lee Harvey Oswald at one point over near the north side of the east elevator with a clipboard in his hand apparently filling an order. That was Oswald's job: gather up books from the upper floors and take them to the first floor to be wrapped and mailed to schools throughout the state of Texas. Bonnie Ray's work crew broke for lunch at about five minutes to twelve noon.

Three men got on the east elevator and three men got on the west elevator to race each other down to the second floor to wash up and eat lunch. As the elevators started down Bonnie Ray heard Oswald yell for them to send an elevator back for him. Plans had been made for Billie Ray and a couple others to wash up, get their lunch sacks, and come back up to the sixth floor and eat their lunch as they watched the motorcade from the sixth floor windows.

Bonnie Ray Williams did just that, but no one else came back up to the sixth floor as planned. Bonnie Ray ate his lunch alone on the sixth floor and then went down to the fifth floor. Bonnie Ray testified that he estimated the time to be from the time they took a lunch break at 11:55 A.M., until after he had gone down to the second floor, washed up, bought a bottle of soda from the soft drink machine in the lunch room, grabbed his lunch, came back up to the sixth floor, ate his chicken sandwich lunch alone on the sixth floor, and then went down to the fifth floor to be five to fifteen minutes.

That would put Bonnie Ray Williams on the sixth floor alone some time between twelve noon and ten minutes after twelve noon. Common sense tells me that it would take more time to duplicate Bonnie Ray's movements than five minutes and it was probably more than fifteen minutes.

An interesting side fact that came from Bonnie Ray Williams eating his lunch on the sixth floor, was that an enterprising reporter, who was able to get into the depository later, took a picture of the chicken bone and Dr. Pepper bottle Bonnie Ray had left behind on the sixth floor. The next morning there was a headline stating: ASSASSIN CALMLY ATE CHICKEN WHILE WAITING FOR KENNEDY, complete with a picture of Bonnie Ray's chicken bone and Dr. Pepper bottle.

CHAPTER THIRTY-THREE

THE STRANGE ACTION OF ROY TRULY

Roy S. Truly had worked for the Texas School Book Depository for 29 years. In 1963 he was on the board of directors, and was the Superintendent of the Depository, a privately owned corporation. Mr. Truly, from everything I could find, was well respected in Dallas.

But ever since November 22, 1963, Truly's actions have left me puzzled and needing an explanation – which never came.

In mid-October, at the request a woman he claims he had never met, he interviewed Lee Oswald, had him fill out an employment application, asked him a couple of questions and then hired Oswald on the spot with no background check.

It was not unusual in 1963 to hire someone without a background check; a convincing face-to-face interview was often all that was needed. But when you connect Mr. Truly's actions 37 days later, November 22, 1963, it raises questions.

In a timed reenactment it was determined that 75 seconds after the first shot, Truly had encountered Lee Harvey Oswald in the second floor lunchroom. Truly's testimony to the Warren Commission stated, "He didn't seem to be excited or overly afraid or anything, he might have been a bit startled, like I might have been if somebody confronted me. But I cannot recall any change in expression of any kind on his face."

The police officer with Truly said almost the same thing: "Calm and not out of breath." About six minutes later the School Book Depository was sealed off, no one could get out, and a few of the employees who had been outside watching the motorcade were locked out.

Truly, in his Warren Commission testimony states that a few minutes after seeing a calm Oswald in the second floor lunch room, Truly called the other Book Depository where the personnel records are kept, and asked for the Oswald's employment application information. As soon as Truly got off the phone he turns to Dallas Assistant Chief of Police Lumpkin, who is standing nearby: "There is one man missing."

Chief Lumpkin said, "Lets go tell Captain Fritz." At 12:45 P.M., just 15 minutes after the assassination a bulletin is put out for a "slender white male about thirty, five-feet-ten, one-sixty five." Contrary to reports, Truly had not yet made a roll call of employee's who were present or not present, when he called the other Depository for Oswald's employment application information, nor had he been asked to do so by the police. Truly's statement that he had only one man missing is false; he had other employees who had been outside watching the motorcade that could not get back in when the Depository was sealed off.

At 12:45 P.M., Officer Tippit was still alive and they had not announced President Kennedy's death.

Roy Truly's actions on November 22, 1963 do not make sense. What was going on in Truly's mind to so quickly finger Lee Harvey Oswald as the assassin of President Kennedy? Truly's actions raise so many questions.

Were Ruth Paine and Roy Truly part of a "need to know" master plan? Was Paine influenced or paid to take Marina and Lee Harvey Oswald in, with no questions asked? Was Paine influenced or paid to call Truly at the School Book Depository to request employment for Lee Harvey Oswald? Was Truly influenced or paid to hire Lee Oswald on the spot with no background check, and no hard questions asked of Oswald? Was Truly also part of a master plan?

In short, did these two people, Ruth Paine and Roy Truly, react to some influence or payment, without having any knowledge or idea of what the end result would be? Could they have been used, without their being aware? Were they minor players in a much larger enterprise?

A master plan to assassinate President John F. Kennedy had to have been at least nearly two years in the planning – down to the last little detail. It is my personal opinion that Roy Truly realized, suspected, and put two and two together in a matter of a few short minutes: That he had been used in the hiring of Oswald, and that the hiring of Oswald was part of the assassination plot of President Kennedy.

Panic caused Truly to tell the Dallas Police that he had one employee missing, when the fact was he had just seen Lee Harvey Oswald in the second floor lunchroom. Truly's Warren Commission testimony regarding his actions after seeing Oswald in the lunch room 75 seconds after the assassination can be found in Volume VII, pages 384-385 of the 26-volume report.

CHAPTER THIRTY-FOUR

THE ZAPRUDER FILM

braham Zapruder, the man who took the movie of the assassination of President Kennedy, was a Dallas businessman whose office was near Dealey Plaza at 501 Elm Street in Dallas. When Mr. Zapruder decided to walk the few steps from his office to Dealey Plaza with his 8mm camera, he did not know that he was about to take the amateur movie of the century.

When the motorcade rounded the corner of Houston and Elm Streets in front of the Texas School Book Depository, Mr. Zapruder was standing on a ledge that was part of the pergola at the rear of the Grassy Knoll, he had his secretary with him, and she helped to steady him so he would not fall. Mr. Zapruder started his camera rolling as the President's limousine turned the corner onto Elm Street. He stopped momentarily and then continued filming until the President's car went under the triple underpass.

Immediately after the shooting, Abraham Zapruder walked back to his office and called the FBI. He then went to WFAA-TV, which was nearby, and did a live interview with Jay Watson. From there he was accompanied by Forrest V. Sorrels, head of the Secret Service in Dallas, to the Eastman Kodak Company at 3131 Manor Way in Dallas to have the film developed.

The film was developed, with the identification number 0183 being made part of the film. Eastman Kodak did not have a way to duplicate the developed movie at that office, and recommended Jamieson Film Company, at 3825 Bryan Street, in Dallas, to have copies made.

Zapruder and Sorrels went to Jamieson, where three duplicate copies were made. They then returned to Mr. Zapruder's office and viewed the film as many as fifteen times; it was now about 4 P.M. The original and at least one copy were then flown to Washington D.C. that same evening, November 22, 1963, and delivered to the National Photographic Interpretation Center in Suitland, Maryland, whose employees are on the payroll of the CIA.

Two employees of NPIC were called at home to come to the Center to do work on the Zapruder film, they were Ben Hunter and Homer A. McMahon.

The Secret Service courier, a Captain Sands, told them the original film and copies were developed by Kodak at Eastman Kodak in Rochester, New York (Yes, that is what these two men were positive they were told by Sands when interviewed in 1997 by the Assassination Records Review Board, that Rochester Kodak developed the film, not Dallas Kodak.)

The original and the copies were in the hands of NPIC until about 3 A.M. EST and arrived back in Dallas at about 6:30 A.M. CST Saturday morning, November 23, 1963 and delivered back to Mr. Zapruder at his office at approximately 7 A.M. Sometime after 8 A.M. CST the film rights were sold to *Life* magazine. The film was then shown to a group of reporters in Mr. Zapruder's office. Dan Rather of CBS was one of those reporters. *Life* magazine published 31 frames of this amateur movie in their November 29, 1963 issue.

At the time, Zapruder's 8mm amateur movie was believed to be the best evidence of the assassination of President Kennedy and the wounding of Governor Connally. The Zapruder film was what the Warren Commission used to determine the timing of the shots, direction of the shots, and other vital information to determine that Lee Oswald was the lone assassin.

Credible researchers over the years have pointed out flaws in this amateur movie suspecting alterations and finding inconsistencies with eyewitness reports and other pictures taken at the same moment. The Assassination Records Review Board (ARRB), a government funded program to preserve the assassination records, did extensive work in the 1990's on this amateur movie and determined that there are indeed problems.

There are at least twenty-four versions in different formants. The so-called original version that was sold to *Life* magazine, a Secret Service version, a FBI version, a CIA version, and other versions that are different. There is a preponderance of evidence that the movie has been tampered with.

There are frames missing, splices, and the unique original perforated I.D. marking 0183 is not on the so-called original today. The head wound as shown in the Zapruder movie is not consistent with Dealey Plaza witnesses, motorcade witnesses, or Parkland hospital witnesses. *There is a dark spot at the back of the head in the movie* where witnesses saw brain debris exit from the rear of the President's head. The movie shows the debris going up and slightly forward with the right side of the President's head exploding.

And most important, this debris is only shown in two frames, while it would take a minimum of three or more frames for this debris to go up and start dissipating as it is coming back down.

The background images are not consistent with a moving vehicle, both are in focus; if the camera is moving on a moving vehicle the background images will be blurry and out of focus while the vehicle is clear or if the camera is stationary the background will be clear while the moving vehicle will be blurry and out of focus. There are those that say that because both the vehicle and the background are clear it is evidence that the limousine had stopped, but the limousine does not stop in the Zapruder movie.

There are people in one place in one frame and a few feet away in the next frame. The secret service agent driving the car turns his head in one frame and in the next frame it is 110 degrees different, something that is not humanly possible in one eighteenth of a second; the blinking lights of the Presidential limousine are out of sync in the movie because of missing frames. There is a long list of these abnormalities.

One needs to view the movie frame by frame to find these abnormalities, but they are there. Today, nearly 50 years later, even the authenticity of the altered original Zapruder amateur movie taken on November 22, 1963 cannot be verified. There is overwhelming and indisputable evidence that the Zapruder film has been tampered with.

I was able to obtain a bootleg 8mm copy of the so-called original 8mm Zapruder movie in the late 1960s, long before the movie became public and I still have that copy today. I have compared the late 1960's bootleg copy and later copies – there is a difference.

If you take the Zapruder film as being authentic, and frames of it have to be, there are still problems. The film shows in graphic detail the fatal shot that rips President Kennedy's head apart. The frames showing the fatal shot, supposedly a single shot coming from the rear, from the School Book Depository Building according to the Warren Commission, shows the President's head and body being thrown violently backward and slammed into the back of the seat of the limousine. This is contrary to all laws of physics.

However a shot fired from behind the picket fence at the back of the Grassy Knoll, would have the exact result that is shown in the Zapruder film head shot, the head and body are blown away from the source of the shot, to the rear and to the left as the sequence of frames in the movie show. It is strong evidence that there was in fact a frontal shot, and at least two shooters.

At first the authorities attributed this violent snap backwards to the limousine's rapid acceleration, this theory was quickly debunked when other photographs showed that the limousine had in reality, almost come to a complete stop after the head shot. Then two new theories were soon advanced to explain why in this instance, the head and body violently reacted toward the direction of the shot. One was a "neuro reaction" and the other a "jet" effect. A careful study of the Zapruder movie does not give credibility to either of these theories.

Why was the Zapruder film put into the hands of CIA photographic employees that night and then sent back to Dallas the next morning? Abraham Zapruder's business partner was one of the persons who viewed the film after it was developed on November 22, 1963, and then viewed the film again the next morning when the magazine was bargaining for the rights to the movie. He remarked that the movie seemed different from when he had viewed it yesterday.

It was years before the public was shown the Zapruder film.

CHAPTER THIRTY-FIVE

ROGER CRAIG, HERO OR?

Deputy Sheriff Roger Craig was a veteran law officer who had worked for Dallas County Sheriff James Eric (Bill) Decker for several years and had been once named the Sheriff's Department officer of the year. Roger lived with his wife Molly and three young children in Dallas.

On the morning of November 22, 1963, at about 10:30 A.M., Sheriff Decker called his plain-clothes men, detectives, and warrant men into his office (Sheriff Decker left the Dallas County Sheriff's patrolmen on duty in the field.). He explained that President Kennedy was in town and that the motorcade would come down Main Street past the Sheriff's office at 505 Main Street. Sheriff Decker advised his deputies to stand out front of the Sheriff's office and represent the Sheriff's Department. The deputies were also advised to take *no part whatsoever in the security of that motorcade.*

These Dallas County Deputies were in place in front of the Sheriff's office by 12:15 and most were not enthusiastic about being forced to watch the President's motorcade. When one of the deputies commented the President was late, another spoke up and said, "Maybe someone will shoot the son of a bitch."

In Roger Craig's unfinished book, *When They Kill A President,* Craig writes that as the President's motorcade approached, he felt something was amiss about the situation: there were no officers guarding the intersections, no crowd control, and a general lack of security in the area.

As the President's limousine passed, Roger Craig was relaxed as he saw the smiling and waving President go by in front of him. Roger watched as the limousine turned right onto Houston Street, went the short block and turned left onto Elm Street in front of the Texas School Book Depository.

Then a shot rang out, Roger bolted toward the Depository; as he ran toward the Depository, two more shots rang out, Rogers mind raced.

Roger saw a Dallas Police Officer run up the Grassy Knoll and behind the picket fence, Roger followed the officer only to find complete confusion and hysteria.

143

Roger Craig did encounter a woman in her early thirties attempting to leave in her car from the parking area behind the picket fence and stopped her. She told Roger she had to leave, but Roger placed her under arrest and turned her over to fellow Deputy Sheriff C.I. (Lummy) Lewis to take her to the Sheriff's office for questioning. Deputy Lewis lost the woman and her car in the confusion.

James
Tague

Roger
Craig

HOMICIDE and ROBBERY BUREAU

Roger
Craig

CHAPTER THIRTY-SIX

ROGER CRAIG AND THE NASH STATION WAGON

A few moments after shots were fired at President Kennedy's limousine, Dallas County Deputy Sheriff Roger Craig heard a shrill whistle and saw a dark complected white male running down the Grassy Knoll from the direction of the Texas School Book Depository and jump into a light-colored Nash Rambler station wagon with a luggage rack on the roof. Vehicle traffic was extremely heavy in Dealey Plaza at that moment and Deputy Craig could not get across the street to stop the Nash station wagon as it drove off.

Later that afternoon, when Roger heard that the Dallas Police Department had a man in custody, Roger called Dallas Homicide and told Captain Will Fritz what he had witnessed about the dark complected man. Captain Fritz asked Deputy Roger Craig to come to Homicide, at the Dallas Police office; Roger identified the man running to the Nash Rambler wagon as Lee Harvey Oswald (evidence was to later prove that the man Roger had seen was not Lee Harvey Oswald).

Unknown to each other, Deputy Sheriff Roger Craig's seeing a dark complected man run down the Grassy Knoll and jump into a Nash Rambler station wagon is corroborated by Marvin C. Robinson.

In a statement taken by the FBI the next day 11/23/1963, Mr. Robinson states he was driving through Dealey Plaza a few minutes after the shooting and as he was driving past the Texas School Book Depository Building a "light-colored" Nash station wagon suddenly appeared before him.

He stated this vehicle stopped and a white male came down the Grassy Knoll and entered the Nash station wagon and drove off to the west toward the Oak Cliff section of Dallas. The existence of this Nash Rambler Station Wagon is fully documented by a picture taken of the Rambler in traffic in Dealey Plaza a few moments after the assassination. This picture shows the Rambler's passenger door is slightly open and the car is near the Grassy Knoll.

Moments before Roger Craig saw the Rambler wagon going west on one-way Elm Street, Richard Carr saw two men hurriedly escort a third man down Houston Street from the School Book Depository, turn onto Main and place this man into a Rambler wagon. Mr. Carr watched this Rambler turn left onto the one-way North Record Street. This Rambler would dead end into Elm Street and would have to have turned left onto one-way going west Elm Street to get out of Dallas, and is probably the same Rambler wagon that Roger Craig then saw stop and a second man get into.

Roger Craig did testify to the Warren Commission, however, when the Warren Commission findings were made public, Roger disputed what the commission had to say about his testimony. Roger Craig said his testimony had been changed. Roger Craig never changed his story about the Nash station wagon.

Sheriff Decker ordered Craig to stop telling his story, but he did not stop talking to reporters and assassination writers about seeing the Nash station wagon, and Sheriff Decker eventually fired Craig in 1967.

In late 1967 a bullet grazed Craig in the head while walking in a parking lot. In 1973 a car forced him off the road causing a back injury. In 1974 he was shot by a shotgun in Waxahachie Texas. In early 1975 he was seriously injured when his car engine blew up. In 1975 he also did a series of radio talk shows talking about the Nash station wagon, someone running down the Grassy Knoll and getting into the Nash station wagon. Soon afterwards on May 15, 1975, he was found dead of a "self-inflicted" gunshot wound.

When it became known that I was writing this book, I was at first contacted by Craig's nephew and then his sister. Jerry Craig the nephew, told me of evidence that Craig had been murdered but Craig's sister told me she thought Roger was trying to shoot himself in the shoulder to get sympathy but misplaced the direction of the self-inflicted injury and the shot hit his heart and killed him.

After Dallas County Sheriff Bill Decker fired Craig in 1967, his life became a living hell. Roger went from job to job, and besides the preceding close calls on his life, whenever someone would hire Craig, Sheriff Decker would make sure he was fired and lost the job.

Penn Jones, owner of a Midlothian Texas newspaper and Kennedy researcher-activist took Craig in and made sure Craig and his family had a place to live and groceries in the house.

CHAPTER THIRTY-SEVEN

JACK RUBY AND THE MURDER OF LEE HARVEY OSWALD

Jack Ruby shot and killed Lee Harvey Oswald in the Dallas Police Headquarters basement less than 48 hours after the assassination of President John F. Kennedy. Ruby's killing of Oswald occurred in front of millions of television viewers. The Dallas Police Department was in the process of transferring accused Presidential assassin Oswald to the Dallas County jail when Oswald was shot and killed by Ruby.

Over the weekend there had been threats on Oswald's life, the Dallas Police had received several crank calls and there were rumors about vigilantes taking action. When Dallas Police chief Jesse Curry arrived in his office that morning, he was told about one of the calls: "About 100 men are going to take the prisoner Oswald and we do not want any policemen hurt."

The Dallas Police made what they thought were intensive security plans to insure a safe transfer of Oswald to the Dallas County Jail. The time of transfer of Oswald was unannounced to the public or the press. The basement was searched, officers were posted to guard all entrances, a decoy armored truck was put in place, and only accredited known reporters were allowed into the basement.

Oswald had been arrested in the Oak Cliff section of Dallas as a suspect in the killing of a Dallas Police officer shortly after the assassination of the President. It was quickly discovered by Dallas Police that Oswald was an employee of the Texas School Book Depository, the building in which it was suspected that the shots were fired that killed the President and injured Texas Governor John Connally.

Oswald was quickly charged with both murders and in less than 48 hours the press had tried and convicted Oswald. On that Sunday morning, November 24, 1963, Oswald was a hated man, already convicted by the Dallas police, the FBI, and the press for the assassination of President Kennedy, the wounding of Texas Governor John Connally, and the killing of a Dallas Policeman. The one and only topic of conversation that weekend was the assassination of our President and his "killer" Lee Harvey Oswald. And in those conversations statements were often made such as: "They ought to just take Oswald and string him up."

Jack Rubenstein, better known as Jack Ruby, a struggling strip club owner, was a small time hustler. He knew underworld characters, had some mob connections, and often sought favor and friendship with members of the Dallas Police Department.

Jack Ruby almost always carried a gun. Texas law allowed a businessman to carry a gun when taking cash receipts to the bank. This law was not strictly enforced when a businessman carried a gun at other times. Although Ruby was known to have a quick temper, he was not considered a dangerous man and he was likable.

I had met Jack Ruby on a couple of occasions; the first time was at his sister's dance hall in the Oak Lawn area. Ruby was going from table to table, introducing himself, handing out business cards, promoting his Carousel Club and giving out free passes to the club. I did use my free pass to his strip club and what I remember most about the visit to his club was his comedian, Wally Weston – he was funny. When the strippers in Ruby's club were through stripping they still had almost as much on as some of the women we see today on prime time television.

Jim Leavelle was the Dallas Police Homicide officer with the white hat, who was handcuffed to Lee Harvey Oswald when Jack Ruby shot and killed Oswald in the basement of the Dallas Police Station two days after the assassination of President Kennedy. Jim Leavelle had known Jack Ruby for many years.

In an interview with Jim Leavelle, at his Garland Texas home, Jim confirmed something to me that I had felt sure of for many years: Jack Rubenstein was not a part of any plot. It was pure happenstance that Ruby was there at that exact moment to shoot Oswald.

In Jim Leavelle's words: "From Friday night on, we had numerous threats that they were going to take Oswald away from us and do all sorts of bodily damage to him, even when it came out we were going to transfer him in an armored vehicle, there were some messages that came in that they were going to barricade the street and turn the armored vehicle over and set it on fire.

"All of this was going through my mind at the time we were coming down the elevator to the basement in the police station with Oswald to transport him to the Dallas County jail, if it, Ruby shooting Oswald had happened outside on the street, I would not of thought too much about it, because I was expecting an attempt on his life, but for it to happen in the basement was a total shock to me and as I have pointed out a lot of times.

"As you can see the expression on my face you know that it was a shock, as I walked out into the basement from the police elevator and they turned on all of those floodlights for the cameras, momentarily I was blinded. But they had told me the car to transport Oswald to the county jail would be cross ways of the entrance, so that all I would have to do was walk right into the back door of the squad car, however it was not there because of the crowd of news people that had gathered and detective Charles Daugherty who was driving the car that we were going to use had parked the car in a different position.

"I might add and I will explain a little later, we had had to abandon the armored vehicle that we were going to use because we could not get it into the basement, because of the air conditioning system on its roof, it would not let it go under the entrance, so we had to revert back to the car as we originally wanted to use anyway.

"As I walked out I was looking to my right to see where the car was and out of the corner of my eye I saw Ruby standing there right in the center of the driveway and he had his pistol by his side and then he took two quick steps and double actioned into the midriff of Oswald and shot Oswald.

"Later, I and Bill Alexander the assistant DA, timed that sequence with the cameras and it took just a little over one second, about a second and a half for Ruby to take that step, those two short steps and double actioned, like one thousand and one is about how much time it took him to make those short steps, so I was not able to react, to prevent him from shooting Oswald. I did, since I had my hand held in his belt, jerk back on Oswald, trying to pull him behind me. But all I did was turn his body so that instead of the bullet hitting him dead center it hit him about 4 inches to the left of his navel.

"The bullet went all the way through Oswald and lodged just under the skin on the other side. If he had had better ammunition the bullet would have gone on through and hit me roughly in the middle of my left side. When I later picked Oswald up along with Officer B.H. Combest and carried him back into the jail hall and laid him down, Officer Combest took my handcuffs off of Oswald.

"I examined Oswald and could see and feel the bullet under his skin, you could roll it around, it was on his right side just under the rib cage. It was just the thickness of his skin from going on through Oswald's body.

"Many times people have said how close did you come from getting shot and I said just the thickness of the skin because if it had gone through him it would have hit me in the left side. The ambulance was there in about three minutes and we loaded him into the ambulance and I rode with him to Parkland.

"In the trauma room at Parkland the doctor pinched the bullet and hit the skin with a scalpel and the bullet popped out into a little silver tray. I had the nurse scratch her initial on the end of the bullet while I watched. The official time of death at the hospital was 1:07 P.M.; but my opinion is that half way to the hospital Oswald stretched and groaned and went completely limp and I always thought that was when he probably expired, I was holding his pulse and I could not find a pulse.

"Oswald lapsed into unconsciousness almost immediately after being shot and was unconscious when he hit the floor. After we carried Oswald back to the hall floor I tried to say something to him but his eyes were closed and he never responded.

"I transferred Jack Ruby on Monday morning to the county jail and on the way there I asked him why he shot Oswald, he told me, "I just wanted to be a hero, but it looks like I just fouled things up good."

"Later on I got to thinking about 13 years earlier when I was new on the department working in uniform patrol, one of the things we did in the evening was go through the night clubs and dance halls and see if there was anybody in there getting drunk that might create a disturbance when the place closed, if so, we would just ease them out.

"It was very seldom that we would have to put anybody in jail; they would leave when we told them that we thought they had too much to drink. On one of those occasions when we were checking the Silver Spur that Ruby owned in 1950, which was located on South Ervay Street here in Dallas, I was talking with Ruby while my partner circulated through the dance hall to see if anybody in there was getting out of hand, Ruby told me that he had had a dream of finding two police officers in a death struggle about to lose their life, so that he could jump in there and save them and be a hero.

"Through the years I have felt that was Jack Ruby's only thought when he decided to kill Oswald, that he would be a hero and people from all over the world would come to the Carousel Club to shake the hand of the man who killed the assassin that killed President Kennedy.

"Several years later I (Jim Leavelle) made this same statement to some television people and it went out on the air. A retired federal agent who had heard what I had said about Ruby on the air, called me and said, Jim you do not know me and asked me where I had come up with this idea about Ruby wanting to be a hero, and I replied just from knowledge of knowing Jack Ruby, I did not get it from anybody.

"The agent said it would be interesting to note that he was the FBI agent assigned to interview all of Ruby's employees after the assassination and that is exactly the same picture that all of Jack Ruby's employees painted of Ruby, that Jack Ruby thought he would be hero for killing Lee Harvey Oswald."

It is important to know that there was no announced or set time to transfer Lee Harvey Oswald to the Dallas County jail on that Sunday morning November 24th 1963. Before being transferred Oswald was to undergo some last minute interrogation by local, state, and Federal authorities and there was no time limit put on how long that interrogation would take. While Oswald was being interrogated, Jack Ruby received a call at his apartment from Teresa Norton, one of his strippers who lived in Fort Worth, asking for money. Jack Ruby agreed he would send Ms. Norton some money and went to the Western Union office down the street from the Dallas Police station and wired $25 to Teresa Norton in Fort Worth. The receipt for this Western Union wire was in Ruby's possession when he was arrested, it was stamped by Western Union at 11:17 A.M. The killing of Oswald was at 11:21 A.M.

That was four minutes from the time the receipt was stamped at Western Union and the shooting of Oswald. A couple of weeks after the assassination, Jim Leavelle went to the Western Union office and interviewed the clerk who was on duty that morning. The clerk explained his procedure was to stamp the receipt at the moment he was paid for the wire. Jim Leavelle then walked off the route from Western Union office to the entrance to the basement of the police station three times and timed himself, once at a fast pace, once at a slow pace, and once at a normal pace. The average time to walk from the Western Union Office to the top of the ramp that led to the police basement was two minutes and twenty seconds, but add on a few seconds to walk down the ramp. That left just a little over a minute unaccounted for. The Dallas Police had not announced the time that they would be transferring Oswald to the Dallas County jail and had in fact not set an exact time for themselves to do the transfer.

They did however initially plan to transfer Oswald earlier that morning, but a last minute interrogation of Oswald took longer than expected. If the questioning of Oswald that morning had not taken so long, Oswald would have already been transferred to the Dallas County jail when Ruby arrived at the Police Station.

As for Ruby getting into the basement, it was too simple, and I will again quote Jim Leavelle as to what Ruby had told him. "I (Ruby) knew that I could not get into the basement but thought I would walk over to the entrance ramp to the basement of the police station and look down the ramp and see what I could see." But as fate would have it, just as Jack Ruby was about to walk up to the ramp to the basement, Lt. Reo Pierce came up the ramp in a squad car. Officer Roy Vaughn who had been assigned to guard the ramp saw Lt. Pierce coming up the ramp and stepped out into the street to hold up traffic on Main Street so Lt. Pierce could make a left turn across oncoming traffic.

The altered plan was for Lt. Pierce to lead the armored car as a decoy to the real transfer. As Lt. Pierce was turning onto Main Street, with Officer Roy Vaughn holding up traffic for Lt. Pierce to make a left turn, Officer Vaughn's back was turned to the ramp. It was at this very moment that Jack Ruby arrived at the ramp from the Western Union office and walked casually and unobstructed down the ramp into the basement of the police station.

There can be only one conclusion. Ruby's shooting of Oswald was not planned, was not a part of any sinister plot to silence Oswald. That Jack Ruby was at the Western Union Telegraph office in downtown Dallas to send a wire to an employee was not planned. Jack Ruby got into the basement by accident because a Dallas policeman momentarily walked out onto the street and stopped traffic for a superior officer to exit the basement of the Police Station onto the street.

Due to an eerie set of unplanned timing circumstances Ruby just happened to be at the right place at the right time to kill Oswald. Ruby always carried a gun, and with Oswald being ushered out into the basement right in front of him, Ruby made a split-second decision that he would be a hero if he killed Oswald.

We did not know for years after the assassination, and only after a long court battle, using the Freedom of Information Act to force the FBI to release their files on the assassination of President Kennedy, that Jack Ruby was a paid FBI informant at the time he murdered Lee Harvey Oswald in front of millions of television viewers. In murdering Oswald, Ruby had acted on a split-second impulse that had absolutely nothing to do with the FBI. But FBI Director J. Edgar Hoover knew that if it got out that Ruby was on the FBI's payroll, when he killed Oswald, the FBI's prestigious public image that had taken years for Hoover to nurture and build, would be seriously questioned, damaged, or even ruined by public outrage if it became public knowledge.

Hoover knew that it did not matter that Ruby had acted alone and on his own, the mere fact that Ruby was on the FBI payroll as an informant was enough to bring suspicion upon the FBI. This writer believes that this revelation, Ruby killing Oswald, along with other facts, was the driving force behind Hoover's haste to wrap up the case. Oswald was the man, close the case.

Jack Ruby was convicted of first-degree murder and sentenced to death for the murder of Lee Oswald by a Dallas County Jury in early 1964. The sentence was reversed by the Texas courts and while Ruby waited for his second trial for the killing of Oswald, Jack Ruby died of cancer while under police guard in a Dallas County Hospital.

I wrote this chapter in 2003 using first hand information from an honorable police source for my book, *Truth Withheld* and I stand by the information as being correct as given to me. However, since writing that chapter ten years ago I have discovered additional information that Jack Ruby was most probably knowledgeable that the assassination of President Kennedy was going to occur in Dallas. I cannot fully document the insiders information I have received on Jack Ruby, so I will leave it to others to document.

However it is well known that when Chief Justice Earl Warren of the Warren Commission visited Jack Ruby in the Dallas County jail, Jack Ruby begged to be taken to Washington so he could tell all and that what he wanted to say was that Lyndon Johnson was behind the assassination of President Kennedy. It is also known that Jack Ruby did not feel safe in the Dallas County jail.

THE DALLAS TIMES HERALD

CONTINUOUSLY PUBLISHED FOR 87 YEARS · THE TIMES 1876 · THE HERALD 1886 · CONSOLIDATED 1888

FINAL EDITION

87th Year—No. 295 ··· ★   DALLAS, TEXAS, MONDAY EVENING, NOVEMBER 25, 1963   Telephones—Classified, RI3-1111 Other Depts., RI-5101   3 Parts   Price Five ¢

Mourning Nation Bids Chief Farewe

Tip to FBI Warned of Oswald Deatl

Copyright, 1963, The Dallas Times Herald—Staff Photo by Bob

The President's accused killer as executioner's bullet pierces body.

Anonymous Call Forecast Slaying During Transfer

The self-appointed executioner of President Kennedy's accused assassin was the materialization of a blunt warning issued police hours earlier, the Times Herald learned Sunday.

An anonymous telephone call to Federal Bureau of Investigation headquarters at 2:15 a.m. warned that Leo Harvey Oswald would be killed during his transfer from the city lockup to county jail.

The FBI said it immediately relayed the warning to police and the sheriff's office.

Oswald, notwithstanding the warning and dozens of riot-gun armed policemen, was brutally wounded in the basement of the police and courts building at 11:20 a.m. as officers prepared to place him in an armored car for the alert ride to the courthouse.

Jack Ruby, nightclub operator and physical culture addict, darted from a crowd of newsmen with cat-like speed, rammed a .38 revolver into Oswald's body and triggered a shot witnessed by the world.

Police stood helpless. One managed only to swear in the split second that added a second explosion to the investigation into the President's assassination.

The FBI's warning that Oswald faced death on the trip between lockups was relayed to both city

and county law-enforcement officials.

Sheriff Bill Decker said his dispatcher received the call from the FBI just after 2:15 a.m.

The city police dispatcher said the call never came to his attention. It could not be determined it was routed to another office or official.

The FBI—which had remained, to all appearances, in the background of the investigation into the President's assassination—stepped into the case openly Sunday on instructions from President Johnson.

The federal agents were seeking to determine if a civil rights

Nation Buries Its Chief

By MERRIMAN SMITH
WASHINGTON (UPI)— America was to bury her dead young President today and a grieving world wept with her.

John F. Kennedy's last journey began with his people, who lingered by the tens of thousands outside the Capitol though out the near-freezing night to pay farewell. Long before dawn, silent crowds formed to wait in the shivering dark along Pennsylvania Avenue.

The grave, at the end of the journey, lies on a sloping Virginia hillside facing the Lincoln Memorial and, beyond it, the

White House that is his no more.

Kings, presidents, premiers and special emissaries from East and West, on both sides of the Iron Curtain, gathered to follow America's fallen leader to the end.

Today Kennedy's soul was to be committed unto God during a pontifical requiem mass at St. Matthew's Cathedral. He was to be committed forever to the land of his people in a hallowed, lonely grave in Arlington National Cemetery.

It was a national day of mourning and millions of Americans across the land flocked to special worship services in Kennedy's memory.

As dawn broke on the third

day after an assassin's bullet cut Kennedy down in Dallas, Tex., and stunned the world, his people still shuffled silently into the great vaulted rotunda of the Capitol to pay their respects before his flag - draped casket. The line outside was several miles long at one point during the night.

The doors were to be closed (at 9 a.m.) and final preparations made for the slain chief's final departure from Capitol Hill.

Ninety minutes later, the black - veiled Mrs. Jacqueline Kennedy and her brother - in - law, Atty. Gen. Robert F. Kennedy, were to arrive at the east front of the Capitol with the Joint Chiefs of Staff.

Military pallbearers will ease the casket down the stairs and place it again on the horse-drawn caisson that brought it to Capitol Hill Sunday before 300,000 persons along Pennsylvania Avenue.

To the dreadful tattoo of muffled drums and hymns sung by the Navy Choir, the solemn procession was to enter the White House driveway and halt.

Mrs. Kennedy and the attorney general were to leave their car at the north portico and follow the caisson on foot for the half-mile to St. Matthew's. Following them were to be President Johnson, foreign dignitaries, former Presidents Dwight D. Eisenhower and Harry S. Truman

and the federal judici net members, congress military leaders and President's personal s

All political and ref ferences were forgotte moment. Among the were listed the leade free world, Sovit P kita Khrushchev's Ya man, Asians, Africa Americans, Arab and

At noon in the na stone cathedral, a po led by Richard Card ing of Boston, a longt

See NATION on

See OSWALD on Page 26

CHAPTER THIRTY-EIGHT

CONVINCE PUBLIC
OSWALD REAL ASSASSIN

Lee Oswald was killed in the basement of the Dallas Police Department only 46 hours after President John F. Kennedy was pronounced dead. Jack Ruby shot Oswald in front of television cameras, as millions of viewers watched their sets at home that Sunday morning just two days after the assassination.

The official reaction in our nation's capitol, Washington D.C., was fast, too fast for FBI Director J. Edgar Hoover, who within minutes of Jack Ruby shooting and killing Oswald, sent out an internal FBI memo to all FBI Department heads, marked *secret* that said, "Our job is to convince the American public that Oswald is the real assassin."

The same day, 11/24/63 Assistant United States Attorney General (under Attorney General Robert F. Kennedy), Nicholas Katzenbach sent a memo to Bill Moyers, one of the our new President Lyndon Johnson's aides, a memo stating: "We must convince the American public that Oswald is the real assassin."

At Dallas Parkland Hospital, minutes after Sunday's shooting Dr. Charles Crenshaw, while working in the emergency room to try and save Oswald's life from Ruby's gunshot, got a patched call to the emergency room from Parkland hospital telephone operator, Phyllis Bartlett, who had just received the phone call from President Lyndon Johnson, who said, "There is a 'Oliver Hardy' standing by in the emergency room, have him get a death bed confession from Lee Harvey Oswald that he, Oswald, shot and killed President Kennedy." Oswald died moments later without ever regaining consciousness.

President John F. Kennedy had not had his funeral, the investigation into his death had not even got off the ground, yet two of the most powerful men in the United States were writing memo's stating: "We must convince the American public that Lee Harvey Oswald is the real assassin," and the new President of the United States was personally calling the hospital emergency room urging the doctor to get a death bed confession from Oswald.

It does not take a smart man to know that something is not right, something is terribly wrong with this scenario. In 1963 we respected and believed what people like the head of the FBI, an Assistant United States Attorney General, and the President of the United States said. The media, the radio, newspaper and television reporters, believed and reported what these respected men said.

It must be noted that Gary Mack, who is curator for the Sixth Floor Museum in Dallas, has gone to great lengths to try and debunk Dr. Crenshaw's every statement. Gary Mack has also tried to debunk Phyllis Bartlett's statement of receiving a call from President Johnson; Ms. Bartlett has never wavered from her original statement. Phyllis Bartlett and Dr. Charles Crenshaw both vividly remember President Johnson's call to Parkland Hospital on November 24, 1963.

CHAPTER THIRTY-NINE

EARLY FBI RESPONSE

At about 5 P.M., November 22, 1963, barely four hours after President Kennedy had been pronounced dead and Oswald was arrested on suspicion of killing officer J. D. Tippit, but before Oswald had been charged with anything, J. Edgar Hoover sent an internal memo stating that the Dallas Police: "Very probably had Kennedy's killer in custody." Hoover in this memo described Oswald as a nut, a radical, and pro-Castro.

On Saturday, November 23, 1963, one day after the assassination, FBI agent James Hosty, who had been in contact with Lee Harvey Oswald, destroys all the information he had concerning Oswald.

On Sunday November 24, 1963 shortly after Oswald's death, FBI Director J. Edgar Hoover calls the White House and leaves a message for President Johnson: "I am most concerned about having something issued so we can convince the public that Oswald is the real assassin."

On Sunday, November 24, 1963, an internal FBI memo was sent by Jenkins to all FBI department heads: Hoover says Oswald alone did it; Bureau must: "Convince the public Oswald is the real assassin."

And there is Hoover's internal FBI memo of November 26, 1963, just four days after the assassination: "Wrap up the investigation; seems to me we have the basic facts now."

Hoover gives orders for the FBI to shut down the Dallas Police investigation and confiscate all evidence that the Dallas Department has.

Hoover internal memo of November 29, 1963, six days after the assassination: "Hope to have the investigation wrapped up by next week."

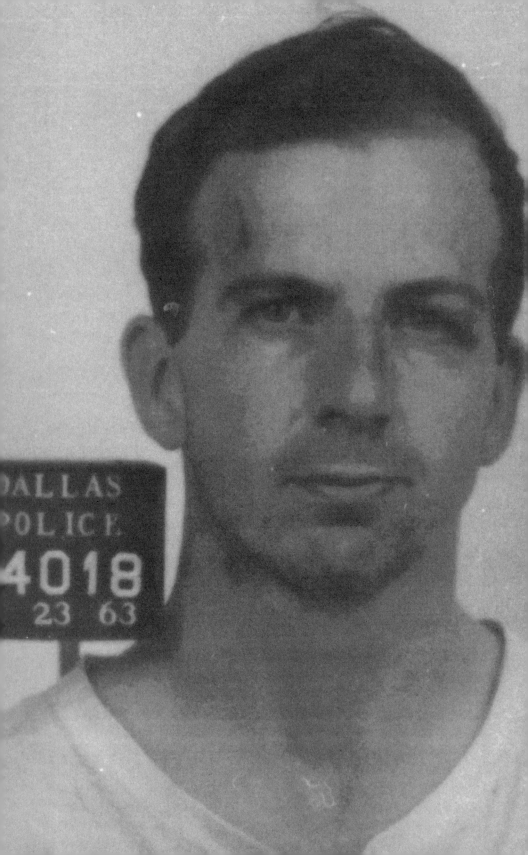

CHAPTER FORTY

PATSY?

There have been millions of words written about Lee Harvey Oswald, and on the surface one can easily make a case for Oswald to be a "lone nut assassin." Then, with open-minded research the case can easily be made that Oswald was innocent of Kennedy's assassination. The FBI, the Press, Dallas County District Attorney Henry Wade, and others had Lee Harvey Oswald tried and convicted within 36 hours of the assassination of President Kennedy.

Jack Ruby finished the conviction of Oswald and executed Oswald in front of national television cameras for the world to see. Lee Harvey Oswald was tried, convicted and executed all within two days.

After Oswald's death, a press conference was held and Dallas County District Attorney Henry Wade told the world that "there is no question that Oswald was the killer."

Lee Oswald was not the person who shot at President Kennedy. Does this clear Oswald of any involvement in the killing of President Kennedy,? No. Does this make him a "patsy?" Maybe. There is evidence that Lee Oswald had connections to the FBI and the CIA. Is this what the government has wanted to hide for so many years? I do not pretend to know the answer to possible connections Lee Harvey Oswald had with the FBI or the CIA. I will leave that to others.

I do know that author Barry Krusch has documented and done a great amount of research on Oswald and written hundreds of words clearing Oswald of Kennedy's murder. Barry Krusch found many answers right in the witness' testimony found in the 26 volumes of the Warren Commission. His three volume's clearing Oswald are *Impossible: The Case Against Lee Harvey Oswald*, Volumes I, II, III.

If you are interested in the truth, I highly recommend Mr. Krusch's volumes.

November 25, 1963

MEMORANDUM FOR MR. MOYERS

It is important that all of the facts surrounding President Kennedy's Assassination be made public in a way which will satisfy people in the United States and abroad that all the facts have been told and that a statement to this effect be made now.

1. The public must be satisfied that Oswald was the assassin; that he did not have confederates who are still at large; and that the evidence was such that he would have been convicted at trial.

2. Speculation about Oswald's motivation ought to be cut off, and we should have some basis for rebutting thought that this was a Communist conspiracy or (as the Iron Curtain press is saying) a right-wing conspiracy to blame it on the Communists. Unfortunately the facts on Oswald seem about too pat—too obvious (Marxist, Cuba, Russian wife, etc.). The Dallas police have put out statements on the Communist conspiracy theory, and it was they who were in charge when he was shot and thus silenced.

3. The matter has been handled thus far with neither dignity nor conviction. Facts have been mixed with rumour and speculation. We can scarcely let the world see us totally in the image of the Dallas police when our President is murdered.

I think this objective may be satisfied by making public as soon as possible a complete and thorough FBI report on Oswald and the assassination. This may run into the difficulty of pointing to inconsistencies between this report and statements by Dallas police officials. But the reputation of the Bureau is such that it may do the whole job.

The only other step would be the appointment of a Presidential Commission of unimpeachable personnel to review and examine the evidence and announce its conclusions. This has both advantages and disadvantages. It think it can await publication of the FBI report and public reaction to it here and abroad.

I think, however, that a statement that all the facts will be made public property in an orderly and responsible way should be made now. We need something to head off public speculation or Congressional hearings of the wrong sort.

Nicholas deB. Katzenbach
Deputy Attorney General

CHAPTER FORTY-ONE

SATISFY THE PUBLIC

Washington D.C. November 24, 1963

The investigation into the assassination of President Kennedy had not yet really begun, there had barely been a preliminary investigation and it had only been 48 hours since our President had been slain on a Dallas Texas Street. The country was in mourning.

Then to our horror, Jack Ruby killed Lee Harvey Oswald in front of millions of television viewers that Sunday morning. Upon the pronouncement of Oswald's death, a closed-door secret meeting was hastily assembled in Washington D.C. We do not know all of those who were in attendance at this meeting. But we do know of at least two men who were there, because both wrote almost identical memorandums.

One of those men was Nicolas Katzenbach, Assistant United States Attorney General, who worked directly under Attorney General Robert Kennedy, the slain President's brother. The other man was FBI Director J. Edgar Hoover.

Katzenbach wrote: "It is important that all the facts surrounding President Kennedy's assassination be made public in a way which will satisfy people in the United States and abroad, the public must be satisfied that Oswald was the assassin."

Attorney General Katzenbach's directive was sent to Bill Moyers, one of the new President's aides. J. Edgar Hoover's directive was written by FBI agent Jenkins and stated: "Hoover says Oswald alone did it, bureau must convince the public Oswald is the real assassin."

The Jenkins/Hoover directive was distributed to internal FBI management. Why this meeting was called so hastily to discuss how information to the public would be handled, concerning the assassination of President Kennedy, is answered when you discover J. Edgar Hoover's motive. The decisions made in this meeting would mold in concrete the outcome of any investigation into the assassination.

It had only been 48 hours since the assassination of President Kennedy when this meeting was held, and no other leads had been followed. No Commission had been named to investigate, and for all practical purposes there had been no investigation. But the results of this meeting would be the key to why the American public would not learn any truths about the assassination of President John F. Kennedy.

Nicolas Katzenbach also wrote in his memo to Bill Moyers, and it must be noted that he was writing this only 48 hours after the assassination: "Oswald did not have any confederates who are still at large ... that the evidence was such that Oswald would have been convicted at trial ... speculation about Oswald's motivation ought to be cut off ... we should have a basis for rebutting thought that this was a conspiracy ... the matter has been handled thus far with neither dignity nor conviction ... *these objectives may be satisfied by making public a complete and thorough FBI report ... there may be inconsistencies between this report and statements by Dallas Police officials ... but the reputation of the Bureau is such that it may do the whole job ...* we need something to head off public speculation or Congressional hearings of the wrong sort.... The only other step would be the appointment of a Presidential Commission of unimpeachable personnel to review and examine the evidence and announce its conclusions."

There it was, two of the most powerful and honored men in the United States Justice Department had decided how the result's of any investigation would be before there was an investigation. There was to be a cover-up before anyone knew what they were to cover up. Their concerns that day, two days after the assassination was not to find the truth, the facts, of the killing of our President but only to use the prestige of the FBI to convince the public that Oswald was "*the real assassin.*"

On November, 26, 1963, only 4 days after the assassination, Hoover issued another secret internal FBI memo (62-109060-1490) to FBI bureau Chiefs, "*wrap up investigation; seems to me we have the basic facts now.*"

FBI Director J. Edgar Hoover also followed up the Katzenbach memorandum to a tee in his report to President Johnson on the assassination of President Kennedy, Oswald was a "lone nut assassin," the killer of both police officer Tippit and President Kennedy, three shots were fired from the School Book Depository, the first shot hit Kennedy in the back, the second shot hit Governor Connally, the third shot hit Kennedy in the head, and there was no conspiracy.

Little did the soon to be named seven members of the Warren Commission know that their job was expected to be a rubber stamp for the evidence that Hoover and the FBI would feed them.

However, we now know that once the Commission was named, and that during one of the Commission's early meetings in January 1964, the newly appointed seven Commission members, to their credit, discussed that they were expected to be Hoover's rubber stamp and one of the Warren Commission members said, "If this is the way it is going to be, we might as well fold up and go home."

Warren Commission members Allen W. Dulles (pointing) and John Sherman Cooper, and staff member David W. Belin in Dealey Plaza during an investigative trip to Dallas in 1964.

CHAPTER FORTY-TWO

THE PRESIDENT'S COMMISSION ON THE ASSASSINATION OF PRESIDENT KENNEDY

On November 29, 1963 President Lyndon Johnson authorized Executive Order 11130, creating a Commission to ascertain, evaluate, and report upon the facts relating to the assassination of the late President John F. Kennedy and the subsequent violent death of the man charged with the assassination and S.J. Res, 137, 88th Congress, a concurrent resolution, conferring upon the Commission the power to administer oaths and affirmations, examine witnesses, receive evidence, and issue subpoenas. The Commission soon evolved as follows.

Chief Justice Earl Warren, Chairman
Senator Richard R. Russell; Representative Gerald R. Ford
Senator John Sherman ; Mr. Allen W. Dulles
Representative Hale Boggs; Mr. John J. McCloy

J. Lee Rankin, General Counsel

Assistant Counsels
Francis W. H. Adams; Albert E. Jenner, Jr.; Joseph A. Ball; Wesley J. Liebeler
David W. Belin; Norman Redlich;William T. Coleman, Jr.; W. David Slawson;
Melvin Aron Eisonberg; Arlen Specter;Burt W. Griffen; Samuel A. Stern;
Leon D. Hubert, Jr.; Howard P. Willens

Staff Members
Philip Barson; Edward A. Conroy; John Hart Ely; Alfred Goldberg;
Murry J. Laulight; Arthur Marmor; Richard M. Mosk; John J. O'Brien;
Stuart Pollak; Alfredda Scobey; Charles N. Shaffer, Jr.

Let us take a close internal look at what the Commission really was like. On November 29, 1963 President Johnson, with only seven days in office, announced the formation of a Commission to investigate the death of President Kennedy, the Commission was to consist of seven men.

Earl Warren, Chief Justice of the Supreme Court was named to head the WC, Chief Justice Warren, at first, flat turned down the appointment, was called to the White House for a meeting with President Johnson and left the meeting accepting the appointment as head of the WC. Two men from the House of Representatives were named, Hale Boggs and Gerald Ford. Two U.S. Senators were named, Richard Russell and John Cooper. Two independent lawyers were also named, John McCloy and Allen Dulles. McCloy was a former President of the World Bank and Dulles was a former Director of the CIA.

The WC held its first meeting on December 5, 1963. They agreed to conduct an independent investigation and not merely depend on reports by State and Federal agencies. They agreed to select a general counsel; Warren suggested J. Lee Rankin, a former solicitor General of the United States, and the members unanimously agreed.

It was also agreed to contact Texas Attorney General Waggoner Carr and ask him to hold off on a Texas court of inquiry into the death of President Kennedy. Carr agreed to hold off. On December 8, 1963 Warren asked J. Lee Rankin to be general counsel for the WC. Rankin's job was to be director and organize the investigation for the WC. Rankin agreed and took the job.

The second meeting was held on December 16, 1963, and J. Lee Rankin was sworn in as General Counsel. The FBI had submitted a summary report on December 9th and the FBI summary report was discussed and it was decided not to take the FBI report at face value, but to reappraise the FBI summary report. It was decided to not employ independent investigators, but to rely on the FBI to be the investigative arm for the WC. Rankin was authorized to hire and organize a staff of independent lawyers to help with the organization and sorting through of the thousands of FBI reports. J. Lee Rankin hired a staff of 14 lawyers from practicing attorneys to law Professors, many young and without investigative experience.

The next five pages show that before the my testimony, the Commission was on track to say that the first bullet hit President Kennedy, the second hit Governor Connally and then the third fatal shot hit the President. No mention of a "magic" bullet.

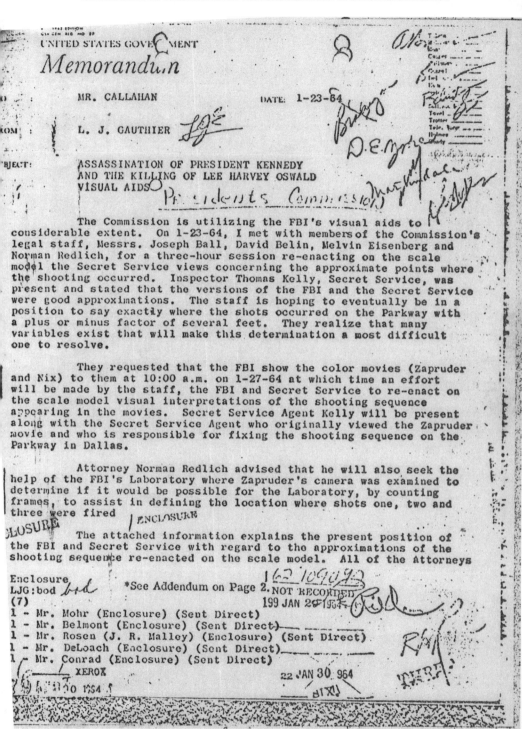

UNITED STATES GOVERNMENT

Memorandum

MR. CALLAHAN   DATE: 1-23-64

FROM : L. J. GAUTHIER

SUBJECT: ASSASSINATION OF PRESIDENT KENNEDY
AND THE KILLING OF LEE HARVEY OSWALD
VISUAL AIDS

Presidents Commission

    The Commission is utilizing the FBI's visual aids to considerable extent. On 1-23-64, I met with members of the Commission's legal staff, Messrs. Joseph Ball, David Belin, Melvin Eisenberg and Norman Redlich, for a three-hour session re-enacting on the scale model the Secret Service views concerning the approximate points where the shooting occurred. Inspector Thomas Kelly, Secret Service, was present and stated that the versions of the FBI and the Secret Service were good approximations. The staff is hoping to eventually be in a position to say exactly where the shots occurred on the Parkway with a plus or minus factor of several feet. They realize that many variables exist that will make this determination a most difficult one to resolve.

    They requested that the FBI show the color movies (Zapruder and Nix) to them at 10:00 a.m. on 1-27-64 at which time an effort will be made by the staff, the FBI and Secret Service to re-enact on the scale model visual interpretations of the shooting sequence appearing in the movies. Secret Service Agent Kelly will be present along with the Secret Service Agent who originally viewed the Zapruder movie and who is responsible for fixing the shooting sequence on the Parkway in Dallas.

    Attorney Norman Redlich advised that he will also seek the help of the FBI's Laboratory where Zapruder's camera was examined to determine if it would be possible for the Laboratory, by counting frames, to assist in defining the location where shots one, two and three were fired / ENCLOSURE

    The attached information explains the present position of the FBI and Secret Service with regard to the approximations of the shooting sequence re-enacted on the scale model. All of the Attorneys

Enclosure
LJG:bod   *See Addendum on Page 2. NOT RECORDED
(7)   199 JAN 29 1964
1 - Mr. Mohr (Enclosure) (Sent Direct)
1 - Mr. Belmont (Enclosure) (Sent Direct)
1 - Mr. Rosen (J. R. Malley) (Enclosure) (Sent Direct)
1 - Mr. DeLoach (Enclosure) (Sent Direct)
1 - Mr. Conrad (Enclosure) (Sent Direct)
    XEROX   22 JAN 30 1964

162 109093

Memo Gauthier to Callahan
Re: Visual Aids
1-23-64

present used the scale model extensively advising they will continue
to do so in the future. The meeting of 1-27-64 will take place in
the same room where the models are maintained, in order that the
versions of those visually examining the movies can be re-enacted
on the model without loss of time.

COMMENTS:

1. Arrangements will be made to show the Zapruder and Nix
movies to the Commission on 1-27-64. A Bureau employee will be
utilized to operate the projector.

2. The points on the Parkway as defined by the FBI are
considered to be the best approximations possible and in line with
the Secret Service version. Inspector Kelly shares the same views.
The FBI has the first shot occurring just before the President's head
emerges from behind the sign while the Secret Service approximates
the location moments after the President emerges. Approximately one
second is involved between the two versions. The Commission realizes
that there is no material difference between the FBI's and Secret
Service's approximations; however, they wish to attempt to fix
shooting sequence with a great degree of accuracy with a plus or
minus factor of a few feet.

RECOMMENDATION:

None; for information only.

ADDENDUM BY I. W. CONRAD 1/24/64:

The FBI Laboratory previously has thoroughly examined the film in question.
Laboratory has been in touch with representatives of the Commission and
arrangements have been made for the Laboratory representative to be present
when the film is shown.

- 2 -

SHOOTING SEQUENCE AS LOCATED ON THE SCALE MODEL

The approximate location of the shooting sequence was determined from an interpretation of the ZAPRUDER movie and from observations made at the site regarding the location of the Stemmons highway sign which was obscuring ZAPRUDER'S line of view while he was photographing the approaching motorcade. The movie also includes details of the surrounding area.

SHOT ONE:

It occurred when the Presidential car was unobserved by ZAPRUDER for approximately twenty feet while moving behind a road sign. Shot one was approximately fixed on the model at a point directly behind the center of this sign. The movie reveals that prior to reaching this sign the President was seen waving and moments later after emerging from behind the sign he was slumped forward. The position on the Parkway where shot one occurred as approximated by the FBI and the Secret Service varies about one car length (13 feet) or about one-half second at 15 mph. The FBI's estimate places the President approximately one-half second nearer to the assassin when shot one was fired.

SHOT TWO:

It occurred approximately at the time Governor Connally was turning his head to the right rear. This point was established through the interpretation of the relative location of trees, shrubs, street lights, curbing, etc. appearing in the movie. The position on the Parkway approximated by the FBI and the Secret Service varies about 1.5 car lengths (22 feet) or about one second at 15 mph. The FBI's estimate places the Governor approximately one second further away from the assassin when shot two was fired.

SHOT THREE:

It occurred approximately at the time a circle of light resembling an explosive blast encircles the President's head. The position on the Parkway approximated by the FBI and the Secret Service varies about 2/3 car length (14 feet) or about 2/3 second at 15 mph. The FBI's estimate places the President approximately 2/3 second nearer to the assassin when shot three was fired.

ENCLOSURE

62-109090

ENCLOSURE

169

COMMENTS:

The FBI's analysis of the shooting sequence was determined independently of a similar study made of the movie by the Secret Service. "WHERE ON THE PARKWAY WAS THE PRESIDENTIAL CAR EXPOSED TO GUN FIRE?" The answer to this question is subject to varying factors such as the speed of the vehicle, the firing position of the assassin and the position of ZAPRUDER. It is a matter of accepting the fact that there will be as many versions as there are analysis made of the shooting sequence. The FBI bases its approximations on an interpretation of the ZAPRUDER movie re-enacted on a scale model. The Secret Service has also used the movie to approximate the shooting sequence; eye-witnesses may vary in locating the car at the time of the shooting; members of the Commission may also have differing opinions regarding this matter.

The ZAPRUDER movie was utilized by the FBI as the best medium for approximating the points on the Parkway where the shooting occurred.

- 2 -

UNITED STATES GOVERNMENT

Memorandum

TO : Mr. Callahan

FROM : L. J. Gauthier

DATE: 4-15-64

SUBJECT: ASSASSINATION OF PRESIDENT JOHN F. KENNEDY
EXAMINATION OF VISUAL AIDS BY
PRESIDENT'S COMMISSION

Reference memo Gauthier to Callahan 4-7-64.

Staff members of the President's Commission and specialists of the armed services, Drs. Humes, Heany, Fink, Light and Olivia (ph.) attended a conference on 4-14-64 for the purpose of reviewing motion pictures and slides of the assassination site. Representatives of the Secret Service and the FBI were present to assist in projecting the film and the use of the scale model.

Dr. Humes, U. S. Navy Commander, who performed the autopsy on the President, appeared to lead the discussion throughout the 4-hour session. All of his associates were generally in agreement with previous findings of the Commission as to where Shots 1, 2 and 3 approximately occurred.

The most revealing information brought out by the doctors is as follows:

1. That Shot 1 struck the President high in the right shoulder area, penetrating the torso near the base of the neck damaging the flesh of the throat but not tearing the throat wall. This bullet, according to the doctors, continued and entered Governor Connally's right shoulder, emerging below the right nipple. The velocity of the missile, according to the doctors apparently was snagged in the coat and shirt, eventually falling out on Connally's stretcher.

2. That Shot 2 struck the wrist of the Governor, continuing on into his thigh

3. That Shot 3 struck the right side of the President's head, carrying much bone and brain tissue away, leaving a large cavity. There is nothing controversial about where Shot 3 occurred inasmuch as the Zapruder movie indicates with much clarity when this happened.

REC- 26   2998

Heretofore it was the opinion of the Commission that Shot 1 had only hit the President, that Shot 2 had entered the Governor's right shoulder area penetrating his torso through the chest area emerging and again entering the wrist and on into his leg.

1 JG:mafi (6)
1 - Mr. Belmont   APR 30 1964
1 - Mr. Rosen (Attention, Mr. Malley)   to APR 30 1964
1 - Mr.   MAY 4 1964 Mr. W. C. Sullivan

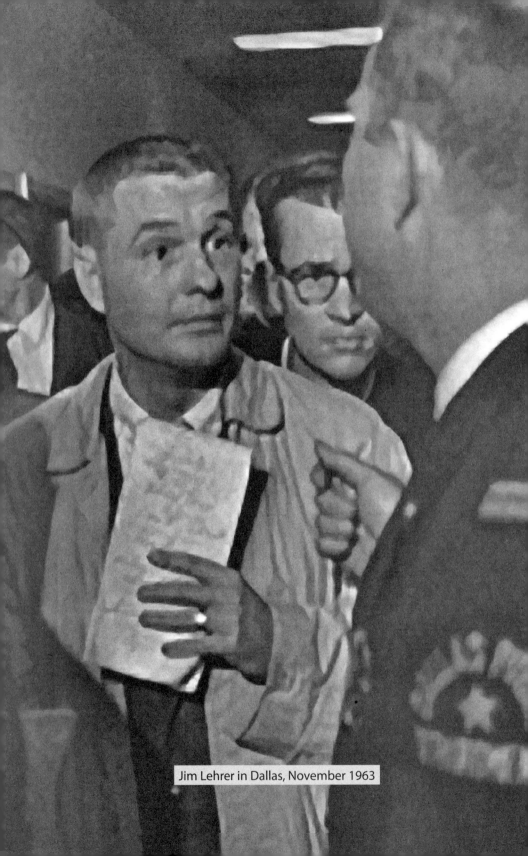

Jim Lehrer in Dallas, November 1963

CHAPTER FORTY-THREE

JIM LEHRER

On June 5, 1964, I had heard on television and read in the newspapers that the Warren Commission was through with their investigation, that three shots had been fired hitting Kennedy, Connally, Kennedy in that order and Lee Harvey Oswald was the lone nut assassin.

I had not been called to testify before the Warren Commission and there was no mention of the missed shot. By accident I came into contact with a young *Dallas Times Herald* reporter that very morning. His name was Jim Lehrer, he came to my place of business. Before I told Jim Lehrer about the missed shot and my minor injury during the assassination, I asked Mr. Lehrer not to use my name. He agreed.

It had been over six months since the assassination of President Kennedy and there had been almost no mention in the media, newspaper or television, of a missed shot or my minor injury. By now if I told someone I had been there in Dealey Plaza when the assassination occurred, and that a bullet had hit the street in front of me throwing debris into my face during the shooting, they would look at me like I was the biggest liar in the world, and turn and walk away shaking their heads.

I told Jim Lehrer how I happened to be in Dealey Plaza by accident, getting stopped by traffic and then the gunshots. It was about 9:30 in the morning on June 5, 1964 when I met Mr. Lehrer. I had just returned from the Indianapolis 500-mile race and had some spectacular film developed the day before that I had taken at the race of the crash that killed Eddie Sachs and Steve McDonald.

I brought my 8mm movie projector to work to show my work buddies the film I had taken of the Indy crash and also the Dealey Plaza film I had taken in early May to show my parents, when I went to the Indy 500.

After the interview about my being in Dealey Plaza, the missed shot, and my minor injury during the Kennedy assassination, I showed Mr. Lehrer the Dealey Plaza film and then I showed the Indy crash. I remember asking

Lehrer if there was any value to the Indy film and he told me no, a week had passed and it was now old news.

About an hour after Lehrer left my office, around 11 A.M., he called me all excited. The *Dallas Times Herald* was an evening newspaper and it had not come out yet, but he had put my story on the wire services. He stated he was getting calls "from all over," including the Warren Commission, wanting to know who I was, and he had to tell them. He assured me he was not using my name in the story in the local paper. It was years before I was able to put the whole story together and realize what Jim Lehrer's interview had triggered.

One thing I found out was that the FBI was at Lehrer's *Dallas Times Herald* office at 4:30 that afternoon and their FBI report was not kind to me. I have a copy of that FBI report of their meeting with Lehrer that afternoon of June 5, 1964.

One of the things in that FBI report that aggravated me was that my asking Mr. Lehrer if the film about the Indy crash I had showed him had any value was now in the FBI report saying I was trying to make money off of the assassination of President Kennedy. There were other non-flattering things in the Lehrer-FBI report. People in the know have told me that is the way the FBI writes their reports when they want to discredit you.

The attempt to discredit me by the FBI was short-lived when two United State Assistant Attorney Generals assigned to the Dallas U. S. Attorney General's office stepped forward with evidence of the missed shot and sent the evidence to J. Lee Rankin, Chief Counsel for the Warren Commission. I was then called to testify before the Warren Commission on July 23, 1964.

I testified, the Warren Report was rewritten and history was changed.

CHAPTER FORTY-FOUR

RESULT OF LEHRER NEWS STORY

My testimony on July 23, 1964, along with other witnesses testimony and photographic evidence, firmly establish that indeed one shot had missed and hit the curb in front of where I was standing near the triple underpass. This caused the Warren Commission a major problem with their "lone-nut single shooter," conclusion, where they had documented two shots had hit President John Kennedy and that one shot had hit Governor John Connally for a total of three shots. Now with two shots hitting Kennedy, one shot hitting Connally and one shot missing and hitting the street, they now had four shots, which equaled two shooters and a conspiracy.

Arlen Specter was the Warren Commission's Assistant Counsel lawyer working on this problem. Specter came up with the original idea that one shot had penetrated both men by hitting Kennedy in the back, then exiting Kennedy's throat and then hitting Connally in the back.

We did not know in 1964 that Arlen Specter could not make this idea work, the first shot had hit President Kennedy in the back 4 and a half inches below the collar line and was on a downward path from a sixth floor window above, and such a bullet would have had to suddenly turn upward to come out Kennedy's neck, the angles would not work.

So the Warren Commission altered evidence and tried to make the public believe that one bullet did go through both President Kennedy and Governor Connally causing all of their injuries and winding up in near pristine condition; thus the *"magic bullet,"* was born *and a big lie* had been perpetrated on the public.

President Lyndon Johnson speaking with Commission member Senator Richard Russell.

CHAPTER FORTY-FIVE

THE FLAWED WARREN REPORT

D ue to the fact I was an eyewitness that day in November 1963 and my Warren Commission testimony had a major impact on the final findings of the Commission, I purchased the full 27-volume set of Warren Commission's investigation of President Kennedy's assassination soon after the set was made available in 1964. Through the years I have probably read most of the 27 volumes. The actual Warren Report is in one volume and the other 26 volumes contain the information that was condensed into the one-volume Warren Report.

WHAT REALLY HAPPENED

W hen the Warren Report came out, Louis Nizer wrote for the *New York Times*, "The organization of the report is a model of clarity. It begins with a Summary and Conclusions, so the reader is not made prey to suspense. The quest for the truth has been long and arduous." Mr. Nizer went on to say the investigation lasted the better part of a year, when in fact the investigation proper lasted less than 10 weeks.

At first, America and myself accepted the report as a true and honest investigation. After all, the Chief Justice of the Supreme Court headed the investigation along with six other prominent Americans. The acceptance of the report by the public did not last, as people like Harold Weisberg, Mark Lane, Sylvia Meagher, and others began questioning the accuracy of the report and raised major questions about the findings.

WHAT WENT WRONG?

T he Commission was made up of two distinct parts, seven prominent men headed by Chief Justice Earl Warren and a group of what started out to be fifteen lawyers headed by Chief Counsel J. Lee Rankin. The real work was done by the Assistant Counsel lawyers working with J. Lee Rankin. A total of 552 witnesses testified, but only 94 witnesses testified with one or more of the seven Commission members present. If only one of the Commission members dropped in on a witness testifying and only stayed for five minutes, it was counted as one of the 94 times a witnesses testified before the full Commission.

The Assistant Counsel took the testimony of 458 witnesses without a "figurehead" being present. With one exception the hearings were closed to the public.

My testimony was taken by Assistant Counsel Wesley J. Liebeler on July 23, 1964 in the office of the U.S. attorney in the Post Office building in Dallas Texas. Only one other person was present, and that was the staff stenographer. It was typical of the way other witness testimony was also taken.

The Chief Justice and the other six prominent Americans played a minor and inattentive role. The staff lawyers were mostly selected by their high academic standing in Law School and most had little or no investigative experience. The FBI was to do the investigating for the Commission. The assignment given to the Warren Commission was: "to ascertain, evaluate, and report upon the facts relating to the assassination of the late President John F. Kennedy."

The seven men appointed by President Johnson and headed by Chief Justice Warren were "front men" who only spent time between their normal daily duties. As an example, Chief Justice of the Supreme Court, Earl Warren, never missed a day on the Court while he was also on the Warren Commission – all seven were part-time Commission members. Chief Justice Earl Warren had, at first, flat turned down President Johnson's request to head up the investigation. President Johnson then called Justice Warren into the White House and after a little chat, Justice Warren agreed to head up the Commission.

The Commission held its first meeting on December 5, 1963 and it was agreed that J. Lee Rankin would be General Counsel. On December 9, 1963 the FBI submitted a summary report to the Commission, this four-volume report summarized the FBI's investigation. It is important to know that this FBI report said Lee Harvey Oswald was the "lone nut assassin."

On December 13, 1963, Congress empowered the Commission to call witnesses and compel their testimony. On December 16, 1963 the Commission had its second meeting. Rankin was sworn in as General Counsel and would sit in on all Commission meetings. It was an organizational meeting. It was decided that nothing would be made public until the investigation was complete. It was also agreed that the Commission would only use Government agencies in their investigation.

On December 20, 1963 the FBI reports (there were nearly 25,000 total) and Rankin was quickly putting a staff together. Howard P. Willens was to be the liaison between the Commission and the Department of Justice. Norman Redlich was to be Rankin's special assistant. Some of the lawyers were given the title of "Senior Counsel" and others "Junior Counsel." On December 28, 1963 Howard Willens drew up a plan that proposed the investigation be divided up into five areas with a Senior Counsel and Junior Counsel assigned to each area. It actually wound up as six two-man teams.

The lawyers started arriving in January and each was given an office and a secretary. The nearly 25,000 FBI reports were divided up among the teams.

On January 22, 1964 Rankin was informed by Waggoner Carr, the attorney General of Texas, that Lee Harvey Oswald had been a paid FBI informant. An emergency meeting was called that was described as most tense. On January 24, 1964 Dallas District Attorney Henry Wade, who had also heard the allegation, and Waggoner Carr flew to Washington, and met with Warren and Rankin. They did not know if the allegation was true but gave details of Oswald's informant number, #179, his salary of $200 a month, and that he had been employed by the FBI since September 1962.

The Commission met again on January 27, 1964 to discuss the problem. J. Lee Rankin told the Commission about the dirty "rumor," how damaging it could be and that it must be wiped out. It was thought that the "rumor" came from a *Houston Post* reporter named Alonzo Hudkins.

Mr. Hudkins was never called to testify. J. Edgar Hoover of the FBI did testify that Lee Harvey Oswald was never an employee of the FBI. The FBI offered their file on Oswald to the Commission, but Justice Warren refused it, and the file was returned to the FBI. In a Secret Service report with control number 767 there was other evidence that showed Hudkins had received his information from Allan Sweatt, Chief of criminal investigations for the Dallas Sheriff's Office.

According to Sweatt, Oswald was being paid $200 a month by the FBI and his informant number was S-172. Sweatt was never questioned by the Commission or staff. In short, the Commission and its staff made no effort to investigate the "rumor" that Oswald was a paid FBI informant. Nowhere in the Warren Report does it mention this dirty rumor that had occupied so much of the Commission's time. It was determined that the best way to get rid of the "rumor," was to not investigate it.

On January 27, 1964 the staff viewed the Abraham Zapruder film of the assassination for the first time. President Kennedy is seen waving and suddenly reaches for his throat slowly slumping over, a second later Governor Connally is hit, about three seconds later the fatal shot hits Kennedy in the head. It was apparent the shots were not evenly spaced.

The question was raised, "Could Oswald have fired two shots in one and one half seconds?" On February 3, 1964 the seven-member Commission had their first hearing with Marina Oswald being the first witness. Three other witnesses were called to testify in February: Marina's business manager, Oswald's mother, and Oswald's brother.

The staff lawyers were held back from any investigation until the Jack Ruby trial was over. Ruby's trial ended on March 14, 1964. On March 18, 1964, almost 4 months after the assassination of President Kennedy, the staff lawyers began their investigation. The investigation was only a few days old when senior lawyer Francis W.H. Adams dropped out, that left Junior Lawyer Arlen Specter to manage area one: to find the basic facts of the assassination and establish the source of the shots. A few days later senior lawyer William Coleman declared he could only work part time for the Commission, and Stuart R. Pollak was appointed to Coleman's area.

In April the investigation continued in Dallas. Almost one half of all the witness testimony was taken in April. In Washington, Specter and Redlich had determined Oswald's bolt-action rifle could not be fired twice in one and one half seconds as shown by the Zapruder film. The seven-member Warren Commission called Governor Connally to testify. Governor Connally testified that it was "inconceivable" that he was hit by the same bullet that hit Kennedy.

In May Rankin told the lawyers to wrap up the investigation and submit their chapters by June 1, 1964. Rankin wanted the report done by June 30, 1964. But there were big problems, the FBI had not answered a lot of questions, most teams had not resolved many problems, and there was new evidence that required more investigation.

The lawyers were told they were not to open up new investigations but to close what they already had. The investigation was not near completion. On May 24, 1964 Rankin, Redlich, and Specter went to Dallas to do a re-enactment of the Kennedy assassination, to try and establish that one bullet hit both Kennedy and Connally.

Only two lawyers had completed their chapters by mid-June. Most of the lawyers had left to go back to their private practices. All five senior lawyers, Adams, Coleman, Ball, Hubert, and Jenner had quit with hardly any contribution to the Commission. The deadline was extended to July 15, 1964. The responsibility of writing the report had diminished to two men (from the original 14), Norman Redlich and Alfred Goldberg. Redlich was working eighteen hours a day, seven days a week. Goldberg told Warren it was impossible to finish the report by July 15 and the deadline was extended to August 1.

The August first deadline was extended. Goldberg and Redlich wrote and rewrote chapters over and over, sometime rewriting a chapter as many as twenty times to get Rankin and the seven member Commission to agree on the facts.

The White House was putting tremendous pressure on to get the report completed. On September 4, a rough draft of the report was finally given to the Commission members for their comments. On September 6, Wesley Liebler submitted 26 pages on the identity of Oswald. This caused more revisions to a key chapter.

On September 7, three Commissioners, Russell, Cooper, and Boggs, went to Dallas to re-interview Marina Oswald. With Senator Russell's hard questioning Marina Oswald changed and altered major issues of her previous testimony. More rewriting was now needed. On September 24, 1964 the final report was submitted to President Johnson. On September 28 the remaining lawyers were told by Chief Justice Warren that the information they had learned was privileged information as in a lawyer-client relationship.

After reluctantly signing off on the report, Senator Russell went to President Johnson in the Oval Office and stated to President Johnson that he: "Did not believe a word in the report." And President Johnson replied, "I don't either," and changed the subject. These comments were taped and still exist today.

Setting the stage for the "magic" bullet.

CHAPTER FORTY-SIX

GERALD FORD'S BIG LIE
AND THE MAGIC BULLET

The *"magic bullet"* did not happen, President Kennedy and Governor Connally were not injured by the same bullet from one shooter. They were injured by separate shots from different shooters. Warren Commission member Gerald Ford had Arlen Specter alter the bullet entry wound evidence by having Specter raise President Kennedy's back-entry wound up into Kennedy's neck so it would appear to line up to look like one bullet had injured both men.

It was a big lie, if you read the whole Ford story. The House of Representatives' Gerald Ford was one of the seven men appointed to the Commission. It was soon found out that every time the Warren Commission had a closed door meeting among themselves, Gerald Ford would immediately report to the FBI and FBI Bureau Chief J. Edgar Hoover what was discussed in those meetings.

It got so bad that sometimes when the Commission wanted something from the FBI and the decision was made to write Hoover a letter and ask him for what they wanted – the Commission would get an answer from J. Edgar Hoover the next morning before they even had the chance to write a letter asking for the information.

Gerald Ford's tipping-off the FBI and J. Edgar Hoover to what the Warren Commission was saying in their closed meetings was confirmed by an FBI internal memo dated December 12, 1963 by Hoover to his deputy Cartha Deloach. The memo stated: "Ford indicated he would keep me thoroughly advised as to the activities of the Commission. He stated that it would have to be done on a confidential basis, however, he thought it had to be done." The *Washington Post* disclosed the memo in 1991. *Newsweek* had previously described Ford as "the CIA's best friend in Congress."

When I gave testimony to the Warren Commission on July 23, 1964 about a missed shot hitting the curb in front of me and spraying my face with debris, and then other witnesses and photographic evidence was presented to back up my testimony, the Warren Commission had a problem. Their pre-conceived theory that the first shot hit President Kennedy in the back, the second shot hit Governor Connally, and the third shot hit President Kennedy in the head, went up in smoke.

In my thinking, the first shot did hit President Kennedy in the back 4 and a half inches below the collar line, slightly to the right of the spine, the autopsy drawing shows that, the President's coat had a bullet hole in it that matched the autopsy drawing, and the President's shirt had a hole in it that matched the hole in the coat and the autopsy drawing, solid evidence that a bullet had hit the President in the back 4 and a half inches below the collar line, slightly to the right of the spine.

Warren Commission Attorney Arlen Specter, who later was to be U.S. Senator Arlen Specter, was in the middle of explaining about this missed shot that caused debris to spray into my face. To outright accept this missed shot would be to accept that there were at least two shooters and that would blow apart the "lone nut gunman" theory.

Then, the theory that one bullet went through both President Kennedy and Governor Connally was developed. But a gunman shooting down from the sixth floor of the School Book Depository and hitting the President in the back 4 and a half inches below the collar line and having the bullet come out the front of the President's throat was an impossibility. The angles were not right.

After hitting the President in the back with a shot in a downward direction, the bullet would then have to turn upward at a 90° angle to come out the neck of the President, and then do another turn downward to hit Governor Connally in the back near his right armpit, not to mention the bullet would have had to jump sideways to accomplish this.

The official report of the Warren Commission said the first shot hit the President "in the base of his neck" and exited from his throat. The very same bullet then proceeded to hit Connally in the back, shattering his fifth rib. The bullet then emerged from the Governor's chest, passed through his right wrist, breaking several more bones, and finally came to rest in his left thigh.

This is known as the single or "magic" bullet theory. Magic because it inflicted so many wounds, broke so many bones and wound up in nearly perfect condition on a stretcher at Parkland Hospital: Commission Exhibit 399.

It was not until 1997 that we found out the truth about the "magic" bullet's big lie. President Bill Clinton appointed an Assassination Record

Review Board, ARRB, to gather up all the records floating around on the assassination of President Kennedy in order to get them into our National Archives and save for future generations.

J. Lee Rankin, who had been chief Counsel for the Warren Commission, turned his Commission notes over to the ARRB. In those notes was an excerpt on the "magic bullet" from the lawyers for the seven Commission members. The excerpt was an attempt to gloss over the back injury. In part it read: "A bullet had entered his back at a point slightly above the *shoulder* to the right of the spine." Gerald Ford marked through it and after Ford's alterations it read "A bullet had entered the back of his *neck* at a point slightly to the right of the spine. It traveled a downward path, and exited from the front of the neck."

An artist drew a picture of a bullet hitting the back of the neck and Gerald Ford falsified evidence that is prominent in the official Warren Report as we see it today. By this time in history the autopsy photos had become public and they showed the back bullet injury 4 and a half inches below the collar line, just like the coat and shirt bullet holes indicated. Some reporters picked up on the altered evidence and approached now retired ex-President Gerald Ford and asked him why he had moved the back injury up into the neck, Ford replied, "For the sake of accuracy."

The President's back injury is represented in the Warren Report by an artist drawing, and in the drawing the President's back injury is moved several inches up into the back of the neck. The Secret Service had not turned over the autopsy pictures to the Warren Commission; artist drawings were all the commission had. There is not one autopsy picture in the Warren Report.

In a July 8, 1964 Dallas police department letter, Detective H.M. Hart to Captain W.P. Gannaway, it was disclosed that Gerald Ford was being investigated by the Dallas County District Attorney for selling Lee Harvey Oswald's diary to the *Dallas Morning News* without the permission of Oswald's widow Marina Oswald. In the letter it also discloses that Ford had taken the diary to executives of *Life* and *Newsweek* magazines.

CHAPTER FORTY-SEVEN

J. EDGAR HOOVER AND THE WARREN COMMISSION

T he Warren Commission held one of its first formal meetings in late January 1964, behind closed doors. At that time the public was unaware of the commission's concerns about what cooperation they would get from J. Edgar Hoover and the FBI. Hoover was adamant that Oswald was a lone nut assassin, and that three shots had been fired from the sixth floor of the School Book Depository.

In the past fifty years since the assassination of President Kennedy, we have learned many new facts about the Warren Commission's investigation of the President's assassination. Also in the last 50 years we have learned many new facts about J. Edgar Hoover. When you put all of these new facts together, it becomes apparent why there is and has been such a controversy over the Warren Commission findings.

We now know that a fair and factual investigation was doomed from the start, caused largely by one man, FBI Director J. Edgar Hoover. There have been many great and honorable men and women who have served in the FBI before and after the assassination of JFK. I do not want to tarnish the reputations of these honorable agents and one cannot deny the fact that Hoover did a commendable job in organizing the Bureau into one of the finest law enforcement agencies in the world.

Washington writer, Jack Anderson once wrote, "Hoover created one of the worlds most effective and formidable law enforcement organizations."

I know as a young man growing up, he was one of my heroes, a man I admired and respected. Now we know, with what has been made public since his death, that by 1963 he had become bigger and more powerful than any man in this country, in his own mind. His self-centered ego had become so big that he referred to *his* FBI as the "Seat of Government," (SOG).

Hoover knew politics and how to control politicians better than most Congressmen and Presidents and he knew how to keep Congressmen and Presidents in line. He kept tabs on up-and-coming politicians, using his field agents to gather information on their sex habits, morals, ethics, associates, and anything derogatory about them. When he died in 1972, at the age of 77, J. Edgar Hoover had amassed over 17,000 pages of secret information he kept locked in his lifelong and trusted secretary's office. She was Helen Gandy and had been his secretary for 54 years.

These private files were not part of the official FBI files. When his domestic employee, James Crawford, found Hoover dead on May 2, 1972, it set off a set of prearranged orders to be followed upon his death. His housekeeper, Annie Fields, called Clyde Tolson, Hoover's number two man in the FBI and a lifelong friend, and confidant. Within minutes Tolson was on the phone to Helen Gandy telling her what to do with the disposition of Hoover's private secret files. Most were destroyed, immediately. Some of the secrets about the investigation of the assassination of JFK that the Warren Commission never saw were in those files.

We now know that Hoover was capable of stonewalling information. He once had evidence on his desk that would have cleared a Boston man of murder before he ever stood trial and he let that man be convicted. That man spent almost 30 years in prison before being cleared. It is well documented and *60 Minutes* ran a story on this in 2002.

Another example of stonewalling was that of Congressman Hale Boggs, who was one of the members of the Warren Commission and who was lost in a plane crash in 1972. In one of the Warren Commission's first meetings in January 1964, Hale Boggs was one of the members questioning the cooperation of the FBI, and their not running out leads, and why Hoover was so adamant that Lee Harvey Oswald was the lone assassin.

When Hale Boggs was lost in an Alaskan plane crash, he had been active in trying to force Hoover's retirement. There was no love lost between Hoover and Boggs. When Boggs, plane went down in Alaska on October 16, 1972, there was a massive 39-day search by 40 military and 20 civilian aircraft. What we have recently learned from an enterprising reporter, using the Freedom of Information Act, is that two days after the plane carrying Hale Boggs went down, J. Edgar Hoover had a Telex on his desk that pinpointed the downed plane and that there were at least two survivors.

That plane or *anyone* from that plane has not been found to this date, 41 years later. It is interesting to note that on the initial leg of this Alaska trip, an up-and-coming young Democrat named Bill Clinton took Hale Boggs to the airport.

In a Warren Commission meeting on January 22,1964, the seven Commission members discussed the fact that it has always been the nature of the FBI to investigate, present the facts, that they do not evaluate, and that they do not make conclusions such as they did about Lee Harvey Oswald being the lone assassin. They also discussed the fact that the FBI had not run out the leads.

The FBI had publicly announced from almost day one that Lee Harvey Oswald was the lone assassin. It is also interesting to note that an FBI secret internal memo two days after the assassination, dated Nov 24, 1963 states that the Bureau must: "convince the public Oswald is the real Assassin." This confidential FBI internal memo two days after the murder of President Kennedy is compelling evidence that something was very wrong inside the FBI, as they had not formally entered the investigation yet. The initial investigation was still in the hands of the Dallas Police department, 48 hours after the assassination of President Kennedy, on November 24, 1963.

When President Johnson announced that he was going to appoint a commission to investigate the assassination of President Kennedy, FBI director J. Edgar Hoover was much opposed to such a commission and beside himself, to say it mildly. Any report on the investigation of the assassination of President John F. Kennedy was the Bureau's business, and this was going over Hoover's head. A cozy chat with President Johnson got FBI Director J. Edgar Hoover back on course; Johnson and Hoover were very close friends.

Hoover did not care for the appointment of Chief Justice Earl Warren to head the commission, and when Warren named J. Lee Rankin as General Counsel for the Commission, Hoover tried to block Rankin's appointment. It was the start of an adversarial relationship between Hoover and the Warren Commission.

Hoover ordered sex dossiers on the members of the Warren Commission and the Commission staff. Hoover also ordered his FBI agents not to volunteer any information to the Warren Commission or its staff. Hoover also ordered that no Bureau official attend the early Warren Commission sessions. J. Edgar Hoover controlled what information the Warren Commission should receive.

To its credit the Warren Commission knew up front what they were into in dealing with Hoover. In that same early January 22, 1964 Commission meeting, the discussion that day ended as follows:

XXX: They (FBI) would like to have us fold up and quit.

Boggs: This closes the case, you see, don't you see.

Dulles: Yes I see that.

Rankin: They found the man; there is nothing more to do. The Commission supports their conclusions, and we can go on home and that is the end of it.

Dulles: But that puts the men right on them, if he was not the killer and they employed him, they are it you see. So your argument is correct if they are sure that this is going to close the case, but it don't close the case, they are worse off than ever by doing this.

Boggs: Yes I would think so. And of course, we are even gaining in the realm of speculation. I don't even like for this to be taken down.

Dulles: Yes, I think this record ought to be destroyed. Do you think we need a record of this?

The record was not destroyed, it was discovered years later, but it does give us a glimpse of why the Warren Commission was doomed from the start from finding the truth about the assassination of President John F. Kennedy. One of the things that the Commission members did not know on that January 1964 day, was that Jack Ruby, Oswald's killer, was an informant for the FBI and Hoover had to keep that a secret at all cost.

Hoover had spent his life building the prestige and image of the FBI, and the fact that the killer of Lee Harvey Oswald, Jack Ruby, was on the FBI payroll as an underworld informant for the FBI was something J. Edgar Hoover could not bear. It would seriously damage the prestige and image of the FBI if it became public.

This was unthinkable for J. Edgar Hoover; that the public might think the FBI had something to do with the assassination. The fact that Jack Ruby was on the FBI payroll as an underworld informant was of no consequence, as we have shown Jack Ruby acted on his own and on impulse only; Ruby's killing Oswald had nothing to do with the FBI, which I cover in another chapter.

Besides the problems with Hoover, the Warren Commission had its own problems. Contrary to popular belief the seven Warren Commission members were only present at a few of the depositions that were taken. And not all of the members were present at those depositions.

A very young staff of 14 lawyers took most of the depositions and did most of the work. These lawyers, as a whole, had very little investigative experience. They had been selected by the Justice Department by sending out letters to law professors at some of the nations law schools and asking the professors to nominate some of their top graduates to be staff members for the Commission. The Warren Commission was also under pressure to "Rush to Judgment" as Mark Lane titled one of the first books written, criticizing the final conclusions of the Warren Commission.

CHAPTER FORTY-EIGHT

SOG & FBI

In 1963 J. Edgar Hoover's ego was bigger than anything else in our United States Government Departments in Washington D.C. He thought that he and the FBI were more important than our Congress or our President. You have to read how he testified to the seven-member Warren Commission to believe it.

"Seat-of-Government," or SOG, is how the Federal Bureau of Investigation referred to itself at the time President Kennedy was assassinated. It was a Washington thing, an insider term, created by J. Edgar Hoover, Director of the FBI for over forty years. A term Hoover now savored and used often to impress his and the FBI's importance.

To show you, the public, an example of Hoover's proud usage of this term, go to Hoover's testimony before the Warren Commission on May 14, 1964, Volume V, page 108. Representative Gerald Ford has been asking Hoover about the possibility of Oswald being an FBI informant and Hoover is explaining the FBI procedure on informants and I quote: "Significant cases, goes to Mr. [Alan] Belmont, and then to my desk for my specific approval. So I, or my seat-of-government staff, have to approve every one of those who are used as informants in all classes of cases." Yes, you read that right, he did not say FBI staff, Hoover said seat-of-government staff.

By all accounts J. Edgar Hoover did an admirable job building the Federal Bureau of Investigation into one of the most powerful and respected law enforcement agencies in the world. The FBI Headquarters in Washington D.C., today, bears his name. But by 1963, after over forty years as the director of the FBI, Hoover had come to believe that he was the most powerful man in the United States, that he was more powerful than the president, that he was bigger than life.

If someone in the Bureau questioned his decisions, it was bye-bye, or on assignment to Timbuktu. He did not hesitate, and it had become a matter of routine to have his agents prepare sex dossiers on politicians and powerful people so he would have a whip to keep them in line if it was needed.

Martin Luther King is a good example of how he used those sex dossiers, but that is another story. *60 Minutes* recently ran a story about a man who had spent 30 years in prison while innocent and J. Edgar Hoover had sat on information that would have cleared this man before the man ever went to trial, and that too is another story.

The majority of time an agent spent in the field was not in chasing bank robbers, but enhancing the image of the FBI. Hoover thrived on image at any cost. Do not get me wrong, some of our best men and women were and are today, FBI agents, a title they could at one time carry with great pride and respect. There is still respect for these agents today, but not the respect that they held in 1963 and that is a shame.

CHAPTER FORTY-NINE

GOOD OR BAD INVESTIGATION

When the Warren Commission published their findings in September 1964 everyone embraced their effort as a great job. And it was a great investigation, considering what was known to the public.

The public was led to believe the investigation was a 10-month effort starting immediately after the assassination of JFK, and ending 10 months later, in September of 1964.

The seven members were appointed by President Johnson were promptly after the assassination. Government Bureaucracy was now going to come into play. A senior counsel was named; he hired fifteen lawyers and divided up 9,000 FBI documents for the lawyers to look at.

These lawyers were mostly attached to law firms and they continued to do their normal work; it had been decided they would do no investigation until the Ruby trial was over and that would be in mid-March.

In February 1964 the first witness, Marina Oswald, was called to testify.

Then on February 10,1964 Lee Harvey Oswald's mother, Marguerite Oswald was called to testify. And on February 20, 1964 Oswald's brother Robert, and then February was gone.

By March 1964, three months since the assassination, the fifteen lawyers who had been hired to do most of the investigation were still waiting for the Ruby trial to be over.

Near the end of March 1964 Rankin's fifteen lawyers meet for the first time. They view the Zapruder film frame by frame and discover that there is more to this than what was thought to be a simple open and shut case. They discover that Governor Connally is hit about a second after President Kennedy and wonder if a bolt-action rifle can be reloaded that quickly. They leave that first meeting with questions.

It only took Francis W. H. Adams a few days to quit the investigation in disgust; he contributed nothing to the Warren Commission, but is still listed in the Warren Report as one of the Assistant Counsels.

The actual full-scale investigation starts April 1964; over 50 percent of all the testimony is taken in April 1964. New leads are discovered and need to be followed up. When the lawyers want to follow up on these new leads, they are told by Rankin, "We are not here to open up something new, we are here to close this case." A few more of the lawyers quit in disgust.

There is plenty of evidence to make the case that Lee Harvey Oswald was the assassin, but other possibilities are ignored. President Johnson continues to pressure the Commission to wrap up the investigation. Rankin pressures the lawyers to be done by the end of May, which would make it a two-month investigation, April and May. It drags on through the summer.

What started out as a simple case of Oswald did it, starts to have its doubts among the staff lawyers, but the doubts are too far-fetched for one to really believe. For the good of the country, forget what you are thinking, and let us get it over with.

If what is being thought is true, it would make this a second-class country, so forget it. Or for the sake of Jackie and the Kennedy family let us get it over with. I can only imagine that when some of the investigator lawyers had thoughts of possibilities bigger than Oswald, the thoughts had to be stifled or quit the Warren Commission; some did just that, quit.

They could not speak up and say what they thought because they had been sworn to silence, that every thing they had learned came under lawyer client relationship.

With the evidence the Warren Commission allowed themselves to use and under tremendous pressure Lee Harvey Oswald was found guilty as stated 24 hours after the assassination of President Kennedy.

CHAPTER FIFTY

SECRECY

The Warren Report came out in September 1964 and it looked good; we accepted it as the truth. We were living in an age of trust, if a public figure made a public statement; it was accepted as being a true statement.

Most of us did not bother to lock our front door at night and the Dallas newspapers were urging people to remove the keys from their car when they went shopping or parked their car in the driveway at night. Lee Harvey Oswald was the lone nut assassin of President Kennedy, end of case.

Now as I look back, I have a question, if Oswald was the "lone nut assassin," case closed: Why was everything to be kept secret? Everyone present at the autopsy were military and government employees except for two FBI Agents. The attending military personnel at the autopsy were told they could not discuss what they had seen at the autopsy or they would be court-martialed if they said anything about what they had witnessed.

The Warren Commission lawyers, also called Counsel and Assistant Counsel, were told that everything they had witnessed or learned in their investigation was considered to come under lawyer-client relationship and could not be discussed or they could face disbarment.

Everything discovered other than what was in the official Warren Report was to be kept secret. J. Edgar Hoover's FBI had become a secret society and every FBI agent knew he would be fired if he talked about any of the FBI's business. Then to top it all off, President Lyndon Johnson ordered every document concerning the assassination of President John F. Kennedy to be locked up for 75 years.

My question is: Why all the Government secrecy if Lee Harvey Oswald was a "lone nut assassin," and that was all there was to it? Now as I sit here in the year 2013, writing about the Kennedy assassination, and President Johnson's order on secrecy to ban the JFK documents from the public for 75 years, I cannot help but think about what might be going on with our government today and President Obama.

CHAPTER FIFTY-ONE

THE ACCUSED
LEE HARVEY OSWALD

There was plenty of evidence to assume Lee Harvey Oswald guilty of being the lone assassin in the killing of John F. Kennedy, and that is what The Warren Commission did. But was he the real killer? Or was there more to it than a "lone nut assassin?" What if the Kennedy assassination had been planned for months ahead and Oswald had been set up, to be the patsy?

The seven members of the Warren commission interviewed and took depositions from the likes of Jackie Kennedy, some of the Secret Service agents, J. Edgar Hoover, etc. There were 15 lawyers hired to take depositions from us common people (about 500 of us). Some of us were good witnesses, some of us were poor witnesses, and some important witnesses were never called.

We common people were asked leading questions and our answers were freely given to help the Commission; we were proud to help. None of us had lawyer's present, lawyers that could recognize there was more to what an eyewitness had to offer than just answering leading questions. Those leading questions only answered what the Commission lawyers wanted us to answer and *how they wanted us to answer.*

When you read your own testimony later, you wondered why you had answered the way you did, not realizing that you had been manipulated to respond to a leading question. Several witnesses who gave testimony claimed that their Warren Commission statement had been changed, not realizing they had been manipulated and did not get to tell their full story.

Oswald never testified: he had been killed in front of millions of television viewers two days after the assassination of President Kennedy. But what if he had lived, charged with the crime, gone to court and had good defense lawyers? Many of us common people would have then been called to testify and when we were asked a leading question, Oswald's defense lawyers would bring out the full story – both sides of what was known.

It only took fourteen minutes after the assassination to start naming Oswald as the assassin. The School Book Depository was sealed off only about seven minutes after the assassination of JFK; no one could go in the building or leave the building, except the police. Some of the Depository workers had gone outside to watch the motorcade and were locked out.

A description of Oswald went out on the Dallas Police radio at 12:44, fourteen minutes after the first shot at President Kennedy.

Roy Truly, after seeing Oswald in the second floor lunch room, and taking Officer Baker to the roof, and then back down to the first floor, Truly estimated the time from when the shots were fired to taking Baker to the roof and back down to the first floor was 5 to 10 minutes.

When Truly got back to the first floor, he testified that he saw police and reporters running all over the place and some of the police were taking names of some of the employees and it was a madhouse.

Truly noticed there were police officer's who had *some* of the "boys" over in the west corner by the shipping department taking their names and addresses. Truly volunteered: Lee Oswald was not among these "boys." (Note: there were other "boys" who had been locked out of the Depository).

Roy Truly's testimony is in Volume III pages 212 to 241 specifically pages 226 to 230, and I quote, "so I picked up the telephone and called Mr. Akin down at the other warehouse (where all employee records were kept) and got the boy's (Oswald's) general description and telephone number and address in Irving." He did not know that Oswald was separated from Marina and living in Dallas. Truly was then asked if he had asked for the name and address of any of the other employees who might have been missing. Roy replied, "No sir."

During the next 46 hours Lee Harvey Oswald was found guilty by the Dallas Police Department, the FBI, The Dallas County DA, etc., and finally less than 48 hours after the assassination of President Kennedy, Lee Harvey Oswald was executed in the basement of the Dallas Police Department by Jack Ruby.

CHAPTER FIFTY-TWO

LEE HARVEY OSWALD

Was the Warren Commission correct in determining that Lee Harvey Oswald was the actual shooter. Of course they could have been absolutely correct with the evidence they used.

Could Lee Harvey Oswald have been a patsy. Of course he could have been a patsy with just as much, if not more, of the evidence that was not used, and could easily prove that he was not the assassin.

My alarm bells went off with Roy Truly's and Dallas Police officer Marrion Baker's Warren Commission testimonies.

Dallas Police Officer Marrion Baker and Depository Superintendent Roy Truly both testified that 75 seconds after the shooting and assassination of President John F. Kennedy, Lee Harvey Oswald was in the second floor lunch room, four floors down from the sixth floor where a gun had been seen sticking out an open window and shots fired and that 75 seconds after the shooting Lee Harvey Oswald was *calm, cool, collected, not out of breath, and appeared normal.*

I sit back and try to picture this; we are to believe that this man, Lee Harvey Oswald, sat in a sniper's nest on the sixth floor, fired off three shots killing the most powerful man in the world, then ran to the other side of the building and hid the rifle, then raced down four flights of stairs.

Throw out the 75 seconds and there is plenty of evidence that Lee Harvey Oswald was the assassin. The rifle found on the sixth floor was traced back to Oswald, the killing of Dallas Police Officer J.D. Tippit, Oswald's actions when he was arrested in the theater. The evidence against Oswald goes on and on. Then I read a couple of small items in the Warren Report.

James Jarman Jr., an employee of the Texas School book depository gave his testimony on Tuesday March 24, 1964. His testimony is recorded in Volume III of the 26 volumes, starting on page 198. Warren Commission Assistant Counsel Joseph A. Ball is taking James Jarman's testimony and on pages 200-201 Mr. Ball asks James Jarman: "Did you talk to him (Oswald) again that morning."

Mr. Jarman: "Yes sir. I talked to him again later that morning?"

Mr. Ball: "About what time?"

Mr. Jarman: "It was between 9:30 and 10 o'clock, I believe."

Mr. Ball: "Where were you when you talked to him."

Mr. Jarman: "In between two rows of bins."

Mr. Ball: "On what floor?"

Mr. Jarman: "On the first floor."

Mr. Ball: "And what was said by him and by you?"

Mr. Jarman: "Well, he was standing up in the window and I went to the window also, and he asked me what were the people – gathering around on the corner for, and I told him that the President was supposed to pass that morning, and he asked me did I know which way he was coming, and I told him, yes; he probably come down Main and turn on Houston and then back again on Elm. Then he said, 'Oh, I see.' And that was all."

Mr. Ball: "Did you talk to him again?"

Mr. Jarman: "No sir."

Then after the shooting, and Oswald had been seen calm and normal in the lunch room by Baker and Truly, Oswald is seen four or five minutes later with a soft drink in his hand calmly walking through the office out the front door.

It was normal for Oswald to ride with Wesley Frazier on weekends to Irving and spend the weekend with his wife Marina at Ruth Paine's house. Mr. Frazier testified before the Warren Commission on March 11, 1963 that Oswald asked for a ride on Thursday November 21, and in Volume II page 222 it states that when Wesley Frazier asked Lee why he was going on Thursday instead of the normal Friday, Oswald said, "I am going home to get some curtain rods."

According to Frazier's testimony on page 226: the next morning Oswald had put a package in the back seat of Wesley's car and Wesley asked Oswald what was in the package and Oswald replied "curtain rods." On the way to work that morning, Wesley Frazier said Lee Oswald was "chuckling" about playing with his babies.

All the above accounts are from actual testimony. Two men said that Lee Oswald was four floors down from where the shots fired and was calm, cool, collected, and normal acting, one minute and fifteen seconds after the President of the United States had been assassinated.

Before the president's motorcade is supposed to pass by where Oswald works, he innocently asks why people are gathering at the corner? On the way to work that morning he is laughing about playing with his children. Does all this sound like a man who is planning to, and/or has assassinated the President of the United States? Common sense tells me something is not right.

Can a man planning to kill the President of the United States be laughing about playing with his children on the way to work that morning?

Would a man with plans to kill the President of the United States not know his motorcade route, and why people were gathering to see the President pass by? Is it possible for a man be the coldest of cold-blooded killers, be calm, cool, normal, not out of breath, and buying a soft drink four floors down from the sniper's nest 75 seconds after killing the President of the United States?

Was Lee Harvey Oswald set up? Was Lee Harvey Oswald a "patsy?"

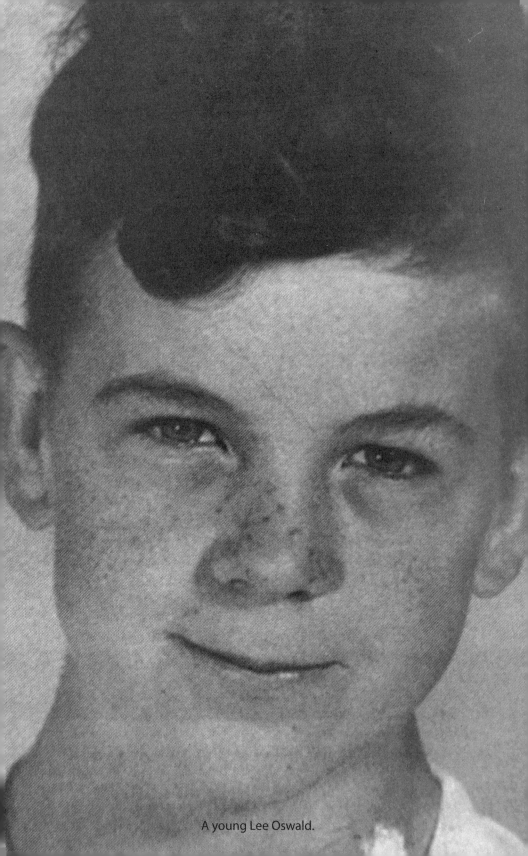

A young Lee Oswald.

Chapter Fifty-Three

Background:
Lee Harvey Oswald

It is evident in the 26 volumes of the Warren Report that the FBI did an intensive background check of Lee Harvey Oswald. He was born in New Orleans. At age three he was placed in an orphanage, taken out of orphanage at age four by his mother and moved to Dallas, where his mother remarried for the third time. Oswald started first grade at Benbrook, Texas.

At Benbrook his mother separated from her third husband and Lee had to restart the first grade in Covington, Louisiana. While still in first grade the family moved back to Fort Worth, Texas for his mother's reconciliation with her husband. At age eight his mother divorced her third husband.

For the next five years Lee's school record in Fort Worth was average. At age twelve, his mother moved the family to New York City. The next year and a half in New York was marked by Lee's refusal to attend school and by emotional and psychological problems. Lee underwent psychiatric study at the Youth House where he was diagnosed as, "seriously detached, and withdrawn," and it was noted on his medical records: "A rather pleasant, appealing quality about this emotionally starved, affectionate youngster. He experiences fantasies about power, hurting people, but not a behavior problem. He appears withdrawn and evasive, a boy who prefers to spend time alone."

He tested above average in intelligence. His mother denied Lee further psychiatric assistance and he returned to school where his grades and attendance temporally improved. In 1954, at age fourteen, while Lee's case was still pending in court, his mother and Lee left for New Orleans, the city of Lee's birth. Upon his return to New Orleans, Lee maintained mediocre grades and had no behavior problems.

Neighbors and others who knew him outside of school remembered him as a quiet, solitary and introverted boy who read a great deal and whose vocabulary made him quite articulate. At sixteen Lee dropped out of school and tried to join the Marines, but was rejected because of his age.

Lee worked at odd jobs during the next few months and started to read communist literature, occasionally praised communism, and expressed a desire to join the Communist party. Another move followed in July 1956, when Lee and his mother returned to Fort Worth. Lee reentered high school, dropped out after a few weeks and enlisted in the Marine Corps on October 24, 1956, 6 days after his 17th birthday.

In basic training with an M-1 rifle, Lee scored a rating of "sharpshooter" on a marksman/sharpshooter/expert scale. Lee received training in aviation fundamentals and radar scanning. Most of those who knew him in the Marines described him as a loner who resented authority. He was court-martialed once for possessing an unregistered privately owned weapon and on another occasion for using provocative language to a noncommissioned officer.

He was, however, generally able to comply with Marine discipline. Oswald served 15 months overseas, most of it in Japan. His final year was spent at Santa Ana, Calif. While in the Marines, Oswald studied the Russian language. Lee was discharged from the Marines on September 11, 1959. He returned to Fort Worth, remained with his mother 3 days and left for New Orleans.

In New Orleans he booked passage to Le Havre, France and sailed on September 20, 1959. On October 16, 1959, Oswald arrived in Moscow by train after crossing the border from Finland, where he had secured a visa for a 6-day stay in the Soviet Union. He immediately applied for Soviet citizenship.

On the afternoon of October 21, 1959, Oswald was ordered to leave the Soviet Union by 8 p.m. that evening. That afternoon, in an apparent suicide attempt, Oswald slashed his wrist. After being released from the hospital, Oswald appeared at the American Embassy and stated he wished to renounce his American citizenship so he could become a Russian citizen.

The Soviet government did not grant his request, but in January 1960 he was given permission to remain in the Soviet Union on a year-to-year basis. He was sent to Minsk where he worked in a radio factory as an unskilled laborer. In January 1961 his permission to remain in the Soviet Union was extended for another year.

In February 1961, he wrote the American embassy in Moscow expressing a desire to return to the United States. In March 1961 Oswald met a 19-year-old Russian girl, Marina Nikolaevna Prusakova, a pharmacist, who had been brought up in Leningrad but was then living with an aunt and uncle in Minsk.

They were married on April 30, 1961. Oswald then corresponded with American and Soviet authorities seeking approval for him and his wife to depart for the United States. Lee Oswald and his wife Marina and new child arrived from Russia in the United States in June 1962 and they settled in Fort Worth, Texas where they met by a group of Russian-born or Russian-speaking persons who lived in the Dallas, Fort Worth area.

These people were very generous to the Oswalds, giving them gifts, food, clothing, baby furniture, and arranging appointments and transportation for medical and dental treatment. When Oswald started looking for employment in October 1962 and when there were marital difficulties, Marina and their child stayed with various members of this group.

Oswald's relationship with the Russian community was strained, he resented the help the "Russian friends" gave to Marina and the child. On April 10, 1963, it is alleged that Lee Oswald took a shot at resigned Major General Edwin A. Walker; the shot missed.

Two weeks later, Oswald went to New Orleans and was later joined by Marina and their daughter. Marina was pregnant with their second child.

In late September 1963, Ruth Paine drove to New Orleans and brought Marina and the child back to Irving, Texas. The Oswald's were still having marital difficulties. Soon after Marina left New Orleans, Oswald supposedly went to Mexico City and supposedly visited the Russian Embassy. Oswald then returned to Dallas, rented a room, and got a job at the School Book Depository on October 15, 1963.

CHAPTER FIFTY-FOUR

THE NOTES OF THE FINAL
INTERROGATION OF
LEE HARVEY OSWALD
AT DALLAS POLICE HEADQUARTERS

For years there has been much criticism over the fact that no notes or tape recordings of the interrogation of Lee Harvey Oswald were made at Dallas Police Headquarters. The fact is that there were detailed notes taken during Oswald's final interrogation.

A memorandum of these detailed notes are in the 26 volumes of the Warren Report. These notes were not taken by anyone with the Dallas Police, the Secret Service, or the FBI, but by a U.S. Postal inspector.

It must be noted that the Assassination Records Review Board in the 1990's did discover some very brief notes made some 30 years earlier by Dallas Police Captain Will Fritz that were taken during these interrogations and these brief notes are now in the National Archives. Captain Fritz's notes do reveal Oswald stated, "He was in the second floor lunch room of the School Book Depository drinking a coke when the assassination occurred." Local, state, and federal interrogators who were present have all stated that Oswald repeatedly denied any guilt.

The brief notes taken by Captain Fritz correspond with the much more detailed notes taken by Harry D. Holmes, a Dallas Postal Inspector who also witnessed the assassination through binoculars from his fifth floor office in the postal building opposite the School Book Depository in Dealey Plaza.

Mr. Holmes was also present and participated in Oswald's last interrogation at Dallas Police Headquarters on Sunday morning November 24, 1963, just before Oswald was killed by Jack Ruby in the basement of Dallas Police Headquarters. Mr. Holmes' memorandum of this interrogation can be found in Volume XXIV, pages 488 to 492 and is labeled Commission Exhibit No. 2064.

This Commission exhibit, 2064, reads as follows: On December 17, 1963, Mr. Harry Holmes, Postal Inspector U.S. Post Office, Terminal Annex, Dallas Texas, made available to Special Agent Charles T. Brown Jr. a copy of a memorandum reflecting results of interview by Inspector Holmes with Lee Harvey Oswald on November 24, 1963, which memorandum is quoted as follows.

"Dallas, Texas December 17, 1963

MEMORANDUM OF INTERVIEW

"Informal memorandum furnished by Postal Inspector H. D. Holmes, Dallas, Texas, of an interview he took part in with Lee H. Oswald on Sunday morning, November 24, 1963, between the approximate hours of 9:25 A.M. to 11:10 A.M. Those present, in addition to Inspector Holmes, were Captain Will Fritz, Dallas Police, Forrest V. Sorrels, and Local Agent in Charge, Secret Service, and Thomas J. Kelly, Inspector, Secret Service.

In addition, there were three Detectives who were apparently assigned to guarding Oswald as none of them took part in the interrogation. "Oswald at no time appeared confused or in doubt as to whether or not he should answer a question. On the contrary, he was quite alert and showed no hesitancy in answering those questions which he wanted to answer, and quite skillful in parrying those questions which he did not want to answer. I got the impression that he had disciplined his mind and reflexes to a state where I personally doubted if he would ever have confessed.

He denied emphatically having taken part in or having any knowledge of the shooting of the Policeman Tippit, or the President, stating that so far as he is concerned the reason he was in custody was because he 'popped a policeman in the nose in a theater on Jefferson Avenue.'

"P.O. BOXES---He was questioned separately about the three boxes he had rented, and in each instance his answers were quick, direct and accurate as reflected on the box rental applications. He stated without prompting that he had rented Box 2915 at the Main Post Office for several months prior to his going to New Orleans, that this box was rented in his own name, Lee H. Oswald, and that he had taken out two keys to the box, and that when he closed the box, he directed that his mail be forwarded to his street address in New Orleans.

"He stated that no one received mail in this box other than himself, nor did he receive any mail under any other name than his own true name; that no one had access to the box other than himself nor did he permit anyone else to use this box. He stated it was possible that on rare occasions he may have handed one of the keys to his wife to go get his mail but certainly nobody else.

He denied emphatically that he ever ordered a rifle under his name on any other name, nor permitted anyone else to order a rifle to be received in this box. Further, he denied that he had ever ordered any rifle by mail order or bought any money order for the purpose of paying for such a rifle. In fact, he claimed he owned no rifle and had not practiced or shot a rifle other than possibly a .22 small bore rifle, since his days in the Marine Corp.

He stated 'How could I afford to order a rifle on my salary of $1.25 an hour when I can't hardly feed myself on what I make.' "When asked if he had a post office box in New Orleans he stated that he did, for the reason that he subscribed to several publications, at least two of which were published in Russia, one being the hometown paper published in Minsk where he had met and married his wife, and that he moved around so much that it was more practical to simply rent post office boxes and have his mail forwarded from one box to the next rather than going through the process of furnishing changes of address to the publishers.

When asked if he permitted anyone other than himself to get mail in box 30051 in New Orleans, he stated that he did not. It will be recalled that on this box rent application he showed that both Marina Oswald and A.J. Hidell were listed under the caption 'persons entitled to receive mail through box.' After denying that anyone else was permitted to get mail in the box, he was reminded that this application showed the name Marina Oswald as being entitled to receive mail in the box and he replied 'well so what, she was my wife and I see nothing wrong with that, and it could very well be that I did place her name on the application.'

He was then reminded that the application also showed the name A.J. Hidell was also entitled to receive mail in the box, at which he simply shrugged his shoulders and stated 'I don't recall anything about that.' "He stated that when he came back to Dallas and after he had gone to work for the Texas School Book Depository, he had rented a box at the nearby Terminal Annex postal station, this being box 6225, and that this box was also rented in his name, Lee H. Oswald. He stated he had only checked out one key for this box, which information was found to be accurate, and this key was found on his person at the time of his arrest.

He professed not to recall the fact that he showed on the box rental application under name of corporation 'Fair Play For Cuba Committee' and 'American Civil Liberties Union.' When asked as to why he showed these organizations on his application, he simply shrugged and said that he didn't recall showing them.

When asked if he paid the box rental or did the organizations pay it, he stated that he paid it. In answer to another question, he also stated that no one had any knowledge that he had this box other than himself.

ORGANIZATIONS-MEMBERSHIP IN – With respect to American Civil Liberties Union he was a little evasive stating something to the effect that he had made some effort to join but it was never made clear whether he had or had not been accepted. He stated that he first became interested in the Fair Play For Cuba Committee, after he went to New Orleans, that it started out as being a group of individuals who, like him, who thought and had like political opinions. They did decide to organize, and did organize after a fashion, but denied that they had any president or elected officers. He stated that he, himself, could probably be considered the secretary since he wrote some letters on their behalf and attempted to collect dues, which, if I recall, were $1.00 per month. He also stated that there was a 'Fair Play For Cuba Committee' in New York that was better organized. He denied that he was sent to Dallas for the purpose of organizing such a cell in Dallas.

"When asked if he was a communist, he stated emphatically not, that he was a Marxist. Someone asked the difference and he stated that a communist is a Lenin Marxist, but that he himself was a pure Marxist, and when someone asked the difference, he stated that it was a long story and if they didn't know, it would take too long to tell them. He stated further that he had read about everything written by or about Karl Marx.

"When asked as to his religion, he stated that Karl Marx was his religion, and in his response to further questioning he stated that some people may find the bible interesting reading, but it was not for him, stating further that even as a philosophy there was not much to the bible.

MARINE CORP SERVICE – Captain Fritz made some mention of his dishonorable discharge from the Marine Corp at which point he bristled noticeably, stating that he had been discharged with an 'honorable' discharge and that this was later changed due to his having attempted to denounce his American Citizenship while he was living in Russia. He stated further that since his change of citizenship did not come to pass, he had written a letter to Mr. Connally, then Secretary of the Navy, and after considerable delay, received a very respectful reply wherein Connally stated he had resigned to run for governor of Texas, and that his letter was being referred to the new secretary, a Mr. Cork, Kurth, or something like that. He showed no particular animosity toward Mr. Connally while discussing this feature.

MAP – Captain Fritz advised him that among his effects in his room, there was found a map of the city of Dallas that had some marks on it and asked him to explain this map. Oswald said he presumed he had reference to an old City map on which he had made some X's denoting location of firms that had advertised job vacancies. He stated that he had no transportation and either walked or rode a bus and that as he was constantly looking for work, in fact had registered at the Texas Employment Bureau, and that as he would receive leads either from newspaper ads or from the bureau or from neighbors, he would chart these places on the map to save time in his traveling.

He said to the best of his recollection, most of them were out Industrial, presumably meaning Industrial Blvd. When asked why the X at the location of the Texas School Book Depository at Elm and Houston, he stated that 'Well, I interviewed there for a job, in fact, got the job, therefore the X. "When asked as to how he learned about this vacancy, he stated that 'Oh, it was general information in the neighborhood, I don't recall just who told me about it, but I learned it from people in Mrs. Paynes neighborhood and that all the people around there were looking out for possible employment for him.

ACTIVITY JUST PRIOR TO AND IMMEDIATELY FOLLOWING ASSASSINATION ATTEMPT – To an inquiry as to why he went to visit his wife on Thursday night, November 21, whereas he normally visited her over the weekend, he stated that on this particular weekend he had learned that his wife and Mrs. Payne were giving a party for the children and that they were having in a 'houseful' of neighborhood children and that he just didn't want to be around at such time. Therefore, he made his weekly visit on Thursday night.

"When asked if he didn't bring a sack with him the next morning to work, he stated that he did, and when asked as to the contents of the sack, he stated that it contained his lunch. Then when asked to the size or shape of the sack, he said 'Oh, I don't recall, it may have been a small sack or a large sack, you don't always find one that just fits your sandwiches. When asked as to where he placed the sack when he got into the car, he said in his lap, or possibly the front seat beside him, as he always did because he didn't want to get it crushed. He denied that he placed any package in the back seat.

When advised that the driver stated that he had brought out a long parcel and placed it in the back seat, he stated 'Oh, he must be mistaken or else thinking about some other time when he picked me up.' "When asked about his whereabouts at the time of the shooting, he stated that when lunch time came, and he didn't say which floor he was on, he said one of the Negro employees invited him to eat lunch with him and he stated 'You go on down and send the elevator back up and I will join you in a few minutes.'

Before he could finish whatever he was doing, he stated, the commotion surrounding the assassination took place and when he went down stairs, a policeman questioned him as to his identification and his boss stated that 'he is one of our employees' whereupon the policeman had him step aside momentarily. Following this, he simply walked out the front door of the building. I don't recall that anyone asked why he left or where or how he went. I just presumed that this had been covered in an earlier questioning.

A. J. HIDELL IDENTIFICATION CARD – Captain Fritz asked him if he knew anyone by the name of A. J. Hidell and he denied that he did. When asked if he had ever used this name as an alias, he also made a denial. In fact, he stated that he had never had heard of the name before.

Captain Fritz then asked him about the I.D. card he had in his pocket bearing such a name and he flared up and stated 'I've told you all I'm going to about that card. You took notes, just read them for yourself, if you want to refresh your memory.' He told Captain Fritz that 'You have the card, now you know as much about it as I do.'

"About 11:00 A.M. or a few minutes thereafter, someone handed through the door several hangers on which there were some trousers, shirts, and a couple of sweaters. When asked if he wanted to change ant of his clothes before being transferred to the County jail, he said, 'just give me one of those sweaters.'

"He didn't like the one they handed him and insisted on putting on a black slipover sweater that had some jagged holes in it near the front of the right shoulder. One cuff was released while he slipped this over his head, following which he was again cuffed.

During this change of clothing, Chief of Police Curry came into the room and discussed something in an inaudible undertone with Captain Fritz, apparently for the purpose of not letting Oswald hear what was being said. I have no idea what this conversation was, but just presume they were discussing the transfer of the prisoner. I did not go downstairs to witness the further transfer of the prisoner."

"s/ H. D. Holmes

CHAPTER FIFTY-FIVE

A BIG LIE AND
A MAJOR DECEPTION

We now know that there were three men on the sixth floor during the assassination of President Kennedy and Lee Harvey Oswald was not one of the three men. Thanks to Barry Ernest, and the urging of my dear friend Harold Weisberg for Barry to keep digging until he found the truth.

Barry Ernest finally did dig up the documentation and witnesses to put this big lie by the Warren Commission into a book titled, *The Girl On The Stairs: The Search for a Missing Witness to the JFK Assassination.* The girl on the stairs was 23-year-old Victoria "Vickie" Elizabeth Adams, an employee of Scott Foreman Co., a company that had its offices on the fourth floor of the Texas School Book Depository on November 22, 1963.

Ms. Adams had been abandoned by her parents when she was eleven and raised within the Catholic Church. One of her first adult jobs was that of a sixth grade teacher at the Immaculate Heart of Mary School in Atlanta Ga. What is important for us to know is that Vicky had no parents or siblings to discuss personal matters or to give her advice.

In 1963 Vickie Adams was on her own like most of us had never experienced and to state that Ms. Adams was naïve and not big-city wise would be an understatement. The women at Scott Foreman Co., Vickie Adams, Sandra Styles, Elsie Dorman, and Dorothy May Garner all decided to watch the President's motorcade from a window in their office on the fourth floor of the School Book Depository, and while waiting for the President's motorcade they opened a window to get the best unobstructed view.

The women watched the motorcade and heard three shots as the President's car drove through Dealey Plaza. After the third shot curiosity got the best of Vickie and Sandra and they ran to the stockroom that led to the stairs and raced down the stairs, in three-inch high heels, to get outside and see what had just happened.

The School Book Depository was an old building that had been erected using huge wood timbers before steel became popular, and the wood stairs creaked and groaned when anyone was using the stairs. As they hurried down the stairs, Vickie and Sandra did not meet, see or hear anyone else on the stairs. The electricity was off so the elevators were of no use.

Soon after the assassination, many of the depository employees were questioned if they had seen anything. Vicky was one of the employees who gave a statement, a simple statement of watching the motorcade and then going down the stairs to see what had happened.

To Vicky, there was nothing in her statement that would help in the investigation, but for some reason, in the days and weeks that followed, Vickie was getting a lot of attention from the FBI and other investigators about seeing the motorcade and then running down the stairs from the fourth floor. Vickie told the same simple story over and over, but did not think much about all the attention she was getting.

Vickie Adams was called to give her testimony to the Warren Commission on April 7, 1964; David Belin was the Assistant Warren Commission Counsel who took her testimony. Vicky Adams told the same simple story about watching the motorcade and then running down the stairs. It is interesting to note in reading her testimony Vickie Adams always answered, "Yes, sir," or "No, sir," to all questions asked by Belin.

At the end of her testimony she was given the same option that all of us who testified before the Warren Commission were given, that she could come back when her testimony was transcribed by the court reporter, read her deposition and sign it before it went to Washington or she could waive the signing and let the court reporter send her deposition directly to Washington.

Vickie replied to Belin that he could use his own discretion and Belin replied "If it doesn't make any difference, we can waive your signing your deposition and you won't have to make another trip down here. Ms. Adams replied, "That's alright."

A couple of important things to note: Ms. Adams always stated the only person she had encountered as she went down the stairs was a black man on the first floor. Her official Warren Commission testimony, however, was changed to state she had run into William Shelley and Billy Lovelady, which would have made the time she ran down the stairs much later.

William Shelley's and Billy Lovelady's Warren Commission testimonies agree with Vicky Adams' verbal statement that she did not run into them on the first floor. The Warren Commission discredited Vicky Adams' testimony on page 154 of the original Government Printing Office publication.

While David Belin was questioning Vicky, he leaned back in his chair and said, "I do not believe a word you are saying." Vicky replied that her co-worker Sandra Styles would back up what she had said as being the truth.

The Warren Commission did not call Sandra Styles to testify. The way Belin reacted to Vicky Adams sounds exactly like the type of rude comment that Belin would make, I know because I met David Belin by accident in 1988, when we shared a ride to the airport and in trying to make polite conversation with him about him being an Assistant Counsel on the Warren Commission.

When I politely asked him if was sure of what he had just said, Belin glared at me and stared out the window the rest of the way to the airport. To this day David Belin stands out as the most egotistical a-hole I have ever met.

Barry Ernest spent years on research and searching for Vicky Adams. When he finally found Vicky, she was leery at first, but did open up to Barry. Her story was still the same: after watching the President's motorcade from a fourth floor window, Vicky and her co-worker Sandra Styles ran down the stairs and out into the open to try and find out what had happened to the President.

Barry Ernest also found Sandra Styles, and Sandra verified that Vicky Adams' recollection of November 22, 1963 was exactly as Vicky had stated.

Dorothy Garner was Vicky Adams' manager and was at the same fourth floor window watching the motorcade with Vicky, but was never called to testify to the Warren Commission. However, in his research Barry found an FBI statement made on March 20, 1964 by Dorothy Garner. In that FBI statement Mrs. Garner states, "After Miss Adams went downstairs she (Mrs. Garner) saw Mr. Truly and the policeman come up."

Barry Ernest located Dorothy Garner and she verified how fast Vicky and Sandra had bolted and run down the stairs. Dorothy was in her 80's, was still sharp, remembered seeing Truly and a policeman coming up the stairs but was hazy in placing the time.

Then came a big break in Barry Ernest's quest for the truth, the discovery of a letter in the National Archives from Martha Joe Stroud, who worked with Assistant United States Attorney General Barefoot Sanders in Dallas. The letter was written on June 2, 1964 by Ms. Stroud to J. Lee Rankin, Chief Counsel of the Warren Commission. The letter was in regard to and enclosed the deposition of Victoria E. Adams, the first paragraph concerned minor changes made in Vicky Adams deposition and the second paragraph stated:

"Mr. Belin was questioning Miss Adams about whether or not she saw anyone as she went running down the stairs. Miss Garner, Miss Adams

Supervisor, stated this morning that after Miss Adams went downstairs she (Miss Garner) saw Mr. Truly and the policeman come up."

Signed by Martha Joe Stroud

PLEASE ADDRESS ALL MAIL TO
UNITED STATES ATTORNEY
P. O. BOX 152

United States Department of Justice *Adams Vicki*

UNITED STATES ATTORNEY
NORTHERN DISTRICT OF TEXAS
DALLAS 1, TEXAS

75221

June 2, 1964

AIR MAIL - REGISTERED - RETURN RECEIPT REQUESTED

Mr. J. Lee Rankin
General Counsel
President's Commission on the
Assassination of President Kennedy
200 Maryland Avenue N.E.
Washington, D. C. 20002

Dear Mr. Rankin:

I am enclosing the signed deposition of:

Victoria E. Adams

The following corrections were made: page 59 line 19 changed to "service"; page 59 line 20 add "and"; page 60 line 18 to "Martin"; page 64, line 14 to "there"; page 75 line 5 add "and"; page 79 line 4 to "officiously."

Mr. Bellin was questioning Miss Adams about whether or not she saw anyone as she was running down the stairs. Miss Garner, Miss Adams' supervisor, stated this morning that after Miss Adams went downstairs she (Miss Garner) saw Mr. Truly and the policeman come up.

Sincerely yours

Barefoot Sanders
United States Attorney

Martha Joe Stroud, Assistant
United States Attorney

Enclosure

There it was, a letter that would clear Lee Harvey Oswald of being on the School Book Depository stairs in the moments after the shooting. The girls, Vicky Adams and Sandra Styles, did not see anyone on the stairs as they ran from the fourth floor down the stairs immediately after the last shot and their Manager, Miss Garner who saw Roy Truly and the policeman coming up the stairs *after* the girls ran down the stair and Truly and the policeman had just seen Oswald in the second floor lunch room calm, cool and collected buying a bottle of soda.

Martha Joe Stroud's letter to J. Lee Rankin Chief Counsel for the Warren Commission, is the solid proof that Lee Oswald was not on the stairs after the assassination of President Kennedy, which also means that Lee Oswald was not on the sixth floor shooting at President Kennedy and had not raced down the stairs to be in the second floor lunch room to be seen by Roy Truly and Dallas Police Officer Marrion Baker, who both testified that Lee Harvey Oswald was calm, normal acting and not out of breath.

It was too simple; Lee Harvey Oswald was in the second floor lunchroom while shots were being fired at President Kennedy. Right where he claimed he was and where he was actually seen a 75 seconds after the shooting.

A note about Martha Joe Stroud: When it became public about a missed shot and my minor injury in early June 1964, FBI Director J. Edgar Hoover started a smear campaign against me, James Tague, to make what I had to say useless and make the missed shot fade away.

Martha Joe Stroud gathered pictures from the photographers who had taken pictures of the spot where the bullet had hit the street and sent the pictures to J. Lee Rankin, Chief Counsel for the Warren Commission. The pictures changed history and stopped J. Edgar Hoover's smear campaign against me.

One thing that distresses me is that J. Lee Rankin, Chief Counsel for the Warren Commission, had a good reputation for being an honest man and when he received the above-mentioned letter from Martha Joe Stroud – he didn't follow up on the information in the letter; it would have changed history and Lee Harvey Oswald would no longer be a "lone nut assassin."

Or was Rankin so buried in documentation on the Kennedy assassination in June 1964 that he never read the letter and just handed it off to the likes of David Belin to read and handle? Whoever altered Vicky Adams Warren Commission testimony, failed to have Sandra Styles and Miss Garner deposed, and failed to act on the information Martha Joe Stroud presented, committed fraud on the American people. Or just maybe Rankin had discovered the deep dark truth about the assassination that was beyond his control.

CHAPTER FIFTY-SIX

HAROLD WEISBERG

O ne evening in the mid-1960s I was home watching television when the phone rang, I answered and the man introduced himself as Harold Weisberg. He wanted to ask me some questions about the Kennedy assassination. I agreed and we talked at length about the assassination.

Mr. Weisberg came across as very knowledgeable about the facts, and I was impressed with his knowledge of the Kennedy assassination. I did not realize it at the time, but some of the things that he told me were things that I had had a gut feeling about. Talking to Harold Weisberg that evening renewed my interest in the assassination. Some of the things he was telling me, he was citing from the 26-volume report. I had an unused 26-volume set that I had bought because my testimony was in Volume VII.

After Harold's phone call, I began reading the full 26 volumes. When I would come across or hear something a witness had said, I would look up the testimony. It was the start of years of personal research on the assassination of John F. Kennedy and a great friendship with Harold Weisberg.

One of the things of great interest to me was Harold's lawsuit against our government using the Freedom of Information Act to get access to the FBI's documents on the Kennedy assassination. It took several years, but with the aid of voluntary legal help by Washington attorney Jim Lesar, Harold won the lawsuit and received thousands and thousands of FBI documents – enough to fill over 60 four-drawer filing cabinets.

During one of the many court appearances of this lawsuit, one of the FBI agent's stated that: "Harold Weisberg knew more about the Kennedy assassination than any person alive."

I must confess that my wife played a major part in corresponding with Harold through the years; my wife Judy and Harold had hit it off while Harold was a guest at our home, and while I was busy making a living, my wife saved and amassed everything new concerning the assassination of John F. Kennedy for me.

We, mostly my wife, corresponded with Harold almost on a weekly basis, with Harold keeping us informed of the latest information available from his research, and with Judy keeping Harold informed of what was going on in Dallas regarding the assassination. She would clip and send Harold any article that appeared in the Dallas papers about the assassination.

It was like having our own personal news source. Whenever Harold discovered something new in the FBI files, he would share it with us and send us copies of what he had found. I never knew of anything that Harold told us that could not be backed up by documentation. Harold Weisberg died February 21, 2002 at the age of 88 at his home in Frederick, Maryland.

Harold Weisberg was often dubbed: "The country's leading authority on the President John F. Kennedy and Martin Luther King assassinations." Those of us who have met and knew Harold, agree.

Harold had been a newspaper and magazine writer, a Senate investigator, and was in intelligence analysis for a spy agency in World War II. His work was of great value to the Justice and Treasury Departments.

During his life Harold had been praised by correspondents, Congressmen, cabinet officers, and the White House. In the late 30's he worked for the chairman of the La Follette Civil Liberties Committee and was consulted by other Congressional Committees, including the War Preparedness Committee, headed by then-Senator Harry S. Truman.

In the late 1940's he turned to farm life with his wife Lillian and they won prizes for their poultry. They named their place the "Coq d'or" farm. They were early participants in the Peace Corps program and their "Geese for Peace" program, which shipped geese world wide to be bred and raised in poverty-stricken countries, brought them world wide acclaim.

Harold was also a gourmet cook, and won many prizes locally and was named National Barbecue King in 1959.

In 1964, when the 26 volumes of the Warren Report became available to the public, Harold purchased the 26-volume Report and poured over the testimony of witnesses and other evidence contained in the 26 volumes.

Friends who knew him stated Harold had a photographic memory. When Harold found contradictions in eyewitness testimony and superficial research into the possibility of a conspiracy, he went to his old friends in the FBI looking for answers to resolve these questions. Harold knew his way around Washington D.C. and expected cooperation in resolving the issues he had discovered in the Warren Report by the FBI making available their files to him.

Harold ran into a wall of secrecy and he was denied any help from the FBI in resolving these issues. This turn-down by the FBI was the start of an obsession to find the truth about the Kennedy assassination, and led to years of financial hardship in his search for the truth.

In 1965 Harold wrote his first book, one of the first books to raise questions about the Warren Report, *"Whitewash: The Report on The Warren Report."* Once the book was finished, he went to publisher after publisher, the editors praised his book with remarks such as: "A convincing document, impressive, certainly worthwhile, valid, reasoned and concerned, could be a best seller," but not one of these establishment presses would publish the book.

In 1965 *you did not* print something that could be considered critical of the Government or the FBI. Harold self-published the book and publicized it himself, it sold over 30,000 copies, and was considered a literary success.

Dell then published the book, and a follow-up called *Whitewash II: The FBI-Secret Service Cover-up* in 1966. Other books were to follow, *Photographic Whitewash, Post Mortem, Oswald in New Orleans, Case of conspiracy with the C.I.A.* (Canyon Books in 1967), *Martin Luther King the Assassination* (Carroll & Graf, 1993), and *Case Open: The Unanswered JFK Assassination Questions* (Carroll & Graf, 1994). Harold also wrote over 30 unpublished books.

Harold Weisberg was the person who brought suits against the United States Government under the Freedom of Information Act that led to the release of the FBI's Kennedy and King files. Harold asked me to join him in one of the lawsuits and I did.

When the files were released by the FBI, Harold was one of the first to receive them. With the help of volunteer students from nearby Hood College, the files were organized into over 60 four-drawer filing cabinets in his basement and remained there until he donated them to the Hood College Library late in his life.

Harold also accumulated thousands of documents from other Government agencies in his home and spent untold hours in the National Archives scouring millions more. Many researchers have spent many hours in Harold's basement, including myself.

I first came to know Harold when he called me one evening asking me questions about the missed shot that hit the curb in front of me. It was the start of a life-long friendship. I have been a guest in Harold's and Lillian's home and Harold has been a guest in my home in Dallas.

Through the years, Harold was constantly going through the hundreds of thousands of pages of FBI files in his basement and when he would find something new and of unusual interest, he would send me a copy. Harold on many occasions – urged me to write the true story about the attempted cover up by the FBI of the missed shot and my minor injury during the assassination of President Kennedy.

Harold spent over 35 years, often seven days a week, in his quest for the truth in the assassination of President John F. Kennedy and this dogged and unrelenting quest for the truth led him to conclude the possibility of a conspiracy or of a different assassin from Lee Harvey Oswald.

Through the years Harold and I debated the many issues that had arisen since the release of the Warren report and one of those issues was that of a government cover-up of some sort. I had many unanswered questions about how the Warren Commission had come to some of the conclusions they had come to. I knew that FBI director J. Edgar Hoover's ego and uncooperative attitude had caused some of the problems, but that someone in our government would make a conscious effort to cover up the facts associated with the assassination of a President was something I had a hard time accepting. I had suspicions of the possibility of a cover-up, but I did not have any cold hard evidence.

Harold had spent hours upon hours in the National Archives with his constant and on-going research on the assassination of President Kennedy and as part of his research he had examined the scar on the curb section where a stray bullet had hit the street near where I was standing during the shooting. Over the years Harold would tell me: "The hole in the curb has been patched." And I would tell Harold that there never was a hole: "That only about an eighth of an inch was scrapped off the curb where the bullet had hit and ricocheted off the round of the curb." And Harold would reply back: "Well, it has been patched."

After years of Harold telling me the hole in the curb had been patched and me explaining there never was a hole, I decided to just go examine the curb section myself in the National Archives and see what Harold was talking about. That was in the spring of 1997.

CHAPTER FIFTY-SEVEN

MISSED SHOT COVER-UP

The FBI made 25,000 reports regarding the assassination of JFK from November 22, 1963 until September 1964, 9000 of those FBI reports were given to the Warren Commission staff. One must remember that it was the staff lawyers who did the majority of the work, not the seven members of the Warren Commission. The seven members of the Warren Commission made decisions on what to use in the report from the summaries given to them by the staff.

There is plenty of evidence that there was bickering, disagreements, and a show of temperament amongst the staff. With all of the depositions taken from witnesses, the staff had little time to fully study the 9000 FBI reports. They were also under pressure from the public, the press, and the White House to get the report out.

I only had contact with two of the Warren Commission staff lawyers. Wesley Liebler took my deposition; he was polite and made a good impression on me. I met another staff lawyer, David Belin, when we rode to the airport together after we both appeared on a talk show in New York City. I tried to make small talk with him and asked him how he happened to get on the staff. He then proceeded to tell me how important he was.

When I asked him how staff lawyer Arlen Specter arrived at the single bullet theory, that one bullet hit both President Kennedy and Governor Connally, he snapped at me in a child-like manner and said, "That was my idea and not Specter's."

And when I asked him why the Commission had ignored the missed shot that hit near me for 6 months, he glared at me, turned to look out the window, and never said another word to me on the way to the airport. He just sat there with a pout like expression on his face.

I can only assume that the staff lawyers were like everyone else; some took there job seriously and others let their ego interfere with their work. The seven Commission members and especially the staff lawyers were handicapped, because they where working under the predetermined conclusions that FBI director J. Edgar Hoover had laid out for them.

The staff lawyers, who as a whole had little investigative experience, were aware of the problem with FBI Director J. Edgar Hoover, and tried to work around it. One problem I do have is with Representative Gerald Ford, who was later to become President Ford.

Gerald Ford had kept J. Edgar Hoover informed about everything that was going on with the Warren Commission. Considering the circumstances the Warren Commission and its staff worked under, it is a miracle that we got any report at all. Was there a cover-up, yes, big time, and I go into that in another chapter.

For years I blamed the FBI for covering up the missed shot and my minor injury. It was over 40 years before I found out what had really happened. It was bureaucracy at work.

In January and February of 1964, J. Edgar Hoover of the FBI was not cooperating with the newly appointed Warren Commission. Hoover was pouting because he felt it was the FBI's job to investigate the assassination. President Johnson had a little man-to-man talk with Hoover and got that straightened out.

Chief Warren Commission Counsel Rankin had not yet gotten his newly hired staff working (they were barely doing anything, waiting for the Jack Ruby trial to be over). The December 14, 1963 FBI interview with me was actually in the 9,000 FBI Kennedy investigation documents that the FBI had turned over to the Warren Commission. The seven-member Warren Commission was trying to do a little preliminary investigation and was using the Secret Service to do their investigating while FBI Director J. Edgar Hoover sulked at being over-shadowed by the appointment of a Commission to investigate the assassination.

The December 14, 1963 FBI report on the interview with me was given to Secret Service agent Forest Sorrels to investigate. Sorrels asked other Secret Service agents if anyone knew about a missed shot, and none of the agents did. Sorrels reported back to the Warren Commission that none of the Secret Service agents knew anything about a missed shot during the assassination of President Kennedy. The FBI report with me was shelved and all but forgotten.

Twelve known witnesses had given statements or testified that they either saw the bullet hit the curb and/or saw debris fly up. It is interesting to note that when some of these witnesses tried to bring up, during their depositions, their seeing debris fly from the street from a bullet hitting the curb during the shooting, the staff lawyer's taking their deposition showed surprise and appeared unfamiliar with the fact that a shot went wild and hit the curb.

Within minutes after the assassination, Deputy Sheriff Buddy Walthers had located where the bullet hit the curb and left a scar. At 12:37 P.M., seven minutes after the assassination, it was called in by police that one man had been hit by debris from a missed shot. During the next few minutes Deputy Walthers took several of his fellow deputies to the spot and showed them where a bullet had hit the curb on the south side of Main Street.

It became instant and common knowledge among the sheriff's deputies that one bullet had missed the President during the shooting. I had been instructed to stick around so I could give a statement. In the excitement of the moment, I suddenly remembered that my car was still parked on Commerce Street. It was about 20 minutes after the shooting when I jumped in my car to move it, but traffic was now bumper to bumper with sight seers and there was no place to re-park my car, so I decided drive on down Commerce to police headquarters.

At Dallas Police Headquarters, Homicide Detective Gus Rose took my statement that afternoon. As Detective Rose was finishing my statement there was a commotion as two policemen brought a handcuffed young man into Homicide and led him into the glassed-in cubicle next to where I was sitting. I could have reached over and touched this man if there had not been glass between us. Detective Rose asked the policemen who they had and one of the policemen replied, "This is the man who killed a policeman over in Oak Cliff."

The statement I made to Detective Rose in Homicide that afternoon was never to be seen again. The next afternoon was a Saturday and Deputy Sheriff Buddy Walthers was in Dealey Plaza and ran into Tom Dillard, chief photographer for the *Dallas Morning News* and Jim Underwood, a television photographer for a local TV station. Walthers led them to where the missed shot had hit the curb and both took pictures of the point where the bullet had hit the round of the curb. The next morning, Sunday the 25th, the *Dallas Morning News* had a small article and picture of the mark, but had the location wrong.

I was interviewed by two FBI agents on December 14, 1963, three weeks after the assassination. Then silence, nothing.

Years later we learn from the forced release of FBI documents under the Freedom of Information Act, that early FBI reports on interviews with Tom Dillard, Jim Underwood, Deputy Buddy Walthers, and other Sheriff's deputies, make no mention of a missed shot.

Then on June 5, 1964, nearly 6 months after the assassination, I tell Jim Lehrer, at that time a reporter for the *Dallas Times Herald*, about the missed shot.

The fact that one shot had missed the President's limousine was now, at last, public knowledge. The FBI acted immediately and had two agents in Jim Lehrer's office by 4 p.m. that afternoon. The FBI report demonized me as someone seeking publicity and money. J. Edgar Hoover then wrote a memo to J. Lee Rankin, Chief Counsel for the Warren Commission, that the FBI knew about me all along and about my "claim" of a missed shot and that they had interviewed me in December of 1963.

When J. Lee Rankin asked Hoover to find the spot where the bullet hit the curb, Hoover reported back that there was no mark to be found on the curb. Rankin had Assistant U. S. Attorney Martha Jo Stroud in Dallas attain pictures of the curb scar from Tom Dillard and Jim Underwood. With pictures of the curb scar in hand, Rankin again asked Hoover to locate the mark. Hoover reported back for the second time that the FBI had no knowledge of a bullet hitting the curb and could not find where a bullet had hit.

We know now from a message sent to the Dallas FBI office on June 5, 1964 Hoover asked the Dallas FBI office to get the original pictures taken of the mark on the curb, yet Hoover told Rankin of the Warren Commission that the FBI was unaware of any missed shot. J. Edgar Hoover's denial of knowledge of a missed shot did not last long, but he continued to say no mark or damage could be found.

I gave my testimony to the Warren Commission on July 23, 1964. The next day, July 24, 1964, the FBI suddenly stated they had found where the missed shot bullet had hit the curb. The curb section was then cut out of the Street on August 5, 1964, more than eight months after the assassination of President John F. Kennedy.

Just before the curb section was removed from the street on that morning of August 5, 1964, FBI agent Lyndal Shaneyfelt took another picture of the curb. FBI agent Shaneyfelt's picture on August 5, 1964 plainly shows that the bullet mark had been patched over.

Since my 8mm movie film taken in early May 1964 showed where the missed shot had hit the curb, and the FBI photo taken on August 5, 1964 showed the missed shot bullet mark had been patched, one can easily conclude that the missed shot bullet mark was patched sometime between early May 1964 and August 5 1964. The last time I viewed my 8mm film of the curb showing where the missed shot hit the curb, was early June 1964.

The film disappeared from the "safe" place, where I kept it – never to be seen again.

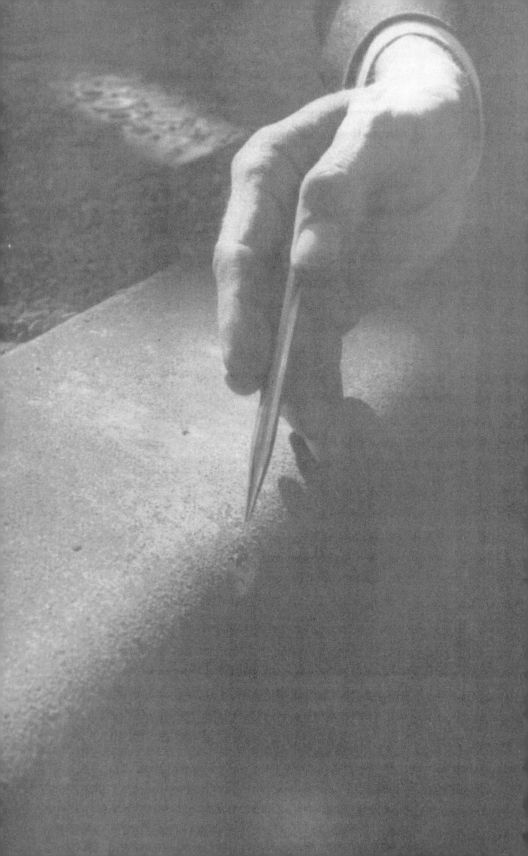

CHAPTER FIFTY-EIGHT

THE BULLET MARK ON THE CURB

In April 1997, I made arrangements to fly to Washington D. C. and visit the National Archives to view the piece of curbing that had been cut out of the street on August 5, 1964.

When I called the National Archives to see if I needed to make an appointment to view the curbing, I was told that it was no longer available for viewing. With the help of my U.S. congressman and my U.S. Senator, Kay Bailey Hutchinson's staff, an appointment was made for me to view the curb in the National Archives in Washington D.C. in April 1997. I armed myself with a high-powered magnifying glass and flew to Washington D. C.

When I arrived at the National Archives at the appointed time, an assistant manager of the Archives led me to a room where the wooden crate containing the curb section had been set out for my inspection. When the assistant manager lifted the curb section out of the crate and placed it on the table, I did not need a magnifying glass, you could plainly see the place where the bullet had hit the curb.

What had been a small gouge with some concrete dislodged, was now smooth and of a different texture from the surrounding concrete. You could plainly see with the naked eye that someone had tampered with the curb where the bullet had hit. And the half-inch by three-quarter inch area where the bullet had hit was darker that the rest of the curb. A close examination of this area revealed that it had been patched by a mortar-like substance.

Concrete has aggregate rock in it and mortar has sand in it. At the point of impact was mortar and the surrounding area was concrete. I remarked to the assistant manager: "It has been patched," and he replied, (gasped) "Yes, it sure has, I can see that."

While at the National Archives the Archive personnel went out of their way to help and assist me in every way. Without asking they gave me many documents and photographs connected with the assassination of President Kennedy. I received clear copies of the photographs that FBI agent Shaneyfelt had taken of the curb just before it was cut from the street on August 5, 1964.

FBI agent Shaneyfelt's FBI photograph C.E. 30, reveals that the mark on the curb was still visible to the naked eye, but had now been visibly patched, in August 1964, 8 months after the assassination of President Kennedy. I forgot to mention in my first book, *Truth Withheld*, that I had taken pictures of the bullet marked curb in early May 1964 with my 8 mm camera to show to my parents when I went to the Indianapolis 500 race at the end of May 1964.

The minor bullet damage to the curb had been patched between early May 1964 and August 5, 1964 when FBI agent Shaneyfelt took a photograph of the curb just before it was cut out of the street. I can only assume that the curb was actually patched after the Jim Lehrer newspaper article about me and the missed shot appeared on June 5, 1964.

That April 1997 I left the National Archives with a handfull of documents and photographs and a mind full of questions as to why someone would patch this curb section with mortar. What was the importance of doing so? It was not until 14 years later that I learned that the FBI had been asked by Warren Commission General Counsel J. Lee Rankin to find where the missed bullet had hit the curbing and FBI Director J. Edgar Hoover had responded back they could not find where a bullet had hit the curb in Dealey Plaza.

I gave my Warren Commission testimony on July 23, 1964 and the next day the FBI announced they had found the bullet mark. Documents discovered in the group of FBI documents released to Harold Weisberg in his Freedom of Information lawsuit in 1977, show that the FBI knew about the curb bullet mark all along and misled J. Lee Rankin and the Warren Commission in Hoover's replies to Rankin.

In plain English, FBI Director J. Edgar Hoover flat lied to General Counsel J. Lee Rankin and the Warren Commission about the curb bullet hit. The curb section is just an ugly piece of cement, boxed in a wooden crate and stored in the National Archives. But it is physical proof that evidence in the assassination of President Kennedy was tampered with.

As I drove my rental car to Frederick Maryland to Harold Weisberg's house, I asked myself who, what, when, why was the bullet mark patched? Harold knew about my appointment at the National Archives and was expecting me. Harold had laid out some papers for me on the table when I arrived and when he handed the sheets of paper to me; he said, "You need to read this."

The most stunning paper that Harold handed to me was a letter addressed to Ms. Sissi Maleki, Research Associate, *Readers Digest*. The letter was from an Engineering firm named Construction Environment Inc, dated March 17, 1983. Reference: Examination of a portion of concrete curb kept at the National Archives, Washington D. C.

The two-page report in summary states: "The dark spot shows visual characteristics which are significantly different from those of the surrounding concrete surface. While any one of the differences, by itself, could be easily explained in terms other than a patch, the simultaneous occurrence of those differences would amount to a rather curious coincidence of characteristics. But the existence of a surface patch would also be consistent with and explain all of the observed differences."

In short, the engineering company is saying the curb has been patched. It does go on to recommend a more through examination using techniques of microscopic petrography be conducted to gain more conclusive information regarding the cement paste, the sand grains and the surface coloration.

There is no record that the *Readers Digest* ever used the report in a story. What Harold Weisberg had been telling me for years, was true, the curb had been patched, but why? Harold and I had a long discussion about my involvement and the missed shot. We reviewed the history of this missed shot. We knew that the Warren Commission was preparing to wrap up its investigation in June 1964 when Jim Lehrer wrote the article in the *Dallas Times Herald* about the missed shot and me. We knew the missed curb shot had not been investigated and I had not been called to testify before that article appeared.

In fact there had been no investigation by the Warren Commission into the fact that one shot had completely missed the Presidential limousine and hit the curb near me. Lehrer's story did stop the Warren Commission from concluding that the first shot hit the President, the second shot hit the Governor, and the third shot hit the President in the head. Their belated investigation, of a shot that missed and hit the curb, concluded that one shot did indeed go astray and hit the curb. But it also forced the Commission to make a faulty conclusion, that one shot had hit both the President and the Governor.

Harold and I asked ourselves many questions. Until the Lehrer article came out in June 1964, was the fact that one bullet had missed its target unknown? No, it was common knowledge, witnesses had made statements in the sheriff's office that very day, about seeing the debris fly off the curb, when a bullet hit the curb and the Warren Commission had those statements.

However, when a couple of these witnesses tried to say something more about the bullet hitting the curb, they were sidetracked and ignored by the Commission staff lawyers taking their depositions. Deputy Sheriff Buddy Walthers was the first to find the scar on the curb and he had also shown several fellow deputies the bullet mark on the curb that day.

James Underwood and Tom Dillard had photographed the scar on the curb. The Sheriff's deputies and the photographers had all testified before the Warren Commission staff, before the Lehrer article appeared, but not one of them was asked about the scar on the curb, nor did they volunteer any information about a bullet hitting the curb.

The statement I had given to the Dallas Police had disappeared into thin air, but the FBI acknowledged they had the statement they took from me in my office on December 14, 1963. The FBI and at least someone on the Warren Commission staff knew about a stray bullet hitting the curb long before June 1964. So why was the scar on the curb patched, ignored? And some of the Commission lawyers acted like there was no missed shot?

It is apparent that at least one person on the Warren Commission staff, J. Lee Rankin, chief Counsel for the Warren Commission, did not know about a bullet hitting the curb. When Rankin became aware of the missed shot in June, he asked Hoover to have his FBI agents find the place where the bullet had hit the curb. When Hoover reported back that they could not find any place where a bullet had hit, Rankin gave Hoover an ultimatum to find the mark. Internally the FBI was gathering information and photos of the curb and finally stated publicly on July 24, 1964 they had located the bullet mark.

Harold and I agreed that a bullet hitting the curb during the shooting was not a secret. So we tried to look at it in another way. Some of the questions we asked ourselves were: Why was I asked, in the middle of my testimony, why I was in Dealey Plaza in May 1964 taking movie pictures? Who knew I took those pictures? Was the FBI tailing me in May for some reason? Why, and how did the innocent film I took in Dealey Plaza disappear from my home? Why did the seven Warren Commission members, in their January meeting, question the fact that Hoover was adamant about Oswald being the lone gunman, there were three shots and all three shots hit men in limousine, and there was no conspiracy?

Why had the witnesses who saw the mark on the curb on November 22, 1963 not been asked about the missed shot or spoke up about the missed shot when they testified before the Warren Commission? Why were the witnesses who saw the debris fly from the curb when the bullet hit the curb ignored? What happened to the statement that I gave at the Dallas Police station? Had the FBI not given the statement I gave to them on December 14, 1963 to the Warren Commission? What reason was there for the curb section to be patched where a bullet had hit during the shooting?

Why did the FBI fight Harold Weisberg's Freedom of Information lawsuit for years over the spectrographic analysis of the curb and then finally state in the court room that this wafer-thin film had been thrown away to make room for storage, and only do so when it looked like the Judge was going to rule in Weisberg's favor? What would this spectrographic analysis plate have revealed? Why did the FBI at first say they could not find the mark where the bullet had hit the curb, and then suddenly find the mark the day after I testified before the Warren Commission? Why did the FBI attempt to discredit me shortly after the Lehrer article?

Harold and I wrestled with these questions and others. Everything pointed to the Federal Bureau of Investigation, but why the bother? Why was covering up this missed shot so important? But, who else had the power and ability to control the outcome of the Warren Commission's investigation? And there is a massive amount of evidence that there was an attempt to cover up the fact that one shot went astray and hit the curb near me.

Harold Weisberg and I could not come up with satisfactory answers to the afore mentioned questions. We did ask a few more questions: Did J. Edgar Hoover fear that if it became public knowledge that one shot had missed, combined with all the other injuries to President Kennedy and Governor Connally, that it would prove that there was a conspiracy to kill President Kennedy? And there were more shots than the three shots heard?

OPTIONAL FORM NO.
MAY 1962 EDITION
GSA GEN. REG. NO. 27

UNITED STATES GOVERNMENT

Memorandum

TO : Mr. Belmont

FROM : A. Rosen

SUBJECT: LEE HARVEY OSWALD
IS - R - CUBA
INTERNAL SECURITY RUSSIA

DATE: June 8, 1964

1 - C. D. DeLoach
1 - W. C. Sullivan
    (R. E. Lenihan)
1 - I. W. Conrad
1 - Mr. Belmont
1 - Mr. Rosen
1 - Mr. Malley
1 - Mr. Shroder
1 - Mr. Rogge

PURPOSE

To advise the United Press International (UPI) release on 6-5-64, relating to a Dallas auto salesman who reported being hit on the cheek by a ricocheted bullet or piece of curbing is probably identical with Jim Tague, who was interviewed by our Dallas Office on 12-14-63, the results of which have been furnished to the President's Commission.

DETAILS

UPI release dated 6-5-64, relates the "Dallas Times Herald" on 6-5-64, reported an unnamed auto salesman had advised one of the three bullets fired during the assassination apparently hit a curb and he was either hit on the cheek by a ricochet or piece of concrete curb.

The UPI release indicates the salesman asked that his identity be concealed and reports the salesman was by a concrete abutment near the triple overpass adjacent to the Presidential Motorcade at the time of the assassination. The auto salesman indicated he heard three reports which he believed to be shots and on the second shot he felt a sting on his cheek. He maintains in the following confusion he forgot about it until a policeman told him his face was "bloody." The salesman states he went back to where he had been standing and saw a fresh crease mark on the curb. This incident according to the salesman was reported to a Dallas detective and later to the FBI, who were more concerned "about whether I knew Jack Ruby." The release concludes that salesman has not been contacted by the Commission.

BACKGROUND

This individual is probably identical with Mr. Jim T salesman for the Chuck Hutton Company, Dallas, who was intervi by our Dallas Office on 12-14-63. The results of this intervi

62-109090
RDR:las
(10)

REC 30

EX-114

64 JUL 13

SOVIET

Memorandum to Mr. Belmont
RE: LEE HARVEY OSWALD

appear on page 31 in the report of SA Robert P. Gemberling
dated 12-23-63, captioned as above. This report has been
furnished to the Commission.

Tague during interview furnished substantially the
same information as reported in the UPI release except it
appears he has become more dramatic and has exaggerated the
incident in an effort to obtain personal publicity or for
other unknown reasons. For example, his interview indicates
Tague reported about "two drops of blood" resulted from this
incident; however, the UPI release now indicates his face was
"bloody." Tague denied knowing Oswald but stated he had been
in Ruby's club on a few occasions and knew Ruby by sight;
however, denied knowing anything about Ruby's associations.

Based on information developed recently, it is
possible that one of the shots fired by Oswald did go wild;
however, efforts to locate the portion of curb where a possible
shot might have hit has been negative.

ACTION

Since this interview has been reported to the
Commission and the UPI release contains substantially the
same information developed by our investigation, no further
action is recommended.

-2-

Other Individuals and Organizations
Involved of Interviewed

Tague, Jim
Rackley, Virgi

AS:mln

MEMORANDUM

(1)

June 11, 1964

TO: Mr. J. Lee Rankin

FROM: Arlen Specter

If additional depositions are taken in Dallas, I suggest that Jim Tague, 2424 Inwood, Apartment 253, and Virgie Rackley, 405 Wood Street be deposed to determine the knowledge of each on where the missing bullet struck. These two witnesses were mentioned in the early FBI reports, but they have never been deposed.

FBI

Date: 6/16/64

Transmit the following in _____

(Type in plain text or code)

Via ___ AIRTEL _____ AIR MAIL _____

(Priority or Method of Mailing)

TO: DIRECTOR, FBI (105-82555)

FROM: SAC, DALLAS (100-10461) (P)

RE: LEE HARVEY OSWALD, aka.
IS - R - CUBA

Re Bureau telephone call from Inspector JAMES R.
MALLEY, 6/5/64, regarding U.P.I. news release concerning
Dallas auto salesman who had stated one of three bullets
fired during the assassination went wild, crashed into a
curb and apparently hit him; and, Dallas teletype 6/5/64,
revealing that Dallas would obtain copy of photograph from
KRLD-TV where a mark appeared on a curb and was in close
proximity to the place where auto salesman claimed he was
standing.

Enclosed for the Bureau are two 8 X 10 photographs
taken from two frames of a 16 millimeter movie film with one
photograph depicting a mark on the top edge of the curb and
the other photograph depicting the Texas School Book Depository Building located at 411 Elm Street in the background.

On June 11, 1964, JAMES UNDERWOOD, newsman,
KRLD-TV, made available the above two photographs taken by
him on the morning of November 23, 1963. UNDERWOOD stated
that immediately after the assassination of President JOHN
FITZGERALD KENNEDY on November 22, 1963, he remained in the
area of the Texas School Book Depository Building taking
movie film for his employer. He advised that a deputy
sheriff, whose name he does not recall, pointed out a spot
on the south curb of Main Street near the triple underpass
which could have possibly been made by a bullet striking
the curb.

Enc. (2)

IDL/ds
(5)

Approved: _____ Sent _____

Special Agent in Charge

237

JLR:HR:ear
r/7/6/64

cc: Mr. Rankin
    Mr. Willens
    Mr. Specter
    Mr. Redlich

Mr. J. Edgar Hoover
Director, Federal Bureau
    of Investigation
Department of Justice
Washington, D. C.

Dear Mr. Hoover:

On June 30, 1964, you forwarded to the Commission two photographs obtained by your Dallas office from James Underwood, a newsman with KRLD-TV in Dallas. Enclosed herewith is a photograph forwarded to the Commission from Martha Joe Stroud, Assistant United States Attorney in Dallas. We are also enclosing a copy of a letter from Miss Stroud indicating the conditions under which this photograph was obtained.

Since the photographs taken by Underwood purport to indicate the exact point on the curb where this nick is located, we request that your Bureau perform the following investigatory steps:

(1) Using either the model of the assassination scene or a diagram, please trace the path which a missile would have taken if it traveled from the sixth floor southeast corner window to the point on the curb indicated in these photographs, and then advise us of the approximate frame in the Zapruder film which would correspond to the point at which this missile would have passed over the President's car.

(2) We would like an analysis made of this mark on the curb to determine whether there are any lead deposits there or any other evidence upon which a conclusion can be reached as to whether this mark was caused by the striking of a bullet.

(3) Please determine whether the photograph forwarded to us by Miss Stroud is a photograph of the same curb mark represented in the Underwood photograph. We suggest that Tom Dillard of the Dallas Morning News be shown the spot on the curb from which the Underwood photograph was taken in order to determine whether the two men had photographed the same mark.

Sincerely,

J. Lee Rankin
General Counsel

PRESIDENT'S COMMISSION
ON THE
ASSASSINATION OF PRESIDENT KENNEDY

200 Maryland Ave. N.E.
Washington, D.C. 20002
Telephone 543–1400

EARL WARREN,
Chairman
RICHARD B. RUSSELL
JOHN SHERMAN COOPER
HALE BOGGS
GERALD R. FORD
JOHN J. McCLOY
ALLEN W. DULLES

J. LEE RANKIN,
General Counsel

AIR MAIL
REGISTERED
RETURN RECEIPT REQUESTED

JUL 9 1964

Mr. Jim Tague
2424 Inwood
Apartment 253
Dallas, Texas

Dear Mr. Tague:

  As you know, this Commission was established by President Johnson on November 29, 1963 to investigate and report upon the facts and circumstances relating to the assassination of our late President, John F. Kennedy, and the subsequent killing of the alleged assassin, Lee Harvey Oswald. Enclosed for your information are copies of Executive Order No. 11130 creating this Commission, Senate Resolution 137 and the Rules of Procedure of this Commission for the taking of testimony.

  Mr. Arlen Specter, a member of the Staff of the President's Commission has been authorized by the Commission to take your deposition or affidavit at the office of the United States Attorney, Dallas, Texas, on July 16, 1964 at 11:50 A.M.

  It would be helpful if upon receipt of this letter you would confirm your appearance at the hour requested by contacting Mrs. Martha Joe Stroud, Assistant U. S. Attorney, Office of the United States Attorney, Dallas, Texas.

  The Commission is authorized to pay your transportation expenses incurred as a result of your appearance before Mr. Specter.

  Thank you for your cooperation in the work of the Commission.

Sincerely,

J. Lee Rankin
General Counsel

Enclosures.

1 - Mr. Belm__   1 - Mr. Con__
1 - Mr. Rosen (Mr. Malley)   1 - Mr. Griffith
1 - Mr. Sullivan (Mr. Lenihan)   1 - Mr. Shaneyfelt
1 - Mr. Rogge

July 13, 1964

REC-15
airtel 62-109060-3659

To: SAC, Dallas (100-10461)

From: Director, FBI (105-82555)

LEE HARVEY OSWALD, aka
IS - R - CUBA

The President's Commission has requested further investigation regarding the nick in the curb along the south curb of Main Street as shown in the photographs you submitted with airtel 6/16/64. Copies of the Commission letter and the photographs you submitted are attached for your guidance. There is also attached a copy of a letter to the Commission from Assistant United States Attorney, Martha Joe Stroud, Dallas, Texas, and an accompanying photograph of a nick in the curb taken by Tom Dillard of the Dallas Morning News on 11/22/63.

You should first attempt to locate the nick in the curb and advise the Bureau whether or not you can locate it. Since the nick area, if located, will be analyzed spectrographically in the Laboratory, you are cautioned not to clean the curb area or otherwise make any alterations that would affect such a Laboratory examination. If the nick is located, you will be furnished detailed instructions regarding photographs to be made before removal of this portion of the curbing as well as instructions for removal after the pictures are made. You should determine through contact with appropriate Dallas officials whether or not there is any objection to the removal of a portion of the curbing. For the spectrographic examination, it will be necessary to have the nick and the curbing approximately four to six inches around it intact. The amount of curbing removed beyond this will be determined by the method of removal that is used in order to retain the pertinent area intact.

To locate the nick in the curb on the south side of Main Street, you should use the photograph made by Mr. Underwood taken from the nick toward the sixth floor window of the Texas School

Enclosures (5)

LLS:kw
(10)

MAILED JUL 13 1964 COMM-FBI

SHANEYFELT 7336

MAIL ROOM ☑ TELETYPE UNIT ☐

Book Depository Building (TSBDB). If you move along the south
curb of Main Street until all objects in view are aligned as
they are in the picture, that point should be within inches of the
nick in the curb providing Mr. Underwood actually made the picture
from the nick as he stated. The best guide to use initially is
the lamp post between the two buildings on the right side of the
photograph. After that is aligned, other objects can be checked
such as the sign on the left and its relation to the steps and
the TSBDB as well as the lamp posts on the north side of Elm Street
and their relation to specific areas of the TSBDB. Sutel results
of efforts to locate the nick on the curb.

The photographers, James Underwood and Tom Dillard, may
be of assistance to you in locating the nick in the curb. In this
regard, you should interview both photographers and submit letterhead
memoranda in compliance with Item 3 of the attached letter from the
Commission. For your further information, Item 1 of the Commission's
letter is being handled by the Laboratory. Item 2 will be handled
by the Laboratory depending upon whether or not the nick in the curb
can be located after which you will be furnished further instructions
relative to submission of the piece of curbing. The Laboratory will
also make a comparison of photographs to be made after the nick is
located, with photographs made by Underwood and Dillard as requested
in Item 3.

- 2 -

241

D. Mr. Shanayfole

7/23/64

Airtal.

To: SAC, Dallas (100-10461)

From: Director, FBI (105-82555)

LEE HARVEY OSWALD, aka
IS - R - CUBA

ReBuairtel 7/13/64 and urtel 7/15/64 regarding The President's Commission request for further investigation of the mark on the curb along the south curb of Main Street, as shown in the photograph submitted with airtel 6/16/64.

Your teletype 7/15 states that the mark was not found but a point along the curb was located. In order to fulfill the request of the Commission, the FBI Laboratory needs certain photographs and additional information and you are requested to do the following:

1. Obtain new prints of the photographs made by Dillard and Underwood, which photographs were described in previous correspondance, requesting that they furnish prints of the entire negative without any cropping.

2. Take a photograph of the curb, including the surrounding reference points, such as the overpass, lamp post and surrounding buildings. You should place a marker of some type at the point on the curb so that it will show in this photograph.

3. Take a photograph of the point located on the curb that will show close detail similar to the Dillard photograph but include slightly more area than the full negative prints of the Dillard and Underwood photographs. It is recommended that a tripod be used with ground-glass focusing for maximum sharpness and composition. It would also be desirable to duplicate the lighting of the Dillard photograph, if possible.

LLS:em
(6)

62-109060-4199 EBF pt

August 12, 1964

By Courier Service

Honorable J. Lee Rankin
General Counsel
The President's Commission
200 Maryland Avenue, N. E.
Washington, D. C.

Dear Mr. Rankin:

Reference is made to your letter dated July 7, 1964, requesting additional examination of the mark appearing on the curbing on the south side of Main Street near the triple underpass at the assassination site in Dallas, Texas. This mark was located and was found to be 23 feet, 4 inches from the abutment of the triple underpass. The Laboratory comparison of the mark as it now appears with the photographs made by James Underwood, a newsman for KRLD-TV in Dallas, and Tom Dillard, a photographer for the Dallas Morning News, establishes they are photographs of this same mark. Four copies of the results of the interviews with Mr. Underwood and Mr. Dillard are attached.

In response to your inquiry, assuming that a bullet shot from the sixth floor window of the Texas School Book Depository Building struck the curb on the south side of Main Street at the location of the mark described above and assuming it passed directly over the President, the bullet would have passed over the President at approximately frame 410 on the Zapruder film. This is 97 frames after the shot that struck the President in the head which is frame 313. At 18.3 frames per second, this represents a lapse of time of 5.3 seconds between frame 313 and frame 410. Based on a direct shot from the sixth floor window to the curb on Main Street, this bullet would have passed over the center of Elm Street at an elevation of about 18 feet from the street level. It is noted that in frame 410 of the Zapruder

62-109060

1 - Dallas (100-10461)

JS:emh (13)

AUG 27 1964

243

Honorable J. Lee Rankin

from the assassin's rifle, the evidence present is insufficient to establish whether it was caused by a fragment of a bullet striking the occupants of the Presidential limousine, such as the bullet that struck the President's head, or whether it is a fragment of a shot that may have missed the Presidential limousine.

This completes the request in your letter dated July 7, 1964. The piece of curbing is available in the FBI Laboratory. A photograph of the mark on the curbing before removal and a photograph of the curbing after removal are attached.

Sincerely yours,

J. Edgar Hoover

Enclosures (0)

- 3 -

Please return to Harold Weisberg via copy owner ??? ??? of Hasting, Univ Wisconsin, Stevens Point, Wisc. 54481

Dear Jim, *L ???*   2/6/78

For spectro/NAA appeal or remand. Soufce FBIHQ #105-82555-4584, the repprt of Robert P. Gemberling dated 8/5/64 covering the investigative period 6/10-7/31/64.

Having tried to ~~pretend~~ protend that there was no "missed " shot when President Kennedy was assassinated - and failed to get the Warren Commission to go along with that particular misrepresentation - the FBI then succeeded in hiding its certain knowledge that proof relating to the missed shot and its cause were forever lost.

Of the possible explanations of what happened to the curbstone on which there was a ballistics impact the more likely is that the hole (also called a nick and a scar at the time of the assassination) was simply patched.

The other alternative is that the section of curbstone was replaced. This is unlikely. It also would have attracted too much attention.

There is no FBI explanation of the shooting in any of its reports or reconstructions that mentions the missed shot of of the wounding of James T. Tague. All these formals statement by the FBI are identical.

Most shocking is the version in its supposedly definitive five-volume report ordered by LBJ before he appointed the Warren Commission. The beginning of those five volumes is a text of 88 numbered pages. (Some have letters added.) It has less than five dozen words on the crime itself.

The first chapter is of but two and a half pages. It is titled "1.THE ASSASSINATION."
                      conclusory and the other irrelevant:
It has two subheadings, one/~~xxxxxxxxxxxxxxxxxxxxxxxxxxxxxxxxxxxxxxxx~~
"A. Assassin in Building" and "B. Patrolman Tippit Killed."(As related to the ~~Tippit killing~~ assassination connecting the Tippit killing also is conclusory.)

"Assassin in Building"is of but two short paragrpahs. The second does not relate to facts of the crime. It is an unfaithful account of what unnamed and unidentified witnesses are represented as having seen.

All there is in five fancy bound volumes on the crime itself is:

"As the motorcade was travelling through downtown Dallas on Elm Street about 50 yards from west of the intersection with Houston (Exhibit 1) three shots rang out. Two bullets struck President Kennedy, and one wounded Governor Connally." (The rest of the paragraph is not on the crime: "The President, who slumped forward in the car, was rushed to Parkland Memorial Hospital, where he was pronounced dead at 1:p.m.")

Before going into the proof of my earlier work I found in the records Gesell ordered the FBI to give me I want to put this together in simpler language.

The FBI states that in all three shots were fired. Of these thre shots two struck the President and a third one struck Governor Connally.

There really is no quibble about the language because if it did not mean this the FBI would be making no other mention at all of the third short. Besides, it does not say "one of these (two) bullets also hit Governor Connally."

On the remote chances some extreme partisan might pretend it meant what it did not say I used other of these records in Post Mortem. They even calculated where the motorcade was when each of the three shots hit. There are a number of such statements. I've used them but they remain unknown because nobody else has.

(The Secret Service tried to pull the same one only its calculations different from those of the FBI by a few foot. Remember the executive session transcript on this that I used in I think WW IV - Rankin said lets split the difference.)

Gemberling's report goes into the curbstone in the synposis:"Additional investigation conducted concerning mark on curb on south side of Main Street near triple underpass..." Of this is states unequivocally what I have said:"No evidence of mark or nick is now visible." Leaving no doubt at all is the next sentence: "Photographs taken of location where mark once appeared." (I have marked this on the copy I've made for you and am sending with this. The original is unmarked.)

With attention this is a blockbuster.

Table of contents shows that pp. 27-39 are on this investigation. The last words of the entry are "and Struck JIM TAGUE."

Jim's name is mentioned one time, as the appropriate page of the index shows. (186) He is on 27. The entire page is a subhead, word-for-word the language of the table of contents. There is no other mention of Tague.

Although the FBI avoided the two Dallas photographers, Underwood and Dillard, for almost nine months, both state there was a visible mark. Their FD302s, not their words but those of FBI agents seeking to play it down, are included.

Agents Barrett and Lee state there was a mark. They were able to locate the point where it "had been." And they go on to say it is not there now, or when they did this July 1964 investigation. (But they do conjecture that rains and cleaning the streets could have work off the concrete!)

Where they talk about Dillard having two pictures they may not be lying but they are wrong. I have these two. I think we used them in deposing the retired agents and that they are in the record.

There was a third, the best. Of it Dillard told me that "the federales did not return it." Maybe this was Shaneyfelt, maybe someone before he was sent down. This is the one I used in Post Mortem.

Now there is a better explanation than the FBI's conjecture about what happened to the spectro plate on the curbstone testing. They conjectured that the lab merely threw it away to save space. Not the other plates, only this one. To save less than an eighth of an inch?

I remind you they claim the spectre detected only two of the dozen elements of a bullet with an inch of specimen to select from when microscopic quantities are adequate for the test. We still do not know of those two if they are even compatible with the results on the bulletOmetal testing.

Another provocative mystery remains: what happened to the movie film Jim Tague took in 5/64, to show his folks when he went to visit them?

Tague still does not know how the Commission knew he had taken any pictures.

But he does know that those movies showed no mark on the curbstone remaining as of 5/64.

This means that someone destroyed the absolute proof of conspiracy prior to the time he took the pictures in May 1964.

It is difficult to x avoid the suspicion that Jim was being watched. NXX Otherwise how would the FBI and the Commission, with both xx avoiding him, have known that he had taken the pictures.

Jim is uncertain of the date his pictures were stolen. When he learned it, which was after we filed the spectro/NAA suit against the FBI, he at first attributed it to some kinds.

What forced interest in Tague is the passing comment of Tom Dillard to then U.S. Attorney in Dallas Barefoot Sanders. Dillard had taken these pictures mentioned in the Gemberling report. He was xixxxi also reading accounts of the solution to the crime that made no mention of this missed shot. So he spoke of it to Sanders when they met at a social function. Sanders office, I believe Martha Joe Stroud, then wrote to Rankin. This again represented Texas knowledge Washington could no longer ignore. Thus the order to the FBI to investigate the curbstone, about early July 1964.

I believe that with this Gemberling report we have enough to go to court and demand a full investigation, with scientific testing of the visible spot to determine if the concrete mix is different. I believe that chemical analysis would have the capability of establishing it. It may be that a concrete expert alone could from the pronounced difference in color and texture. With so small a chip to obliterate it was not possible to use a normal concrete mix. There could be no coarse aggregate because one piece of it would be larger than the hole that was to be hidden. Perhaps a parging mix was used, maybe even mortar or plastering sand size rather than concrete size, which is much coarser.

I've had many calls and interruptions. I hope this is clear. If not let me know.

                                                        Best,

FEDERAL BUREAU OF INVESTIGATION

REPORTING OFFICE	OFFICE OF ORIGIN	DATE	INVESTIGATIVE PERIOD	
DALLAS	DALLAS	8/5/64	6/10-7/31/64	
TITLE OF CASE		REPORT MADE BY		TYPED BY
LEE HARVEY OSWALD, aka.		ROBERT P. GEMBERLING		ds
		CHARACTER OF CASE		
		IS - R - CUBA		

REFERENCE:
Report of SA ROBERT P. GEMBERLING, 7/2/64, at Dallas.

- P -

LEADS:

All leads in this case have been set forth by teletype or airtel and are not being restated herein.

NEW ORLEANS AND SAN ANTONIO: (INFORMATION)

One copy of this report is being furnished each of the New Orleans and San Antonio Offices for information in view of the extensive investigation conducted in those Divisions.

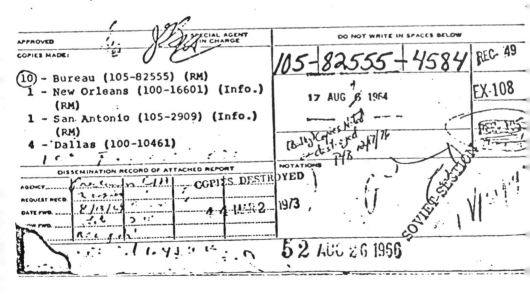

APPROVED	SPECIAL AGENT IN CHARGE	DO NOT WRITE IN SPACES BELOW

COPIES MADE:

(10) - Bureau (105-82555) (RM)
1 - New Orleans (100-16601) (Info.) (RM)
1 - San Antonio (105-2909) (Info.) (RM)
4 - Dallas (100-10461)

105-82555-4584   REC-49

17 AUG 6 1964   EX-108

DISSEMINATION RECORD OF ATTACHED REPORT

COPIES DESTROYED

NOTATIONS

AGENCY		COPIES DESTROYED
REQUEST RECD.		1973
DATE FWD.		
HOW FWD.		

52 AUG 26 1956

UNITED STATES DEPARTMENT OF JUSTICE
FEDERAL BUREAU OF INVESTIGATION

Copy to:

Report of: ROBERT P. GEMBERLING   Office: DALLAS
Date: 8/5/64

Field Office File No.: DL 100-10461   Bureau File No.: 105-82555

Title: LEE HARVEY OSWALD

Character: INTERNAL SECURITY - RUSSIA - CUBA

Synopsis:

CLOTILE WILLIAMS heard assassination shots while standing on
northwest corner of Houston and Elm Streets, Dallas, Texas,
but did not see anything that aroused her suspicion and did
not know from where the shots came. Supplemental listing of
exhibits by item number and description prepared. Additional
investigation conducted concerning mark on curb on south side
of Main Street near triple underpass, which it is alleged was
possibly caused by bullet fired during assassination. No
evidence of mark or nick on curb now visible. Photographs
taken of location where mark once appeared, together with
other photographs reflecting angle of such location in relation to the sixth floor window of the Texas School Book
Depository (TSBD) from which assassination shots fired.
Photographs also taken from inside sixth floor of TSBD southeast corner window from which assassination shots fired,
showing distance between floor and window sill and height of
opening in the window when window half open. Photographs
taken of person approximate height of OSWALD showing relative
position of window ledge and window to such person. Photographs taken at Methodist Hospital of Dallas of bone specimen
allegedly from skull of President KENNEDY obtained. Additional investigation conducted with negative results concerning claim by Mrs. EDITH WHITWORTH that she directed OSWALD
family to Irving Sports Shop, Irving, Texas, in early November
1963, which investigation consisted of interviews of certain
parents of female babies born 10/20/63, in the Irving and
Dallas, Texas, area to determine if they were the individuals

DL 100-10461

TABLE OF CONTENTS

- 1 -

250

DL 100-10461

II. INVESTIGATION RELATING TO PHYSICAL EVIDENCE AND CRIME
     SCENES

     A. Listing By Item Numbers and Description of
         Additional Exhibits

     B. Information to the Effect One Bullet Fired
         During Assassination Went Wild, Crashed Into
         a Curb, and Struck JIM TAGUE

     C. Photographs Taken From Inside The Sixth Floor
         of the Texas School Book Depository Southeast
         Corner Window From Which Assassination Shots
         Fired

     D. Photographs Taken At Methodist Hospital of
         Dallas of Bone Specimen Allegedly From Skull
         of President KENNEDY

     E. Repair Tag For Gun in Name "OSWALD" At Irving
         Sports Shop, Irving, Texas, and Alleged Visit
         By LEE HARVEY OSWALD and His Wife and Children
         to Furniture Mart of Mrs. EDITH WHITWORTH at
         Irving, Texas

9

DL 100-10461

B. Information to the Effect One Bullet Fired
During Assassination Went Wild, Crashed Into
a Curb, and Struck JIM TAGUE

67

1
DL 100-10461
RPG:vm

By letter dated July 7, 1964, the President's Commission requested additional investigation concerning an alleged mark on the curb in the vicinity of the Texas School Book Depository (TSBD), Dallas, Texas, which had been photographed by JAMES UNDERWOOD, a Newsman with KRLD-TV, Dallas, Texas. In connection with this request, the President's Commission letter made available a photograph of the curb made by TOM DILLARD of "The Dallas Morning News" which had been forwarded to the President's Commission by MARTHA JOE STROUD, Assistant United States Attorney, Dallas, Texas.

FD-302 (Rev. 1-25-59)

╰──ᴏᴇʀᴀʟ BUREAU OF INVESTIGAT╮

1

Date ___7/15/64___

JAMES UNDERWOOD, residence, 9751 Parkford Drive, Dallas, Texas, a Newsman for KRLD-TV, Dallas, was shown two photographs. One of these photographs is of a mark on the curb on the south side of Main Street near the triple under-pass and shows a hand shielding the light from this mark. The second photograph was taken looking across Main Street and up Elm Street towards the Texas School Book Depository (TSBD) Building. Mr. UNDERWOOD identified these photographs as frames taken from a 16 mm movie film, which film was taken by him on the morning of November 23, 1963. Mr. UNDERWOOD advised he had been told by a Deputy Sheriff, whose name he could not recall, that there was a mark on the curb on the south side of Main Street near the underpass, which was possi-bly made by a ricocheting bullet. The photograph of the hand shielding the mark on the curb was made by UNDERWOOD squatting down in the gutter to get a close-up view of the mark, and the picture of the TSBD Building was taken by placing the handle attached to the underneath side of UNDERWOOD's movie camera on the curb near the mark and pointing the camera back towards the TSBD Building, in order to get a low-level shot.

Mr. UNDERWOOD repeated what he had told Bureau Agents on June 11, 1964, that he could not be positive the mark was made by a richocheting bullet, but appeared to him that it could have been, based on knowledge acquired by him while in the mili-tary service. He further stated it was definitely a mark on the curb and not a nick in the curb. He repeated that the concrete was not broken and that the mark appeared to have possibly been made recently, but he could not judge how much time had passed since the mark was made when he took the photographs of it.

Mr. UNDERWOOD stated that, prior to taking the photo-graphs, he met TOM DILLARD, a Photographer for "The Dallas Morning News," near the entrance to the Dallas County Jail, and had told DILLARD about the information he had received from the Deputy Sheriff about the mark on the curb. DILLARD indi-cated he would possibly also take a still photograph of this mark.

on ___7/15/64___ at ___Dallas, Texas___ File # ___DL 100-10461___

by Special Agents ___ROBERT M. BARRETT & IVAN D. LEE___ Date dictated ___7/15/64___
eah

FD-302 (Rev. 3-3-59)

FEDERAL BUREAU OF INVESTIGATION

Date _1/15/64_

1

TOM C. DILLARD, residence, 7022 Merrilee Lane, Dallas, Texas, a Photographer for "The Dallas Morning News," advised that on the morning of November 23, 1963, while at the Dallas County Jail entrance, he had received information from JAMES UNDERWOOD, a Newsman for KRLD-TV, to the effect there was a mark on the curb on the south side of Main Street near the triple underpass. UNDERWOOD had told DILLARD that the mark was possibly made by a bullet. Later during the afternoon of November 23, 1963, DILLARD, using a Mamiyaflex 120 Camera, took a picture of a mark on the curb on the south side of Main Street about twenty feet east of the triple underpass. DILLARD stated he was of the opinion the mark very possibly could have been made by a richocheting bullet and that it had been recently made.

Mr. DILLARD was shown a photograph of a mark on the curb with a hand holding a pencil pointing towards the mark. He identified this photograph as a copy of the one he had taken on the afternoon of November 23, 1963.

Mr. DILLARD stated he definitely recalls it was a mark on the curb, rather than a nick in the curb, and the concrete was not broken or chipped.

21

on _7/15/64_ at _Dallas, Texas_ _____ File # _DL 100-10461_

by Special Agents_ROBERT M. BARRETT & IVAN D. LEE_ Date dictated _7/15/64_
eah

FD-302 (Rev. 3-3-59)

FEDERAL BUREAU OF INVESTIGATION

Date _____ 7/15/64

1

        Special Agents ROBERT M. BARRETT and IVAN D. LEE, of the Federal Bureau of Investigation, accompanied by TOM C. DILLARD, a Photographer for "The Dallas Morning News," and JAMES UNDERWOOD, a Newsman for KRLD-TV, went to the area approximately twenty feet east of the triple underpass and on the south side of Main Street. Through the use of the same camera used by Mr. UNDERWOOD on November 23, 1963, and by aligning three reference points in a photograph of the Texas School Book Depository (TSBD) Building taken by Mr. UNDERWOOD on November 23, 1963, from this same area, it was ascertained the mark observed and photographed by Mr. UNDERWOOD and Mr. DILLARD had been at a point on the curb twenty-one feet and eleven and one-half inches east of a point where Main Street passes under the triple underpass. This same point where the mark had been observed by Mr. UNDERWOOD and Mr. DILLARD was seventy-three feet and five inches west of the first lamp post on the south side of Main Street, which lamp post is the first one located east from the triple underpass on Main Street.

        The area on the curb from this point for a distance of ten feet in either direction was carefully checked and it was ascertained there was no nick in the curb in the checked area, nor was any mark observed.

        Reference points in the photograph taken by Mr. UNDERWOOD used to locate this point were a lamp post located in the right of the photograph, which appears to be midway between two buildings, a lamp post located on the north side of Elm Street, which is in line with the third row of windows from the southwest corner of the TSBD Building, and which face south, and a traffic sign located on the left side of the photograph, which is to the west of the TSBD Building.

        It should be noted that no nick or break in the concrete was observed, in the area checked, nor was there any mark similar to the one in the photographs taken by UNDERWOOD and DILLARD observed in the area checked either by Special Agents

2

on _____ 7/15/64 _____ at _____ Dallas, Texas _____ File # _____ DL 100-10461

by Special Agents ROBERT M. BARRETT & IVAN D. LEE Date dictated _____ 7/15/64
eah

2
DL 100-10461

BARRETT and LEE, nor by Mr. UNDERWOOD or Mr. DILLARD. It should
be noted that, since this mark was observed on November 23, 1963,
there have been numerous rains, which could have possibly washed
away such a mark and also that the area is cleaned by a street
cleaning machine about once a week, which would also wash away
any such mark.

33

257

FD-302 (Rev. 3-3-59) **FEDERAL BUREAU OF INVESTIGATION**

Date _____7/27/64_____

JAMES UNDERWOOD, residence, 9751 Parkford Drive, Dallas, Texas, a Newsman for KRLD-TV, Dallas, on July 23, 1964, was requested to furnish a copy of the movie film taken by him on November 23, 1963, of a mark on the curb, which was located at a point on the south side of Main Street just east of the triple underpass.

On July 24, 1964, Mr. UNDERWOOD furnished a reel of 16 mm movie film, in which the footage depicting the above-described mark is located. He stated there were other scenes taken by him on November 23, 1963, also set out in the same reel of film, but that this reel of film would show the print made from the original negative in its entirety and without any cropping.

34

on __7/23,24/64__ at _____Dallas, Texas_____ File # ___DL 100-10461___

by Special Agent __IVAN D. LEE/eah__ Date dictated __7/24/64__

FD-302 (Rev. 3-3-59)

FEDERAL BUREAU OF INVESTIGATION

Date _7/27/64_

TOM C. DILLARD, residence, 7022 Merrilee Lane, Dallas, Texas, a photographer for "The Dallas Morning News," was requested on July 23, 1964, to furnish prints of any photographs he took on November 23, 1963, of a mark on the curb, which mark was located on the south side of Main Street, just east of the triple underpass. Mr. DILLARD was requested to furnish a print of the entire negative of each photograph taken without any cropping.

On July 24, 1964, Mr. DILLARD furnished two 8" x 10" glossy prints on each of which there is a 7½" x 7 3/8" photograph. These photographs are identified on the back by the letters "A" and "B". He stated these were prints made from the entire negative, without any cropping, and were copies of two photographs he took of the mark on the curb.

From photograph "A", a blowup was made and a copy of this blowup had been previously furnished by Mr. DILLARD to an Assistant United States Attorney in Dallas. A copy of photograph "B" is differentiated from photograph "A", in that in the upper left-hand background of photograph "B", there can be seen a manhole cover.

75

on _7/23,24/64_ at _Dallas, Texas_ _____ File # _DL 100-10461_

by Special Agent _IVAN D. LEE/eah_ _____ Date dictated _7/24/64_

259

Above: The picture was taken by FBI agent Shaneyfelt of the curb just before the section was cut out of the street on August 5, 1964. This picture shows that the point of impact where a bullet had hit the curb has been patched.
Below: The curb as I saw it in April 1997 in the National Archives.

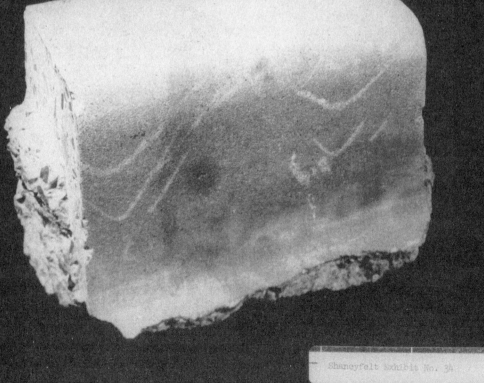

Picture taken from point where bullet hit curb with School Book Depository in background.

CONSTRUCTION ENVIRONMENT, INC.

5655-D GENERAL WASHINGTON DRIVE • ALEXANDRIA, VIRGINIA 22312 • (703) 750-0525

March 17, 1983

Ms. Sissi Maleki
Research Associate
Reader's Digest
Pleasantville, NY 10570

Reference: Examination of a portion of concrete curb kept at the
National Archives, Washington, D. C.

Dear Ms. Maleki:

On March 10, 1983, the undersigned conducted a visual examination of
a portion of concrete curb at the National Archives in Washington, D. C.
The specimen was kept in a padded wooden box and was made available
for examination by Mr. Marion Johnson of the Judicial, Fiscal and Social
Branch. The purpose of the examination was to look for external signs
which might indicate that the concrete curb had been patched.

The section of concrete curb was approximately 12 in. long and was
generally gray in color. There were several marks of higher color
along the vertical face of the curb; those marks could have been caused
by wheels of vehicles parking too close to the curb or by construction
equipment during removal of the section of curb. The scratch marks
were not considered significant relative to the purpose of the examination.

At the center of the concrete curb section, on the vertical face just
below the curbed transition between the horizontal and vertical surfaces,
there was a dark gray spot. The dark spot had fairly well-defined boundaries, so that it stood out visually from the surrounding concrete surface.
The spot was roughly ellipsoidal in shape, approximately 1/2 in. by
3/4 in. in principal dimensions.

The surfaces of the curb which would normally have been exposed in service
were visually examined with the aid of a 10X illuminated magnifier,
with special attention given to the dark spot. It is significant to
note that no other areas of any size were found anywhere on these surfaces with characteristics similar to those of the dark spot. These
characteristics are described below.

The most obvious characteristic of the dark spot was the difference
in color. The boundaries of the darker area were as well defined under
the 10X magnifier as they were to the unaided eye. It is considered
probable that the difference in color is due to the cement paste; however,
the possibility of a surface-induced stain cannot be ruled out.

Another difference was noted in the color of the sand grains. The sand
grains in the surrounding concrete surface were predominantly semi-translucent
light gray in color, but there was also a significant amount of light brown
sand grains. The dark spot contained only semi-translucent light gray
sand grains. It is possible that the difference in sand color may be
due to a different kind of concrete; i.e., a patch, existing in the
dark spot area. However, given the ratio of light gray sand grains
to light brown sand grains in the surrounding concrete surface, and
the relatively small size of the dark spot area, it is also possible
that the difference in color of sand grains may be explained in terms
of the statistical variations in the distribution of sand grains throughout the concrete mass.

The upper edge of the dark spot appeared to show marks of some sand
grains having been dislodged along the boundary between the dark spot
and the surrounding concrete area. This is consistent with the relatively
weaker zones that normally occur in the thin, or "feathered", edges
of a surface patch. Again, however, the dislodgement of sand grains
could be due to other causes.

In summary, the dark spot shows visual characteristics which are significantly different from those of the surrounding concrete surface.
While any one of the differences, by itself, could be easily explained
in terms other than a patch, the simultaneous occurrence of those differences would amount to a rather curious coincidence of characteristics.
But the existence of a surface patch would also be consistent with and
explain all of the observed differences.

While the results of this visual examination must necessarily be considered
inconclusive, it would certainly appear that further investigation is
warranted. Since the methods of investigation must be strictly non-
destructive in nature, it is recommended that a more detailed visual
examination, using techniques of microscopic petrography, be conducted to
gain more conclusive information regarding the cement paste, the sand grains
and the surface coloration.

If there are any questions with regard to this report or if we can be
of further service to you in any way, please do not hesitate to contact us.

Very truly yours,

CONSTRUCTION ENVIRONMENT, INC.

Jose I. Fernandez, P.E.
Chief Engineer

JIF/vdd

7-2

FEDERAL BUREAU OF INVESTIGATION
UNITED STATES DEPARTMENT OF JUSTICE

Laboratory Work Sheet

Re: Lee Harvey Oswald; ak
15 - R - C

File #
Lab. #

Examination requested by: J. Lee Rankin, Pres Comm.

Examination requested: Firearms

Date received: 8/5/64

Result of Examination:

Examination by: Shaneyfelt
Heilman
Frazier

Slight lead residue on curb
corner which could be bullet (lead) or
core of MC - previously mutilated -
non-positive bullet - Very little
damage to concrete

Specimens submitted for examination

Curbing Section from South
Side of Main Street

C321

CHAPTER FIFTY-NINE

A FAULTY FBI LAB REPORT

A brief summary of how a faulty lab report almost altered history: The section of curbing where a missed shot hit the street during the assassination of JFK was cut out of the street on August 5, 1964 and sent to the FBI laboratory.

On August 12, 1964, J. Edgar Hoover sent the lab report of the spectrographic analysis on the curb mark with a letter to J. Lee Rankin, Chief Counsel for the Warren Commission. The report states that traces of lead and antimony were found at the point of impact on the curb. Strangely, there is no mention that the point where the bullet hit the curb had been tampered with, or patched.

The letter reads: "The absence of copper precludes the possibility that the mark on the curbing section was made by an unmutilated military-type full-jacketed bullet such as the bullet from Governor Connally's stretcher, C1, or the bullet or bullets represented by the jacket fragments, C2 and C3, found in the presidential limousine. Further, the damage to the curbing would have been much more extensive if a rifle bullet had struck the curbing without first having struck some other object. Therefore, this mark could not have been made by the first impact of a high velocity rifle bullet."

To the Warren Commission's credit, it dismissed the implications of Hoover's letter and found that one shot did go wild and hit the street. The Warren Report states on page 117, titled CONCLUSION: "Since the preponderance of evidence indicated that three shots were fired, the Commission concluded that one shot probably missed the Presidential limousine and its occupants."

But let us analyze Hoover's FBI lab report letter in detail, for it could have had a great bearing on the outcome of the Warren Report, if Hoover had had his way.

Did Hoover not look at the Dillard photograph of the scar on the curb or read his own agent's description of the mark? The bullet had hit at the very round of the curb at the point where the side of the curb rounds into the top of the curb and it had hit at a forty-five degree angle to the street. The only thing this bullet could do was ricochet off the curbing.

At the angle the bullet hit the curb there was not a flat surface of concrete for the bullet to dig into and do major damage. The hint that it was a mutilated fragment that hit the curb will not hold water. The mark was a half-inch wide, the size a full-sized bullet would make. If it had been a fragment from a hit in the car, it would have had to come through the windshield of the car and there was no hole in the windshield of the car.

That Hoover stated there was an absence of copper in his report on the curb becomes intriguing when you go to Volume XX, page 2 of the 26-volume Warren Report and read the letter to Rankin from Hoover dated March 18, 1964, concerning the analyses of President Kennedy's shirt and tie, in part it reads: "During the course of the spectrographic examinations previously conducted of the fabric surrounding the hole in the front of the shirt, including the tie, no copper was found in excess of that present elsewhere in undamaged areas of the shirt and tie. Therefore, no copper was found which could be attributed to projectile fragments."

No copper found in the exit wounds of the President's shirt or tie? Comparing these two reports of the spectrographic examinations of the curb and President Kennedy's clothing could lead one to some wild speculation. Were there two different types of bullets used? Commission exhibit 399, was a pristine copper-jacketed bullet found at Parkland Hospital and the bullet fragments found in the President's limousine were from a copper-jacketed bullet or bullets. The bullet that came out the throat of the President was not copper jacketed and the bullet that hit the street was not copper-jacketed. Were there two guns, two shooters?

In the 1970's Harold Weisberg brought suit against the FBI to make available the spectrographic plate that was made to analyze the curb section. The FBI Attorneys fought for years against releasing this wafer-thin spectrographic plate for examination. The FBI Attorneys finally announced in court that the plate had been lost or thrown away to make room for storage. Why did the FBI go to such lengths to cover up the fact that one shot did in fact go astray and then eight months later when that fact was forced down their throat, say that it was a fragment that hit the curb because there was no trace of copper? How did the FBI lab do an examination on the "patched" over mark on the curb that sits as tampered – with evidence in the National Archives today?

What is interesting is that the spectrographic analysis of President Kennedy's clothing also showed no trace of copper. They had my statement in December 1963 about the missed shot. They had the statements taken by the Sheriff's Department the day of the assassination. They had interviewed photographers who had taken pictures of the mark on the curb. They knew I had taken pictures in Dealey Plaza in May 1964. Why were they that interested in me and what I did? Somebody patched that curb before it was cut out of the street in August 1964 – why?

Over 50 years after the assassination we have now learned that the spectrographic analysis used by the FBI laboratory in 1964 was junk science and the above-mentioned lab reports by J. Edgar Hoover's FBI were worthless.

Today, knowing that the 1960's FBI lab reports were faulty, one can only speculate on how it would have changed the Warren Report.

Robert Gemberling was the main FBI agent gathering evidence in Dallas.

CHAPTER SIXTY

FBI AGENTS?

Before November 22, 1963, I was in awe of J. Edgar Hoover, his FBI and his FBI agents. There was no question that only the best and brightest young men and women our country had to offer became FBI agents. My nephew Daniel, a young man with a law degree, was one of those who became a member of the Federal Bureau of Investigation. Daniel quit the FBI after 5 years; his years in the FBI were long after J. Edgar Hoover had died.

In a conversation I had with my nephew, his dissatisfaction with the FBI seemed to be with their old-fashioned ideas and bureaucracy. I remember Dan mentioning their filing system, it was still on index cards almost 40 years after the Kennedy assassination, and his citing the way the FBI was managed, that most of the agents were unhappy, reminded me of Dallas Special Agent Robert P. Gemberling.

FBI agent Robert Gemberling first came to my attention in an FBI memo dated 8/5/64; it was one of the many FBI documents that Harold Weisberg had received from the FBI after winning his Freedom of Information suit that he later sent to me. I believe Gemberling was the assistant FBI agent in charge of the Dallas FBI office on August 5, 1964. His memo stated that the location where the mark on the curb once appeared was no longer visible.

What is interesting to note is *that at the same time* FBI agent Shaneyfelt, this very day, August 5, 1964, is supervising a crew that is cutting the cement curb from the street, where a stray bullet had hit the curb during the assassination of President Kennedy. My first thought upon reading the 8/5/64 Gemberling memo to (name whited out), was that it was okay for the FBI to now cut the curb from the street because the mark had been patched over and was no longer visible. The further I go with my research, the more positive I am that the Gemberling memo is just what I thought, a memo to say that the mark on the curb has now been patched and no longer visible to the naked eye, so it is now safe to proceed with an FBI examination of the mark.

It was in 2003, when I received a call from Robert Gemberling, early on a Saturday morning; there was panic in his voice and he stated he needed some help from me and wanted to see me. I told Robert to come on over, he lived in north Dallas and I lived in Plano next to north Dallas. He was at my home in minutes.

Gemberling had been retired from the FBI for years and he had just turned 80, he told me he had been hired to do documentation for a new movie and wanted to know if I could identify a man in a picture that had been taken 10 minutes after President Kennedy had been assassinated.

The picture was that of a man picking up something out of the grass and putting an object in his pocket near where I had been standing when the President was killed. I told Robert that I was sorry, but I did not know who the man was. It was a picture that researchers had been speculating on for years.

Gemberling could not hide the anxiety in his voice that bordered on panic. A few days later I was talking to Mark Oakes, and Mark told me he had finally found out who the mystery man in the aforementioned picture was.

Mark's hobby was interviewing people who had been associated with the Kennedy assassination. Mark had been interviewing Robert Gemberling a few days before Gemberling's visit to my home, when Robert blurted out the name of the FBI agent who had picked up something out of the grass.

Mark said that Gemberling wanted to retract his identification of the man in the picture and was begging Mark not to use the footage Mark had taken of Gemberling telling Mark who the person was. Robert Gemberling died of cancer soon after and may have taken a secret to the grave with him. As an FBI agent under J. Edgar Hoover, keeping secrets were part of an agents life.

UNITED STATES DEPARTMENT OF JUSTICE
FEDERAL BUREAU OF INVESTIGATION

Copy to:

Report of: ROBERT P. GEMBERLING   Office: DALLAS
Date: 8/5/64

Field Office File No.: DL 100-10461   Bureau File No.: 105-82555

Title: LEE HARVEY OSWALD

Character: INTERNAL SECURITY - RUSSIA - CUBA

Synopsis:

CLOTILE WILLIAMS heard assassination shots while standing on
northwest corner of Houston and Elm Streets, Dallas, Texas,
but did not see anything that aroused her suspicion and did
not know from where the shots came. Supplemental listing of
exhibits by item number and description prepared. Additional
investigation conducted concerning mark on curb on south side
of Main Street near triple underpass, which it is alleged was
possibly caused by bullet fired during assassination. No
evidence of mark or nick on curb now visible. Photographs
taken of location where mark once appeared, together with
other photographs reflecting angle of such location in relation to the sixth floor window of the Texas School Book
Depository (TSBD) from which assassination shots fired.
Photographs also taken from inside sixth floor of TSBD southeast corner window from which assassination shots fired,
showing distance between floor and window sill and height of
opening in the window when window half open. Photographs
taken of person approximate height of OSWALD showing relative
position of window ledge and window to such person. Photographs taken at Methodist Hospital of Dallas of bone specimen
allegedly from skull of President KENNEDY obtained. Additional investigation conducted with negative results concerning claim by Mrs. EDITH WHITWORTH that she directed OSWALD
family to Irving Sports Shop, Irving, Texas, in early November
1963, which investigation consisted of interviews of certain
parents of female babies born 10/20/63, in the Irving and
Dallas, Texas, area to determine if they were the individuals

271

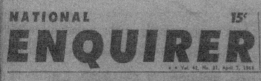

EXCLUSIVE

MAN WOUNDED IN ASSASSINATION OF JFK FINALLY TALKS

A few minutes after the shooting, while blood was still streaming from the wound in my face, I showed police the mark on a curb where a bullet or bullet fragment hit near me. (Continued in centerfold)

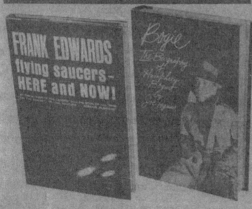

DOUBLE BOOK BONUS:

FRANK EDWARDS flying saucers— HERE and NOW!

Rock 'n' Roll Causes Serious Hearing Loss

How You Can Beat the Blues When Depression Sets In

CHAPTER SIXTY-ONE

JIMMY KERR

I was at work one day in 1968 when I got a call from a man who identified himself As Jimmy Kerr. It was now over 4 years since the assassination of President Kennedy. Kerr was a Dallas reporter with many local police and Sheriff's Office connections. I first met Jimmy in January 1968, he wanted to interview me for a story he was doing on the Kennedy Assassination. At first I turned him down. I had recently done an interview that I did not care for the way it been done and had decided not to do any more interviews.

Jimmy was persistent, he called me three or four times offering $200 for an hour of my time, and I repeatedly turned him down. Jimmy was a good talker, and I finally did formally agree to do the interview.

We did the interview, and Jimmy took notes. Jimmy also wanted a picture of me standing in Dealey Plaza at the same spot I was in at the time of the President's assassination. After the picture was taken Jimmy pulled out a piece of paper for me to sign that said he could use my interview and picture in his story. I quickly scanned the piece of paper and signed it without giving much thought to it.

A couple of months later, while at work one day, a fellow employee approached me and stated, "That is quite an article you wrote for the *National Enquirer* on the Kennedy Assassination."

I replied, "What article, I didn't write any article for the *National Enquirer*."

He said, "Well your name is on it as the author and it contains your picture."

I went straight to the nearest 7-11 and bought a copy of the *National Enquirer*, and there on the April 7, 1968 issue was a screaming headline that took up half of the front page.

MAN WOUNDED IN ASSASSINATION OF JFK FINALLY TALKS, with a sub headline: "A few minutes after the shooting, while blood was streaming down my face, I showed police the mark on the curb where a bullet or bullet fragment hit near me."

It was a five-page article, and had my picture in it along with President Kennedy's and Governor Connally's pictures. The article was full of stretched quotes and many exaggerations. The sub-headline about blood streaming down my face was a total fabrication; there was never blood streaming down my face and I had never made that statement. I only had a few drops of blood on my face from being peppered by the debris from a missed shot. The article was signed "James Tague" as if I had personally written it.

It did not take me long to put together that this was the result of the Jimmy Kerr interview. I was initially very upset with Mr. Kerr, but later became very good friends with Jimmy for many years. I found out years later that Jimmy had been paid a large fee for this story, but by then, I could laugh about it. Through the years Jimmy would call me and say, "Hey mystery man, what's going on?"

You could usually find Jimmy hanging around Sheriff Bill Decker's office, and Jimmy always had a lot of inside information about what was going on around the town; it was fun and interesting to hear his stories. One of his stories, that I believe to be true, was about him going to the Dallas Police Station the evening of the assassination and walking into the property room. The door was open and no one was there, they were all over in another section of the police station watching Oswald being paraded before reporters.

There were articles laid out on the counter that had been taken from the garage in Irving where Marina Oswald had been living with the Paines. There were also some duplicated photos lying on the counter and Jimmy helped himself to a copy of each.

Another story I believe to be true from Jimmy was about the official photographs that were taken of the sniper's nest on the sixth floor of the School Book Depository. According to Jimmy; the official photographs that we see today were not taken on Friday shortly after the assassination, but were taken on Monday, three days after the assassination. That the officials arranged the boxes and spent shell casings as they felt they would look best for the official pictures. The Warren Commission exhibits seem to confirm that Jimmy knew what he was talking about. Commission exhibits 509, 724, and 733 are supposed to be of the sniper's nest. But, they show three different versions of the boxes stacked around the sniper's nest.

CHAPTER SIXTY-TWO

JAMES TAGUE FINGERED AS MARTIN LUTHER KING'S ASSASSIN

It was not until 10 years after Martin Luther King had been assassinated in Memphis Tennessee that I learned that I had been fingered by a Memphis resident as the killer of King. The matching of my picture by a Memphis resident with a possible sketch of Kings assassin caused the FBI to investigate me, James Tague, as the assassin of Martin Luther King.

Harold Weisberg called me one evening shortly after he had won his lawsuit against the United States Government. Harold was almost laughing as he told me he was mailing me something I would get a kick out of. I kept trying to get Harold to tell me what was so funny, but he would not, saying only that he was going to mail it to me.

A few days later I received a large envelope in the mail from Harold, and enclosed were five pages of FBI reports concerning the Martin Luther King Assassination dated 4/7/68, with me named as a suspect in the King assassination. Two men, Billy Northern and Sidney Joiner, had read Jimmy Kerr's *National Enquirer* article of 4/7/68 about me at a bus station in West Memphis, Arkansas.

They saw my picture in the *National Enquirer* and determined that my picture matched a description and sketch of King's Assassin that had appeared in the *Memphis Commercial Appeal* newspaper on 4/6/68. Northern and Joiner then went to the *Commercial Appeal* newspaper office and talked to Metro Editor Angus McCarren, who called the FBI after hearing their story.

This initiated an investigation by the FBI of me, as the possible assassin of Martin Luther King. The file on me was closed in July 1968 with a hand-written notation by the FBI agent in charge, and at the bottom of the last page of the FBI memorandum "Northern is a nut." It was a little scary to find out 10 years after Martin Luther King's assassination that I was investigated as his assassin.

CHAPTER SIXTY-THREE

JIMMY KERR AND THE
TWO SHELL CASINGS

I was about 400 feet from the School Book Depository, and standing near the Triple Underpass when I heard the first shot; it sounded like the pop of a "firecracker," the next sounds, coming three or four seconds later and in rapid succession (about a second apart) were that of the crack, crack of two rifle shots and I felt something sting me in the face. Counting the pop of a "firecracker" as a shot and the crack-crack of two rifle shots, I heard three shots. Almost every witness in Dealey Plaza that day said the same thing: they heard three shots.

The "sniper's nest" on the sixth floor was found almost immediately and almost as fast, homicide Captain Will Fritz was on the scene. After visually taking in the "sniper's nest," Captain Fritz picked up the spent cartridges and put them in his pocket. A few moments later he put the spent cartridges back on the floor for the evidence gathering crew that had just arrived and later, before he went back to police headquarters, he pocketed the spent cartridges once again.

When the chaotic and scrambling media heard about a "sniper's nest" being found, and that spent cartridges had been found, the media assumed in the excitement of the moment that the three spent shell casings found at the "sniper's nest," matched the "fact" that three shots were heard.

The early reports coming out of Dallas on the wire services were of an attempted assassination of President Kennedy, it was soon changed to the President had been assassinated, Governor Connally seriously injured, three shots had been fired and three spent shell casings had been found in a "sniper's nest" on the sixth floor of the School Book Depository.

It has been verified by more than one officer present, that the head of Homicide, Captain Will Fritz, had picked up the empty shell casings from the floor and put them in his pocket, and then tossed them back down in the same area where he had found them a few minutes later for someone to take a picture.

When Captain Fritz returned to Dallas Police headquarters he put the shell casings in his desk drawer. Before the Captain had time to digest what he had seen at the School Book Depository, Lee Oswald was brought in and Captain Fritz was consumed with interviewing Oswald. That evening Captain Fritz gave the empty cartridges to Lt. J.C. Day and went back to questioning Oswald.

The Warren Report does not tell you about Captain Fritz picking up the empty shell casings and putting them in his pocket that Friday afternoon, nor does the Warren Report tell you that the official photographs of the sniper's nest and the empty shell casings were taken on Monday.

My friend, reporter Jimmy Kerr, was the one who told me about the official photographs of the sniper's nest in 1968. Jimmy also told me in 1968 that Friday afternoon after the assassination of President, there were only two empty cartridge cases found on the floor of the sniper's nest, and that a third spent cartridge was added on Monday for the official photographs. This was done to match the fact that witnesses had heard three shots, and three empty cartridge cases matched the number of shots heard.

In 1968 I did not give much thought to what Jimmy Kerr told me about Captain Fritz, that only two empty shell casings were found on Friday 11/22/63, and then three empty shell casings were laid out for the official photographs on Monday. I just shrugged it off as something of little or no importance. It had been four and a half years since the assassination of JFK and I was putting that November day behind me.

Now fast forward to 40 years later, my family is raised and my career is over, I am thinking about writing this book and I mention to my friend and Kennedy assassination researcher Phil Singer what Jimmy Kerr had told me years ago about only two spent shell casings being found on the floor of the sniper's nest.

Phil told me to take a look in J. Gary Shaw's and Larry R. Harris' book *Cover-Up* and go to the Texas Department of Public Safety (D.P.S.) evidence sheet on the Kennedy assassination. I had *Cover-Up* in my library, so I pulled the book off the shelf, opened it up, and there it was on the D.P.S. evidence sheet just as Phil had told me, half way down and right in the middle of the page, it states: "1 live round 6.5, and 6.5 spent rounds (2)."

Finally, I had verification of what Jimmy Kerr told me in 1968, *there were only two empty shell casings found in the sniper's nest*. This was explosive evidence, only two shots had been fired from the sixth-floor sniper's nest. There was at least one more shooter. Did the Warren Commission know this? Yes, read on.

What is most interesting is that this same D.P.S. evidence sheet is also Warren Commission exhibit CE2003, but in the Warren Report the (2) spent rounds has now become a distorted (3). Exhibit CE2003 is several pages long and the D.P.S. exhibit can be found on page 260 of Volume XXIV (24) of the 26-volume set of the Warren Report. Further confirmation of only two shell casings being found in the sniper's nest" can be found in Dallas Police Chief Jesse Curry's book *JFK Assassination File* on page 53. There is a picture of the window and floor of the sniper's nest with the two cartridge cases circled, the lack of a third being seen is evaded by the statement that the third casing is hidden by a box, Curry's picture is Commission exhibit 511.

The extra cartridge case, Commission Exhibit 543, that shows up in Monday's official photos has been dented in such a way it could not have been fired from a rifle in the condition it is in. Furthermore Commission Exhibit 543, the dented shell casing, does not have a chambering mark on it such as the two shell casings that were found on the floor of the sniper's nest that Friday afternoon.

Another interesting thing in studying Commission exhibits #310, 311 and 312 which are in Volume XVII (17) pages 221-223, is that the spent cartridge cases are lying in different positions in each photograph, confirming the spent cartridge cases have been moved around.

What Jimmy Kerr had told me in 1968 about the official shooting scene, being altered within three days of Kennedy's assassination, took me years to document. Once you understand that a cover-up was underway the moment JFK's blood was spilled that day in Dealey Plaza, you will start to know how simply and easily the public was fooled.

Further documentation about only two shots being fired from the Sixth Floor sniper's nest can be found in Barry Krusch's new book *Impossible: The Case Against Lee Harvey Oswald* (there are three volumes to this set). Starting in Volume one on page 250, Mr. Krusch has found Warren Commission testimony in Volume IV (4), on pages starting 254, given by Lt. Day of the Dallas Police on April 22, 1964, that three cartridge shells found and marked by Lt. Day is a lie.

Warren Commission Assistant Counsel David Belin, who had taken Lt. Day's testimony, recalled Lt. Day, and Lt. Day recanted his three shells found and admitted he only found two shells, and further he stated he did not put his initials on these two shells until 10 o'clock that evening after the shells had been in unknown hands. *Author Barry Krusch, is offering $25,000 to anyone who can successfully refute his findings.*

That only two spent cartridge cases or shells were found in what was assumed to be the sniper's nest on the sixth floor of the School Book Depository, means without any doubt whatsoever that there was a minimum of two shooters and the evidence points to even more during the assassination of President Kennedy. There are strong testimonies that there were two shooters on the sixth floor, and the second shooter was at the other end of the sixth floor, which I will cover in another chapter.

EVIDENCE

1 Italian make 6.5 rifle, serial # C 2766, blue steel, wood stock, brown
  leather sling with 4 x 18 Coated Ordinance Optics Inc. Hollywood
  California. O 10 Japan telescopic sight.

                                     Found by Dept. Sheriff Weitzman on
                                     6th floor, 411 Elm, 5' from west wall
                                     and 8' from stairway.

1 Green and brown blanket   Found by Dets. Rose, Stovall, Adamcik
                                     2515 W. 5th, Irving, Tex. taken from garage

1 .38 slug   (Taken from body of J. D. Tippit at
                                     (Methodist Hospital by Dr. Paul Moellenhoff
1 button   (at 1:30 pm. He gave them to R. A. Davenport

1 homemade paper bag resemblin gun case   Found by Johnson and Montgomery at 411 Elm
                                     and brought to Crime Lab.

1 .38 Cal pistol, 2" barrel   M. N. McDonald, DPD, took it from Oswald
                                     at 231 W. Jefferson, gave it to Sgt. Jerry
                                     Hill who gave it to Det. Baker.

Bullet fragments taken from body of   Mrs. Audrey Bell, Operating room nurse, to
Governor Connally   Bob Nolan, D.P.S., to Capt. Fritz, to Crime
                                       lab, to FBI.

Live round 6.5   (Recovered by Dept. Sheriff Luke Mooney at
                                     (411 Elm, 6th floor, southeast window.
6.5 spent rounds (2)   (

1 Man's brown sport shirt "Taken from
  Lee Harvey Oswald

1 Piece cardboard containing palm print of suspect

3 Empty cardboard boxes marked A, B, & C

1 cardboard box, empty, size: 11 3/4" x 13 x 17½" "From which thumb print
  of suspect was found"

1 Partial palm print "off underside gun barrel near end of foregrip"
  on rifle C 2766

3 Negatives of partial prints "found on trigger housing of rifle
  nor. # C 2766.

Taken from 6th floor, 411 Elm, by Lt. Day and Detective Studebaker and taken to
Crime Lab, City Hall.

Paraffin test made on Oswald, was positive on both hands and negative on face.

443A

EVIDENCE

1 Italian make 6.5 rifle, serial # C 2766, blue steel, wood stock, brown leather sling with 4 x 18 Coated Ordnance Optics Inc. Hollywood California. O 10 Japan telescopic sight.

    Carcano carbine

                                         Found by Dept. Sheriff Weitzman on 6th floor, 411 Elm, 5 ' from west wall and 8' from stairway.

1 Green and brown blanket

                                         Found by Detr. Rose, Stovall, Adamcik 2515 W. 5th, Irving, Tex. taken from garage

1 .38 slug

1 button

                                         (Taken from body of J. D. Tippit at (Methodist Hospital by Dr. Paul Moellenhoff (at 1:30 pm. He gave them to R. A. Davenport

2 homemade paper bag resembling gun case

                                         Found by Johnson and Montgomery at 411 Elm and brought to Crime Lab.

1 .38 Cal pistol, 2" barrel, S&W, Rev. sandblast finish, brown wooden handles ser.# 510210. Rel. to FBI Agent 11-22-63 and again 11-26-63

                                         M. N. McDonald, DPD, took it from Oswald at 231 W. Jefferson, gave it to Sgt. Jerry Hill who gave it to Det. Baker.

Bullet fragments taken from body of Governor Connally

                                         Mrs. Audrey Bell, Operating room nurse, to Bob Nolan, D.P.S., to Capt. Fritz, to Crime Lab, to FBI.

Live round 6.5

                                         (Recovered by Dept. Sheriff Luke Mooney at

6.5 spent rounds (3)   (411 Elm, 6th floor, southeast window.

                                         Found by Dep. Sheriff Mooney. Picked up by

1 Man's brown sport shirt "Taken from   Det. R. M. Sims. See pages L-130 and P-262. Lee Harvey Oswald

* 1 Piece cardboard containing palm print of suspect

* 3 Empty cardboard boxes marked A, B, & C

* 1 cardboard box, empty, size: 11 3/4" x 13" x 17½" "From which thumb print of suspect was found"

* 1 Partial palm print "off underside gun barrel near end of foregrip" on rifle C 2766

* 3 Negatives of partial prints "found on trigger housing of rifle nor. # C 2766.

* Taken from 6th floor, 411 Elm, by Lt. Day and Detective Studebaker and taken to Crime Lab, City Hall.

130

The second Texas Department of Public Safety (D.P.S.) Evidence report showing three spent rounds.

CHAPTER SIXTY-FOUR

MORE ABOUT THE BIG LIE

Jimmy Kerr, a Dallas reporter and friend, was the person who told me that there were only two spent bullet hulls found in the sniper's nest, not three as reported in the Warren Report. Jimmy also said the official photographs of the sniper's nest were taken on the following Monday and a third bullet hull was added, the hull that was damaged.

I have seen those Monday pictures and it shows the three hulls and one of them is flattened a little bit. In studying these official photographs that were taken three days after President Kennedy was assassinated and then reading the Warren Commission testimony of Capt. Will Fritz and Lt. Day, discrepancies appear in the photographs and the testimonies of Fritz and Day.

The first example is a photograph, Commission exhibit 482, taken by *Dallas Morning News* photographer Tom Dillard of the exterior of the Depository about the moment of the shooting. The exterior photograph, Commission Exhibit 482 shows two boxes sitting on the windowsill of the eastern most window of the sixth floor.

The photographs that Lt. Day testified to that Detective R.L. Studebaker had taken from inside the sixth floor of the sniper's nest about an hour after the shooting only show one box on the windowsill. Lt. Day testified that nothing had been moved in the sniper's nest. This testimony can be found in Volume IV(4) pages 249-251. What is obvious is that in re-creating the sniper's nest for the official photographs taken on Monday 11/25/1963, the second box that had been sitting on the windowsill, as pictured in Tom Dillard's photograph taken within seconds of the shooting from outside the School Book Depository, is now missing.

The second example is Lt. Day's Warren Commission testimony that he gave on April 2, 1964, it is found in Volume IV starting on page 249. I discovered in vol. XVII of the 26 Volume Warren Report, that on page 499, was Commission exhibit 715, a picture taken of the two spent bullet hulls.

In the background of this picture you can see through the window a crowd standing on the sidewalk on Houston Street where they had watched

281

the motorcade go by. Being able to see the crowd through the window dates the picture as being taken moments after the assassination of Kennedy and the discovery of the alleged sniper's nest. This picture only shows one box, not two boxes, sitting on the windowsill. On page 500 of Volume XVII, is Commission exhibit 716 and it is a picture taken from the opposite direction and it now shows three spent bullet hulls, but it also only shows one box, not two boxes, on the window sill.

When questioned about the discrepancy of one or two boxes by Warren Commission Attorney David Belin, Lt. Day had no explanation for the difference in the pictures. The third example is that Lt. Day at first stated that at about 1:20 P.M., 40 minutes after the assassination of JFK, he fingerprinted and marked the three spent bullet hulls with his name "Day."

Later, under close questioning by Commission lawyer David Belin, Lt. Day stated that he only marked two of the hulls and that was done at 10:00 P.M. that evening. It must be noted that if Lee Oswald had ever come to trial, the chain of possession of the bullet hulls was a nightmare that would have never been admitted in a trial.

Gary Shaw tipped me off that there was additional information to be found in Barry Krusch's new book, *Impossible: The Case Against Lee Harvey Oswald, Volume One*, published in 2012. In this book, Barry Krusch also documents by using actual Warren Commission testimony that there were only two spent shell casings found on the floor of what has been described as the sixth-floor sniper's nest in the assassination of JFK.

To sum it all up, my friend who was a witness to the discovery of the sniper's nest told me there were only two shell casings found, the Texas Department of Public Safety who also investigated the murder of JFK stated there were only two shell casings found, Lt. Day of the Dallas police department got caught misstating that he had marked three casings 40 minutes after the shooting when it was discovered he had only marked 2 casings at 10:00 that evening, the official Dallas police photographs that were supposed to have been taken right after the assassination have been found to be faulty, the next day when all the evidence was supposedly turned over to the FBI there were only two hulls in the evidence turned over to the FBI, there were matching rifle chambering marks on only two of the three spent bullet hulls claimed by the Dallas Police to have been found on the floor of the sniper's nest, and lastly a book using step-by-step details from Warren Commission testimony by Barry Krusch tells the full story of only two spent bullet hulls being found in the sniper's nest. Barry Krusch offers a $25,000 reward to anyone who can disprove that only two spent bullet hulls were found on the floor of the sniper's nest in the assassination of President Kennedy. From the solid evidence that has been developed through the years following the assassination, and most important, by using the Warren Commission's own evidence and exhibits found in the original 26 volumes of the Warren Commission, we can document that only two shots were fired through the eastern-most sixth-floor open window of the Texas School Book Depository that has been designated the sniper's nest.

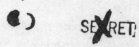

SECRET

The Federal Bureau Of Investigation

I. Early Bureau Response To The President's Assassination

    A. November 22-25, 1963

        1. Early teletypes; instructions to field;
Hoover, Sullivan, Belmont memos; 80 agents to Dallas

        2. Jenkins memo of Nov 24: Hoover says Oswald alone did
it, Bureau must "convince the public Oswald is the real
assassin."

        3. Hoover memo on Nov 26: "wrap up investigation; seems
to me we have the basic facts now" 62-109060-1490

        4. Hoover memo on Nov 29: "hope to have investigation
wrapped up by next week"

    B. Lee Harvey Oswald

        1. Establishing chain of evidence, bullet to gun, etc.

        3. Rosty note destruction: handling by Bureau on Nov 24
and effect in subsequent days

        4. Interviews of Oswald associates, Marina wiretap
Mr MARINES, ETC

    C. Jack Ruby

        1. Basic facts, early memos

        2. Hoover suspicion of basement entry and assistance

        3. extensive teletypes and reports on organized crime
connections, also Hoover's own memos

        4. contacts in 1959 as P.C.I - for use as informer
on criminal element in Dallas

REFERRAL DOCUMENT
FOI/PA # 24 326
APPEAL #
CIVIL ACT. #
E.O. # 12356
DATE 4/5/84

5-1
5-2

Referred

SECRET

Doc #1

The first page of the FBI "burn or destroy" list.

CHAPTER SIXTY-FIVE

FBI FILE CLEAN UP LIST

Kennedy researcher Harold Weisberg called the FBI's documents, on page 284 and the pages following 286, the FBI's "Burn and Destroy Lists." Neither Harold nor anyone else was supposed to see this list of the FBI's secret internal documents; they were to be withheld from Harold or to be destroyed.

The documents you see, the "burn or destroy" list, slipped out of the FBI's possession by mistake, when they were preparing to send Harold Weisberg a court ordered, over 200, 000 FBI documents. It is not known if the FBI has any of the secret documents listed.

These "secret FBI clean up our files" documents tell many stories that the public was not supposed to see. My friend Harold Weisberg had won a "Freedom of Information Act" lawsuit against the FBI to attain their documents on the Kennedy and King assassinations.

Winning this Freedom of Information lawsuit by Harold was the first crack in President Lyndon Johnson's order to seal everything pertaining to the Kennedy assassination for 75 years. Through the years as Harold found a document he thought I would be interested in, he would send it to me, and my collection of FBI files grew through the years thanks to Harold.

I find under November 22-25, 1963, item A-2, it is very interesting to see what FBI Director J. Edgar Hoover was thinking. The Jenkins memo of Nov. 24: Hoover says Oswald alone did it; Bureau must "convince the public Oswald is the real assassin."

The Dallas Police Department turned the Kennedy assassination investigation over to the FBI the night before the Jenkins memo. Kennedy was killed on Friday afternoon, November 22, the FBI took charge of the investigation Saturday night, November 23. The next morning, Sunday November 24, Jack Ruby killed Lee Harvey Oswald on TV.

It had not even been 48 hours since the assassination, and a top FBI official was distributing an internal memo where Hoover says, "We must convince pubic Oswald is the real assassin." Something is wrong here, The

FBI is supposed to investigate, not wage a campaign to convince the public of what J. Edgar Hoover wants the public to believe.

Maybe there was an investigation, because two days later Tuesday November 26, the day after President Kennedy was buried on Monday and only four days after the assassination, item A3 Hoover memo states, "Wrap up investigation; seems to me we have the basic facts now."

The C4 item on Jack Ruby is also very interesting. The FBI did not want the public or anyone else to know that Jack Ruby had been a paid FBI informer since 1959. Making public that Oswald's killer, Jack Ruby was on the FBI's payroll would have made interesting news.

On page two, there is B3: lack of communication with Domestic Intelligence? And B4 FBI official Rosen characterization of the FBI: "standing with pockets open waiting for evidence to drop in." And C3, Soviet experts handled Oswald investigation? It sure would be interesting to read all these FBI reports.

On page three: the Bureau relationship with Warren Commission 3 A1 through five. Hoover opposition? Adversary relationship? Hoover blocking Warren's Choice for General Counsel? Preparation of dossiers on staff and members.

On page 4: B2 through 9. Early friction over informant allegation? Withholding of Hosty name from Oswald notebook? *Hoover instruction to agents not to volunteer info to Warren Commission?* Destruction of Hosty note; implications? Withholding of secret "Cale report" on Bureau mistakes in earlier Oswald probe? *Hoover instruction ordering that no Bureau official attend earliest WC session, despite Katzenbach request?*

Apparent withholding of "Oswald imposter" memos of 1960-1961.

On page 4: C, 1 through 8, Sullivan relationship with Angleton: pre-arranging of answers to Commission questions? Secret plan to distribute Oswald-Marxist posters in Bureau plan to discredit Communist Party; prejudicial aspects? Hoover reaction to Warren Report? *Subsequent preparation of sex dossiers on those critical of probe.* Questions regarding FBI's continual pledge that "case will remain open for all time;" actual designation of it is "closed in internal Bureau files?"

Wow, was the FBI going to frame and discredit Oswald and Communist Party by distributing fake Marxist posters? If you are critical of the FBI they will prepare a sex dossier on you? As we read this secret list of FBI documents to be burned and destroyed, you get a sick feeling in the pit of your stomach. Is this an example of the way our Government did business back in the 1960s and the 1970s? Is this the way our Government is still doing business today, 2013, 50 years after the assassination of President Kennedy? We know the answer and the answer is yes, our Government has grown too big and it is out of control, we need to shake up and wake up America.

SE~~CR~~ET

2. Structure and Methods of the Bureau Investigation

A. Basic Organization and Jurisdiction

1. Legal basis of FBI involvement in probe, statutes,

2. Hoover and Belmont memos

3. Organization chart

B. General Investigative Division GID.

1. Rosen testimony on "ancillary nature" of probe; lack of meetings; assignment to bank robbery desk

2. Supervisors Senate testimony on physical evidence chain

3. Sullivan on lack of communication with Domestic Intelligence - the Division running the probe of LHO
LACK OF COORDINATION BETWEEN DIV 5 - 6.

4. Rosen characterization of FBI "standing with pockets open waiting for evidence to drop in"

5. Supervisors testimony on LHO not being included in G.I.D. probe other than in relation to physical evidence

6. Rosen didn't know of "Gale Report" which found deficiencies in Bureau coverage of Oswald
D=O ML INITIAL IT.

C. Domestic Intelligence Division D.I.D.   DIV. 5 ;

1. LHO background established, prior coverage

2. Sullivan testimony on chaotic process, lack of input

3. Soviet experts handled Oswald investigation

4. Secret disciplining of DID officials who handled pre-assassination investigation of Oswald

5. Incident of Sullivan's people copying GID files

6. Hosty note destruction: Sullivan lack of knowledge

7. Assignment of Ruby probe to Civil Rights Division - outside of DID jurisdiction, thus not a part of general Oswald investigation.

SE~~CR~~ET

( ) ( )

SECRET

D. Investigation of Potential Cuban Aspects

1. Cancellation of orders to contact Cuban sources on Nov 23

Referred

3. Deletion of [REDACTED] from memo provided to Commission (S-1)(5)

(S-2)(5)

4. Cuban experts and supervisors excluded from investigation

5. Church Committee findings on narrow Cuban focus

6. [REDACTED]

(S-1)(5)

E. Investigation of Potential Organized Crime Aspects

1. Hoover memos and teletypes on Ruby connections

2. Ruby phone records

3. Justice Dept. interest in probing O.C. aspects

4. Chicago interviews with Ruby associates

5. Evans and Staffeld (and Denahy and Stanley) statements on not being consulted

6. Use of Ruby as informant on Dallas criminal element

7. LCN sources available at time

3. Bureau Relationship With Warren Commission

A. Formation of Warren Commission

1. Hoover opposition: memo and Jenkins memo

2. Katzenbach testimony and Sullivan statement

3. Early memos - adversary relationship

4. Hoover blocking Warren's choice for general counsel

5. Preparation of dossiers on staff and members.

 SECRET

SECRET

B. Assistance To Warren Commission

1. Basic scope of official relationship

2. Early friction over informant allegation (LHO)

3. Withholding of Hosty name from Oswald notebook

4. Hoover instructions to agents not to volunteer info. to WC

5. Destruction of Hosty note: implications

6. Withholding of secret "Gale Report" on Bureau mistakes in earlier Oswald probe; disciplining of officials

7. Hoover instructions ordering that no Bureau official attend earliest WC session, despite Katzenbach request

8. Delay in sending information to Commission regarding Bureau's past nine contacts with Ruby

9. Apparent withholding of "oswald imposter" memos of 1960-1961

Referred ███████████████████████████████

11. Handling of Ruby polygraph

C. Related Bureau Actions and Activities

SEPT. 24 '64

1. Preparation of dossiers on WC staff after the Report was out

2. Hoover's leaking of early FBI report (Sullivan statement)

3. Hoover views on Communism and Oswald (Kronheim letter)

4. Sullivan relationship with Angleton: pre-arranging of answers to Commission questions.

5. Secret plan to distribute Oswald-Marxist posters in Bureau plan to discredit Communist Party; prejudicial aspects

6. Hoover reaction to Warren Report

7. Subsequent preparation of sex dossiers on critics of probe

8. Questions regarding FBI's continual pledge that "case will remain open for all time;" actual designation of it as "closed in internal Bureau files.

SECRET

This picture was taken inside the Late Chevrolet showroom in the early 1980s. The showroom would hold up to forty cars. There was a seperate building and showroom for trucks. Mr Late was an oil man and when he built the dealership he used hard steel oil drilling pipe to hold up the roof over the showroom. As you can see there are stairs to the right in the picture, the stairs lead up to an extra 10,000 square feet of office space for over forty corporations Frank Late owned.

CHAPTER SIXTY-SIX

LESSONS FROM
A BILLIONAIRE OIL MAN

To help you understand some knowledge gained, I must include the lessons learned in the most interesting years of my life. Those years were spent working directly under and answering only to billionaire oilman Frank Late.

Frank Late owned several corporations and these corporations employed a total of over 10,000 employees. To show their respect, everyone called Frank Mr. Late, even his closest and most powerful friends. The years with Mr. Late were a lesson in money and power, and a good look at his Texas oilmen friends.

Mr. Late was a self made man, at the age of 20 he borrowed $5,000 from his dad, fibbed to General Motors that he was 21, and bought a hole-in-the-wall Chevrolet dealership in Claremore, Oklahoma. It was in the depression, and it was just he and a mechanic – a two-man dealership.

By his everyday actions and demeanor, you would never know Frank Late was a billionaire, a successful businessman maybe, but not one of the richest men in America. In the mid 1970s, I was a sales manager for a Chevrolet dealership in Dallas. Our general manager was not feeling well and our dealership owner was out of town, and I was asked to represent our dealership at a big advertising kick-off meeting for all the Dallas County Chevrolet dealerships (13) to sponsor the Dallas Cowboys football team for the coming season.

At this meeting we had all had a few drinks and I was in a small group of Chevrolet dealers with this Frank Late doing the talking about how hard it was to find good managers. I had never met Frank before, but had heard he was a tough man to work for. While listening to Late talk about the disappointing managers he hired and fired, the drinks in me spoke up and said, "I have heard you were a tough SOB to work for."

It was obvious to the Chevrolet dealers standing there that you did not talk to Frank Late that way. Mr. Late cornered me for several minutes and gave me a friendly talking to. I never said a word, just listened. Mr. Late's final words to me were: "If you ever need a job, you come and see me." Under the circumstances, I did not give his parting words much of a thought. The word spread around town with a chuckle about me, a lowly sales manager, talking back to Frank Late, the richest man in town, but it was soon forgotten.

A couple years later, I had become unhappy with what was going on at the dealership I worked for, and had quit in disgust. As I was sitting at home one day trying to decide what I wanted and needed to do, I recalled Late's words about seeing him if I ever needed job. I had not thought much about these last words to me, other than it had come from some drinking words. I started to brush it off, it was a Friday afternoon, but with nothing better to do, I called his dealership and asked for Mr. Late; the call went right through.

I started the conversation by saying, "You probably do not remember me but you told me a couple of years ago that if I ever needed a job to come and see you."

Mr. Late replied, "You are either the man who carried me home one night when I had too much to drink, or the man who told me off at a Chevrolet dealer meeting."

I replied that I was not the one that drove him home one night and Mr. Late told me to get right to his dealership now. As I drove to his dealership, Late Chevrolet in Richardson Texas, a suburb of Dallas, I was thinking to myself and wondering why I was going to see this old man who had such a bad reputation for hiring and firing managers.

I was soon in Late's splendid office and listening to him talk about the oil and drilling business for two hours; my skills and abilities were never mentioned. It was soon after 5 P.M. when his secretary reminded him of somewhere he needed to be. He asked his secretary for an employment application, which he gave to me and told me to get the application back to him.

As I drove home I was puzzled, Mr. Late had not asked me one question about my background or knowledge of the automobile business. When I got home I dropped the employment application on the dining room table and forgot about it until I received a phone call Monday morning from a Les C., who said he was General Manager of Late Chevrolet, and that I was supposed to have an employment application for him.

He was sarcastic in stating he would like to meet new employee's before they went to work. I quickly filled out the application and met GM Les C. for lunch. At lunch Les asked, "What position do you want, you can have any one but mine." I was very uncomfortable as I asked, what position are you needing filled? We soon decided that I would be the new truck sales manager, and I was to come in the next day at 10 A.M., giving Les time to fire the present new truck sales manager.

Late Chevrolet was a very large dealership in every way. The new car showroom would hold 40 cars and the separate new truck show room would hold eight trucks. I had eight truck salesmen and it did not take a day for me to discover I was not one of GM Les C's team members; he had been ordered to hire me.

It was a tough situation; Mr. Late would call me into his office and ask me to do some things that the GM should do. It bounced along like that for about three months, then one day when Mr. Late was out of town and the GM Les C. called me into his office and stammered around until I finally asked him: "Les, are you wanting to firing me?"

He stammered, "Yes." I went to my office and told my assistant sales manager what was going on and to hold the fort down, that I was going home. When I got home, my wife met me at the door and said, "What is going on? Mr. Late's secretary just called and said for you to get back to work in the morning."

The next morning I went to work to find out that Les was gone and that I was now the general manager and was told I was to have a dual job of GM and new truck sales manager. My salesmen had become energized by me, their sales manager, being an ex-sales manager myself, and wehad been setting new truck sales records: Mr. Late liked that.

In the main dealership building we had an extra 10,000 square feet of office space on the second floor of the dealership for some of Mr. Late's other companys' headquarters. The Chevrolet dealership fit in as just a hobby.

Mr. Late had always owned one or more Chevy dealerships since buying his first dealership during the 1930's depression. One of his largest corporations was his Coca Cola bottling operations. His plants were bottling over 15% of all the Coca Cola in the United States. His Coca Cola business had also started back in the 1930s in Claremore, Oklahoma when he bought the town's small bottling plant.

Back then every town in America of any size had a Coca Cola bottling franchise. Coca Cola liked Mr. Late as an operator, and every time a local bottling plant came up for sale, Coke made sure Frank Late wound up with it.

For example, by the 1960's he owned all of Oklahoma and Kansas and built one huge plant to serve each state, Mr. Late stated more than once that the Oklahoma bottling plant had a bad year if it did not net 15 million dollars after taxes. When I worked for him, all of Late's 42 Corporations were paid for, he did not owe a dime to anyone, and he had not given out any credit information (Dunn & Bradstreet) on his net worth since the 1930s.

You never saw him listed as one of the United States richest men. I was working in a dream world.

As an example of what it was like: one time a few days before Christmas I was walking by Mr. Late's office and he called me into the office and joking said, "I want you to meet this wetback, Roberto," and he introduced me to a man of obvious Spanish decent, and we chatted for a few minutes and then I excused myself. Later that afternoon after the man had left I asked Mr. Late who the man was and Mr. Late said that he was Roberto Goizueta, President of Coca Cola Bottling Co.

It was constantly like that, people of prominence, CEOs, company presidents, oil tycoons, most of these men were like that, down to earth and just like the guy next door. Another of Mr. Late's hobbies was his Granite Hills Hereford ranch, a 38,000-acre ranch down by Llano Texas; the ranch bred some of the finest Hereford cattle in the world and shipped bull semen all over the world. He kept his prize bull "Grand Slam" out in front of the ranch headquarters; Mr. Late paid $250,000 for this bull. Grand Slam is now buried on the Ranch with a 6-foot high head stone.

At the edge of his ranch, Mr. Late had a huge lodge. The lodge served a dual purpose, a place for rich cattle and sperm buyers to stay while they observed ranch operations, and a place for many his business friends to stay while they went deer hunting on the ranch. The lodge was on Lake LBJ around the bend from Lyndon and Ladybird Johnson's lake home.

Frank Late was a Republican but he had one Democratic acquaintance, Lyndon Johnson. Keith Calvert had a favorite story about Frank Late and President Johnson. Keith was Vice President of Mr. Late's Cactus Drilling Company (Mr. Late sold Cactus Drilling in 1980 for $124,000,000).

A story that Keith told over and over was about what he had witnessed one night when President Johnson came to visit Mr. Late at the lodge. The event happened before I went to work for Mr. Late. As Keith told it everyone was there already, and had had a drink or two or more before President

Johnson arrived. Lyndon's favorite drink was put in his hand upon arrival and everyone was joking around. President Johnson was wearing his $500 Stetson western hat, and Mr. Late told him that he should not be wearing his hat inside and reached over and took the President's $500 Stetson off and tossed it on the end table and everyone chuckled.

A couple of minutes later Lyndon picked up his Stetson and put it back on. A few minutes after that Mr. Late noticed that Lyndon had put his Stetson back on and repeated yanking the President's Stetson off with the warning, "Damn it Lyndon, you do not wear your hat inside the house."

According to Keith there was a tense chuckle this time and the Secret Service Agents were at attention. The drinks were flowing freely. Lyndon put his Stetson back on and soon, Mr. Late yanked his $500 Stetson off for the third time. This time Frank Late tossed President Johnson's expensive $500 Stetson on the floor and stomped on it until it was flat and then said, "Let's see you wear that damn hat in the house now Lyndon?" Keith said that even President Johnson had to laugh at Mr. Late's antics.

One of my favorite things to do was going to the ranch with Mr. Late. My relationship with Frank Late went beyond friendship; it was more like a father-son relationship. My telling Mr. Late he was a tough SOB to work for at the Chevrolet Dealer meeting had hit a chord. All he wanted was honesty from me. Mr. Late knew and accepted that sometimes mistakes were made by a manager who made dozens of decisions every day. If you did screw up, just admit it, correct it, and go on; that is what made our relationship work.

The importance of my working with and for Frank Late did not dawn on me until years later when I started putting the true facts together about the assassination of President Kennedy. Frank Late would never have been involved in any way with such a plot to kill someone. Mr. Late was probably the most honest man I had ever known in my life. But learning about the power, the men he knew in the oil and drilling business, and learning about these men, gave me an insight from a different view that no one else close to the assassination possessed.

Man grazed by JFK bullet spreading gospel of cover-up

Author tells story to Longview Public Library audience

BY MAGGIE SOUZA
msouza@longview-news.com

In the hours after John F. Kennedy was assassinated, James T. Tague went down to the Dallas police station to give a statement of what he had seen.

Speaking Tuesday night to a group of about 20 people at the Longview Public Library, Tague once again recounted the afternoon: Late for a date, he had gotten out of his car to find out why traffic had stopped. He soon realized it was because of the president's motorcade.

As Tague watched the procession make its way down the street, he heard what sounded like a firecracker go off, followed by rifle shots. The next thing he knew, a man standing on the grassy knoll nearby yelled out, "His head exploded! His head exploded!"

Kennedy had been shot.

Caught up in the commotion, it took Tague a moment to realize that his face had been grazed by shrapnel after a bullet struck the curb near where he was standing.

See AUTHOR, Page 4A

Maggie Souza/News-Journal Photo

James Tague was grazed by a bullet near where President Kennedy was assassinated in Dallas. Tague wrote a book on what he believes was a government cover-up. He spoke Tuesday at the Longview Public Library.

296

CHAPTER SIXTY-SEVEN

MY HEALTH & A DECISION

Since my discharge from the Air Force, I had lived around Dallas for nearly 50 years, with 30 of those years in the Dallas suburb of Plano. But I was born and raised on a farm and getting tired of the city traffic in Plano.

I had bought a house in Plano when it was 15,000 people and now it was over 275,000 people. I had been looking for a couple of years in East Texas and finally bought a place with a few acres four miles south of Pittsburg, Texas. I added two bedrooms and a small library to the house and soon found I had a house-full with three of my children, a daughter in-law, plus two grand children living there.

I had a 30 x 40-foot steel work shop to spend idle time in, a separate garage, a 150-foot dog run for our two German Shepherds and two small dogs. I even built a heated doghouse for the dogs. There were over twenty-five large sassafras trees in a grove in the backyard to keep the area shaded. I called it my retirement ranch.

I had many Kennedy researchers, writers, and media people make the two-hour drive from Dallas and visit the "ranch," even had a couple of documentaries made there. I guess my favorite was George Michael Evica who wrote a couple of very serious scholarly books in regards to the Kennedy Assassination, *And We Are All Mortal* and *A Certain Arrogance,* and his delightful wife, Alycia. They brought a filming crew with them from New York. The girls prepared a feast for lunch and we all had a wonderful time. Professor Evica died shortly after the visit; I do not think anything was ever done with the filming we did that day.

I had been toying with writing another book, a book that would tell the true story about the assassination of President John F. Kennedy, what and who was behind the assassination, the corruption, the greed and the planning. I had not gone looking for the story; it had come to me, little bit by little bit, the pieces had been dropped in my lap.

I am one of those people who save everything and I had made notes starting from the evening of the day I had witnessed President Kennedy murdered in front of my eyes in Dealey Plaza.

Then one morning in 2008, I woke up with my ankles so swollen I could not put my shoes on and my entire body was broken out in a rash. I thought I had caught some children's disease. My daughter drove me to a doctor. The doctor ordered me to take a blood test and sent me home. At 7:30 A.M. the next morning the phone rang and it was my doctor. He stated they were waiting for me in the emergency room at the hospital in Tyler Texas 50 miles away, right now, do not bother to shave or shower.

My daughter drove me to the hospital and an hour and a half later I was on dialysis. My kidneys had failed me and my body had started to shut down. I fully expected to make a full recovery; this was surely just a minor thing for a healthy man.

I soon found out that you do not recover from kidney failure, it is permanent, and for me to live would mean dialysis for the rest of my life.

I was assigned to a dialysis clinic three days a week for four hours each day. During the four hours I sat hooked up to the machine, my blood would be removed from my body and cleaned of impurities by the machine; the machine did the work of my kidneys. The clinic was like a factory with kidney dialysis machines lined up in a row and nurses hooking up and unhooking patients three shifts a day, starting at 4 o'clock in the morning.

You have a lot of time to think about your life with the misery you are feeling for four hours three times a week while on dialysis. Dialysis saps your energy, when you drive to the clinic, the time it takes to hook up to the machine, the four hours of dialysis, unhooking from the machine, driving back home, is a full day lost in your life. I was ready to give up on any thoughts of writing a new book that would name names, when a friend asked if I would speak to the Historical Society in Longview, Texas about the John F. Kennedy assassination.

I spoke to the Historical Society at the Longview public library on the evening of October 7, 2008 to a crowd of about 50 people. The lady who had organized this speaking engagement for me had also invited a reporter from the *Longview News-Journal* daily newspaper. I spoke briefly about being a witness and then went into detail about what I had learned about who was behind the assassination of John F. Kennedy and the cover-up.

When I finished there was silence, no reaction from the audience, and the thought raced through my mind, there was no interest in what I had to say: "The public is not ready for the cold hard truth." The silence hurt for a moment, and as I started to leave the podium the audience stood in unison and gave me the longest applause I could remember, and I was soon surrounded by the audience asking questions.

The next morning my phone started ringing with calls from people from all over the country: they were asking questions about the speaking engagement in Longview, and what I had said. The story had been printed in local newspapers across the country. The reporter who had heard me speak about who was behind the assassination of President Kennedy and the cover-up, had put my story on the wire services nationwide. I drove into town and bought a copy of the October 8, 2008 Longview newspaper, there was the story on the front page, with the headline: MAN GRAZED BY JFK BULLET SPREADING GOSPEL OF COVER-UP. And to my surprise my picture was on the front page along with the two 2008 presidential candidates, John McCain and Barack Obama.

One thing about being a kidney patient and being on dialysis is that the medical doctors and nurses coddle you. Your urine and blood are checked every few days and your diet is adjusted accordingly. I had read and checked every thing I could find about kidney failure; recovery was so rare it was not worth thinking about. Getting a kidney transplant did not happen to a man in his 70's, and kidney dialysis was something I was going to have to accept as part of my life until the day I died.

I regard myself as a God-fearing man who has tried to live an honest and decent life. As an adult I did not attend church. I had been brought up going to church as a child and had continued into my mid-twenties. To this day I always say a prayer for my family and their welfare, a thank you God for their safety, a couple times a week: it is something I have done for years and not a big deal.

Then it happened – I was having my normal monthly check-up for January 2010 and I could hardly believe what I was hearing. The doctor was telling me my kidneys were now working again and he was taking me off dialysis. That was January 16, 2010. My kidney doctor guessed that the odds of a person's kidneys recovering from failure are more than 10,000 to one.

As I left the doctors office and in the days that followed, I thought about all that had happened in my life, especially my being in Dealey Plaza at that exact moment when President Kennedy was killed, my minor injury during the shooting, the inside information that had just fell into my lap through the years about the assassination, and now my recovery from kidney failure.

The thought hit me and did not go away, God wants the American people and the world to know the truth and I am to be the messenger. No, I was not a being born again Christian; I just had this overwhelming feeling that the American people and the world had to know the truth.

Chapter Sixty-Eight

Jackie Kennedy – Her Thoughts?

I think it was in 2010 that Caroline Kennedy Schlossberg, Jackie and John F. Kennedy's daughter, announced she was going to publish some of her mother's writings. One of the statements Caroline made in her press release was that her mother, Jackie Kennedy Onassis, thought Texas oil money was behind the assassination of her husband President John F. Kennedy.

Jackie was partially right when you consider that Lyndon Johnson's main backers were Texas oilmen and the military-industrial complex. President Kennedy was going to ask Congress to do away with the oil depletion allowance and Texas had a big interest in the military aircraft industry.

I do not have the time (years) it would take to unravel all the unsavory dealings and politics of big Texas oil money that were connected to the assassination of President Kennedy. I had worked for several years directly under billionaire oilman, Frank Late of Late Oil Company and Cactus Drilling Company.

Frank Late was as honest as any man you would find, and had absolutely nothing to do with Kennedy's killing. My boss' favorite activity was the weekly Dallas Petroleum Club meetings. Working in this big-money environment gave me an insight into these men in how they thought and acted. Most were humble and just like everyday people.

This is another chapter that I am writing for present and future Kennedy assassination researchers to connect the loose dots. Connecting the dots was one of the problems the Warren Commission lawyers ran into. When they discovered something that needed further investigation, they were told to ignore it, that is not what we are here for, we are here to close the case against Lee Harvey Oswald. Many of the lawyers quit.

A little bit of information I was able to verify was about David Harold Byrd, better known as D.H. Byrd, an oil man and also a business man in the military-industrial complex in Texas. D.H. Byrd was a close friend of politicians: Sam Rayburn, who ran the U.S. House of Representatives,

Lyndon Johnson, who ran the U.S. Senate, and John Connally, Governor of Texas. If D.H. Byrd needed a favor from one of these powerful men, it was as easy as you or I asking to borrow our neighbor's lawn mower.

What I found most interesting was D.H. Byrd's close friendship with Lyndon Johnson and D.H. Byrd being the co-founder of LTV. When Mac Wallace was given a 5-year suspended sentence for the first degree murder of John Kinser in Austin, Texas, Mac Wallace walked out of the court room and went to work for Byrd's LTV. Mac Wallace had killed Kinser for Lyndon Johnson. Johnson thought Kinser was going to cause a scandal over Johnson stealing the 1948 U.S. Senate election.

Mac Wallace continued working for Byrd at LTV with special privileges, like extended leaves from work, and no security clearance. Mac Wallace was one of the assassins, probably the main shooter from the Texas School Book Depository in the assassination of President John F. Kennedy. *D.H. Byrd owned the Texas School Book Depository.*

Some of the richest and most active men with big concerns over the oil depletion allowance were Clint Murchison Sr., H.L. Hunt and Sid Richardson. Murchison and Hunt were part of a closed-door meeting with Johnson and J. Edgar Hoover at the Murchison Estate in north Dallas the night before Kennedy was killed.

Another of the dots that need to be connected is the Suite 8F Group, named after a room that these rich and powerful met at in the Lamar Hotel in Houston, Texas. Most meetings were to coordinate political activities. When talking about Suite 8F, Jack Ruby's name pops up as handling and placing the big wagers for these men. There have also been many rumors about the General Dynamics, 6.5 billion dollar TFX scandal.

John F. Kennedy was aware of the political corruption that now had deep roots in our country, political corruption that dated back into 1930s. John F. Kennedy had set a goal for himself as President, to rid our country from this corruption, but if President Kennedy had lived, he would have been facing possible blackmail over his affair with Judith Exner.

Ms. Exner's apartment had been bugged and she was sleeping with both President Kennedy and Chicago mobster Sam Giancana. Judith Exner finally talked years later and wrote a fascinating book, *My Story,* about her affair with Kennedy. Sam Giancana's daughter, Antoinette, wrote a book, *JFK and Sam,* about her father. (Antoinette mentions me and the missed shot on page 182 of her book and kindly sent me an autographed copy).

CHAPTER SIXTY-NINE

50 YEARS OF CHANGE & NEW INFORMATION?

In 1963 I did not think about or realize how the world was going to change in the next 50 years. I had just recently been honorably discharged from the Air Force after five years of service and had settled into my first real non-military employment selling new cars.

At that time, you could go to a cafeteria down the street for lunch and get all you could eat, including dessert, for a dollar, a McDonald's Big Mac was 15 cents, gas was 19 cents a gallon, a six-pack of beer was $1.00, cigarettes 25 cents a pack, and after work you could pull into the gas station next door, get 10 gallons of gas, a six pack of beer, and a pack of cigarettes, give the attendant a $5.00 bill and get change back. You could rent a nice one bedroom apartment, fully furnished with all bills paid for $100 a month. You could live a decent single life in Dallas, Texas for $500 a month.

Lucille Ball, Ed Sullivan and the Beverly Hillbillies dominated our black and white TV sets; it would be years before we would have cell phones, Facebook and the Internet. In January 1963 we had three advisors killed in Viet Nam. Our space program was just getting off the ground, integration was coming into focus, Alfred Hitchcock's *The Birds* was the shock movie of the year, Harvard Professor Timothy Leary was dismissed from Harvard for using the drug LSD, Willie Mays signed a $100,000 contract to play baseball, *Playboy* magazine showed Jayne Mansfield nude from the waist up, women wore dresses to work, Martin Luther King made his famous "I Have A Dream" speech, discount stores were something new, and The Beatles gave a Royal Performance in England.

Our President John F. Kennedy, his wife Jackie and their children made headlines on everything they were involved in; they were in the news daily, on every magazine cover. They had become the United States royal family, loved and admired by a nation of Republicans, Democrats and Independents alike.

Then at 12:30 P.M. Central Standard time on November 22, 1963, it ended, the world changed. John Kennedy was assassinated right in front of my eyes here in my beloved Dallas, Texas. This laid back and serene Texas city had becomen in an instant, a city of hate. I could not believe what I was reading in the newspapers about the hate this country had for Dallas because of what one lone nut named Lee Harvey Oswald had done.

It finally sank in one day when I stopped into a filling station in St. Louis Missouri. As I got out of my car to open the gas cap, the attendant was looking at my Texas license plate and said, "You need to find another filling station, and we do not serve cars from a state full of hate."

I can still look back at that very moment, November 22, 1963, at Dealey Plaza in Dallas Texas and still see in my mind President John Kennedy's limousine coming down Elm Street directly toward me and hearing the pop of what sounded like a firecracker.

It was actually the first shot that was to be the start of a change in America and the world. Make no mistake about it, no matter what history may claim, the assassination of John F. Kennedy changed America and the world.

As the days, months and years came and went I did not let my being in Dealey Plaza that day affect my personal life. I had a family to raise and a career to follow and they came first in my life.

I did keep up with what was new and thanks to my wife, she saved my notes and items of interest and I think I knew in the back of my mind, that I would write this book some day. I am proud that I did not allow myself to be influenced by some of the junk being said and written about the assassination of JFK.

CHAPTER SEVENTY

TOO SIMPLE NOT TO SOLVE

I did not realize it for years, but the Kennedy assassination was too simple to not solve. But the government had their bureaucratic way of doing business and had to make it look like there had been a superb and thorough investigation into the death of our President.

The cover-up appears to have been planned well ahead of time and began within an hour of the pronouncement of JFK's death. The FBI was monitoring the news coming out of Dallas that afternoon. Nothing was supposed to be allowed that would suggest there was more than one shooter.

What happened to *Dallas Times Herald* reporter Connie Kritzberg is a good example. She had interviewed two Parkland Hospital doctors, who had attended to the President, and they had told her how the back of the President's head had been blown out. The *Times Herald* was an evening paper and the last edition for the day had been published when Connie turned her story into her editor.

The *Times Herald* put the Kritzberg story on the wire services that evening, November 22, 1963. The next day, Connie read her story in the *Times Herald* and the fact that the back of Kennedy's head had been blown out had been deleted. Connie called her editor and asked him why, and he told her: "You need to ask the FBI about that."

It has taken me years to accept that so much information about the assassination has just been dumped in my lap. I did not go looking for the information, it came to me. In the nearly 50 years since President Kennedy was killed, I had not gone looking for details of the assassination. What I am presenting in this book is first-hand information. I still find it hard to accept that I was a witness, and what I have learned about the killing of Kennedy.

That day, President Kennedy's Dallas visit was the last thing on my mind; I was headed downtown to take a cute red-head to lunch when I was stopped in traffic, as my car was about to emerge from the triple underpass.

I stepped out of my car to see why traffic was stopped, walked three or four steps into the open to see what was going on, and there was a car

305

rounding the corner across Dealey Plaza from me with flags on the front fenders. Then it dawned on me, I had read where the President was going to visit Dallas, and this was the President's motorcade.

Then the gunshots rang out and something stung me in the face, I had been hit by debris from a missed shot, it was minor. There was one small item in Sunday's paper about an inch by two inches in size about the possibility of a missed shot, then nothing until the next June when the Warren Commission announced they were winding up their investigation.

They said three shots had hit in the car, Kennedy, Connally, Kennedy, but nothing about the missed shot. Later, I was at work and an employee of the *Times Herald* that I had sold a car to, had his car in for service and was waiting for it to be finished. We struck up a conversation about the latest news from the Warren Commission and I told him about my being stopped in traffic, the missed shot and my minor injury. He said they had a young reporter with the *Times Herald* that needed to hear what I had to say.

The next thing I knew a guy from the Dallas paper named Jim Lehrer was there wanting to interview me. I told him what had happened, it was put on the wire services and history was changed forever.

Connally was now hit by the same bullet as Kennedy and we had a "magic" bullet and a missed shot. Then came a call one evening from a Harold Weisberg and a 30-year friendship full of inside information is established.

For those that do not know, up until his death, Harold was respected as the most knowledgeable person alive about the assassination of JFK. Harold was the person who originally filed under the Freedom of Information act and got the Kennedy and King FBI documents released. I joined Harold in one of his suits. Harold sent me key FBI documents of interest. And one by one I met three of Lyndon Johnson's closest friends, all by accident. Then I was reading a Kennedy article one day and discover that one of the actual shooters of President Kennedy was himself killed a mile down the road from where I now lived in east Texas, 3 miles south of Pittsburg, Texas.

I am not a writer, never claimed to be, but I found out something when I wrote my first book, *Truth Withheld* ten years ago. At first in trying to write that book, I made several false starts by referring to how professional authors wrote, then by accident I discovered something: the truth was easy to write, there was nothing to make up, just tell the truth and the truth *is* the story.

CHAPTER SEVENTY-ONE

ANOTHER LOOK

Through the years I had studied many books and opinions. There many were doubts about what really happened to bring about John Kennedy's assassination; I did not close the door on the possibilities. But there were some very credible thoughts that I needed to clarify in my mind.

There were the claims that more than one person had been seen on the sixth floor at the time of the shooting. The "wild" tale Madeleine Brown had told me. What Billie Sol Estes had told me. What Jimmy Kerr had told me. What Barr McClellan had said. What Harold Weisberg had told me. What Ed Hoffman had to say. LBJ's attorney Edward Clark's involvement. The Malcolm Wallace killings. Who J. Edgar Hoover really was. The constant rumors/facts that Lyndon Johnson was involved in the assassination of JFK. What Gaylon Ross had told me. The unknown fingerprint on a sixth-floor box. My reviews of witness testimony in the 26-volume Warren Report.

In short, I needed to go back to that day in November 1963, make a chart and add or eliminate what could be found to be true or false and keep an open mind.

CHAPTER SEVENTY-TWO

USCA

USCA is short for United States House Select Committee on Assassinations. Continued fault finding of the Warren Commission and the King assassination findings brought public pressure on our government to re-open the investigation into the assassination of President John F. Kennedy, the Martin Luther King assassination and the Governor George Wallace shooting. There had been hundreds of books and magazine articles printed since 1963 critical of the Warren Commission. The Hart-Schweiker and Church Committees had turned up problems with the CIA being involved with other assassinations. The Abraham Zapruder film had it first public airing on TV in March 1975. It was made public that the CIA had teamed up with Organized Crime in a plot to assassinate Cuban leader Fidel Castro. The public was demanding answers.

The USCA was formed in 1976 with authorization coming from the House of Representatives with a vote of 280 to 65 for the investigation and G. Robert Blakey was named Chief Counsel. In looking back, the big problem the USCA had was holding its meetings in secret and that it sealed much of its secret evidence for 50 years.

The USCA concluded that the Soviet Union, Cuba, Organized crime (mob), and the anti-Castro Cuban's had nothing to do with the assassination of JFK. The USCA found fault with the FBI, CIA, DOJ for withholding information from the Warren Commission. Both Lee Harvey Oswald and James Earl Ray were confirmed as shooters of JFK and MLK. The USCA did conclude that President Kennedy was killed as a result of a conspiracy and that there were at least two shooters and four shots fired in the assassination of John F. Kennedy.

The USCA evidence shows that by August 1978 all FBI files on me, James Tague, the missed shot, and the curb where the missed shot hit the street were asked for from the FBI, but I was never called to testify before the USCA.

The USCA used acoustics from an old Dallas Police Department dictabelt to determine the number of shots and from where the shots came,. In 2001 the acoustics were found to be faulty by a government scientist, but the fourth shot was found to be a fact.

It is now well known that the FBI and the CIA did not cooperate with the committee. In fact in 2003 Chief Counsel for the USCA, G. Robert Blakey issued a statement that he could no longer believe anything the CIA had provided to the USCA investigation. At first Blakey had relied on Special CIA liaison George Joannides as a go-between for the CIA and USCA. Blakey trusted Joannides to be honest with him only to find out later that Joannides and Lee Harvey Oswald had worked together on CIA operations involving the anti-Castro groups before the Kennedy assassination. *The sad part is that by 2003 the general public was no longer interested in finding out that Lee Harvey Oswald had connections to the CIA.*

CHAPTER SEVENTY-THREE

THE THREE TRAMPS

The mysterious three tramps that were infamously pictured being marched off to jail after they were apprehended in a boxcar in the railyard adjacent to the School Book Depository, is a perfect example of all the misleading information that has been publicized about the assassination of President Kennedy.

When one looks closely at one of the tramps, he has a new haircut, shave, and freshly shined shoes. Suspicious until you learn that he had spent the night in a homeless shelter and before he checked out of the shelter, they gave him a shave, haircut, and shoe shine. There have been thousands of words written about these three men. Their arrest records were thought to be non-existent, hidden, or destroyed.

There were authors who tried to connect the tramps to assassination of the President. Some even said one of the tramps looked like Watergate burglar E. Howard Hunt. Others thought one of the tramps looked like Watergate burglar Frank Sturgis. And still others thought one of the tramps looked like Charles Harrelson, actor Woody Harrelson's father, who was later convicted of murdering a Federal Judge.

The House Select Committee on Assassinations in 1979 spent a lot of time and money trying to identify who these three men really were. The three tramps played a role in the murder of John F. Kennedy in Oliver Stone's early 90's movie *JFK*. Author after author and others have, for year after year, made these three tramps out to be infamous and sinister figures in the assassination of John F. Kennedy.

The showing of Oliver Stone's movie *JFK* in the early 1990s made Dallas City officials uneasy about Dallas' image and they ordered all of the city's police files on the assassination of President Kennedy released to the public. In January 1992 researchers searched through these newly released files only to find hardly anything new.

One of the researchers was Mary La Fontaine who was doing research for a new book she and her husband were planning to write. As she looked through these newly-released police files she noticed a second set of police files that had been released a couple of years earlier.

One of the first things she noticed in the second set of police files was a folder marked: "Arrest sheets on persons arrested 11-22-63." The first 3 sheets in the file were for the 3 tramps arrested for vagrancy in the railroad yard behind the School Book Depository.

According to the arrest records the three tramps were Harold Doyle, Gus Abrams, and John Forrester Gedney. Records show that the FBI had also interviewed these men and they had been cleared of any involvement in the assassination of JFK.

In that 11-22-63 arrest file there were three more arrest sheets and an arrest sheet for a fourth tramp arrested in the railyard behind the School Book Depository that day, he was 31 year-old John Elrod. These three (or four) tramps were just that – three or four tramps.

The fact that Mary La Fountaine had discovered the arrest records of these four tramps made the news and as normal for the media to do, caused Mary La Fountaine to be labeled a "conspiracy theorist." By 1992 anyone who gave an opinion on anything to do with the assassination that was not in the Warren Report was labeled a "conspiracy theorist," which was a code name for conspiracy "nut."

Today nearly 50 years later if you say or write something other than what the Warren Commission wrote in their report there are still those who will call you a "conspiracy nut" no matter how much documentation you present. I fully expect that label to be put on my book and me by these same people before they ever read a word in my book.

Now here is the problem with the above: the three tramps who were photographed were not the only men rounded up that day in the vicinity of the railyard beside the school book depository.

There were at least 12 to 15 or more men brought to the sheriff's office for questioning that could have been labeled "tramps." In the confusion of that afternoon, not every man's name was recorded before they were released as not having a part in the assassination of JFK. Dallas police Sargent David V. Harkness brought in six to eight men who could have been labeled hobos or tramps, but none of the ones Sgt. Harkness arrested are the tramps in the famous "three tramps photos."

Other police officers brought in other men that afternoon that could be called "tramps" because of the work clothes they were wearing. There were poor and/ or no records kept that day during the excitement of the moment. I have only brought up the three tramps story because it is an example of the blind alleys and misinformation that has blocked our country and the world from knowing the full truth about the assassination of President John F. Kennedy for 50 years.

CHAPTER SEVENTY-FOUR

CONNIE KRITZBERG
& THE COVER-UP

For many years after the assassination of President Kennedy, there were cries of a cover-up regarding the assassination. Those thoughts of cover-up were dismissed by most as just an idle thought. But there was a nagging feeling that something was just not right about the Warren Report.

It did not take much of an investigation to verify that there was indeed a cover-up involving the assassination. Once I discovered what was behind the cover-up, who was involved in the cover-up, and why there was a cover-up, the long sought answers soon came pouring forth one right after another.

The murder and cover-up of President John F. Kennedy's assassination had been planned out to the last small detail over a period of two years. The cover-up was already waiting for Kennedy when the first shot was fired in Dealey Plaza at 12:30 P.M. November 22, 1963, and it was fully in force before his brain tissue and pieces of skull bone hit the street. Carefully selected FBI agents at FBI headquarters in Washington D.C. were sitting in front of their wire service terminals ready to monitor all the news of President Kennedy's trip to Texas.

Connie Kritzberg, a reporter for the old *Dallas Times Herald*, was one of the first reporters to interview Mary Moorman and Jean Hill that fateful day. These women had been standing side by side in Dealey Plaza when the President was shot just a few feet from where they were standing, however they gave opposing eyewitness views of what they had heard and witnessed. But they did agree that they both thought they had heard four to six gunshots.

At about 3:30 P.M., Connie's editor asked her to interview the Parkland Hospital doctors who had worked on President Kennedy in the emergency room. Malcolm Kilduff, Assistant Press Secretary to the President, had announced the President's death earlier, but Parkland officials were not sure whether the local press had been present and allowed Kritzberg to do an interview by phone with Drs. Malcolm Perry and Kemp Clark.

The doctors had just gone through a lot of stress, but answered Connie's questions without hesitation or qualification. Part of what she wrote: "One of the things that Dr. Perry stated there was an entrance wound in the front of the neck below the Adam's apple and either an exit wound or tangential entrance wound in the back of the President's head. Dr. Clark described the back of the head wound as a large gaping wound with considerable loss of tissue. Dr. Clark said the main wound was on the right rear side of the head."

Later, Kritzberg read her Moorman and Hill story in the *Dallas Times Herald* and then started to read her Parkland Doctors story. The story as she had written it had been changed. The first change Connie noticed was in the third paragraph, and not written by Connie: "A doctor admitted that it was possible there was only one wound." Connie jumped up and phoned the city desk and asked where that sentence had come from in her Parkland Doctors story.

Connie's editor answered matter-of-factly, you need to ask, "The FBI about that." Connie Kritzberg's Parkland Doctors story had been put on the wire services immediately after being turned in. The FBI, within minutes of the President being pronounced dead, was monitoring in the FBI Headquarters in Washington D.C. the wire services of the assassination stories coming out of Dallas. A cover-up was in place with the FBI controlling as much of the assassination news as they could, as soon as they could. Every last detail of the murder had been planned out to the smallest detail.

CHAPTER SEVENTY-FIVE

THE JOHNSON SENATE YEARS

When Lyndon Johnson was sworn in as a United States Senator, he was soon nicknamed "Landslide Lyndon." Senator Johnson had but one goal, and that was to be President. His every action was to help him attain that goal, and in the 50's, he became the leader of the Senate. He took care of his political allies, the big money Texas oilmen and the big money that backed his elections. Rumors followed him, but no big scandal such as the stealing of the election in 1948. The killing of his sister Josefa's boyfriend John Kinser in 1951 had taken care of one possible leak, and the killing of Kinser had gotten Lyndon's sister Josefa's attention: she was now watching what she said.

That all changed in 1959 when Senator Johnson announce he was running for President. The announcement for President brought the spotlight on Johnson. *Time* magazine mentioned "suspicious votes" and the "notorious box 13." *Look* magazine mentioned "fraud" in reference to his first Senate election in 1948, and so it went. Senator Johnson's character came under intense attack by the media, his reputation for honesty and integrity was questioned. But a strange thing happened – the public paid no attention.

It was not until 1977, 29 years after Johnson had stolen the 1948 Senate election and was now dead, that Luis "Indio" Salas admitted in an interview with reporter James W. Mangan of the Associated Press, that he had lied about box 13. Salas told Mangan how he had been summoned to George Parr's office (The Duke of Duval) three days after the election (in 1948 it took a few days to hand count votes in Texas in 1948) where others were gathered including Lyndon Johnson and told to manufacture 200 more votes for Lyndon Johnson, to put him ahead of his opponent Coke Stevenson.

There were 200 names in alphabetical order from the poll tax sheet certified by Luis Salas and added to the box 13 vote for Lyndon Johnson, and Lyndon won the election by 87 votes. In March 1986 Robert Caro located an aged Luis Salas in Houston living in a nice mobile home with his wife Tana. The home was well kept, had a nice yard and belonged to Mr. Salas daughter Grace. Robert Caro was asking questions for a book he was writing about former President Lyndon Johnson.

In the middle of the questioning Luis produced a rough draft of a book, 80 typed pages and nine handwritten pages, he had written about the box 13 affair. When Mr. Caro asked Luis why he had written it all down, Luis replied number one was to "show the corruption in politics." Luis went on to say that if a vote was for Stevenson, he would change it to a vote for Johnson. The second reason was for his children to know the true story of box 13, that he had lied under oath and it had led to a man becoming President.

Luis Salas allowed Robert Caro to go to a stationery store and make a copy of Luis's writing for Mr. Caro to use in his book *The Years Of Lyndon Johnson, Means Of Ascent*. Robert Caro interviewed some of the names in Luis Salas' writing that were still alive and they confirmed as true what Salas had stated about Lyndon Johnson stealing the 1948 Senate election.

When he first became a U.S. Senator, Lyndon would introduced himself as "Landslide Lyndon."

CHAPTER SEVENTY-SIX

VICE PRESIDENT JOHNSON

The 1960 Democratic Convention was held in Los Angeles California. There were twelve candidates running for President at this Democratic National Convention. The top two candidates were both sitting senators, John F. Kennedy and Lyndon Johnson. The main Democratic platform was for the loosening of tight money and to end high interest rates; also on the platform was national defense, civil rights, immigration, foreign aid, and tax reform.

Robert F. Kennedy led a highly efficient Kennedy campaign and John Kennedy was nominated,. None of the other candidates could match the Kennedy campaign. However it was not a clean win, as dirt was thrown back and forth. The surprise of the convention was Kennedy asking Lyndon Johnson to be his running mate as Vice President. Despite being a powerful Senate leader, Johnson accepted to run as Kennedy's running mate, a demotion in power for Johnson.

Insider information told me that mega-rich oilman, H.L. Hunt and John F. Kennedy's father, Joe Kennedy, made the deal for Johnson to be on the ticket. John Kennedy wanted someone else to be his running mate, but Joe Kennedy overruled his son.

Robert Kennedy had tried to dissuade Lyndon Johnson from accepting the nomination to be Kennedy's running mate; this meeting caused extremely bitter feelings between RFK and LBJ. In a close race between Richard Nixon on the Republican ticket and Kennedy on the Democratic ticket, Kennedy won the 1960 election.

In 1960 votes were counted by hand and could still be bought in some parts of the country. Nixon felt that Kennedy had stolen the election. It was a close election, but Nixon could not say anything – his people had bought some fake votes also. Lyndon Johnson, while a Senator and giving out insider information made some of his friends rich and richer, with Bobby Baker, Billie Sol Estes, topping the list. Lyndon's sister Josefa had become a major liability with her alcohol addiction, prostitution rumors, and loose lips.

CHAPTER SEVENTY-SEVEN

PRESIDENT LYNDON JOHNSON

In Ronald Kessler's book, *In The Presidents Secret Service*, the author interviewed Secret Service sources who were in charge of protecting President Johnson. It is a close look at Johnson's presidency, and what went on behind closed doors and sometimes in public.

One of the Secret Service agents is quoted as saying: "If he (LBJ) wasn't president, he'd be in a mental hospital." Lyndon Johnson was out of control, he was often drunk and he had a stable of secretaries that he would have sex with while he was President.

One time, his wife, Lady Bird Johnson, caught him with one of the secretaries in the Oval Office. After that LBJ set up a system to warn him when Lady Bird was around. The Secret Service agents reported that Lyndon Johnson would spend hours in the President's cabin on Air Force One with one of these secretaries. This crazy behavior had started long before LBJ became President.

LBJ, it appears, was bi-polar with a psychopathic personality and was an alcoholic. While he was Vice President, one of his secretaries was Mary Margaret Wiley who also worked in his Austin Texas office. The story goes that Mary Wiley became pregnant in 1962 and Vice President Johnson convinced one of his loyal aides and confidant, Jack Valenti, to marry Ms. Wiley to make the child legitimate.

Mary Wiley and Jack Valenti were married on June 1, 1962. Linda Courtney Valenti was the child born of this pregnancy. To everyones surprise, this "shotgun marriage" stuck until Jack Valenti's death in April 2007.

As Linda was growing up, she had special favor from President Johnson and was often seen in the White House, Lyndon treated Linda better than his own two daughters he had with Lady Bird. It is interesting to note that after leaving LBJ's employ, Jack Valenti became President of the Motion Picture Association in California and held that position for 38 years.

As an adult, Linda Courtney Valenti is aware of who her biological father is (LBJ). As I write this story, Linda Valenti is Vice President of Production for Warner Brothers in Hollywood. She is in charge of production on a new movie to be released in 2013 named, "Legacy of Secrecy."

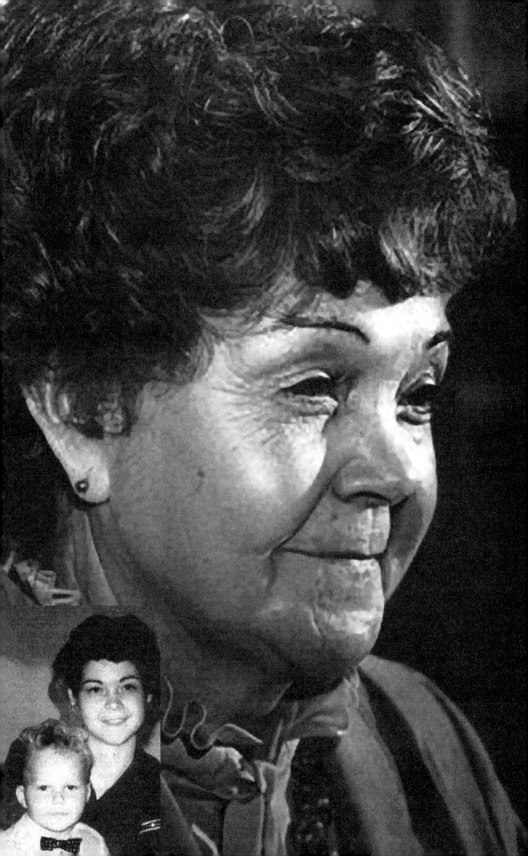

Chapter Seventy-Eight

The Mistress, the KGB and Me

I believe it was 1988 and I was on a plane from Dallas to New York. I had been asked to be on another TV talk show and was sitting beside another witness who was also going to the same TV program. We exchanged our nice to meet yous and a short conversation when she said, "You need to talk to Madeleine Brown, Lyndon Johnson's mistress, she is also on this plane, let me trade seats with her."

A moment later a lady sat down next to me and introduced herself as Madeleine Brown. Ms. Brown was a pleasant woman in her sixties at that time. I had read about her and her son in the paper connecting them to President Johnson, but that was all I knew. I mostly listened as to what she had to say about ex-President Lyndon Johnson; it was hard to grasp what she said: Lyndon Johnson knew before the assassination that President Kennedy was going to be killed and the others involved.

She related that Lyndon had had a few too many drinks on New Year's Eve 1964, and he confirmed to her what the inside facts were about the killing of President Kennedy: what really happened. My mind was racing, but was she telling the truth?

At that time it had been 25 years since the Kennedy assassination and I had learned not to believe everything I had read or heard about what people had to say about the Kennedy assassination. But I have always been open minded, and I was about to leave Madeleine Brown's chat at that. As we approached New York City for a landing, Madeleine pulled her billfold out of her purse and showed me a picture of her son Steven Mark Brown, who she said was hers and Lyndon Johnson's son. I was stunned when I looked at the picture, her son, Steven Mark Brown, was the exact image of Lyndon Johnson.

That day was hectic, and I was invited to spend the night in New York City in a nice hotel at the TV shows expense, but I had turned the invitation down as I had an appointment in Denver, Colorado the next day, and another appointment in Louisville, Kentucky the day after that.

I did not have the time to dwell on what Madeleine had told me about Lyndon Johnson being involved in the killing of John Kennedy. I was now in my fifties and unemployed, finding out that highly skilled well paid new car dealer general managers my age were being replaced by younger men at half the salary.

I had two nice homes (one was rented out), with mortgages on both homes and had a lot more on my mind than what Madeleine had related to me about Lyndon Johnson.

During the early 1990s I had not spent much time thinking about the Kennedy assassination. I had become a single parent and that was my number one job. I was still in constant contact with Harold Weisberg, and we had a point we disagreed on.

At the turn of the century (2000) I was being urged to write a book and tell my story about what really happened in my experience. I would start to write, look up how others wrote, and tear up what I had written. This went on for a couple of years, then one day I just started writing in my own words and wrote, *Truth Withheld, Why We Will Never Know the Truth About the JFK Assassination*. I self-published the book in time for it to come out on the 40th anniversary of the Kennedy assassination. It was a success and is still selling nearly 10 years later as I write this new book.

Then, I believe it was in early 2004, and unplanned, I met Billie Sol Estes for the second time, who was another insider friend of Lyndon Johnson. This time we were able to have a serious talk, with me mostly listening to what Billie Sol Estes had to say. It was 15 years after I had first talked to Madeleine Brown. Billie Sol Estes verified exactly what Madeleine Brown had said about Lyndon Johnson's involvement in the Kennedy assassination. It got my attention big-time.

Then I came in contact with a Mr. X, he is still alive, as I write this book and in his 80's. Mr. X is and was a friend of both Madeleine Brown and Billie Sol Estes, and he verified what both Madeleine Brown and Billie Sol Estes had told me about Johnson's involvement in the Kennedy assassination.

Now, with this additional inside information, it was all falling into place, why Kennedy was killed, who was behind having Kennedy killed, who actually pulled the trigger, who handled the cover-up, how easy the cover-up was.

So after years of documenting and assembling the facts of JFK's assassination and as this book was being readied to go to a publisher. I was in Dealey Plaza finishing up an interview for the coming 50th anniversary of the assassination. A man walked up to me and said his name was

Casper and that he understood I was writing a new book on the Kennedy assassination.

When I told him yes I was, Casper handed me a large envelope and said, "You might want to use this." I thanked Casper and put the envelope in my car. When I got home I opened the envelope and found several JFK assassination documents. A copy of a letter from the Defense Intelligence Agency caught my eye. The subject was a translated copy of the Russian KGB's investigation of President Kennedy's assassination.

The 1965, nineteen page, 81 paragraph, Soviet Intelligent Report was enclosed with the letter. As I read it I was stunned, the KGB had come to the same conclusion in 1965 that it had taken me nearly 50 years to come to: Lyndon Johnson was behind the assassination of John F. Kennedy.

The KGB Intelligent Report is next, then later a United States Marshall is going to blow the whistle, then I will take you person by person, step by step, to the long sought answers about President John F. Kennedy's assassination.

CHAPTER SEVENTY-NINE

KGB AND THE SOVIET UNION

Within 24 hours after the assassination of President Kennedy, one of the first accused of the assassination was the Soviet Union and their intelligence agency, the KGB. History now tells us that blaming Russia and the KGB, as being behind the assassination of President Kennedy was far from the truth, in fact the Soviet Union had great respect for John F. Kennedy and admired him as president of the United States.

To give you an example of how the USSR felt about President Kennedy, the Russians broadcast country wide President Kennedy's June 10, 1963 peace speech at American University. Airing a U.S. President's speech was something the Russians were not known to do. The Premier of the Soviet Union, Nikita Khrushchev, openly cried upon hearing of Kennedy's death. The Russians were very aware that some Americans were going to be quick to blame the USSR, and that blame had to be cut off. It could lead to war with the United States, they reacted accordingly the day of the assassination.

The assassination was quickly blamed on Lee Harvey Oswald and his murder live on television just 46 hours after President Kennedy's assassination stopped the accusations against the Soviet Union. Nikolai T. Fedorenko, who was the permanent Representative of the Soviet Mission to the United Nations in New York City, on Nov. 27th, called a meeting of the diplomatic personnel who were on duty at the Soviet Mission in New York and advised that Kennedy's death was officially regretted by the Soviet Union, and that it was a shock to the Soviet government. He further stated that Russia preferred to have President Kennedy leading the United States and that Kennedy had a mutual understanding with Russia. He also stated that the Soviet Union had no knowledge of who Lyndon Johnson was or what his policies might be.

The KGB was assigned to find out who this new U.S. President Lyndon Johnson was and how Johnson thought. The KGB's assignment was two-fold, finding out about Lyndon Johnson, how he thought, and finding out who was behind the assassination of President John F. Kennedy.

Colonel Boris Ivanov was chief of the Soviet Committee for State Security (KGB) and resided in New York with United Nations Mission group. Colonel Ivanov felt that the assassination of Kennedy was done by a well organized group rather than being the act of "a lone nut assassin." Colonel Ivanov stated to his personnel that it was important to act with speed to find out what group or groups were behind Kennedy's assassination and get the true facts.

By September 16, 1965, the Soviet KGB had concluded that Lyndon Johnson was responsible for the Kennedy assassination. Four decades later, buried in our National Archives, a memo was discovered that was from J. Edgar Hoover to President Johnson, dated 12/1/66, the memo from Hoover states:

"On September 16, 1965, this same source reported the KGB Residency in New York City received instructions approximately September 16, 1965 from KGB headquarters in Moscow to develop all possible information concerning President Lyndon Johnson's character, background, personal friends, family, and from which quarters he derives his support in his position as President of the United States. Our source added that in the instructions from Moscow, it was indicated that the KGB was *now* in possession of data purporting to indicate President Johnson was responsible for the assassination of the late President John F. Kennedy.

"KGB headquarters indicated that in view of this information, it was necessary for the Soviet Government to know the existing relationship between President Johnson and the Kennedy family, particularly between President Johnson and Robert and 'Ted" Kennedy.'"

There you have it, history now tells us the Kennedy assassination was solved, not by our own FBI or our own CIA, or any other United States law enforcement agency, but by the Russians and their KGB.

Lyndon Johnson and his buddy, FBI Director J. Edgar Hoover had been made aware that, as of December 1, 1966, the Soviet Union and the KGB knew that he, President Lyndon Johnson, was the man behind the killing of President Kennedy.

Immediately after the assassination Johnson was telling everyone that it was an international conspiracy, and to his confidants that it was Fidel Castro who had President Kennedy killed. To his mistress, Madeleine Brown and his Chief of Staff, Marvin Watson, Johnson said: the CIA had murdered President Kennedy.

During the last couple of years of Lyndon Johnson's Presidency his approval rating dropped to 38% and both his physical and mental health was deteriorating. He was distressed, and alcohol had become a big problem. One of the Secret Service agents who was a Presidential guard for President Johnson stated: "If he was not the President, they would have him locked up in a mental institution." The full *Soviet Intelligent Report* translated into English is the next chapter.

20 April 1978

SUBJECT: Soviet Intelligent Report on Assassination of President KENNEDY

TO: Director

The following report has been prepared at your request in response to a
Soviet report on the assassination of President John F. KENNEDY on 22 Nov 1963.
The Soviet document (see Enclosure a) has been obtained from a fully reliable
source and duly authenticated.

This report is an analysis of the Soviet document and is done on a
paragraph-by-paragraph basis.

Material in this analysis has been taken from a number of sources indicat
in the Appendix and is to be considered classified at the highest level.
Nothing contained in this report may be disseminated to any individual or agenc
without prior written permission of the Director or his appointed deputy.

This agency does not assume, and cannot verify, the correctness of the
material contained herein, although every reasonable effort has been made to do
so. Any use of information contained in this report must be paraphrased and
sources, either individual or agency, must not be credited.

VEDDER B. DRISCOLL
Colonel, USA
Chief, Soviet/Warsaw Pact
   Division
Directorate for Intelligence
   Research

1 Enclosure
Appendix

NOTE: The Russian language file is not attached to this report and exists in
      official translation only.

CHAPTER EIGHTY

SOVIET INTELLIGENCE DOCUMENTS

ENCLOSURE A

THE SOVIET INTELLIGENCE STUDY (translated)

1. On 22 November, 1963, America President John Kennedy was shot and killed during a political motor trip through the Texas city of Dallas. The President was riding at the head of the procession in his official state car, seated in the right rear with his wife on his left side. Seated in front of him was the Governor of Texas and his wife, also on his left side. The vehicle was an open car without side or top protection of any kind. There was a pilot car in front, about 30 meters, and the President's car was flanked by motorcycle outriders located two to a side roughly parallel with the rear wheels of the State care.

2. The President and his party were driving at a speed of about 20 kilometers per hour through the built-up area of Dallas and greeted the many people lining the streets along his route. Security was supplied by the Secret Service supplemented by local police. There were two Secret Service agents in the front of the car. One was driving the car. Other agents were in cars following the Presidential vehicle and Dallas police on motorbikes were on both sides of the Presidential car but at the rear of it. There was a pilot car in front of the President's car but it was some distance away.

3. The course of the journey was almost past all the occupied area. The cars then turned sharply to the right and then again to the left to go to the motorway leading to a meeting hall where the President was to speak at a dinner. It is considered very bad security for such an official drive to decrease its speed or to make unnecessary turnings or stops. (Historical note: It was just this problem that led directly to positioning the Austrian Heir in front of waiting assassins at Sarajevo in 1914). The route was set by agents of the Secret Service and published in the Dallas newspapers before the arrival of the President and his party.

4. After the last turning to the left, the cars passed a tall building on the right side of the street that was used as a warehouse for the storage of school books. This building was six stories tall and had a number of workers assigned to it. There were no official security people in this building, either on the roof or at the windows. Also, there were no security agents along the roadway on either side. All security agents were riding either in the Presidential car (two in the front) and in the following vehicles.

5. As the President's state car passed this building, some shots were heard. The exact source and number of these shots was never entirely determined. Some observers thought that the shots came from above and behind while many more observers in the area stated that the shots came from the front and to the right of the car. There was a small area with a decorative building and some trees and bushes there and many saw unidentified people in this area. Many people standing in front of this area to watch the cars stated that shots came from behind them.

-1-

6. When the first shots were fired, the President was seen to lean forward and clutch at his throat with both hands. Immediately when this happened, the Secret Service driver of the President's state car slowed down the vehicle until it was almost stopped. This was a direct breech of their training which stated that in such events where firing occurred, th driver of the President's car would immediately drive away as quickly as possible.

7. At the same time as the first shot, there was a second one, this one from above and behind. This bullet struck the Governor, sitting in fr of the President and slightly to his right, in the right upper shoulder. bullet went downwards into the chest cavity, breaking ribs, struck his wrist and lodged in his left upper thigh. There were then two shots fired the President's car. The first shot initiated the action and this one app to have hit the President in the throat. If so, it must have been fired f in front of the car, not behind it.

8. Right at this moment, there was one other shot. The shell, obviou struck the President on the upper rear of the right side of his head, throwing him back and to the left. Also, at this time, blood, pieces of skull and brains could be seen flying to the left where the motorbike poli guard was struck with this material on his right side and on the right si of his motorbike.

9. Immediately after this final shot, the driver then began to incre his speed and the cars all went at increasing speed down under the tunnel.

10. The fatally injured President and the seriously injured Governor were very quickly taken to a nearby hospital for treatment. The President was declared as dead and his body was removed, by force, to an aircraft a flown to Washington. The badly wounded Governor was treated at the hospita for his wounds and survived.

11. Within moments of the shots fired at the President, a Dallas motorcycle police officer ran into the book building and up to the second floor in the company of the manager of the establishment. Here, the police man encountered a man later positively identified as one Lee Harvey Oswald an employee of the book storage company. Oswald was drinking a Coca-Cola and appeared to be entirely calm and collected. (Later it was said that he had rushed down four flights of steps past other employees in a few moment after allegedly shooting the President. It is noted from the records that none of the other employees on the staircase ever saw Oswald passing them. The elevator which moved freight and personal between the floors was halte at the sixth floor and turned off so that it could not be recalled to persons below wishing to use it.

12. After meeting the police officer and apparently finishing his dri Oswald went down to the main floor and left the building, unnoticed.

13. Oswald then went to his apartment by a public bus and on foot, d in new clothes and left the building. His apartment manager observed that

—2—

330

Police car stopped in front of the building and blew its horn several times. She was unaware of the reason for that.

14. Oswald was then stated to have been halted by a local police officer whom he was alleged to have shot dead. The only witness who positively identified Oswald as the shooter was considered to be unstable and unreliable.

15. Oswald then entered a motion picture house and was later arrested there by the police. He was beaten in the face by the police and taken into custody.

16. When the captured Oswald was photographed by the reporters, he claimed that he was not guilty of shooting anyone and this was a position he maintained throughout his interrogation.

17. All records of his interrogation, carried out by the Dallas police and the Secret Service, were subsequently destroyed without a trace.

18. During the course of the interrogation, Oswald was repeatedly led up and down very crowded corridors of the police headquarters with no thought of security. This is an obvious breach of elementary security that was noted at the time by reporters. It now appears that Oswald's killer was seen and photographed in the crowds in the building.

19. The American Marine defector, Lee Harvey Oswald, entered the Soviet Union in October of 1959. Initially, Oswald, who indicated he wanted to "defect" and reside in the Soviet Union, was the object of some suspicion by Soviet intelligence authorities. He was at first denied entrance, attempted a "suicide" attempt and only when he was more extensively interrogated by competent agents was it discovered that he was in possession of material that potentially had a great intelligence value.

20. Oswald, who as a U.S. Marine, was stationed at the Atsugi air field in Japan, had been connected with the Central intelligence Agency's U2 intelligence-gathering aircraft program and was in possession of technical manuals and papers concerning these aircraft and their use in overflights of the Soviet Union.

21. The subject proved to be most cooperative and a technical analysis of his documentation indicated that he was certainly being truthful with Soviet authorities. In addition to the manuals, Oswald was able to supply Soviet authorities with a wealth of material, much of which was unknown and relatively current. As a direct result of analysis of the Oswald material, it became possible to intercept and shoot down a U2 aircraft flown by CIA employee Gary Powers.

22. On the basis of the quality of this material, Oswald was granted asylum in the Soviet Union and permitted to settle in Minsk under the supervision of the Ministry of the Interior. This was partially to reward him for his cooperation and also to remove him from the possible influence of American authorities at the Embassy in Moscow.

23. Oswald worked in a radio factory, was given a subsidized apartment in Minsk and kept under constant surveillance. He was very pro-Russian, learned

-3-

to speak and read the language, albeit not with native fluency, and behaved himself well in his new surroundings.

24. Although Oswald was a known homosexual, he nevertheless expressed an interest in women as well and his several casual romantic affairs with both men and women were duly noted.

25. Oswald became involved with Marina Nikolaevna Prusakova, the niece of a Minsk-based intelligence official. He wished to marry this woman who was attractive but cold and ambitious. She wished to leave the Soviet Union and emigrate to the United States for purely economic reasons. Since his marrying a Soviet citizen under his circumstances was often most difficult, Oswald began to speak more and more confidentially with his intelligence contacts in Minsk. He finally revealed that he was an agent for the United States Office of Naval Intelligence and had been recruited by them to act as a conduit between their office and Soviet intelligence.

26. The official material on the CIA operations was entirely authentic and had been supplied to Oswald by his controllers in the ONI. It was apparent, and Oswald repeatedly stated, that the CIA was completely unaware of the removal of sensitive documents from their offices. This removal, Oswald stated, was effected by the ONI personnel stationed at Atsugi air field. Oswald was unaware of the reasons for this operation but had been repeatedly assured that the mission was considered of great national importance and that if he proved to be successful, he would be afforded additional and profitable future employment. It appears that Oswald was considered to be a one-time operative and was expendable. His purpose was to establish a reputation as a pro-Russian individual who would then "defect" to the Soviet Union and pass over the U2 material. He did not seem to realize at the time he "defected" that once he had been permitted to live in the Soviet on an official governmental subsidy, returning to America would be very difficult, if not impossible.

27. Now, with his romantic, and very impractical, attachment to Prusakova, he was being pressured by her to marry and then take her with him back to the United States. Oswald was informed that this was not a possible option for him. He became very emotional and difficult to deal with but finally made the suggestion that if he were allowed to marry and return to the United States, he would agree to work in reality for the Soviet Union.

28. After referring this matter to higher authority, it was decided to accede to Oswald's requests, especially since he was of no further use to Soviet intelligence and might well be of some service while resident in America.

29. Marriage was permitted and his return was expedited both by the Soviet authorities and the Americans who were informed, via a letter from Oswald, that he was in possession of intelligence material of value to them. This valuable information was duly given to him, a reversal to be noted on his original mission!

30. Oswald was given prepared information of such a nature as to impress American intelligence and permitted to contact intelligence officials in the American Embassy in Moscow. He was then permitted by the Americans to return to the United States with his new wife.

—4—

31. In America, Oswald no longer worked with the ONI because he was not able to further assist them. Besides, he was viewed as dangerous because he had knowledge of the ONI theft and use of CIA documents.

32. While in America, Oswald then worked as a paid informant for the Federal Bureau of Investigation who had contacted him when he returned and requested his assistance with domestic surveillance against pro-Soviet groups. He was assigned, in New Orleans, the task of infiltrating the anti-Castro groups which were normally under the control of the CIA.

33. It is noted that there exists a very strong rivalry between the FBI and the CIA. The former is normally in charge of domestic counterintelligence and the latter in charge of foreign intelligence. They have been fighting for power ever since the CIA was first formed in 1947. Oswald has stated that the FBI was aware of this ONI-sponsored defection with stolen CIA U2 documents but this is not a proven matter.

34. Later, Oswald was transferred to Dallas, Texas, by the FBI and he then secured a position in a firm which dealt in very secret photographic matters. Here, he was able to supply both the FBI and Soviet intelligence with identical data.

35. FBI reports, kept secret, show clearly that Oswald was paid by the FBI as an informant.

36. In New Orleans, a center of Cuban insurgent activity, Oswald was in direct contact with FBI officials and worked for a guy Bannister, former FBI agent. Oswald infiltrated the ranks of Cuban insurgents and reported his findings to the FBI.

37. At that time, the FBI was involved, at the request of the Attorney General, Robert Kennedy, in watching the clandestine activities of the CIA and its Alpha and Omega special commando groups, some of whom were in training in the New Orleans area.

38. The American President was greatly concerned that continued and fully unauthorized para-military action against Cuba might upset the balance he had achieved in seeking peace with the Soviet Union.

39. It is know from information inside the CIA and also from Cuban double agents that the CIA was, in conjunction with the highest American military leadership, to force an American invasion of Cuba.

40. These joint plans, which consisted of acts of extreme provocation by American units against American property and citizens, were unknown to Kennedy.

41. When the American President discovered the Cuban insurgents, under the control of the CIA and with the support of the highest military leadership, were embarked on a course of launching military action against American naval bases under the cover of being Cuban regular troops, he at once ordered a halt.

-5-

42. Kennedy also informed the Soviet Premier directly of these planned actions and assured him that he had prevented them from being executed. The Premier expressed his gratitude and hoped that Kennedy would be successful in enforcing his will and preventing any other such adventures.

43. The American President, unsure of the depth of his influence with the leadership of the American military and the CIA, ordered the FBI to investigate these matters and ordered the Director, Hoover, to report directly to him on his findings.

44. Oswald was a part of the FBI surveillance of the Cuban insurgents in the New Orleans area.

45. Oswald made a number of public appearances passing out pro-Castro leaflets in order to ingratiate himself with the insurgents.

46. At the FBI request, a local television station filmed Oswald passing out these leaflets and had this film shown on local stations in order to enhance Oswald's image. When his mission was finished, Oswald was then sent to Dallas to observe and penetrate the Russian colony there.

47. Two days after the shooting of the American President, the alleged assassin, Oswald was shot to death in the basement of the Dallas Police Department while he was being transferred to another jail. On the day of the assassination, November 22, FBI Chief Hoover notified the authorities in Dallas that Oswald should be given special security.

48. This killing was done in the presence of many armed police officers by a known criminal and associate of the American Mafia named Jack Rubenstein, or "Ruby" as he was also known. "Ruby" had a long past of criminal association with the Mafia in Chicago, Illinois, a major area of gangster control in America. "Ruby" had once worked for the famous Al Capone and then for Sam Giancana. This man was head of the Chicago mob at the time of the assassination.

49. "Ruby" was the owner of a drinking establishment in Dallas that specialized in dancing by naked women and was also a close friend of many police officers in Dallas. "Ruby" had been seen and photographed in the Dallas police department while Oswald was being interrogated. It should be noted here that suspect Oswald was very often taken by Dallas police out into the completely unguarded hallways of the building and in the presence of many persons unknown to the police. This is view as either an attempt to have Oswald killed or a very incompetent and stupid breach of basic security.

50. The timing by "Ruby" of his entrance into the guarded basement was far too convenient to be accidental. Also, the method of his shooting of Oswald showed a completely professional approach. "Ruby" stepped out from between two policemen, holding a revolver down along his leg to avoid detection. As he stepped towards the suspect, "Ruby" raised his right hand with the revolved and fired upwards into Oswald's body. The bullet severed major arteries and guaranteed Oswald's death.

51. Although "Ruby" subsequently pretended to be mentally disturbed, his actions showed professional calculation to a degree. This play-acting was continued into his trial and afterwards. "Ruby" was convicted of the murder of

-6-

334

and sentenced to death. H died in prison of cancer in January of 1967 after an appeal from his sentence had been granted by the court judge. Information indicates that he was given a fatal injection.

52. "Ruby's" statements should not be confused with his actions. He was a professional criminal, had excellent connections with the Dallas police, had been involved with activities in Cuba and gun running into that country and some evidence has been produced to show that he and Oswald had knowledge of each other.

53. Like Oswald, "Ruby" too had homosexual activities and one public witness firmly placed Oswald in "Ruby's" club prior to the assassination.

54. In view of later developments and disclosures, the use of a Chicago killer with local Mafia connections to kill Oswald is not surprising. Stories of "Ruby's" eccentricity were highlighted by American authorities to make it appear that he, like suspect Oswald, was an eccentric, single individual who acted out of emotion and not under orders.

55. As in the case of Oswald, there was never a proven motive for "Ruby's" acts. Oswald had no reason whatsoever to shoot the President, had never committed any proven acts of violence. Although he was purported to have shot at a fascist General, it was badly presented and in all probability was a "red herring" to "prove" Oswald's desire to shoot people. "Ruby", a professional criminal with a long record of violence, claimed he shot Oswald to "protect" the President's wife from testifying. This statement appears to be an obvious part of "Ruby's" attempt to defend himself by claiming to be mad.

56. It is obvious that "Ruby" killed Oswald to silence him. Since Oswald was not involved in the killing of the President, continued interrogation of him leading to a court trial would have very strongly exposed the weakness of the American government's attempt to blame him for the crime.

57. Silencing Oswald promptly was a matter of serious importance for the actual killers.

58. That Oswald could not be convicted with the evidence at hand, his removal was vital. He could then be tried and convicted in public without any danger.

59. Rubenstein was not a man of intelligence but was a devoted member of the American criminal network.

60. Just prior to the assassination, Rubenstein was in a meeting with representatives of the criminal network and was told that he was to be held in readiness to kill someone who might be in Dallas police custody.

61. It was felt that Rubenstein was a well-connected man with the Dallas police department and that he might have access to the building without a challenge. He was also informed that he could be considered a "great hero" in the eyes of the American public. Rubenstein was a man of little self-worth and this approach strongly influenced him in his future actions.

-7-

62. A very large number of published books about the assassination have appeared since the year 1963. Most of these books are worthless from a historical point of view. They represent the views of obsessed people and twist information to suit the author's beliefs.

63. There are three main ideas written about:
    a. The American gangsters killed the President because his brother, the American Attorney General, was persecuting them.
    b. Cuba refugees felt that Mr. Kennedy had deserted their cause of ousting Cuban chief of state Castro;
    c Various American power groups such as the capitalist business owners, fascist political groups, racists, internal and external intelligence organization either singly or in combination are identified.

64. American officials have not only made no effort to silence these writers but in many cases have encouraged them. The government feels, as numerous confidential reports indicate, that the more lunatic books appear, the better. This way, the real truth is so concealed as to be impenetrable.

65. It was initially of great concern to our government that individuals inside the American government were utilizing Oswald's "Communist/Marxist" appearance to suggest that the assassination was of a Soviet origin.

66. In order to neutralize this very dangerous theme, immediately after the assassination, the Soviet Union fully cooperated with American investigating bodies and supplied material to them showing very clearly that Oswald was not carrying out any Soviet design.

67. Also, false defectors were used to convince the Americans that Oswald was considered a lunatic by the Soviet Union, and had not been connected with the Soviet intelligence apparatus in any way. He was, of course, connected but it was imperative to disassociate the Soviet Union with the theory that Oswald, an American intelligence operative, had been in collusion with them concerning the assassination.

68. The false defector, Nosenko, a provable member of Soviet intelligenc was given a scenario that matched so closely the personal attitudes of Mr. Hoover of the FBI that this scenario was then officially supported by Mr. Hoover and his bureau.

69. Angleton of the CIA at once suspected Nosenko's real mission and subjected him to intense interrogation but finally, Nosenko has been accepted as a legitimate defector with valuable information on Oswald.

70. Because of this business, Angleton was forced to resign his post as chief of counter intelligence. This has been considered a most fortunate byproduct of the controversy.

71. The FBI has accepted the legitimacy of Nosenko and his material precisely because it suited them to do so. It was also later the official position of the CIA because the issue dealt specifically with the

involvement, or non-involvement, between Oswald, a private party, and the organs of Soviet intelligence. Since there was no mention of Oswald's connection with American intelligence, this was of great important to both agencies.

72. It is known now that the American gangsters had very close relations with the Central Intelligence Agency. This relationship began during the war when the American OSS made connections with the Sicilian members of the American gangs in order to assist them against the fascists. The man who performed this liaison was Angleton, later head of counter intelligence for the CIA. These gangster contacts were later utilized by the CIA for its own ends.

73. American foreign policy was, and still is, firmly in the hands of the CIA. It alone makes determinations as to which nation is to be favored and which is to be punished. No nation is permitted to be a neutral; all have to be either in the U.S. camp or are its enemies. Most often, the wishes of American business are paramount in the determination as to which nation will receive U.S. support and which will not only be denied this support but attacked. It is the American CIA and not the Soviet Union, that has divided the world into two warring camps.

74. American, and most especially the CIA, attempts to destabilize a Communist state i.e., Cuba, could not be permitted by the Soviet leadership. Castro was a most valuable client in that he provided an excellent base of intelligence and political operations in the American hemisphere. As the CIA had been setting up its own ring of hostile states surrounding the Soviet Union, Cuba was viewed officially as a completely legitimate area of political expansion. Threats of invasion and physical actions against Cuba were viewed by the Chairman as threats against the Soviet Union itself. It is an absolute fact that both the American President, Kennedy, and his brother, the American Attorney General, were especially active in a sexual sense. A number of sexually explicit pictures of the President engaging in sexual acts are in the official file as are several pictures of the Attorney General, taken while on a visit to Moscow in 1961.

75. The President was aware that a number of these pictures were in Soviet hands and acted accordingly. In addition to a regular parade of whores into the White House, it was also reliably reported from several sources that the President was a heavy user of various kinds of illegal narcotics. It is also known from medical reports that the President suffered from a chronic venereal disease for which he was receiving medical treatment.

76. In order to better cooperate with the Soviet Union, President Kennedy used to regularly keep in close, private communication with the Chairman. These contacts were kept private to prevent negative influences from the State Department and most certainly from the Central Intelligence Agency. The President said several times that he did not trust this agency who was bent on stirring up a war between the two nations. Through this personal contact, many matters that might have escalated due to the interference of others were peacefully settled.

-9-

337

77. The pseudo-defector, Oswald, became then important to the further-ance of the plan to kill the American President. He had strong connections with the Soviet Union; he had married a Soviet citizen; he had been noticed in public advocating support of Fidel Castro. His position in a tall building overlooking the parade route was a stroke of great good fortune to the plotters.

78. Oswald was then reported by the CIA to have gone to Mexico City on 26 September, 1963 and while there, drew considerable attention to his presence in both the Soviet and Cuban embassies. What Oswald might have done in the Cuban embassy is not known for certain but there is no record of his ever having visited the Soviet embassy in Mexico at that time. CIA physical description as well as photographs show that Oswald was not the man depicted. This appears to be a poor attempt on the part of the CIA to embroil both the Soviet Union and Cuba in their affairs. It is understood that the actual assassins were subsequently removed in a wet action but that one apparently escaped and has been the object of intense searches in France and Italy by elements of the CIA.

79. From this brief study, it may be seen that the American President was certainly killed by orders of high officials in the CIA, working in close conjunction with very high American military leaders. It was the CIA belief that Kennedy was not only circumventing their own mapped-out destruct-ion of Fidel Castro by assassination and invasion but actively engaged in contacts with the Soviet Union to betray the CIA actions.

80. The American military leaders (known as the Joint Chiefs of Staff) were also determined upon the same goals, hence both of them worked together to ensure the removal of a President who acted against their best interests and to have him replaced with a weaker man whom they believed they could better control.

81. President Johnson, Kennedy's successor, was very much under the control of the military and CIA during his term in office and permitted enormous escalation in Southeast Asia. The destruction of the Communist movement in that area was of paramount importance to both groups.

338

ANALYSIS OF THE SOVIET INTELLIGENCE REPORT

    1. The Soviet analysis of the assassination of President John F. Kennedy contains material gleaned from American sources both official and unofficial i.e., media coverage, etc. Some of this material obviously stems from sources located inside various agencies. To date, none of these have been identified.

    2. It has long been a concern of the leadership and intelligence organs of the Soviet Union that blame has been attached to them for this assassination.

    3. The Soviet felt in the days immediately following the assassination that a plot was being developed, or had been developed prior to the act, that would serve to blame either the Cuban government or themselves for this action.

    4. It was felt that the identification of Lee Harvey Oswald as the sole assassin was intended to implicate the Soviet Union, in the act because Oswald had been a very vocal supporter of the Marxist theory; had defected to the Soviet Union and had married a Soviet woman with intelligence connections.

    5. The strongly stated official policy of putting Oswald forward as the sole assassin greatly alarmed the Soviet Union which had already weathered the very serious Cuban Missile Crisis, a situation that came perilously close to an atomic war between the two powers.

    6. The Soviet leadership had established a strong, albeit secret, connection between themselves and the American President but with his death, this clandestine communications channel was closed.

    7. The Soviet promptly dispatched a number of senior intelligence personnel and files to Washington in order to reassure President Johnson and his top aides that the Soviet Union had no hand in the assassination.

    8. Johnson himself was a badly frightened man who, having witnessed the murder of his predecessor, lived in constant dread of a similar attack on himself. He also had no stomach for the kind of international brinkmanship as practiced by Kennedy and immediately assured the Soviets that he did not believe they had anything to do with the killing.

    9. The Soviets had learned of the plan formulated by the JCS to create a reason for military intervention in Cuba in 1962-1963. They believed then, and still believe, that the killing of Kennedy was done partially to create a causus belli insofar as the Soviet Union itself was concerned.

    10. Their information indicated that while Kennedy had not permitted these provocations to influence his policy, such could not be said for Johnson. He was viewed as an untried individual and best reassured.

    11. One of the strongest supporters of the Soviet point of view was FBI director Hoover.

-11-

12. Because of the involvement of his agency with Oswald, it was in Hoover's best interest to absolve the Soviets of any complicity and maintain the accepted fiction of Oswald as a deranged person working without assistance of any kind and certainly without any connection to any U.S. agency.

13. It has been alleged that Oswald had also worked for the CIA. This has not been proven although it should be noted that Oswald was in direct contact with CIA agents, associated with the U.S. Embassy in Moscow, while in Russia and had been debriefed by that agency after his return from Russia.

14. Oswald was also intimately connected with De Mohrenschildt who was certainly known to be a CIA operative. Oswald's connections with this man were such as to guarantee that the CIA was aware of Oswald's movements throughout his residence in the Dallas area.

15. When Oswald secured employment at the Texas Book Depository, De Mohrenschildt, according to an FBI report, reported this to the CIA.

16. The existence and location of Oswald's mail order Mannlicher-Carcano rifle in the garage of his wife's friend, Ruth Paine, was also known to De Mohrenschildt at least one week prior to the assassination.

17. The background and development of the Presidential trip as hereinafter set forth is in parallel with the Soviet report.

18. The Dallas trip had been in train since late July of 1963. Texas was considered to be a key state in the upcoming 1964 Presidential elections. It was the disqualification of over 100,000 Texas votes, in conjunction with the known fraudulent voting in Chicago in 1960 that gave President Kennedy and his associates a slim margin of victory.

The actual route of Kennedy's drive through downtown Dallas was made known to the local press on Tuesday, November 19. The sharp right turn from Main St. onto Houston and then the equally sharp left turn onto Elm was the only way to get to the on ramp to the Stemmons Freeway. A traffic divider on Main St. precluded the motorcade from taking the direct route, from Main St. across Houston and thence right to the Stemmons Freeway exit.

20. Just after the President's car passed the Texas Book Depository, a number of shots were fired. There were a total of three shots fired at the President. The first shot came from the right front, hitting him in the neck. This projectile did not exit the body. The immediate reaction by the President was to clutch at his neck and say, "I have been hit!" He was unable to move himself into any kind of a defensive posture because he was wearing a restrictive body brace.

21. The second shot came from above and behind the Presidential car, the bullet striking Texas Governor Connally in the upper right shoulder, passing through his chest and exiting sharply downwards into his left thigh.

-12-

340

22. The third, and fatal, shot was also fired at the President from the right front and from a position slightly above the car. This bullet, which was fired from a .223 weapon, struck the President above the right ear, passed through the right rear quadrant of his head and exited towards the left. Pieces of the President's skull and a large quantity of brain matter was blasted out and to the left of the car. Much of this matter struck a Dallas police motorcycle outrider positioned to the left rear of the Presidential car.

23. Photographic evidence indicates that the driver, SA Greer, slowed down the vehicle when shots were heard, in direct contravention of standing Secret Service regulations.

24. Reports that the initial hit on the President came from above and behind are false and misleading. Given the position of the vehicle at the time of impact and the altitude of the alleged shooter, a bullet striking the back of the President's neck would have exited sharply downward as did the projectile fired at Governor Connally purportedly from the same shooter located in the same area of the sixth floor of the Texas Book Depository.

25. The projectile that killed the President was filled with mercury. When such a projectile enters a body, the sudden decrease in velocity causes the mercury to literally explode the shell. This type of projectile is designed to practically guarantee the death of the target and is a method in extensive use by European assassination teams.

26. The disappearance of Kennedy's brain and related post mortem material from the U.S. National Archives was motivated by an official desire not to permit further testing which would certainly show the presence of mercury in the brain matter.

27. Official statements that the fatal shot was fired from above and behind are totally incorrect and intended to mislead. Such a shot would have blasted the brain and blood matter forward and not to the left rear. Also, photographic evidence indicates that after the fatal shot, the President was hurled to his left, against his wife who was seated to his immediate left.

28. The so-called "magic bullet" theory, i.e., a relatively pristine, fired Western Cartridge 6.5 Mannlicher-Carcano projectile produced in evidence, is obviously an official attempt to justify its own thesis. This theory, that a projectile from above and behind struck the President in the upper back, swung up, exited his throat, gained altitude and then angle downwards through the body of Governor Connally, striking bone and passing through muscle mass and emerging in almost undamaged condition is a complete impossibility. The bullet in question was obtained by firing the alleged assassination weapon into a container of water.

29. Three other such projectiles were recovered in similar undamaged condition. One of these was produced for official inspection and was claimed to have been found on Governor Connally's stretcher at Parkland Hospital. As a goodly portion of the projectile was still in the Governor's body, this piece of purported evidence should be considered as nothing more than an official "plant".

-13-

30. Soviet commentary on Oswald is basically verified from both KGB and CIA sources. Oswald, however, was not being run by the ONI but instead by the CIA. Their personnel files indicate that Oswald was initially recruited by ONI for possible penetration of the very pervasive Japanese Communist intelligence organization. Atsugi base was a very important target for these spies.

31. Because of a shift in their policy, the CIA found it expedient to exploit their U2 surveillance of the Soviet Union as a political rather than intelligence operation.

32. The Eisenhower administration's interest in the possibility of achieving a rapproachement with the Soviet Government created a situation that might have proven disasterous to the CIAs continued functions.

33. Internal CIA documents show very clearly that as their very existence was dependent on a continuation of the Cold War, any diminution of East-West hostility could easily lead to their down sizing and, more important, to their loss of influence over the office of the President and also of U.S. foreign policy.

34. It was proposed, according to top level CIA reports, to somehow use their U2 flights to create an increase in tension that could lead to a frustration of any détente that might result from a lessening of international tensions.

35. It was initially thought that certain compromising documents could be prepared, sent to the CIA base at Atsugi, Japan, and then somehow leaked to the aggressive Japanese Communists. However, it was subsequently decided that there was a strong possibility that the documents might not be forwarded to Soviet Russia and kept in Japan for use in the anti-west/anti-war domestic campaigns.

36. CIA personnel stationed at Atsugi conceived a plan to arrange for select documents to be given directly to the Soviets via an American defector. It was at this point that Oswald's name was brought up by an ONI man. A CIA evaluation of Oswald convinced them that he would be the perfect defector. Psychological profiles of Oswald convinced them that he was clever, pro-Marxist, a person of low self-esteem as manifested in his chronic anti-social attitudes coupled with homosexual behavior.

37. As Oswald had developed a strong friendship with his ONI control, it was decided to allow him to think that he was working for the U.S. Navy rather than the CIA.

38. Oswald was told that he was performing a "special, vitally important" mission for the ONI and would be given a very good paying official position when he "successfully returned" from the Soviet Union. CIA and ONI reports indicate that he was never expected to return to the U.S. after he had fulfilled his function of passing the desired documents to the Soviet intelligence community.

39. The subsequent interception and shooting down by the Soviets of a U2 piloted by CIA agent Gary Powers using the leaked CIA material was sufficient to wreck the projected Eisenhower/Khruschev meeting and harden the Soviet leader's attitude towards the West.

-14-

40. It should be noted that the Powers U2 was equipped with a delayed action self-destruct device, designed to be activated by the pilot upon bailing out. This device was intended to destroy any classified surveillance material on the aircraft. In the Powers aircraft, the device was later disclosed to have been altered to explode the moment the pilot activated it. This would have resulted in the destruction of both the pilot and his aircraft.

41. After his return to the United States, Oswald was a marked man. He was a potential danger to the CIA, whose unredacted personnel reports indicate that Oswald was considered to be unstable, hostile, intelligent and very frustrated, He was, in short, a loose canon.

42. While resident in Dallas, Oswald became acquainted with a George S. De Mohrenschildt, a CIA operative. De Mohrenschildt, a Balt, had family connections both in Poland and Russia, had worked for the German Ausland Abwehr and later the SD during the Second World War. He "befriended" Oswald and eventually an intimate physical relationship developed between the two men. This infuriated Marina Oswald and their already strained relationship grew even worse. She had come to America expecting great financial rewards and instead found poverty, two children and a sexually cold husband.

43 It was De Mohrenschildt's responsibility to watch Oswald, to establish a strong interpersonal relationship with him and to learn what information, if any, Oswald might possess that could damage the CIA if it became known.

44. The CIAs subsequent use of Oswald as a pawn in the assassination was a direct result of this concern.

45. The connections of Angleton, Chief of Counter intelligence for the CIA with elements of the mob are well known in intelligence circles. Angleton worked closely with the Sicilian and Naples mobs in 1944 onwards as part of his duties for the OSS.

46. The connections of Robert Crowley, another senior CIA official, with elements of the Chicago mob are also well known in intelligence circles.

47. The attempts of the CIA and the JCS to remove Castro by assassination are also part of the official record. These assassination plots, called RIFLE show the connections between the CIA and the Chicago branch of the Mafia.

48. This Mafia organization was paid nearly a quarter of a million dollars to effect the killing of Castro but apparently kept the money and did nothing.

49. Subsequent to the assassination, the CIA put out the cover story that Castro has planned to act in retaliation for the attempts on his life. This is not substantiated either from U.S. or Soviet sources.

50. While the American Mafia had numerous reasons for wishing the removal of the President and, especially, his brother, the Attorney General, it does not appear that they were participants in the assassination.

-15-

51. It is evident that contact was made between the Chicago Mafia and its counterpart in Sicily in an effort to locate putative assassins.

52. French intelligence sources have indicated that a recruitment was made among members of the Corsican Mafia in Marseilles in mid-1963.

53. French intelligence sources have also indicated that they informed U.S. authorities in the American Embassy on two occasions about the recruitment of French underworld operatives for a political assassination in the United States.

54. It is not known if these reports were accepted at the Embassy or passed on to Washington.

55. In the event, the Corsicans were sent to Canada where they blended in more easily with the French-speaking Quebec population.

56 Although the Chicago Mafia did not supply the actual assassins, they did provide the services of one of their lesser members, Jack "Ruby" Rubenstein, a small-time mob enforcer, in the event that Oswald was taken alive.

57. The use of Jack Ruby to kill Oswald has been explained by the official reports as an aberrant act on the part of an emotional man under the influence of drugs. The Warren Commission carefully overlooked Ruby's well-known ties to the Chicago mob as well as his connections with mob elements in Cuba.

58. Ruby's early Chicago connections with the mob are certainly well documented in Chicago police files. This material was not used nor referred to in the Warren Report.

59. Ruby's close connection with many members of the Dallas police infrastructure coupled with a very strong motivation to remove Oswald prior to any appointment of an attorney to represent him or any possible revelations Oswald might make about his possible knowledge of the actual assassins made Ruby an excellent agent of choice. If Oswald had gained the relative security of the County Jail and lawyers had been appointed to him, it would have proven much more difficult to remove him.

60. The Warren Commission was most particularly alarmed by attempts on the part of New York attorney Mark Lane, to present a defense for the dead Oswald before the Commission. Lane was refused this request. A written comment by Chief Justice Earl Warren to CIA director Allen Dulles was that "people like Lane should never be permitted to air their radical views... at least not before this Commission..."

61. Ruby had been advised by his Chicago mob connections, as well as by others involved in the assassination, that his killing of Oswald would "make him a great hero" in the eyes of the American public and that he "could never be tried or convicted" in any American court of law.

62. Ruby, who has personal identity problems, accepted and strongly embraced this concept and was shocked to find that he was to be tried on a capital charge. Never very stable, Ruby began to disintegrate while in custody and mixed fact with fiction in a way as to convince possible assassins that he was not only incompetent but would not reveal his small knowledge of the motives behind the removal of Oswald.

-16-

344

63. In the presence of Chief Justice Warren, Ruby strongly intimated that he had additional information to disclose and wanted to go to the safety of Washington but Warren abruptly declared that he was not interested in hearing any part of it.

64. A polygraph given to Ruby concerning his denial of knowing Oswald and only attempting to kill him as a last minute impulse proved to be completely unsatisfactory and could not be used to support the Commission's thesis.

65. During his final illness, while in Parkland Hospital, Ruby was under heavy sedation and kept well supervised to prevent any death bed confessions or inopportune chance remarks to hospital attendants. An unconfirmed report from a usually reliable source states that Ruby was given an injection of air with a syringe which produced an embolism that killed him. The official cause of Ruby's death was a blood clot.

66. It was later alleged that Ruby had metastated cancer of the brain and lungs which somehow had escaped any detection during his incarceration in Dallas. It was further alleged that this terminal cancer situation had existed for over a year without manifesting any serious symptoms to the Dallas medical authorities. This is viewed by non-governmental oncologists as highly unbelievable and it appears that Ruby's fatal blood clot was the result of outside assistance.

67. Following the assassination, a number of persons connected with the case died under what can only be termed as mysterious circumstances. Also, the FBI seized a number of films and pictures taken by witnesses. These were considered to be too sensitive to leave in private hands.

68. Statements by Dallas law enforcement personnel, as well as similar statements by witnesses, that there had been "several" men in the area of the railroad yard adjacent to the roadway and that these men had "Secret Service" identification, created considerable confusion.

69. According to Secret Service records, the only Secret Service agents at the scene were in the motorcade itself and they had no agents in the railroad yard.

70. Witness and Witness statements introduced before the Warren Commission were carefully vetted prior to introduction as evidence. The home movie of the assault was turned over to the FBI and a spliced version of it was released to the public. This doctored version showed Kennedy reacting in a way that was diametrically oposed to his actual reactions.

71. The concerns of Soviet intelligence and governmental agencies about any possible Soviet connection between defector Oswald and themselves is entirely understandable. It was never seriously believed by any competent agency in the United States that the Soviet Union had any part in the assassination of Kennedy.

72. Because of the emotional attitudes in official Washington and indeed, throughout the entire nation immediately following the assassination, there was created a potentially dangerous international situation for the

-17-

Soviets. Oswald was an identified defector with Marxist leanings. He was also believed to be a pro-Castro activist. That both his Marxist attitudes and his sympathies and actions on behalf of the Cuban dictator were enhanced simulations was not known to the Warren Commission at the time of their activities.

73. To bolster their eager efforts to convince the American authorities that their government had nothing to do with the assassination, men like Nosenko were utilized to further support this contention. It is not known whether Nosenko was acting on orders or whether he was permitted access to created documentation and given other deliberate disinformation by the KGB and allowed to defect. A great deal of internal concern was expressed upon Nosenko's purported defection by Soviet officials but this is viewed as merely an attempt, and a successful one, to lend substance to his importance.

74. James Angleton's attitude towards Nosenko is a commentary on the duality of his nature. On the one hand, Angleton was performing as Chief of Counter Intelligence and openly showed his zeal in searching for infiltraters and "moles" inside his agency while on the other hand, Angleton had very specific personal knowledge that the Soviet Union had nothing to do with the Kennedy assassination.

75. The senior Kennedy, it is known, was heavily involved with rum-running during the Prohibition era and had extensive mob connections. He had closely been associated with Al Capone, mob boss in Chicago, and had a falling out with him over an allegedly hijacked liquor shipment. Capone, Chicago police records indicate, had threatened Kennedy's life over this and Kennedy had to pay off the mob to nullify a murder contract.

76. Anti-Castro Cuban militants view Kennedy's abandonment of their cause with great anger and many members of these CIA-trained and led groups made calls for revenge on the President for his abandonment of their cause.

77. Soviet attempts to gain a strategic foothold in close proximity to the United States and certainly well within missile range, was intolerable and had to be countered with equal force. At that time, the threat of a major war was not only imminent but anticipated. In retrospect, all out nuclear warfare between the United States and the Soviet Union was only barely averted and only at the last minute.

78. The President's highly unorthodox form of personal diplomacy vis a vis the Soviets created far more problems than it ever solved. When it came to light, both the DOS and the CIA were extremely concerned that sensitive intelligence matters might have been inadvertently passed to the Soviets.

79. Reports from the CIA concerning Oswald's September/October visit to Mexico City are totally unreliable and were rejected by the FBI as being "in serious error." The reasons for Oswald's visit to Mexico are completely obscure at this writing but the individual allegedly photographed by CIA surveillance in Mexico is to a certainty not Lee Oswald. As the CIA had pictures of the real Oswald, their reasons for producing such an obvious falsity are not easy to ascertain at this remove.

80. The hit team was flown away in an aircraft piloted by a CIA contract

pilot named David Ferrie from New Orleans. They subsequently vanished without a trace. Rumors of the survival of one of the team are persistent but not proven.

81. A study of the Soviet report indicates very clearly that the Russians have significant and very high level sources within both the Central Intelligence Agency and the Federal Bureau of Investigation. Their possession of material relating to certain highly classified American military papers has been referred to the CIC for investigation and action.

-19-

Edwin Aubrey Clark
LBJ's attorney

CHAPTER EIGHTY-ONE

PLANNING AND CORRUPTION

T he total number of people involved in the planning of Kennedy's killing will probably never be known. Many had a task to do, not knowing that the end result was murder; there were others who had roles to play on a need-to-know basis. And still others were used having no idea they were involved in a murder plot.

Ruth Paine and Roy Truly were probably two of the most prominent minor individuals used in this plot. It was most likely that it was suggested to Paine to take in the Oswald family, and later, to call Truly to attain a job for Lee Oswald.

Truly had probably been told to expect Ruth Paine's phone call about hiring Oswald and did the hiring as a favor to someone. It has been established that Oswald had at least minor connections to the CIA and FBI, and that Oswald took the School Book Depository job at somebody's suggestion or orders, not knowing he was being set up as a "patsy."

Roy Truly's actions immediately after the shooting, stating that he had "one man missing," when he had several men locked out of the building because the police had sealed off the building, indicate to me that Truly snapped to the fact he had been used and reacted accordingly, pointing to Oswald.

The best information I have indicates that the planning of the assassination started with LBJ and Edward Clark, LBJ's main attorney in Austin, Texas. President Kennedy had decided that the Vice President (LBJ) should have the same Secret Service protection as the President, and gave Lyndon Johnson a Secret Service manual. That was about two years before the assassination.

A string of murders that Lyndon Johnson ordered began with Mac Wallace killing John Kinser in 1951.

The financial kickback deals with Bobby Baker and Billie Sol Estes were not exactly legal, and they were catching up with Vice President Johnson. The most prominent murder victim was that of Federal Agriculture agent

Henry Marshall. Marshal was looking into Billie Sol Estes' dealings with LBJ and when Henry Marshall would not accept a bribe, Lyndon Johnson ordered Mac Wallace to "take care" of Marshall.

Lyndon Johnson ran his life on bribery and corruption. When he was a Senator he ran the Senate the same way. And when he was Vice President, the Vice President's job called for him to run the Senate.

Money talked: if you wanted a bill passed, you made sure Johnson was taken care of. LBJ did not keep it all for himself; if he needed a vote from a reluctant senator, Lyndon made sure that senator was taken care of.

While the Viet Nam war was being waged, money was flowing like water. If you were Edward Clark, and Johnson's lawyer, major corporations flocked to your law office for the influence that you had with your client.

When you are told an interesting story about Lyndon Johnson and the assassination of President Kennedy by an insider, you think, well, that was an interesting story. When you hear that same story from another insider years later, you remember what that first insider told you, and it starts you to wondering if there is any truth to what you have been told by these people.

Then you hear the same story again from a third and fourth insider, and I am talking about face-to-face conversations, you decide you are probably onto the trail of truth, and you start digging for additional information to document what you have been told. In the process of digging for the additional documentation you stumble onto others, who have also discovered what you have discovered.

Now, once you know that Lyndon Johnson and his cronies were behind the Kennedy killing you start connecting the dots in such a way as to make sense and then putting the evidence you are aware of in a neat tidy way, so that anyone can fully understand what really happened, in everyday terms.

Standing in a crowded theater and screaming, "Johnson did it," is not enough. It takes time to tie up loose ends in a way as to be able to answer most of the questions that people have been asking for years.

I know I can now answer most of the main questions, but there are still some I cannot answer. And I hope and pray there are people who are still alive that can add to the story of this book.

In searching for documentation, it became too easy to find hard evidence that Lee Oswald was not the shooter. J. Lee Rankin, Chief Counsel for the Warren Commission, had information on his desk before the Warren Report was ever published, that Lee Harvey Oswald could not have been the shooter. *Had J. Lee Rankin already realized that President Johnson and his cover-up buddy, J. Edgar Hoover were behind the assassination,* and that he,

Warren Commission Chief Counsel, could do nothing, but go along with Hoover's FBI report that Lee Harvey Oswald was the "lone nut assassin?"

We may never know the full truth about who Lee Harvey Oswald really was, and did he or did he not have some minor role in the assassination of President Kennedy?

What we do know is that Lyndon Johnson and his cronies were behind the organized and well-planned killing of President Kennedy, and that the cover-up was in place before Kennedy's head exploded. We also know that the cover-up appears to be mainly handled by the Director of the FBI, Hoover.

It was too simple, when the day was over, two of the most powerful men in the world were in control, the President of the United States and his buddy who ran the most prominent law enforcement agency in the world.

When the smartest, most intelligent, and sharpest men in our government snapped to, to what had just happened and figured it out, a coup de' etat, a government take-over had just occurred, there was no one to go to. To speak out would surely mean some kind of "accident" or "freak" death.

Three FBI agents who were going to give evidence to the House Select Committee on Assassinations (HSCA) in the late 1970's were dead before they could speak a word to the HSCA. When Federal Marshall Clint Peoples said he was going to announce to the public who was behind the Kennedy assassination, he was killed in a one-car automobile accident four days later.

Maybe the people who did face the truth square on, decided, *for the good of the country*, to just let Lee Harvey Oswald be the lone nut assassin, when what they really felt, and felt with great fear, was *for the good of their health*, to forget what they had learned.

The best example of that fear is of the lawyers closest to the evidence, those who were on the Warren Commission and, when they figured out what had really happened to our country, quit the Warren Commission and went home. They had no choice; they had been sworn to secrecy, with the threat of losing their law license if they spoke of anything they had discovered while on the Warren Commission.

The evidence has been there all along, various writers and authors have written about the assassination with those bits and pieces of the truth in their writing. Let us take those bits and pieces and put them together with what insiders have told me, so you can see the full story.

TIME

THE WEEKLY NEWSMAGAZINE

CLINT MURCHISON
A big wheeler-dealer.

Chapter Eighty-Two

Clint Murchison's Party

The famed Clint Murchison Sr. party and the secret meeting afterwards was held on November 21, 1963, supposedly to honor FBI Director J. Edgar Hoover, who was a close friend of Clint Sr. The party and secret meeting was held at Murchison's six-acre estate in north Dallas. Clint Murchison Sr. is not to be confused with his son Clint Murchison Jr., who owned the Dallas Cowboys football team.

I must tell the reader that there is controversy over the meeting held at Clint Murchison Sr.'s estate on November 21, 1963. I am talking about the meeting, not the party that was held before the closed meeting started.

A maid and butler did identify many of those at the party. Timing is crucial; the secret meeting was held after midnight, after many of the party guests had left. The controversy is mainly over who was in attendance at the secret meeting after the party.

The meeting actually started after midnight on November 22, 1963. The naysayers try to say the meeting started much earlier, as early as 10:30 or 11 P.M. Wealthy oil men do not throw a party that has alcohol served that only lasts a couple hours. I know, I have been there.

I started to leave this chapter out of this book, until I learned that Caroline Kennedy Schlossberg, President Kennedy's daughter, had made a public statement that her mother Jackie Kennedy Onassis accused Texas oil men of being behind the assassination of her husband, President "Jack" Kennedy.

I am leaving this chapter in my book because I trust the word of Clint Murchison Sr.'s butler and maid above all others. I am also taking the word of Madeleine Brown, Lyndon Johnson's mistress for 21 year, with certain reservations. Madeleine was at the party; I have no reservations about her presence. But one must remember this was not a tea party where they served soft drinks – alcoholic drinks were served.

A writer-researcher friend of mine has verified at least six who were at the Murchison meeting. My personal reservations concern Madeleine's perhaps clear or unclear memory of who was at the party versus her clear or unclear memory after a few alcoholic drinks as to who was in the closed meeting.

This chapter is for current and future historians to sort out. If anyone who was at the party or meeting is still living they would be in their 90's or over 100 years old now in 2013. The dinner party was held on the pretext of honoring J. Edgar Hoover. Clint Murchison's friendship with Hoover was close and well documented. It has been said that Clint bought Del Mar horse racing track in La Jolla California just so J. Edgar Hoover and Hoovers companion Clyde Tolson had a place to go bet on the horses. When Hoover and Tolson frequented the racetrack, Murchison took care of all their expenses.

Clint Murchison was a well-known philanthropist in Dallas; his favorite philanthropy was helping bright young men pay for their college education. He was a Presbyterian, a Mason, a Democrat, and belonged to many prestigious organizations. But there was another side to Clint Murchison: he had deep ties to the Mafia, and organized labor, plus CIA and FBI connections.

Murchison, a close friend of Lyndon Johnson, was also a co-conspirator in the plot to assassinate Kennedy. President Kennedy's plans to do away with the oil depletion allowance could cost Clint Murchison and other oilmen like H. L. Hunt millions of dollars.

At approximately 12:30 A.M. the early morning of November 22, 1963 Vice President Lyndon Johnson walked in and the party soon broke up.

Many of those at the dinner party, but who were not included in the closed door secret meeting were:

Madeleine Brown, Philip K. Elliot, Shirley Pauling, Ted W. Powers, Val Imm, Dave Blair, Gordon McClendon, Lex Dale Owens, Dick Kantazer, Neal Spelce, Don Newbury, Cactus Prior, Helen Thomas and Frank Cormier

This list was supplied by party attendee Madeleine Brown to Robert Gaylon Ross Sr. for Mr. Ross's book, *The Elite Serial Killers*.

As stated, the above list and a following list of people was supplied by Madeleine Brown. I also have Murchison's maid and butler, on tape, who were there that evening, and they verify a few of the attendees. Murchison's maid and butler were not in the same inner circle as Madeleine and as expected, they did not know the names of all the guests.

I have been skeptical of Madeleine's recall of the names of those attending this party, especially her list of those attending the secret meeting. But Madeleine Brown's recall of the names of the guest who were at Clint Murchison Sr.'s mansion the evening of November 21, 1963 has never varied and was unshakable until her death.

Gaylon Ross, a friend of mine, has been able to verify six people in attendance at the secret meeting. There has to be a son, daughter, niece, nephew, grandson, or granddaughter of those listed who would step forward and relate what a parent or grandparent told them in secret about this meeting. Of course there will be a chorus of denials to protect family names, but maybe just one relative, with verifiable secret information would step forward with what they have learned from a relative.

Those who were at the private meeting according to Madeleine Brown:
Clint Murchison Sr. a billionaire oil man
H.L. Hunt a billionaire oil man
Vice President Lyndon Johnson
Texas Governor John Connally
FBI Chief, J. Edgar Hoover
Clyde Tolson, Hoover's lover and second in command of the FBI
ex-Vice President Richard M. Nixon
ex-Dallas Mayor R.L. Thorton
Dallas Mayor Earle Cabell
Dallas County Sheriff Bill Decker
Night Club owner and killer of Lee Harvey Oswald Jack Ruby
Mobster Carlos Marcello
Texas Ranger and U.S. Marshall Clint Peoples
W.O. Bankston, local new car dealer
Joe Yarbrough, construction
George Brown, of Brown and Root construction
Millionaire Amon G. Carter Jr.
John Currington, an H.L. Hunt advisor
John McCloy, CIA, Chairman of Chase bank and later named to the Warren Commission
B.R. Sheffield, military construction
Cliff Carter, Executive Director Democratic National Committee
Joe Civello, Dallas Mafia
Larry Campbell representing Jimmy Hoffa
Don Smith G.M. Del Mar race track
Mac Wallace, assassin

The main reason for the meeting was to make sure all the bases had been covered. National Democratic Director Cliff Carter ran the meeting and did the talking; the main purpose of the meeting was for everyone to know their part in the cover-up of the murder of President Kennedy that was to occur within hours. Hardly anyone had anything to say. J. Edgar Hoover said, "Any information that gets out will have to come through me," and "I have it 'wired' from the Police Force to the CIA."

Madeleine Duncan Brown was Lyndon Johnson's mistress for twenty-one years and had a son Steven by Lyndon. She was well recognized in Dallas social circles because of her prominence in commercial advertising and closeness to Lyndon. It was normal for media people like Madeleine Brown and Helen Thomas to be invited to parties such as this at the Murchison estate as a mixer with the prominent guests.

It was expected that these media people would not discuss any gossip overheard at such parties. Although Madeleine was Vice President Lyndon Johnson's mistress, she did not know he would show up until he walked in to the mansion after midnight.

When the private meeting was assembled in the private dining room, Madeleine waited for Lyndon in the living room. When the meeting was over and Lyndon came out of the meeting he walked over to Madeleine grasped her hand so hard it hurt and stated in a grating whisper: "After tomorrow those goddamn Kennedy's will never embarrass me again."

Three witnesses who were at this party, the butler, the maid, and Madeleine Brown, made statements on tape about who attended the "Hoover" dinner party, and who stayed to attend the closed meeting after the "Hoover" party broke up. The preceding list was made by Madeleine Brown. The butler and the maid, who did not want their names publicized, could only recognize the prominent people at the party/meeting such as J. Edgar Hoover.

Through the years, the naysayers in trying to discredit Madeleine Brown, use the fact that Clint Murchison Sr. had a stroke in 1958, and due to that stroke could not have had this November 21, 1963 party and meeting. While it is true Clint Murchison had a stroke in 1958, it is also true that he made a full recovery from the stroke. An interesting note about this full recovery is that in the summer of 1963 he took John McCloy to his farm in Mexico to hunt whitewings on Murchison's Mexican farm. It must also be noted that this John McCloy is the same John J. McCloy who was at the 11/21/1963 Murchison meeting, and was later named by President Johnson to be on the Warren Commission.

Chapter Eighty-Three

J. Edgar Hoover & the Cover-up

John Edgar Hoover was Director of the Federal Bureau of Investigation, the FBI, from its start, and for nearly 50 years until his death in 1971. He built the world's greatest law enforcement agency. The FBI headquarters in Washington D.C. has Hoover's name on it.

To Hoover's credit, he only hired the brightest and best young men in America to be his agents. J. Edgar Hoover's orders were law, as an agent you obeyed Hoovers rules to a tee, you never questioned him; if you did, you might be assigned to Timbuktu or out of a job. I remember as a kid growing up, one of my favorite TV programs was about the FBI. J. Edgar Hoover and the FBI were about honesty and truth. I even had a nephew that was in the FBI for five years.

But there was another side to J. Edgar Hoover, an "evil" side that was hidden from the public. So that you can understand the evil that was part of J. Edgar Hoover's life and what he was capable of, I will relate a true story about Hoover that was featured on the TV program *60 Minutes* in the early 2000's. It is a true story about FBI Director J. Edgar Hoover and a man who had just been cleared of murder after spending almost 30 years in prison in Massachusetts.

Joseph Salvati was 21 when he married 19-year-old Marie Moschella. In 1967. Joe drove a truck and Marie took care of their four children. They lived in the North End, the Italian section of Boston.

On October 25, 1967, while waiting to pick up her children from school, a neighbor told Marie her husband had been arrested for murder. Marie was 32 when her husband went to prison. Three others were convicted for the same murder, two of these innocent men died in Prison, a third, Peter Limone spent 32 years in prison before being cleared. Marie and the children stood behind Joe for all those years he was in prison.

The truth came out later, when Special U.S. Attorney John Durham and U.S. District Court Judge Mark L. Wolf conducted a vigorous investigation into corrupt relationships between FBI agents and the Boston mob in the Boston FBI office.

For all those years the FBI had concealed documents that proved an FBI informant, a Boston mobster, had committed the murder. FBI director Hoover knew before Joseph Salvati ever went to trial that Salvati was an innocent man, yet he did not intervene. Hoover felt it was more important to protect his mob informant than to clear an innocent man. Hoover chose to let Joseph rot in prison while Joe's wife and children lived in misery and shame for 30 years.

This was just one of the outrages Hoover and the Boston FBI was guilty of. In 1995 FBI agent John J. Connally warned James "Whitey" Bulger, who had murdered 19 people, that he was about to be indicted. Whitey fled and it was not until 16 years later that Whitey Bulger was captured in California in 2011.

We now know J. Edgar Hoover blackmailed members of Congress, threatened the life of Dr. Martin Luther King, ordered illegal wiretaps, used Government funds to enhance his residence, ignored too much about organized crime, hid information from judges, spied on political adversaries, and kept secret files. That FBI building in Washington D.C. with J. Edgar Hoovers name on it, is honoring a scumbag. Hoovers name does not deserve to be on FBI headquarters or anywhere except his gravestone.

Many old-time FBI agents admit that most of their time and duties were used to enhance the image of the FBI. Once in a while they would try to run down a bank robber, but organized crime was off-limits in many cases.

I am telling you who FBI Director J. Edgar Hoover really was, so you can understand the evil that was involved in the assassination. Because when you understand the simple fact that Hoover handled the cover-up, the answers come flooding forward in droves and you can understand how easily the American people were fooled.

There were and are some good men in the FBI, but not at the top echelon in 1963. Under Hoover the FBI laboratories were an arm for prosecutors, and off-limits for defense experts. The FBI worked for the prosecution and no one else. The pro-prosecution bias was evident, and the FBI controlled the evidence.

One of the FBI's tricks was to discredit witnesses that had any evidence they did not want presented. When Jim Lehrer wrote the June 5, 1964 article about me and my statement about a missed shot during the assassination of President Kennedy, the FBI was in Jim Lehrer's office that afternoon.

At that time, FBI agents were not allowed to write their own reports; Hoover had trained report writers that could slant the investigating agents' reports any way he wanted. Hoover's report on the Kennedy assassination to the Warren Commission did not contain any information about a missed shot or me and my minor injury.

My statement was unwanted by Hoover, and in the FBI report on the Lehrer article I was no longer a new car salesman, but was now portrayed as a used car salesman just trying get publicity (I had asked my name not be used) and trying to make money off the assassination.

I had never asked for, was offered, or received a dime from anyone.

J. Edgar Hoover was one of the most morally corrupt men to ever serve our country. The information in this chapter is a short summary of all that has been written about FBI Director Hoover for the last 40 years.

Hoover, born in Washington D.C. January 1, 1895, was Director of the Federal Bureau of Investigation for almost half a century. Wherever Hoover went, so did his live-in lover, Clyde Tolson.

Hoover's power as head of the FBI attracted other powerful men, such as ultra-rich oil men Sid Richardson and Clint Murchison Sr. Murchison's friendship with Hoover was so enthusiastic that he bought the Del Mar horse racing track in La Jolla California so that Hoover and his lover Clyde Tolson would always have a place to go for their favorite pastime, the sport of kings, horse racing. When you add politician Lyndon Johnson and his cronies to this group, you have the money, power, and political force to almost do whatever they pleased.

Now back to 1963. These men kept company, they had much in common. At the top of their list of things in common was a mutual dislike of JFK, in short, they hated John F. Kennedy's guts. President Kennedy was going to do away with the oil depletion allowance, Vice President Johnson was going to dropped from the 1964 ballot. The Kennedy brothers, President John and Attorney General Robert were going to force J. Edgar Hoover to retire, Hoover was over the mandatory government employee retirement age.

This group's closeness went all the way back to 1948. When Lyndon Johnson was elected to the U.S. Senate in 1948, there were two major celebrations, one was at the Adolphus hotel in Dallas, Texas, and the other was at the Driskill hotel in Austin, Texas. Besides Johnson, Hoover, Tolson, Richardson, and Murchison were at both victory celebrations

These men were the core of the two years of planning to assassinate President John F. Kennedy. The oil men had an unlimited supply of money, and J. Edgar Hoover's power, except for the Kennedy's, was unlimited. Lyndon Johnson had access into the deepest part of the CIA and more, one of Clint Murchison's closest friends was Mafia Boss Carlos Marcello. There you had it, evil men with money, power and burning desire to pull off the crime of the century. Did they think they would get caught,? Of course not, they made sure there were layers of men between them and the actual assassination.

How would they cover-up the assassination and the investigation of the murder of President Kennedy? That would be too easy: the FBI would be in charge of any investigation and Director of the FBI J. Edgar Hoover would control the outcome of that investigation. The assassination of President Kennedy was planned down to the last detail.

There were a couple of minor snags after the killing, getting Kennedy's body out of Dallas was one, Dallas wanted to do the autopsy in Dallas. A whisper to a secret Service agent, "for Jackie's sake let us get this body out of here and back to Washington," was all the Secret Service needed to take control of Kennedy's body at Parkland Hospital. The second was the Dallas Police Department wanting to handle the investigation. A call to Homicide Captain Will Fritz of the Dallas Police Department by new President Johnson sent Captain Fritz scurrying to Sheriff Bill Decker's office for advice. Sheriff Decker, who had inside information, told Captain Fritz the FBI should take over the investigation and for Fritz to go back to Dallas Police Headquarters and tell Dallas Chief of Police Jesse Curry that the Dallas Police needed to bow out of the investigation and turn it over to the FBI. Dallas did turn it over to the FBI at once.

Then, less than 48 hours after the assassination, the plotters hit the jackpot, Jack Ruby killed Lee Harvey Oswald, the "lone nut assassin" was now dead and could not defend himself – mission accomplished. But there was one more snag to come up in the plans. President Johnson bowed to public pressure and appointed a Commission to investigate the assassination. J. Edgar Hoover was fit to be tied, President Johnson called Hoover to the Oval Office, had a heart-to-heart chat with Hoover and convinced Hoover that every thing the new Commission needed would have to come through the FBI and J. Edgar Hoover, that he, Johnson would not authorize anyone other than the FBI to investigate. Of the 25,000 documents generated by the FBI agents, only 9,000 were ever turned over to the Warren Commission.

On December 9, 1963, the FBI leaked to the press an FBI summary report in which the FBI concludes that Lee Harvey Oswald acted alone in assassinating President Kennedy. The FBI's leak was intentional so the United States government could put their spin on the murder of JFK by a "lone nut assassin" to the public.

The crime of the century had been solved in two days by the press and the FBI. Lee Harvey Oswald was tried, convicted and himself murdered and silenced in less than 48 hours.

CHAPTER EIGHTY-FOUR

A COVER-UP EXAMPLE

Sometimes years later and by accident we find out critical information about the assassination of JFK. Tip O'Neill was a popular political figure with a career spanning 50 years, including a decade as Speaker of the House, in Washington D.C.

When Speaker O'Neill retired he wrote his life story, *"Man of the House, The Life And Political Memoirs of Speaker Tip O'Neill,"* in 1987, 24 years after the assassination of JFK. On page 178 of that book, Speaker O'Neill writes: " I was never one of those people who had doubts about the Warren Commission's Report on the President's death. But five years after Jack (JFK) died, I was having dinner with Kenny O'Donnell (JFK's Special Assistant riding in the car directly behind JFK) and a few other people at Jimmy's Harborside Restaurant in Boston, and we got to talking about the assassination.

"I was surprised to hear O'Donnell say that he was sure he had heard two shots that came from behind the fence.'

'That's not what you told the Warren Commission, I said.'

'You're right he replied, I told the FBI what I had heard, but they said it couldn't have happened that way and that I must have been imagining things. So I testified the way they wanted me to. I just didn't want to stir up any more pain and trouble for the family.'

'I can't believe it, I said. I wouldn't have done that in a million years, I would have told the truth. '

'Tip you have to understand. The family – everybody wanted this thing behind them.'

"Dave Powers (Assistant to JFK and also in the car behind JFK) was also with us at the dinner that night, and his recollection of the shots was exactly the same as O'Donnell's. Kenny O'Donnell is no longer alive, but during the writing of this book I checked with Dave Powers. As they say in the news business, he stands by his story."

O'Neill goes on to write, "And so there will always be some skepticism in my mind about the cause of Jack's death. I used to think that the only people who doubted the conclusions of the Warren Commission were crackpots. Now, however, I'm not so sure."

Tip O'Neill's reflection on a conversation at a dinner five years after the assassination of President Kennedy pretty much tells the story of the influence J. Edgar Hoover had on his agents, and how those FBI agents carried out that influence with the public. Kenny O'Donnell and Dave Powers were the top two assistants to President John F. Kennedy.

CHAPTER EIGHTY-FIVE

TWO MEN SEEN ON THE SIXTH FLOOR

One of the saddest actions of the Warren Commission was in trying to crucify a young man's testimony who saw two men on the sixth floor of the School Book Depository shortly before the assassination of President Kennedy and then, for reasons we once could only guess at, the Commission did not call the other witnesses who also saw two men on the Sixth floor.

We will never know how many witnesses saw at least two men on the sixth floor moments before our President was assassinated. When I first connected the dots, it appeared to me that the Commission had covered up facts and was corrupt.

The Warren Commission called for Arnold Rowland to testify because he had made public statements about seeing two men on the sixth floor of the School Book Depository moments before the assassination. The lawyers questioning Arnold could not get him to change his story so they called his teen-age wife Barbara to testify.

They did not ask Barbara Rowland what she had seen as a witness to the assassination of JFK, they only asked her questions about her husband's character.

Of all the witnesses who had seen people or movement on the sixth floor before and after the shooting, the Rowlands were the only two witnesses called to testify other than those who had seen the rifle sticking out the window. It is unknown how many people did see someone on the sixth floor of the School Book Depository before, during, and after the shooting. I was able to compile a partial list of witnesses who saw more than one person on the sixth floor at the time President Kennedy was assassinated.

The list is as follows: Arnold Louis Rowland testified on March 10, 1964 to the Warren Commission, he was 18, married, attended High School part time, worked at Pizza Inn part time and lived in Dallas. He planned to go to college with Rice as his first choice.

Warren Commission lawyer Arlen Specter took Mr. Rowland's testimony. His testimony is in Volume II, pages 165-190. Arlen Specter did most of the questioning with Commission member Gerald Ford occasionally asking questions. The questioning of Mr. Rowland is intense and it established that Mr. Rowland has good eyesight and is standing about 150 feet from the open window, where he can see a man with a rifle with a big telescopic sight standing back from the window a few feet in the far west sixth floor window. The rifle is seen for 15 to 20 seconds and reminds him of his step-dads 30-06 deer rifle.

Rowland guesses the man is in his early 30s and on the slender side. Mr. Rowland's answers are direct, without hesitation, and look very good on paper. Mr. Rowland also states that he saw "an elderly Negro" hanging out the far east sixth floor window (the window where the sniper's nest was found). He also describes other windows on lower floors with various people looking out raised windows.

Rowland is asked about his eyesight, school grades, and I.Q., and he answers 20-20 eyesight, straight As except for a couple Bs, and an I.Q. of 147. He states he cannot positively ID Lee Harvey Oswald, and that he gave a statement immediately after the assassination at the Sheriff's office, and to the FBI 6-8 times in the following days at his home and at his work.

His testimony is 25 pages long, and has many questions repeated by Commission lawyer Arlen Specter. Despite the repeated questions, Rowland does not change his story. He does stretch his school grades a bit and possibly his eyesight just as many a teenager might do.

Barbara Rowland, Arnold Rowland's wife testified on April 7, 1964 and her testimony is in Volume VI pages 177-191. Her entire testimony is devoted to Commission Lawyer David W. Belin trying to get Barbara Rowland to discredit her husband. You can tell Mrs. Rowland is getting tired of the questioning of the honesty of her husband, when she states: "Well, he may have had an A average overall. A average, but some of his cards didn't have A's altogether."

Under intense questioning Mrs. Rowland, sensing what the questioning was about, finally said, "My husband might exaggerate sometimes." And then she asked, "Is that what you want me to say?" The lawyer agreed and dismissed her from further testimony.

The questioning of the Rowlands was very biased and in reading the "interrogation," the bias jumps out at you. The two Warren Commission lawyers, Specter and Belin, acted like prosecutors, and there was no "defense" lawyer present to keep the questioning of these two young people fair. This hard questioning of Mrs. Rowland finally succeeded in discrediting her husband's claim about seeing two men on the sixth floor.

The above information was taken from the Rowland's testimony in the 26 volumes of hearings. I then compared the Rowland's 39 pages of testimony to what the official, available to the general public, 888-page condensed Warren Commission Report said.

It was on pages, 250-251 of the official Warren Report, I read what the final Report had to say about Arnold Rowland in dismay. It stated Arnold had lied about his grades, lied that he had graduated from High School, and that he had lied about being admitted to College. That every thing Arnold Rowland had said was false.

In fact in his testimony, he stated his grades were straight As, with a couple of Bs and in fact it was only an A average. In his testimony he stated he was going to school part-time and working part-time, and that he would like to get into Rice.

The Warren Commission lied. They also lied in saying that he had not told anyone about seeing two men on the sixth floor until he testified on March 10, 1964, when in fact he had told Deputy Sheriff Roger Craig about the two men on the sixth floor ten or fifteen minutes after the assassination, and he mentioned the two men also to an FBI agent.

Mrs. Carolyn Walthers reported to the FBI soon after the assassination that she saw two men in an upper floor window of the Texas School Book Depository: one man was holding a rifle pointed at the street below and was wearing a white shirt and had blond or light-colored hair. The other man wore a brown suit coat.

The FBI tried to make her think that all she saw was boxes. Mrs. Walthers was never asked to give testimony to the Warren Commission about her observations, thus escaping the danger of defamation by the Commission. The FBI also ignored her observations.

Mrs. Ruby Henderson was standing across the street from the Depository and recalled seeing two men in the window on the sixth floor. One of the men wore a brown suit coat, and the other wore a white shirt. She could only see their head and shoulders, it was not like they were leaning out. She noticed one man had dark hair and a darker complexion than the other. She was unable to determine if either man was holding anything. Mrs. Henderson was not called to give testimony to the Warren Commission about what she had witnessed moments before the shots rang out, thus avoiding being defamed by the Commission.

Johnny L. Powell was on the sixth floor of the Dallas County Jail across the intersection and on the opposite corner of Houston Street from the

School Book Depository (he was serving three days in jail for a minor misdemeanor). He and other inmates had a clear view of the sixth floor window sniper's nest, shortly before the shooting. One man was dark skinned and appeared to be Latin. The other man had a rifle and seemed to be fooling with the rifle's telescope.

Neither Powell, nor any of the other men who had witnessed two men on the sixth floor of the Depository were called to testify about what they had seen.

Stanley Kaufman, a lawyer and friend of Jack Ruby's, testified that he had a client that was in the county jail at the time of the assassination named Willie Mitchell. Willie Mitchell had told Kaufman that his fellow inmates congregated at the jail windows to watch the motorcade and had witnessed the President being murdered. When Mr. Kaufman was deposed, Volume XV pages 525-526, he tactfully suggested that the Commission might want to interview the jail inmates who witnessed the killing, and had a clear view of the sixth floor of the Depository. There is no record in the Warren Commission Hearings that any of these inmate witnesses were called to testify.

Charles I. Bronson, an amateur photographer innocently filmed moving images in three of the sixth floor windows of the Depository, including the sniper's nest window and next two windows closest to the sniper's nest window with the movements being behind each of the three windows all at the same time about six minutes before the assassination.

However the FBI said the film was not conclusive and Charles Bronson was not called to testify, nor was his film seen by the Warren Commission. I have personally watched this film, and the movement behind the three sixth-floor windows is plain to see.

Robert Hughes filmed the motorcade as it was turning off Houston Street onto Elm Street with the TSBD in the background, and his film shows the same movement in the same windows as the Bronson film. Robert Hughes was not called to testify nor was his film used by the Warren Commission.

Tom Dillard, a photographer for the *Dallas Morning News* was riding in the press car, eight cars back in the motorcade and about fifteen seconds after the shooting stopped, he took a picture of the Depository.

His picture was widely published with the west window cropped off. The un-cropped Dillard picture of the west window shows the figure of a large person in that window. A shot from this window would also match the trajectory of Governor Connally's injury.

After the shooting Howard L. Brennan saw what appeared to be a pipe being withdrawn from this most westward window of the sixth floor of the School Book Depository. Mr. Brennan also stated that moments later he saw someone looking out the window as if to, "admire his handiwork."

Richard R. Carr

Richard R. Carr had a birds-eye view of Dealey Plaza at the time of the shooting and this view allowed him to see into the sixth-floor windows of the Depository. Mr. Carr was working on the new Courts building being constructed at the corner of Main and Houston Streets.

In an interview with the FBI, Mr. Carr told the FBI that he saw a heavy-set man wearing a hat, a tan sports coat, and wearing horned rim glasses, standing in one of the sixth-floor windows of the Depository a minute or so before the assassination. Moments after the shooting, Carr climbed down from where he was working and saw the same man along with two other men walking at a fast pace away from the Depository south down Commerce Street to Main Street and then east one block to Record Street where the heavy-set man wearing the brown jacket and horned rim glasses got into a 1961 or 1962 gray Rambler station wagon, which was parked down Commerce Street and then drove onto Record Street.

The Rambler station wagon had Texas license plates, was driven by a young Negro man, and drove off north on Record Street. According to Richard Carr, the FBI told him: "If you didn't see Lee Harvey Oswald in the School Book Depository with a rifle, you didn't see it."

After Mr. Carr told the FBI what he had observed, he received phone threats ordering him to leave Texas or else. He moved to Montana. In Montana he once found dynamite taped to his car's ignition and had someone take a shot at him.

With the help of a policeman neighbor, Carr and the policeman captured the shooter. Mr. Carr testified at the Jim Garrison New Orleans trial of Clay Shaw and was attacked again by two men. Mr. Carr was stabbed but managed to shoot and kill one of the men by shooting him three times; after the assailant was shot he managed to say, "Doodle Bug, he has killed me."

Mr. Carr received more threats when he was called to testify to the House Select Committee on Assassinations in 1975.

For the first five minutes after the assassination, from my personal knowledge of being in there in Dealey Plaza during the assassination, I can say without any doubt whatsoever, it took at least five minutes of total confusion for the police to decide that the shots may have come from the School Book Depository and then make a move to seal off the Depository.

The fact is that Inspector Herbert V. Sawyer ordered the Depository sealed off at 12:37, seven minutes after the assassination had occurred. James Worrell was killed in a motorcycle accident two years later.

Carolyn Walthers, Ruby Henderson, Johnny L. Powell, Charles I. Bronson, Richard R. Carr, county jail inmate witnesses, Dallas city street worker witnesses, and many unknown other witnesses were *not* called to testify before the Warren Commission nor was the Bronson film introduced into Warren Commission evidence.

Arnold Rowland and James Worrell were both called to testify, but the Warren Commission did not accept either Rowland's or Worrell's testimony as honest, even though there were other witnesses who backed up their testimony.

The best view of all was from the sixth floor of the Dallas County Jail, cater-corner across from the School Book Depository. The Warren Commission interviewed not one inmate who had that view.

Chapter Eight-Six

Preliminary Report

The previous chapter, "Two Men On The Sixth Floor" presents facts that were omitted or ignored by the Warren Commission. The fact that a man ran out the back door of the School Book Depository moments after the assassination of President Kennedy can now be an established fact and that the person who ran out the back door was wearing a brown coat can also be an established fact.

Three witnesses, we know of, saw a man with a brown sport or suit coat on the sixth floor, and it can now be stated as fact that there was a man on the sixth floor of the Texas School Book Depository at the time of the assassination of President Kennedy wearing a brown coat.

A minimum of at least five people saw at least two men on the sixth floor moments before the assassination of President Kennedy. We can now accept as fact that there were at least two men on the sixth floor of the Texas School Book Depository at the time of Kennedy's murder.

Other things that need to be considered about who was on the sixth floor of the Depository at the time of the assassination: A man that has a bald spot at the top of his head. A heavy set man that wears horn-rim glasses. A man was seen hurrying away from the Depository and seen getting into a Rambler station wagon. And one of the men seen on the sixth floor of the Depository at the time of the shooting was either a dark-skinned white man, Latino, Black man, or an Indian.

There was only one witness, Arnold Rowland, called to testify about seeing two men on the sixth floor of the Depository and the Warren Commission wrote in their Report that what was considered normal information he had given was false.

There was only one witness, James Worrell, called to testify that had seen a man run out the back door of the Depository moments after the assassination. His testimony was extremely credible, but ignored.

There were dozens of eyewitnesses, such as the county jail inmates across from the sixth floor, Dallas city street workers on Houston street, and the group of onlookers who may have seen two men on the sixth floor or witnessed a man tear out the rear door who were not sought out to testify about what they had observed.

Bystander Charles Bronson was standing on the southwest corner of Main and Houston Streets about six minutes before the assassination. When an unidentified man had an epileptic type seizure near the corner of Elm and Houston Streets, Bronson filmed this man's medical problem with his 8mm camera.

The filming of the man having the seizure inadvertently showed the Depository and its sixth floor in the background. The film clearly shows people moving behind the three windows, the alleged sixth-floor sniper's nest, and the two windows to the left of the sniper's nest.

The movement being seen behind these three windows is simultaneous, indicating that there are three people at and next to the sniper's nest six minutes before shots were fired.

Robert Hughes was also standing at the corner of Main and Houston Streets in Dealey Plaza. Robert Hughes filmed the President's motorcade as it turned off Houston Street onto Elm Street in front of the School Book Depository, his film showed the Depository including the sixth floor about two seconds before the shooting started. Robert Hughes' film clearly shows simultaneous movement behind the three easternmost windows on the sixth floor of the School Book Depository, two seconds before the shooting.

Charles Bronson called the FBI immediately after the assassination and told the FBI about a film he had taken. The FBI supposedly reviewed the film, but said it did not contain anything of interest.

In 1978, Earl Golz, a reporter and assassination researcher discovered the FBI's notes on the Bronson film and was able to borrow the film from Charles Bronson.

After optically enhancing the Bronson film, one could plainly see the movement behind the sniper's nest window and two windows next to the sniper's nest window. For anyone who would like to see the Bronson and Hughes films that show this movement behind the sixth floor windows as the assassination was about to take place, Robert Groden has put both of these films in his DVD's, JFK, *The Case For Conspiracy* and *JFK Assassination Films*, which can be found online for under $30.00 each.

Both titles have both the films. When you add up the known witnesses 'description of a little bit here and a little bit there, a bald spot at the top of his head, heavy set, horn-rim glasses, you have described Mac Wallace.

CHAPTER EIGHT-SEVEN

THE ESCAPE

FBI Director J. Edgar Hoover said Lee Harvey Oswald did it, three shots were fired from the sixth floor "snipers nest," case closed. The Warren Report hardly varied from what Hoover had dictated two days after the assassination of President Kennedy. The problem with the Report was that there were too many witnesses who had not been called to testify and too many questions left unanswered. We now know that there is overwhelming evidence that Lee Harvey Oswald was not the shooter, which leaves the question of how did the assassin or assassins escape and a seemingly minor question of why the electricity went off as the President's motorcade approached the School Book Depository. The answer to how the escape was made can be found in the 26 volume Warren Commission set, in Volume VII page 386.

On that page, Texas School Book Depository Manager Roy Truly is giving sworn testimony that when he and Dallas Police Officer Marrion Baker start to use the elevator to go to the roof, the electricity is off and both elevators are stuck on the fifth floor. They race up the stairs and when they get to the fifth floor, Roy Truly notices the electricity is back on and one of the elevators has now moved down. Everyone is accounted for except for who took one of the elevators down the moment the electricity came back on. There is no eyewitness to who took that elevator down but it is safe to assume that it could in fact have been the assassination crew from the sixth floor.

Who took that elevator down was never investigated by the Warren Commission and the mystery of why the electricity went off was never investigated by the Warren Commission. I do not like to speculate, but a scenario has jumped out at me to address. All evidence points to the assassination as being a well-planned professional undertaking.

The scenario that jumps out at me is that the elevators were deliberately placed at the fifth-floor level and the electricity was cut off so no one could move them. When the assassin or assassins were through with the killing,

371

they could walk down one flight of stairs to a waiting elevator that had now had the power restored as planned for their escape. That would be too easy, but let me go one step further. In the overall plan there was a preplanned secret place on the fifth floor where the weapon or weapons used in the killing could be stashed to be secreted out of the building later. Again too easy, all the attention was on the sixth floor and finding the "patsy's" rifle planted there. The assassins, once down and out the door of the Depository, had the men with the fake Secret Service badges waiting to rush them away.

Roy Truly's testimony has been right there in the 26 volumes of the Warren Commission since 1964. At first glance Roy Truly's third time to be deposed does not look important. But when you put it together with the known facts it completes the picture of a clean get-a-way by the assassins. Let us look at the known facts, facts that seem to be unimportant by themselves.

The Charles Bronson and Robert Hughes amateur home movies show movement behind the three easternmost windows of the sixth floor of the School Book Depository. Both movies show this movement to be simultaneous, indicating that there were at least 3 people on the sixth floor before and during the assassination of President Kennedy. These windows were dirty and with the sun's glare you could not see into them but you could see the "shadow" of someone moving behind the windows. Charles Bronson caught the School Book Depository on film because a man had an epileptic-type seizure near the Depository about 6 minutes before the assassination and in filming this minor event, he inadvertently filmed the front of the sixth floor. Charles Bronson was standing at the corner of Main and Houston Streets when he took the movie. Robert Hughes was also standing at the corner of Main and Houston Streets and he started filming on Houston Street as the motorcade was turning onto Elm Street. His movie film also shows the sixth floor and the movement behind the "snipers nest" window and the two windows next to it.

A little-discussed and mentioned fact was that the electricity had strangely gone off just moments before the President's motorcade appeared. Roy Truly and other School Book Depository employees who gave testimony mentioned the fact about the electricity being off at the moment President Kennedy was killed.

When Roy Truly and Dallas Motorcycle Officer Marrion Baker tried to use the elevator only to discover the electricity was off, they took the stairs. There was a moment when they stopped on the second floor when Baker saw Oswald in the lunch room, they then resumed racing on up the stairs to the fifth floor. Roy truly noticed one of the elevators had now gone down and the electricity was now back on. Truly and Baker took the other elevator to the seventh floor to get to the roof.

The ignored third deposition of Roy Truly can be found in Volume VII, and on page 386 of the 26 volumes of the Warren Report. Roy Truly has been called to testify for the third time on May 14, 1964 and is winding up his testimony that started on page 380.

In the middle of the page Mr. Truly's testimony is continued in Mr. Truly's office In the Texas School Book Depository at 411 Elm Street, Dallas Texas. Assistant Counsel Joseph A. Ball takes Roy Truly's deposition.

Mr. Ball: Mr. Truly, when you came into the building with Officer Baker you tried to look up the elevator shaft, didn't you?

Mr. Truly: Yes, I sure did.

Mr. Ball: And where did you see the elevators?

Mr. Truly: On the fifth floor – both of them on the same floor.

Mr. Ball: They were both on the fifth floor?

Mr. Truly: Yes.

Mr. Ball: You are sure of that?

Mr. Truly: I am sure because their bottoms were level.

Mr. Ball: When you went up to the floor, was there an elevator on any of the floors?

Mr. Truly: When I reached the fifth floor, the east elevator was there, but west one was not.

Mr. Ball: Do you know where it was?

Mr. Truly: No I don't. I didn't look. I just remember it wasn't upstairs. So it was down below somewhere.

Mr. Ball: You took the east elevator?

Mr. Truly: I took the east elevator load to the seventh floor.

Mr. Ball: That's all.

Mr. Truly: Fine.

One more fact. There were three young black men who had been watching the motorcade from the fifth floor, James Jarman Jr., Bonnie Ray Williams and Harold Norman, after they heard the gun shots they ran to a west window to watch the activity in the rail yard. They testified that they did not see or hear Roy Truly or Officer Baker when they came up the stairs (cartons of books were stacked high). When these three young men finally decided to go down, the elevators had both already gone down and so they ran down the stairs.

It might seem a little complicated but it is not: some unknown person or persons took one of the awaiting elevators down from the fifth floor immediately after the electricity was turned back on about two minutes after the assassination of President Kennedy for a clean escape in the pandemonium of the moment. You must note that there were several companies on the first four floors doing business in the School Book Depository. These companies were there to do business and there were strangers coming and going all day every day, it would be too easy for the assassins to just walk out the door.

I was never inside the School Book Depository that day, I was outside in Dealey Plaza and I can tell you that when the crowd discovered what had just happened, reactions went crazy for the civilians and police alike. The pandemonium was unlike anything you will ever see in your lifetime. You were so distracted with the immensity of the thought of what and you had witnessed, that so very much could escape your attention. I am told that is human nature.

CHAPTER EIGHTY-EIGHT

LYNDON BAINES JOHNSON

We should all know by now what a flawed person Lyndon B. Johnson was. Lyndon Johnson had a lifelong struggle with a bi-polar, manic-depressive disorder and was an alcoholic. He was able to hide much of this from the public, but could not hide the mental problems and alcoholism from his aides or those close to him.

At an early age he had been determined to be President at any cost, but when he finally became President, and it came time to run again for President in 1968, the mental collapses had become progressively worse and President Lyndon Johnson announced he would not seek re-election.

Lyndon Johnson retired to his ranch in Texas, where his mental health rapidly deteriorated, to the point that all Lyndon wanted to do was sit at the window of his ranch house and wait for a tour bus to drive by so he could wave at the bus.

Doctors were called, heavy medication was given, but the weight of the thousands of war dead and the murders he had ordered were too much of a load for one man to carry. Lyndon Johnson was completely nuts when he died at the age of 64, four years after he left the Presidency.

I cannot describe the agony his daughters must have gone through watching their father in his last years. Like any child, they loved their father no matter what. Now, these same daughters with children of their own must hear what they probably already know about their father over and over. I am so sorry.

There have been dozens of books telling the good side of Lyndon Johnson, and there are some good things he has done. In looking back at those good deeds, they were most likely done to give him a political advantage or to boost his ego. There have been a couple of negative books but they have been mostly ignored. The public has not known the really deep dark side of this man who was our 36th President.

Lyndon Baines Johnson was born on August 27, 1908 near Stonewall, Texas. He graduated from Johnson City High School in 1924, attended

Southwest Texas State Teachers College and graduated with a Bachelor of Science degree.

At the age of 20 he was teaching poor Mexican-American kids in a poorest of poor schools. He made an effort to teach these kids English. By 1930 he was teaching public speaking and debate at a high school in Houston, Texas.

In 1932-1935 he was Secretary to U.S. Representative Richard M. Kleberg of Texas. On November 17, 1934 he married Claudia "Lady Bird" Taylor. In 1935-1937 he was Director of the National Youth Administration in Texas.

In 1937, at the age of 28, he was elected to the U.S. House of Representatives from Texas. In 1941-1942 he served on active duty in World War II as a Lieutenant Commander in the U.S. Navy.

In 1948 he was elected U.S. Senator from Texas (it has now been documented that Johnson stole that 1948 Senate election). Lyndon Johnson served as a U.S. Senator until he was named as Vice Presidential running mate to John F. Kennedy in 1960.

Johnson was majority leader of the Senate from 1955-1960. From 1961-1963 he was Vice President of the United States. From November 22, 1963 to January 1969 he was President of the United States. Johnson died at his Texas ranch on January 22, 1973.

When President Kennedy was assassinated in Dallas on November 22, 1963, Vice President Lyndon Johnson was immediately sworn in, that afternoon, on Air Force One as the airplane sat at Dallas Love Field.

At that time in history, November 1963, Vice President Johnson had learned that he would not be on the ticket with Kennedy in the Presidential election of 1964, meaning his political career would be over. He also knew a scandal was about to erupt over his Bobby Baker and Billie Sol Estes dealings, and that he, could be facing criminal indictment's upon his return to Washington D.C.

By becoming President, Lyndon Johnson stopped the criminal investigation over the kickbacks from Baker and Estes at once. There was no news of what Johnson becoming President meant to him, the media was only concerned with JFK assassination news for the days and months following the assassination.

We now know that much of the Warren Commission's evidence was twisted or fabricated to fit the FBI chief J. Edgar Hoover's short two-day assessment of President Kennedy's assassination, and Hoover's naming of Lee Harvey Oswald as the "lone nut assassin."

The FBI then coerced the Dallas Police Department into turning the investigation over to the FBI the next evening, Saturday 11/23/1963. The next morning, 11/24/1964, a FBI internal and marked secret memo (yes I have a copy), by FBI official Jenkins states: "Hoover says Oswald alone did it, Bureau must convince the public Oswald is the real assassin."

According to the Jenkins memo, Hoover and the FBI had overnight solved the assassination of President Kennedy. Two days later and only four days after the assassination, 11/26/1963, J. Edgar Hoover sends out another internal FBI memo marked secret and it states: "Wrap up investigation, seems to me we have the basic facts now."

What we did not know then, was that the Kennedy killing was a well-planned coup by Lyndon Johnson and his cronies with FBI director J. Edgar Hoover in charge of the cover-up. It was too simple, two of the most powerful men in the world were now in charge and if you were a poor civilian or government employee that discovered the truth, there was no one to tell.

The Warren Commission never had a chance to get to the truth with Lyndon Johnson as President and J. Edgar Hoover's FBI feeding the Warren Commission only slanted information.

Lyndon Johnson liked to make people think that nearby Johnson City, Texas was named after his family, but Johnson City was not named after anyone in his family. Lyndon was from a poor family in what is known as Hill Country in Texas.

J. Edgar Hoover and President Lyndon Johnson

Johnson's granddaddy and family did not enjoy a good reputation. He was a tall gangling big-eared youth and was the butt of humiliation and ridicule in high school. To his credit he did get a college teaching degree, and at the age of 20 he started teaching Mexican children on the wrong side of the railroad tracks in Cotulla, Texas.

These poor Mexican children did not have lunches or lunch money, so Lyndon persuaded the School Board to buy bats, balls, and volley ball nets. He organized sports for the children to play during lunch hour. These children did not speak good English or any English at all. Lyndon insisted they speak English and formed English debating teams. He won the hearts of these poor Mexican children. Lyndon Johnson learned a valuable lesson on winning the downtrodden over.

In 1937, at the age of 28 he put the compassion lesson he learned from teaching these poor children to work. Lyndon ran for Congress in the tenth Texas Congressional District. The district had two-hundred thousand ranchers and farmers living a terrible bleak life of toil and sweat. Most of them had no electricity. He ran on the slogan "bring the lights," and was elected to the United States House of Representatives at the age of 28.

It is important to know that Lyndon had become friends with a young lawyer named Edward Clark who had helped Lyndon in the election. Lyndon was now known as a boy wonder and political genius.

CHAPTER EIGHTY-NINE

MADELEINE BROWN

Madeleine Duncan Brown (July 5, 1925 – June 6, 2002) was a media buyer for Glenn Advertising in Dallas when she met Lyndon Johnson. She would later become an executive with the advertising firm.

It was in the Crystal Ball Room at the Adophus Hotel shortly after Lyndon Johnson had won election to the United States Senate in 1948, that she met Lyndon. Madeleine was 23 years old, had a young son, and had been separated for a while from her husband and childhood sweetheart who had come back from World War II and the Marines a changed man.

Madeleine's husband, Glynn, had become an abusive drunkard and was institutionalized in a Veterans Hospital as a chronic paranoid schizophrenic. Madeleine was about to leave her office late one evening when one of her business associates, Jesse Kellam, who managed Lyndon Johnson's radio station KTBC in Austin Texas, called and asked her to come to a party at the Adolphus Hotel that evening honoring Lyndon Johnson's Senate victory.

There was no way Madeleine could turn down an invitation to a party at one of Texas and the country's plushest hotels, and a chance to mingle with some of Texas' richest oil men and their wives.

Madeleine was a very pretty young lady and it was normal for a cute young media personality to be invited to swank social parties as a conversationalist to mingle with the guests. It was also a good place to attain new business contacts for a young businesswoman.

When Madeleine entered the ball room, Jesse Kellam stood up and waved her to his table. Already seated at the table was Mrs. Kellam, Fort Worth oil man and bachelor Sid Richardson, Charles Marsh, Alice Glass, John Connally who was to become a Texas Governor, H.L. Hunt who was on his way to becoming the world's richest man, and oil billionaire Clint Murchison. With everyone now present, the waiter brought a large dish of caviar and a bucket of chilled champagne to their table and placed it near Jesse Kellam.

As the waiters brought in big trays of food to the ballroom's crowded tables, Madeleine and Alice Glass chatted away like old friends, then something caught Alice's eyes and Madeleine followed Alice's gaze to see a big hunk of a man with a petite simply dressed shy looking woman at his side.

The man was formally dressed except that he was wearing western cowboy boots. Alice nudged Madeleine and whispered "that's Lyndon Johnson." Lyndon's presence dominated the ballroom. Johnson came walking over to Jesse Kellam's table, and he startled Madeleine with his presence; he was a big man and he looked every bit like a Texan and a Congressman.

Lyndon greeted the men with a handshake and bowed slightly to Ms. Glass and Mrs. Kellam, Lyndon then walked around behind Madeleine, put his hands on her shoulders and said to Jesse: "Aren't you going to introduce me to this lovely young lady Jesse? Where are your manners Jesse?"

Jesse was embarrassed and jumped up with arms outstretched toward Madeleine and said, "Mr. Johnson this is Madeleine Brown, one of my favorite people in the advertising business." Lyndon leaned over to Madeleine and spoke in his Texas accent: "So you are the beautiful redhead at Glenn Advertising that Jesse has been hiding from me. It is about time that I have the honor to finally meet you."

Stunned and overwhelmed, Madeleine managed to say, "The honor is all mine, Mr. Johnson."

Lyndon asked if he could call her Madeleine and told her to call him Lyndon.

Madeleine replied, "Well of course." Lyndon Johnson then kissed her hand and asked Madeleine to be at a victory party at the Driskill hotel in Austin in three weeks.

Before Madeleine could answer; Jesse spoke up and said, "She'll be there Mr. Johnson, I'll see to it."

Suddenly the band started playing and Lyndon pulled Madeleine to the dance floor. Lyndon held her tight and looked into her eyes the whole time they danced. When the music ended, Lyndon escorted Madeleine back to the table and excused himself to mingle with the other guests. Madeleine could barely go to sleep that night thinking about the warmth in Lyndon's voice, the tenderness in his eyes, and the intimate dance. She knew Lyndon wanted her and she felt desirous, sensual, and beautiful as she fell asleep that night.

When Madeleine got to work Monday morning there were two dozen red roses waiting for her with a card that read: "Here's to new beginnings," and a formal invitation to the party at the Driskill hotel in Austin, on October 29, 1948.

It was about all a naive 23-year-old redhead could handle. Madeleine counted the days hours and minutes till she boarded Trans Texas Airlines at Love Field for Austin and the Maximilian Room at the Hotel Driskell.

Some of the most influential men in Texas and America were there with their women, wives and mistresses. Even FBI Director J. Edgar Hoover was there with his lover Clyde Tolson. Out of the blue, Lyndon startled Madeleine with "Madeleine Brown! May I have the honor?"

"You look absolutely beautiful," said Johnson.

With Lyndon teaching, Madeleine learned to dance that night. As the party broke up, Lyndon discreetly placed a key in the palm of Madeleine's hand and said, "Go on up to my suite and take a bath."

The suite was luxury like Madeleine had never seen; she ran a steamy bath and soaked for 45 minutes and then, standing in the doorway was Johnson. She tried to cover her breast and cried, Lyndon undressed, got in the bath with Madeleine and kissed the tears away. He then picked Madeleine up soaking wet and carried her to the bed. Their lovemaking was the start of a 20-year affair, with Madeleine being the mistress of this man while he was a Senator, a Vice President, and a President.

Steven Mark Brown, who died at the age of 39 under mysterious circumstances, was born of this affair. The manager of Lyndon Johnson's Austin TV station was the go-between for the affair: he would call Madeleine and tell her that there was a plane ticket waiting for her at Love Field. That was the signal that Lyndon was going to be in Austin.

They always had the same hotel room. One morning Lyndon threw open the shades and looked out and said, "I love Texas in the morning."

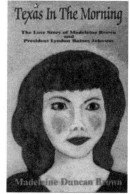

Later, Madeleine, years after Johnson had died, named her tell-all book, *Texas In The Morning*. It is a good book and goes into great detail about the affair with a good insight into who LBJ was, but it should be read by adults only. *Texas In The Morning* has become a collector's item.

I met Madeleine in 1988 and listened to her stories. At the time I did not take her seriously except for her and Lyndon's son, Steven. The picture of Steven was an exact image of Lyndon Johnson.

Steven found out that Johnson was his father after Johnson had died. Steven decided that part of Lyndon's estate was his and filed a lawsuit. Madeleine begged Steven to leave it alone, and suddenly Steven died mysteriously at the age of 39.

A few years later, and after I had met and talked to three other Johnson insiders, and these other insiders told me independently of each other the same damning stories about Johnson that Madeleine Brown had told me, I accepted what Madeleine and the others had to say as the truth.

On New Years Eve 1963, Lyndon Baines Johnson had been President for six weeks, and with Madeleine Duncan Brown present, Lyndon got rip roaring drunk and told the whole corrupt story of the coup d'état and how he had become President.

CHAPTER NINETY

MALICIOUS DIRT

While discussing Madeleine Brown it is a good time to talk about how malicious it can become if one goes against what the Warren Commission, FBI, CIA, or certain media or Government groups can do if they want to keep you from telling the truth.

I am James Tague, an eyewitness to the assassination of President Kennedy and the author of this book, and I felt it when I raised my hand in June of 1964 and asked what about the missed shot.

FBI Director J. Edgar Hoover did not want any missed shots. When an article appeared in newspapers nationwide on June 5, 1964 about a missed shot and the article did not use my name (at my request), the FBI responded that they knew exactly who I was.

I was no longer portrayed as an Air Force veteran trying to make a living selling new cars, but as a lowly used car salesman trying to make money off the assassination of President Kennedy.

Thankfully two Assistant United States Attorney Generals and some others stepped in and verified what I was saying as true: there was at least one shot that missed during the gunfire at the President.

New Orleans District Attorney Jim Garrison was not as lucky. The full force of the United States Government, especially the CIA, tried their best to vilify Garrison and what he had found out about Clay Shaw and others in New Orleans.

Another example is Penn Jones, who owned and published the Midlothian, Texas newspaper. Penn was outspoken about the flaws in the Warren Commission and did not mince words about how he felt about those flaws. One thing Jones did every year until his health failed him was to hold a prayer every November 22, at exactly 12:30 P.M., in Dealey Plaza for the deceased President Kennedy.

One year a few Dallas tourists joined in with Penn at this annual prayer and knelt with Penn on the grass. The next day the Dallas newspaper wrote an article about those crazy radical conspiracy theorists that show up in Dealey Plaza every year. There is now a nearly 50-year history of our government and the press trying to, at the very least, make sport of anyone who disagrees with the Warren Commission.

I know as I write this book that those same people will try to vilify me once again. I can almost hear the first words about my being a car salesman at the time Kennedy was killed. Those first words will be: "What does a car salesman know about the Kennedy Assassination?"

Many of those, with a closed mind to anyone that disagrees with the findings of the Warren Commission, have a strong passion against anyone who has information other than what the government has officially said.

This hatred I am trying to describe is still alive today in the year 2013, fifty years after the assassination of President Kennedy. I will use Madeleine Brown, Lyndon Johnson's mistress for over 20 years as a prime example.

When I first talked to Madeleine, I found her to be a very nice lady, a lady with some class and easy to talk to. I must note that when I first talked to Madeleine Brown, I was not seeking information for a book and as I look back it was difficult for me at that time to appreciate her first-hand information.

Then, as time passed, I met and talked to others who verified what Madeleine Brown had to say. Madeleine worked for a very reputable advertising company for several years and she had an executive position with that company. There is no question that Madeleine Brown knew Lyndon Johnson intimately and knew secrets that only a lover would know.

The *Dallas Morning News,* and *Morning News* reporter Hugh Aynesworth are examples of how lasting and to the extent this hate will go with lies to ruin a person's reputation. I am reprinting an article for you to read that appeared in the *Dallas Morning News* on Sunday November 18, 2012. It was on the front page of section two and started below a picture of an older man, Dave Perry, smiling into the camera, and the headline: "Assault On Conspiracies."

The story starts off about Dave Perry, age 69, disproving one conspiracy theory after another until it gets to perhaps the most titillating of the conspiracy stories, at least for Dallas residents.

It was published in the *Morning News* on November 6, 1982 under the headline: "Dallas Woman Claims She Was LBJ's Lover." Perry had disproved the allegation years ago, and only this year found new evidence he said bolsters his conclusions.

The 1982 story told of a Dallas woman who alleged she had been a longtime lover of former President Lyndon B. Johnson. Madeleine Duncan Brown had told a packed news conference that for many years, before Johnson died in 1973, she had met LBJ in various places for love trysts.

Brown said the affair lasted from 1949; the year Johnson became a Senator, until the late1960's. Obviously enjoying the attention, Brown spun quite a tale that day about an alleged party held at the Preston Road home of the late multimillionaire Clint Murchison Sr. the night before Kennedy was assassinated in Dallas.

It was a party she said, attended not only by LBJ, but FBI Director J. Edgar Hoover, former Vice President Richard Nixon, the late oil tycoons H. L. Hunt and Sid Richardson, and a handful of other rich and famous men.

Brown said several of the men met in a private room at the Murchison home on the evening of Nov. 21, 1963. Afterward, she said, LBJ took her hand and growled into her ear: "After tomorrow those (expletive) Kennedy's will never embarrass me again. That's no threat, that's a promise."

Hours later, on Nov. 22, Kennedy was dead.

Brown's allegation, denied by several close LBJ associates, still reverberated amid the Kennedy conspiracy crowd. "See," chortled several who had written conspiracy-tinged books about the case, "We told you Oswald didn't act alone."

Over the years her story has drawn national attention and became part of a dozen or more conspiracy theories. As Brown became more and more famous, some noted that she may have embellished the tale. She even outlined an alleged meeting she said she witnessed at Jack Ruby's Carousel Club between Oswald and his eventual killer, Ruby.

Here is Hugh Aynesworth's article:

FINDING THE SCENT

Dave Perry, a former insurance investigator who had moved to the Dallas area from Glens Falls N.Y. in 1986, originally volunteered at the JFK Assassination Information Center in downtown Dallas. It was there that several leading conspiracy believers promoted and exchanged theories.

As the different theories came and went, often becoming more and more bizarre, Perry began to realize that many of his friend's presumptions often weren't bolstered by facts.

"In some cases I saw authors and self-professed researchers reaching absurd conclusions, and then providing historically inaccurate proofs to prop up their theories," Perry said.

After that original news conference, Brown, basking in the light of those willing to believe her "love story" with LBJ and her allegations that he was involved with Kennedy's death, decided to add a bit more spice to her story.

Four years later she claimed LBJ was the father of her son, Steven Mark Brown who was born in 1951. Perry and his wife, Nikki, met Madeleine Brown at a social function a few years after she first drafted the LBJ stories. Though they thought she was "a nice woman," neither believed her ever-growing tales.

Perry decided to investigate the party story first. Rather quickly, he determined that LBJ could not have been at a Dallas party the night of November 21, 1963. The Vice President had been seen at a political rally in Houston with JFK until about 10 that night. He then flew to Carswell Air Force Base near Fort Worth, and after touching down at 11:07 P.M. he was driven to the Texas Hotel in Fort Worth, where he and Lady Bird were photographed at 11:50 P.M. on their arrival.

Further investigation proved to Perry that Murchison had moved from his Dallas home four years earlier after a stroke and declining health. On Nov. 21 he was living in East Texas at his Glad Oaks Ranch between Athens and Palestine. Murchison died in 1969. With the help of another area researcher, Greg Jaynes, Perry soon found two longtime employees who recalled being with their boss when a friend telephoned him Nov. 22 at the ranch to tell him the President had been shot.

Warren and Eula Tilley, Murchison's longtime chauffeur, and his housekeeper, said they recalled the day distinctly.

Checking further on the alleged party list, Perry determined that Hoover had been in Washington on Nov. 21 and 22.

And Tony Zoppi, the longtime entertainment columnist for the *News*, said he had seen Nixon introduced at the bottlers convention at a downtown Dallas hotel about 11 P.M. on Nov. 21. That sighting made it virtually impossible that Nixon could have attended the alleged Murchison party.

STILL DIGGING

Perry in October 2002, reported the entire investigation on his website in a lengthy piece called "Texas in the Imagination," a takeoff of a Brown book. But his pursuit of evidence did not stop there. In June 1987, Steven Mark Brown filed a $10.5 million lawsuit against Lady Bird Johnson claiming as LBJ's son he had been deprived of much of the Johnson estate.

Already in possession of evidence that Madeleine Brown, who died in June 2002, had lied about various aspects of her early life, Perry at that time began digging around on the paternity claim. Based on articles in the *News* dated Oct. 3, 1990, he soon determined that the son's suit had been tossed out of court because the plaintiff had not appeared at a scheduled hearing.

While meandering through old legal files that same year, Perry found that Madeleine Brown had been convicted of forging the will of Guy Duncan, an elderly relative, three months after his death in 1988. She was sentenced to 10 years in prison, but the conviction was later reversed on a technicality. She had not personally signed the original will but had induced a lawyer friend to do so. The real shocker came that summer.

In July, Perry came across a lawsuit that Steven Mark Brown filed in 1980 that ended up in Bastrop County. Brown claimed that a Dallas lawyer, Jerome Ragsdale, was his real father, and that he should share his estate. The case would later be dismissed by an appeals court for lack of evidence.

One of the most downloaded features from Perry's website is a list he calls "Rashomon To The Extreme," a reference to Oliver Stone's movie, *JFK*.

Perry compares the list to the 1950 Japanese film classic *Rashomon*, in which several witnesses see the same event differently.

In Perry's offering, he lists 68 individuals who have claimed to have shot the president, been accused of shooting him or been recognized as part of an assassination plot.

"I did not pick these names at random," Perry said. All are footnoted to a specific conspiracy author, researcher, research group, tabloid, newspaper, or self-proclaimed witness.

"It shows the level of absurdity some theorists have reached while claiming they only want to get to the real truth about the assassination."

WHAT REALLY HAPPENED

Like the conspiracy within a conspiracy theory, some Perry foes claim the CIA sent him to Dallas to "turn" Gary Mack, who at the time was a serious conspiracy believer.

Mack is now curator of the Sixth Floor Museum at Dealey Plaza, and many conspiracy folks consider him an abomination. "Some conspiracy theorists just want confirmation of their versions of truth," Mack said.

"It is satisfying when folks like Dave Perry step forward with documented evidence and information that sheds additional light on what really happened."

    – End of Aynesworth article –

Yes, what really happened?

Documented evidence that two ranch hands can recall a certain day several years after the fact, when reliable witnesses have already stated differently. Forgetting that Lyndon Johnson arrived after the party was over and it was after midnight. Saying that Madeleine Brown was given a 10-year prison sentence because a lawyer she knew forged a will.

Incidentally, any of us who have seen Madeleine's son Steven Mark Brown, or a picture of Steven, know that Steven is the spitting image of Lyndon Johnson. C'mon Hugh Aynesworth, this is the type of spin the public has been reading for 50 years and you still think they will believe whatever you put into print.

I must admit that there have been too many false conspiracy theories advanced over the last, 50 years, and that the public does not know what to believe. I will be the first to say that these theories need to be carefully read for documentation. What I have found in many of these theories is that some author has come upon some small truthful fact and in trying to get that true fact out to the public, has fabricated a dishonest theory into a book around that lonely true fact.

CHAPTER NINETY-ONE

TEXAS LAWMAN CLINT PEOPLES

O ne of the most over looked men with inside knowledge about the assassination of President Kennedy was Clinton Peoples, a lawman who wore many badges in his career. Clint Peoples was born in 1910 and in his career was a deputy sheriff, a Texas Special Investigator, a Texas Highway Patrolman, a Texas Ranger, a Texas Ranger Captain, and rounded out his career with an appointment from President Nixon to serve as a Federal Marshall.

One of his assignments had been investigating the 1951 murder of John Kinser (Senator Lyndon Johnson's sisters boyfriend) by Mac Wallace. Clint was stunned when Mac Wallace was found guilty of First Degree murder for Kinser's death, and the judge gave Mac Wallace a five-year suspended sentence. Senator Johnson's influence was suspected by many.

Ten years later in 1962 Clint Peoples was asked by Colonel Homer Garrison, director of the Texas Department of Public Safety to look into the mysterious death of Federal Agriculture agent Henry Marshall.

Henry Marshall's death had been ruled a suicide. The physical evidence was that Henry Marshall had been shot in his side five times with a bolt-action rifle, there was blood on Marshall's pickup truck, a new dent was found in the door of his pickup, and there was a bump on Marshall's head.

No pictures, no fingerprints were taken, and the pickup was washed and waxed the next day. The undertaker did not believe a man could shoot himself like that. The Sheriff ordered the Justice of the Peace to put suicide on the death certificate and JP Farmer signed off: death certificate, "death by gunshot, self inflicted."

Clint Peoples reported back to Colonel Homer Garrison that it: "would have been utterly impossible for Mr. Marshall to have taken his own life."

The Sheriff, the JP, and the judge would not talk to Ranger Peoples.

Peoples interviewed Nolan Griffin, a gas station attendant near Marshall's ranch. Griffin stated that on the day of Marshall's death a stranger had stopped in the gas station and asked directions to Henry Marshall's ranch.

Peoples had Thadd Johnson, a Texas Ranger artist, draw a facial sketch, at Nolan Griffin's direction, of the stranger who had asked directions to Henry Marshall's ranch the day of Marshall's death.

When the sketch was completed, Clint Peoples had an eerie feeling that he knew the man that Thadd Johnson had drawn. Then it came to Ranger Peoples, the sketch was that of Mac Wallace, the convicted murderer of John Kinser, whom Clint Peoples had investigated 10 years earlier. The Henry Marshall investigation led Ranger Peoples to Billie Sol Estes, and that led to Billie Sol and Clint Peoples becoming friends.

The Estes-Peoples friendship brought out a Lyndon Johnson tie-in to a cotton allotment scheme that lead Henry Marshall to investigate Billie Sol Estes. The investigation was pointing to corruption in Washington D.C.

Henry Marshall's investigation concerned Billie Sol Estes being paid millions of dollars by the United States Government not to grow cotton on hundreds of acres of farm land that Billie Sol had leased. Senator Johnson had tipped off Billie Sol that they were going to pass a bill to pay farmers not to grow cotton and Billie Sol had leased 100's of acres in anticipation.)

Lyndon Johnson was Vice President now, and it was decided that he could use his influence to get Henry Marshall promoted to a major position in the Agriculture Department in Washington D.C. with a big raise in pay.

It did not work, Henry Marshall saw through the bribe and turned down the promotion to D.C.

Billie Sol Estes was indicted by the U.S. Government and went to prison. His Lawyer did not allow a defense in his trial. Billie Sol Estes told me personally, in a face-to-face conversation that if his attorney, who was also President Lyndon Johnson's attorney, had tried to put up a defense it would have opened up Pandora's box.

Senior Ranger Captain Clint Peoples retired from the Texas Rangers in March of 1974 and President Richard Nixon appointed Clint as a U.S. Marshall for the Northern District of Texas. Clint Peoples continued to investigate Henry Marshall's death and visited Billie Sol Estes in prison.

U.S. Marshall Clint Peoples arranged for immunity for Billie Sol Estes and three month after Billie Sol got out of prison in December 1983, Billie Sol appeared before a Grand Jury in Robertson County Texas.

On June 19, 1992 U.S. Marshall Clint Peoples went public and stated that he now had documentary evidence that Malcolm "Mac" Wallace, Lyndon Johnson's hit man, was one of the gunmen in The Texas School Book Depository in Dealey Plaza when President John F. Kennedy was assassinated in Dallas on November 22, 1963. Four days later Clint Peoples was killed in a one-car automobile accident.

CHAPTER NINETY-TWO

BARR MCCLELLAN

B arr McClellan is a most interesting person for his life, his career, his family history and for being in the unique position of being one of Lyndon Johnson's lawyers.

Barr had a brilliant youth, he was his senior class president in high school, and had many awards in college. One of his sons, Scott McClellan was press secretary for President Bush and his ex-wife, Carole Strayhorn ran for governor of Texas.

Barr McClellan was one of the few men who were insiders to the events of big Texas oil money and that money's connection to Lyndon Johnson. McClellan was an attorney for the Edward Clark law firm in Austin Texas. Edward Clark and Lyndon Johnson were close friends as well as Clark handling Lyndon's legal problems going back before Lyndon stole his 1948 Senate race.

When Barr joined the Edward Clark law firm in 1966, he was soon doing legal work for President Johnson, such as advising on labor disputes and political strategy. Barr also did work for the Democratic Party and Texas oilmen.

When McClellan went to work for the Edward Clark law firm, it had been nearly three years since John F. Kennedy had been killed. What Barr soon found out was that the Kennedy assassination was still a topic of conversation with the other lawyers in the firm. There were conversations over coffee and lunch, and if there was a court case in another county, it was a common practice for the two lawyers assigned to the case to have conversations while riding together.

The names that kept popping up over and over were Mac Wallace, Cliff Carter and their own boss Edward Clark. As time went on, these insider's conversations had a story to tell about the constant closed-door visits Johnson had with Edward Clark and big cash payments paid by billionaire oil men to Edward Clark.

The old time lawyers who had been with the firm for years were not dummies, they had seen characters come and have secret meetings with their boss Edward Clark and Lyndon Johnson. And when President Kennedy was assassinated, it all came together. They could not talk about it openly, but away from the office it was *the* topic of constant conversation.

In researching for his book, Barr used hundreds of newly released documents, insider interviews, court papers, and the Warren Commission to document the story.

Barr McClellan had the story down pat; Lyndon Johnson was behind the assassination of John F. Kennedy. The most prominent person talked about was Mac Wallace. On a hunch, Barr got Wallace's fingerprints from Wallace's first murder trial and then got the only unidentified print found on a box on the sixth floor after the JFK assassination.

Barr then gave the prints for a blind test (the tester did not know whose prints they were checking) to one of the best-recognized print experts in the country, Nathan Darby. The prints were a match: Mac Wallace had been on the sixth floor when Kennedy was killed.

Barr McClellan had now verified what the Russian KGB had done in 1965; Lyndon Johnson was behind the assassination of President Kennedy. Barr then wrote the book *Blood, Money & Power: How LBJ Killed JFK*. The book finally came out in 2003 and was a best seller.

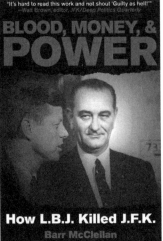

Nigel Turner, who had interviewed witnesses, including myself, for his TV series *The Men Who Killed Kennedy* interviewed Barr McClellan for his last segment (number 9); Barr goes into detail about Lyndon Johnson being behind the assassination of JFK.

The segment was broadcast on the History Channel on November 18, 2003 and all hell broke loose. Former Presidents Gerald Ford and Jimmy Carter, former LBJ staff workers Bill Moyers and Jack Valenti all raised heck with the History Channel for broadcasting the episode.

We do not know what went on in secret, but three "historians" on the assassination were called in and the History Channel issued a press release April 2, 2004 stating that the claim of LBJ's involvement in the assassination of JFK is entirely unfounded and does not hold up to scrutiny, and the History Channel apologizes to its viewers and Ladybird Johnson and her family.

The naysayers who always attack someone who comes up with positive documented evidence that the Warren Commission came to a wrong conclusion came out in full force against Barr McClellan. The first and foremost thing was that he was a convicted forger and made up the story about LBJ being behind the Kennedy assassination. Barr McClellan was convicted of forgery in 1982, but what the naysayers forget to add is that the forgery charges against Barr were later dismissed and as far as making up the story about LBJ being behind the assassination of JFK, Barr was there right in the middle of the story, the exact place where the murder was planned out in detail.

Madeline Brown   Billy Sol Estes

CHAPTER NINETY-THREE

BILLIE SOL ESTES

After President Kennedy and Vice President Johnson's trip to Texas in November 1963, Johnson was facing the possibility of a criminal indictment when he returned to Washington D.C. for receiving kickbacks from Billie Sol Estes on a cotton allotment scheme, and for receiving kickbacks from Bobby Baker on a vending machine deal.

A criminal indictment would mean the end of Lyndon Johnson's political career. Billie Sol Estes and Lyndon Johnson were close friends. While Johnson was a U.S. Senator, he gave Estes inside Government information. This connection helped in making Billie Sol Estes a multi millionaire, a "Wheeler Dealer."

In the late 50s too much cotton was being grown in the U.S., and it had driven the value of cotton down. Unknown to the public, the U.S. Congress was preparing to pass a law to pay farmers to not grow cotton. Senator Johnson tipped off his pal Billie Sol Estes about what was about to be enacted into law.

Estes then simply leased hundreds of acres of farmland from cotton farmers (the farmers were happy for the lease, they were not making money growing cotton). The law was passed and Estes was then paid to not grow cotton on the leased farmland.

A small amount of cotton could be grown but it was highly regulated. Billie Sol personally told me he had taken suitcases with as much as $200,000 to Senator Johnson's office for Lyndon's share of the scheme.

Billie Sol Estes funneled millions back to Johnson. In 1961 U.S. Department of Agriculture field agent, Henry Marshall, was looking into Billie Sol's dealings and discovered a possible link to the now Vice President Johnson in the scheme. He reported this to his superiors in Washington D.C.

The word quickly got back to Vice President Johnson. He had an easy answer to solve the problem, he would simply arrange to have Henry Marshall promoted to the Agriculture Department headquarters in Washington D.C. with a big increase in pay.

Marshall turned down the promotion. A short time later, Marshall was found dead on his farm with a rifle lying at his side. The coroner ruled that Marshall had taken a bolt action rifle and shot himself in the side five times. An awkward thing to do since he would have had to turn the rifle around pointing it at his side, stretched his arm to the trigger and with his thumb squeeze off a shot, then take the gun away from that position and work the bolt action to reload a bullet into the chamber, then point the rifle at his side again and do this 5 times.

A very difficult thing to do *since any of the 5 shots would have killed him.* The coroner ruled that Henry Marshal had committed suicide.

In 1984, after receiving immunity, and under oath in the Robertson County Texas court house, Billie Sol Estes told the court that Lyndon Johnson, Cliff Carter, Malcolm Wallace, and himself had met several times to discuss the issue of Henry Marshall. It was finally decided that Wallace should handle the problem. Estes testified that Wallace had murdered Marshall on Lyndon Johnson's orders to "get rid of him."

Later, it was discovered that just before Marshall "committed suicide" a man had stopped at a nearby service station and asked directions to Marshall's farm. A police drawing of that man created a picture of Malcolm Wallace. Billie Sol Estes was indicted for the cotton scheme, convicted and went to prison. Lyndon Johnson was now President and Estes kept his mouth shut and served his sentence.

Billy Sol Estes knew that if he did not keep his mouth shut, Johnson would have him killed. Estes' agriculture business collapsed while he was in prison causing him yet another offense and conviction. The U.S. Supreme court overturned his first wrongful conviction.

Billie Sol Estes later told the Grand Jury that he met Mac Wallace and Cliff Carter at his home in Pecos after Henry Marshall was killed. Wallace told how he waited for Marshall at his farm. He planned to use carbon monoxide from Marshall's truck exhaust to make it look like a suicide, but Marshal fought back and Mac had to shoot him with his own gun. Billie Sol quoted Cliff Carter as saying that Wallace: "Sure did botch it up." Lyndon Johnson was forced to use his influence as Vice President to get Texas authorities to cover up the murder.

The undertaker, Manley Jones, reported, "it looked like murder to me, a man can't shoot himself like that." Justice of the Peace, Judge Lee Farmer, said the Sheriff, Howard Stegall, told him to put suicide on the death certificate. Sybil Marshall, Henry Marshall's wife, finally convinced the Robertson County authorities to change the death certificate to murder.

Cliff Carter was a life-long friend who had gotten Estes involved with Lyndon Johnson. From all accounts before getting involved with Lyndon Johnson, Estes was a very good businessman. At the age of 18 he was presented with an award at the White House by President Roosevelt in 1943 for being America's most outstanding young farmer. He was a church-going Christian and was known as a Robin Hood to the poor.

Estes morals were such that he did not allow boys and girls to swim in his pool at the same time. He helped pay for hundreds of young men's college expenses – many were young black men. Billie Sol Estes was worth $400 million in 1962.

In speaking to Estes today (he is in his 80's), he sometimes gets carried away. An acquaintance recently (2010) told me she had taken Billie Sol to a mutual friend's wedding and when they were checking out of the hotel, Estes started to write a check for the bill and the clerk said they did not take checks, Billie Sol replied in an agitated voice, "I'll just buy this place." My acquaintance paid the bill by credit card and got Billie Sol out of there and every one had a good laugh, Billie Sol was still living like he was back in the 1960's.

I have no time for those who say: "You cannot believe a word an ex-convict tells you." Estes has paid for his mistakes by keeping his mouth shut and going to prison to protect Lyndon Johnson. Billie Sol did not rob a bank; he took advantage of insider's information and borrowed money more than once on the same fertilizer tanks, a white-collar crime.

Billie Sol Estes swears that what has kept him alive is some old recorded telephone conversations he taped.

When I met Madeleine Brown, Lyndon Johnson's mistress for 21 years, she talked fondly of Billie Sol Estes and he talked fondly of Madeleine and both talked fondly about the wild drinking times they had with Cliff Carter (Cliff Carter was Lyndon Johnson's campaign manager), Mac Wallace, and Lyndon Johnson; they were a small group that enjoyed each others company.

When I mention Billie Sol Estes to some people, the first thing they say, "You cannot believe a word a convicted criminal says," and Billie Sol was convicted of a white collar crime.

Before he got tangled up with Lyndon Johnson he was a model citizen who was a church-going Christian and never let a family go hungry in his territory. He was well respected and a sharp businessman who built a fortune worth 300 to 400 million dollars. Today in his 80's, he has fun with some northern writer who wants to ask him questions about his relationship with Lyndon Johnson.

Billie Sol would rather tell a Yankee writer the tallest tale you ever heard than eat a rib-eye steak, and then go home laughing all the way. You could write a whole book about Billie Sol Estes's life. The main thing to tell about Estes was his friendship with Texas Ranger Clint Peoples who arranged immunity for Estes and convinced him to tell all he knew.

Billie Sol Estes did go before the Robertson County Grand Jury and testify about the murders committed by Malcolm Wallace upon orders by Lyndon Johnson. Billie Sol learned of these murders from direct conversations with Cliff Carter and Mac Wallace. Mac Wallace had the habit of bragging about the murders.

There were nine murders that Billie Sol Estes knew of that Mac Wallace had committed, but Cliff Carter told Estes there were other murders done while he was in prison and that the total killed by Wallace was seventeen.

Mac Wallace was only arrested for his first murder and then he was given only a 5 year suspended sentence for first-degree murder by a bought and paid for judge in Austin, Texas. The first murder was Lyndon's sister's boyfriend, John Kinser, the others were:

Henry Marshall
George Krutilek
Ike Rogers and his secretary
Harold Orr
Coleman Wade
Josefa Johnson (Lyndon's sister)
President John F. Kennedy

Billie Sol Estes stated that Cliff Carter told him that the Mafia did not participate in the assassination of JFK, but that their participation was discussed and the Mafia was willing, but LBJ nixed their participation; Johnson felt the Mafia would wind up blackmailing him.

On November 21, 1963, the day before President Kennedy was assassinated, Vice President Lyndon Johnson was not only facing being indicted on the Bobby Baker scandal and the Baker kickbacks, but also the kickbacks from Billie Sol Estes. The only thing to save LBJ's political career would be for LBJ to suddenly become President.

Chapter Ninety-Four

Bobby Baker

R obert (Bobby) Baker was born in 1929 in Pickens, South Carolina and rumors are that he is still alive today as I write this chapter in 2012. Bobby was a page in the Senate at the age of 14 and was befriended by Lyndon Johnson. It was the start of a lifelong friendship: Bobby was known as Little Lyndon. Baker was a hard worker and when he was an adult became a full-time Senate aide to Johnson.

Lyndon Johnson schooled Bobby on body language and how to read a person, mainly politicians.

In the 1950s Bobby Baker arranged for Ed Levinson, an associate of mobsters Meyer Lansky and Sam Giancana, to get involved in establishing casinos in hotels in the Dominican Republic. Bobby Baker and Lyndon Johnson were invited to the grand opening of the first casino in the Dominican Republic, where Lyndon met some Mafia hoods in 1955.

The Dominican Republic was to be a replacement for the loss of Cuba as a gambling mecca. That ended when the CIA murdered Dominican Republic Dictator Rafael Trujillo. President Kennedy then supported Juan Bosch who was elected as President of the Republic in 1962. Bobby Baker with the help of Lyndon Johnson and mobsters Ed Levinson and Benny Sigelbaum formed Serve-U-Corporation, a vending company.

They bought their vending machines from a company in Chicago secretly owned by Sam Giancana. The vending machines were placed in places with federally granted programs. The money rolled in and Bobby Baker was getting rich and kickbacks went to Lyndon Johnson.

Bobby Baker's official income was from his job as Secretary to the Senate Majority leader Lyndon Johnson. When Lyndon Johnson became Vice President, President John F. Kennedy also named his brother Robert F. Kennedy as Attorney General of the United States.

The bitterness between Robert and Lyndon went back to the 1960 Democratic Convention. Rumors of corruption about Bobby Baker and Lyndon Johnson were floating all around Washington D.C. That was the excuse Bobby Kennedy needed to investigate Bobby Baker and Lyndon Johnson.

The Attorney General Robert F. Kennedy soon found out that Bobby Baker was a very rich man, and that he had connections to Dallas oil billionaire Clint Murchison and the Mafia and that Lyndon Johnson was right in the middle of it all, that Johnson was a corrupt politician.

RFK discovered Johnson had pushed through getting General Dynamics, a Fort Worth Texas Company, a seven billion dollar contract to build the F-111 fighter plane, received a $100,000.00 kickback.

On October 7, 1963 Bobby Baker was forced to resign his post. The coming scandal also caused Fred Korth, Secretary of the Navy, to resign. According to Anthony Summers, Baker had also arranged women for President Kennedy; Ellen Romesch was one of those women.

When J. Edgar Hoover, who was head of the FBI, got wind of the relationship between Ellen and President Kennedy, he had Ellen Romesch investigated by his agents. It was determined that Ellen was probably a Russian spy – that she worked for the Communist leader Walter Ulbricht of East Germany. When Ellen Romesch told Robert Kennedy about this communist connection, Robert Kennedy ordered her deported.

CHAPTER NINETY-FIVE

OILMAN INDUSTRIALIST – D. H. BYRD

D.H. Byrd was the owner of the School Book Depository, the building where a sniper's nest was found and shots were fired at President Kennedy on November 22, 1963.

What makes D. H. Byrd a person of interest is his many other connections to the assassination of President Kennedy. Byrd was co-founder of Ling Temco Vought Corporation; LTV became one of the largest government contractors in the United States.

Byrd was the employer of Lyndon Johnson's hit man, Malcolm Wallace at LTV; Wallace was to become purchasing manager at LTV. Byrd had hired Wallace immediately after he had been convicted in Austin, Texas of first degree murder and given a five-year suspended sentence for killing John Kinser, who was Lyndon Johnson's sister's boyfriend.

Speaker of the House Sam Rayburn and Lyndon Johnson were close friends of D.H. Byrd. One of Byrd's employees at LTV was Mac Wallace, whose fingerprint was found on a box on the sixth floor of the School Book Depository, by an FBI agent shortly after the assassination of President Kennedy. We can now document that Mac Wallace was one of the shooters when Kennedy was assassinated.

In a short summary, Byrd was a close friend of Lyndon Johnson, Byrd owned the School Book Depository, Byrd had the assassin Mac Wallace on his payroll at LTV, and D.H. Byrd was out of town on a two-month long safari in Africa when President Kennedy was assassinated.

D.H. Byrd started out in the oil business by drilling 56 dry holes before hitting oil in a big way. When the millions started rolling in he became a major business investor, and when you become filthy rich like Byrd, men with influence come to you like a magnet.

Byrd was a member of the Dallas Petroleum Club where he met and made friends with George DeMohrenschildt, David Atlee Phillips, and George H.W. Bush. The main topic of conversation in the early 1960s at the Petroleum Club, was President Kennedy's wanting to do away with the oil depletion allowance (oil men did not have to pay tax on the first 27% of their oil income).

The most active members in the oil depletion allowance conversations were Clint Murchison Sr., H.L. Hunt and Sid Richardson. It was not until years later that I figured out why my employer and the man whom I worked directly under, oil Billionaire Frank Late, had some negative words to say about a couple of his rich oil men friends.

Frank Late, my boss, never missed a Petroleum Club meeting; it was a place where he could light up a cigar, have a drink and talk about old times in the oil field. I do not want to infer that my boss, Frank Late had anything to do with the likes of Clint Murchison and his bunch, Frank Late was as straight and honest as any man alive, and I would have trusted him with my life. Not only was he my employer, he was my friend.

Frank knew I was an eyewitness to the Kennedy assassination, but whatever tidbit of Kennedy conversation he might have picked up at the Petroleum Club he never told me.

David Harold Byrd was born on April 24, 1900 and presents a serious challenge to Kennedy Assassination researchers. I think D.H. Byrd went to his grave with many secrets.

Once Byrd finally hit oil in a big way, there are many interesting facts about D.H. Byrd and his connections. Byrd bought Texas School Book Depository building in the 1930s as an investment.

Byrd was one of the founders of the LTV Corporation, which became one of the biggest government contractors in the nation, thanks to President Lyndon Johnson and a cost plus 10% "buddy" deal during the Viet Nam war.

D.H. Byrd's close friends included Lyndon Johnson, House Speaker Sam Rayburn and Governor John Connally. Byrd had hired convicted murderer Mac Wallace almost straight from the courtroom and a trial in which Wallace was found guilty of first degree murder and given an unheard of 5 year suspended sentence for first degree murder for killing Lyndon Johnson's sister's boyfriend. I would guess that Byrd's hiring of Mac Wallace to work at LTV was at the urging of Byrd's close friend Lyndon Johnson.

Mac Wallace was given a major position in purchasing at LTV, and was able to come and go as he pleased. Mac Wallace was a felon, but somehow he received a "Top Secret" U.S. Government security clearance. The file on how Wallace attained this security clearance was marked secret. Wallace's fingerprint was found on one of the boxes on the sixth floor and Wallace fit the description of a man seen on the sixth floor and leaving the building soon after the assassination of President Kennedy.

CHAPTER NINETY-SIX

CLIFF CARTER

Clifton C. Carter was managing a small 7-Up bottling company in 1937 when he volunteered to help Lyndon Johnson in Johnson's bid for a U.S. House of Representative seat in 1937.

By 1948 Cliff Carter was running Johnson's campaign for the Senate. Johnson stole the 1948 Texas U.S. Senate election, Johnson and Cliff Carter had hit it off, and Cliff Carter was to become a lifetime Johnson flunky.

It is important to note that during World War II, Cliff Carter served under Captain Edward Clark. After the war Edward Clark was to become one of the most powerful attorneys in the nation and became Lyndon Johnson's attorney.

As a reward for helping Johnson steal the 1948 Senate election, Carter was appointed to be a Federal Marshall in July 1949 only six months after Johnson was sworn in as a U.S. Senator. When Cliff Carter was appointed a U.S. Marshall, he had no law enforcement experience, but kept the title for five years until 1954.

Cliff Carter also ran Johnson's re-election campaign in 1954 and by 1957 Carter was heading up the Democratic Party in Texas. Cliff Carter was now firmly a part of Lyndon's inner circle and was soon known by members of the Democratic Party as Senator Johnson's bagman because of his ability to collect cash from the Washington lobbyist's.

Senator Lyndon Johnson's corrupt Texas "friends" besides Carter included his Austin, Texas attorney Edward Clark, and Malcolm Wallace who had killed John Kinser and was Lyndon Johnson's hit man.

When federal agriculture agent Henry Marshall became a major problem because of his investigation into Billie Sol Estes' cotton growing scheme and then Marshall turned down a promotion to Washington D.C. to get Marshall out of Texas and off of Billie Sol's back, a meeting was held on January 17, 1961 with Senator Johnson, Billie Sol Estes, Cliff Carter, and Mac Wallace in attendance.

The meeting ended with Senator Johnson ordering Mac Wallace to get rid of Henry Marshall. When Billie Sol Estes' cotton growing problems became a major problem after Senator Johnson became Vice President, Cliff Carter became the go-between for orders from VP Johnson to Mac Wallace.

Billie Sol Estes and three of his employees were indicted in April 1962 in Robertson County, Texas; Cliff Carter was given orders to relay to Mac Wallace to get rid of Billie Sol's indicted employees. Three of Estes's employees separately committed "suicide" by carbon dioxide poisoning in their automobiles.

Billie Sol Estes personally told me that the deaths of his employees had scared the hell out of him, and that keeping his mouth shut and his recordings of telephone conversations is what had kept him alive. Billie Sol had feared that Lyndon Johnson would give orders to get him out of the way

At this time, 1962, the planning to assassinate President Kennedy was well underway, with VP Johnson's attorney in the middle of the planning. It can be safely assumed that Clifton C. Carter was also right into the middle of plans to assassinate Kennedy.

Upon John F. Kennedy's assassination, Lyndon Johnson was immediately sworn in as President of the United States. Part of Cliff Carter's reward by President Johnson was to be named national Executive Director of the Democratic Party. This appointment by President Johnson was short-lived; Cliff Carter was forced to resign as Executive Director of the Democratic Party in 1966 due to illegal fund raising methods.

When Billie Sol Estes kept his mouth shut, served a prison sentence to protect Lyndon Johnson, Johnson had died, Mac Wallace had died in a car accident, and Billie Sol was given immunity to testify about Mac Wallace's killings. Billie Sol knew of eight murders that Wallace had committed for Lyndon Johnson, which included Johnson's own sister Josefa and John Kennedy. Later, Billie Sol, after his Robertson County Grand Jury testimony and in a conversation with his old acquaintance Cliff Carter and the two talking about old times, Cliff Carter told Billie Sol Estes that Malcolm Wallace had killed a total of 17 people for Lyndon Johnson that he knew of. Clifton C. Carter died September 22, 1971 and took many secrets with him.

LBJ and crew waiting for Jacqueline Kennedy to board aircraft for flight to D.C.

Cliff Carter

CHAPTER NINETY-SEVEN

MALCOLM E. WALLACE - ASSASSIN

Madeleine Brown (Lyndon Johnson's mistress for 21 years) was the first to tell me about Mac Wallace. That was in 1988, and I did not take Madeleine serious at that time. Then fourteen years later in a conversation with Billie Sol Estes (one of Lyndon Johnson's closest friends), Billie Sol told me the same thing about Mac Wallace.

A year later in 2003, Barr McClellan's book *Blood Money & Power* came out. Barr had worked for the Edward Clark law firm in Austin, Texas, (Lyndon Johnson's old law firm). Barr McClellan had worked at the Edward Clark law firm from 1966 to 1971, and was at times representing some of Lyndon Johnson's personal interests.

What is important to know is that Barr at times worked side by side with some of the firm's older attorneys who were there in the Lyndon Johnson Senate and Vice President era. Barr heard old Lyndon Johnson stories from the firm's older lawyers over coffee and while working cases together. You can call it office gossip, but the stories were about what Madeleine Brown and Billie Sol Estes had told me: Mac Wallace.

Unbeknownst to me, when I bought my east Texas country place in 2005, my property was less than a mile from where Mac Wallace hit a bridge abutment and died on the way to the hospital on January 7, 1971 at 7:30 in the evening. Finding out that Mac Wallace had been killed down the road from my country place was intriguing. His name had popped up, off and on over the years, and now I had been told by three insiders, who named Malcolm Wallace as the real assassin of President John F. Kennedy.

The Warren Commission dismissed the testimony of Arnold Rowland who saw two men on the sixth floor just before the shots were fired. The Warren Commission did not call Carolyn Walthers or Richard R. Carr to testify; both had seen two white men on the sixth floor just before the assassination.

Richard R. Carr reported to police and other officials that he had seen a heavy-set man wearing horn rimmed glasses and a tan coat standing in one of the sixth floor windows of the Texas School Book Depository a minute before the assassination, a few minutes later Carr saw this same man walking away from the Depository. Carolyn Walthers also saw a man in a brown coat standing next to another man with a rifle. She was not sure on which upper floor she saw the two men with a rifle. James Worrell Jr. saw a man in a suit tear out the rear door shortly after the shooting.

For several years there was an unidentified fingerprint (Warren Commission print 29) on a box that was on the sixth floor near the sniper's nest on November 22, 1963. Barr McClellan became suspicious of a Johnson-Clark connection named Malcolm Wallace.

In early 1998, using a fingerprint card from Malcolm Wallace's Austin murder trial and the Warren Commission's print # 29, a Nathan Darby was contacted to review the prints. Mr. Darby had over 30 years experience, and was the director of the Austin Texas Police Department identification unit, was certified by the International Association for Identification, had testified in court on many occasions, and never had a case reversed. He was well recognized as being an expert on fingerprint identification.

Mr. Darby was not made aware of who or why he was comparing the prints. Mr. Darby concluded the prints were a match. After Mr. Darby matched the prints he was told of the importance of his findings and the connection of the prints to the assassination of President Kennedy. An affidavit of Mr. Darby's findings was drawn up and sent to the Dallas Police Department, the FBI, and The Assassination Records Review Board.

After 18 months, the FBI voiced the opinion that the prints were not a match. In a filmed interview I have in my possession, Nathan Darby was totally shocked that the FBI waited 18 months, and then stated there was no match between Wallace's murder trial fingerprint and the unidentified print found on a cardboard box on the sixth floor near the sniper's nest.

Mr. Darby stated that there was absolutely no doubt that a 34-point fingerprint match was a lay-down match. Darby was disturbed and could not understand why the FBI had verbally stated the Wallace murder trial print and the longstanding unidentified print found on the sixth floor were no match, when it was a positive match and there was no question about it being a match.

Malcolm E. "Mac" Wallace was the son of a farmer and was born in Mt. Pleasant, Texas in October 1921. Four years after his birth the family moved to Dallas. In 1939 Mac joined the Marines and a year later Mac had a bad fall from a ladder, injured his back and was medically discharged.

In 1941 he entered the University of Texas in Austin, Texas and soon took an interest in politics. He was active in the American Socialist Party and led a protest against the firing of the President of the University of Texas, who was also active in the American Socialist Party; the protest failed.

Mac was elected President of the Student Union in 1944. Mac Wallace graduated in 1947 and a month later married Mary DuBose Barton, a well-to-do preacher's daughter. While working on his Doctorate Degree, Mac taught at Columbia University, Long Island University, Texas University, and University of North Carolina.

While teaching at the University of Texas, Wallace was introduced to Senator Lyndon Johnson by Johnson's lawyer, Edward Clark. In October 1950 Malcolm Wallace was working for the United States Department of Agriculture in Texas, due to the efforts of Lyndon Johnson. Mac Wallace soon met Senator Lyndon Johnson's sister, Josefa Johnson, and began having an affair with her. Josefa was also sleeping with John Kinser who managed a miniature golf course in Austin.

John Kinser and Josefa Johnson wanted to start a business together and Josefa asked her brother, Lyndon for a loan. Senator Johnson turned Josefa down and thought that was the end of it. But Josefa persisted with her request for a loan and said something that scared Lyndon into thinking his sister and her boyfriend could cause him a scandal over his stealing the 1948 U.S. Senate election.

With great concern, Senator Johnson consulted with Edward Clark, his confidant and lawyer, about Josefa's on-going loan requests. Johnson and his lawyer Clark had been living with the fear of a public scandal over the 1948 election since the contest. Senator Lyndon Johnson had shamelessly stolen the Senate election in 1948 and his sister Josefa was aware of the details of the fraudulent results.

Josefa Johnson was known to drink too much, slept around, and had loose lips. It was feared by Johnson and Clark that Josefa had told Kinser too much of her brother Lyndon Johnson's illegal activities and the stealing of the 1948 election.

Senator Johnson and Edward Clark decided that Josefa's request for a loan was a blackmail attempt. A scandal over the 1948 election results was something they could not afford to become public. Lyndon Johnson's ego was such that he had plans to be President someday and Edward Clark was going to help him.

Lyndon Johnson and Edward Clark plotted a scheme to enrage Malcolm Wallace about John Kinser being in a threesome with Malcolm's wife (she had stayed in Austin while Mac went to Washington) and Josefa Johnson. Johnson and Clark promised Wallace legal protection if he did something about Kinser.

On October 22, 1951, Wallace went to John Kinser's miniature golf course office in Austin, Texas and shot Kinser several times, killing him. A customer on the miniature golf course heard the shooting, saw Wallace walk out of the office and took down Wallace's Virginia license plate number on his station wagon. The Austin Texas Police Department within minutes arrested Wallace and he was charged with first-degree murder.

In 1950 first-degree murder in Texas often meant death in the electric chair. Bond was at first set at $30,000 and then reduced to $10,000 on this potential death penalty case. Two of Senator Johnson's supporters, M. E. Ruby and Bill Carroll posted bond for Wallace and he was released on bail. One of Senator Johnson's attorneys, John Cofer, agreed to defend Wallace.

On February 1, 1952 Mac Wallace resigned from his U. S. Department of Agriculture job to distance himself from LBJ. His trial started February 18, 1952, Wallace did not testify. His lawyer, John Cofer, admitted Wallace's guilt but claimed it was revenge for Kinser sleeping with Mac's wife. Senator Johnson stayed in a hotel nearby during the ten-day trial and had a runner going back and forth to the trial to keep Lyndon posted.

The jury found Malcolm Wallace guilty of premeditated murder with malice. Eleven jurors wanted the death penalty and one argued for life in prison.

The Judge, Charles O. Betts, overruled the jury and pronounced a sentence of five years imprisonment, suspended, and Malcolm Wallace walked out of the courtroom a free man. Some jurist's claimed there had been threats made against their families.

A conviction for first-degree murder normally meant the death penalty in Texas at that time. Lyndon Johnson's attorney Edward Clark, who owned the powerful Edward Clark law firm in Austin, Texas, contacted Johnson's friend D.H. Byrd, who had co-founded LTV, they met and arrangements were made for Mac Wallace to go to work at what would become Ling-TempcoVought (LTV), a major U.S. military contractor.

LTV was a conglomerate partially owned by rich oilmen besides co-founder D.H. Byrd who were also clients of Edward Clark. What one must remember is that Malcolm Wallace, now a convicted murderer, had been a teacher/professor at Columbia University while working on his Doctorate Degree. Mac Wallace was not a dummy, he was smart and he was sharp, and he soon was named head of purchasing for LTV, one of the United States Government's largest contractors.

The murder of John Kinser was the first and only murder Mac Wallace was ever arrested for. There were at least four individuals involved in or with knowledge of the next eight murders committed by Mac Wallace. They were Lyndon B. Johnson, Cliff Carter, Billie Sol Estes, and Mac Wallace.

Johnson would suggest to Cliff Carter that something should be done with so and so and Cliff Carter would tell Malcolm Wallace to get rid of so and so. Billie Sol had a deep personal friendship with Lyndon Johnson and had obligations to Johnson for helping Billie Sol become a multi-millionaire. Billie Sol Estes was a loyal friend, kept his mouth shut and went to prison twice to keep Lyndon from being indicted for fraud.

One was an indictment of Billie Sol Estes in 1963, which would have ended Johnson's political career, and probably would have happened as soon as Vice President Lyndon Johnson returned to Washington D. C. with President Kennedy after their Texas trip in November 1963.

When Billie Sol Estes first got out of prison in January 1971, he and Cliff Carter reminisced about what had occurred in the past. Malcolm Wallace had just died on the way to the hospital after an automobile accident (less than a mile from my East Texas property) on what is now the old Gilmer Highway, three and a half miles south of Pittsburg, Texas, on January 7, 1971.

Billie Sol knew of nine murders by Mac Wallace. Texas Ranger Clint Peoples arranged for Billie Sol Estes to have immunity, if he would testify about what he knew about Mac Wallace. Billie Sol did testify, as promised, to the Grand Jury in Robertson County, Texas about the nine murders Billie Sol knew of that Mac Wallace had committed for Lyndon Johnson, (the nine murders, including President Kennedy, are listed in the Billie Sol Estes chapter). Lyndon Johnson and Malcolm Wallace were dead, and there was no one to indict.

Billie Sol Estes told me that Cliff Carter bragged to him, that Carter knew the details of seventeen total murders that Mac Wallace had committed for Lyndon Johnson, many of those murders Estes was unfamiliar with.

It is evident to me from what Estes said, that Wallace had bragged about the details of the murders he had committed for Lyndon Johnson. A witness, Kyle Brown of Brady Texas, was also present during this conversation between Billie Sol Estes and Cliff Carter.

In 1970 Mac Wallace had moved to back to Mt. Pleasant, Texas and was working for Harry Lewis and L & G Oil Co. He was pressing Edward Clark for more money. It was decided Wallace needed to be eliminated. After driving to see his daughter in Troup, Texas he stopped at the L & G Oil Company office in Longview, Texas.

While in the office of L & G Oil, his car was rigged so that the exhaust would flow back into the car. While driving back from Longview to Mt. Pleasant he passed out and hit a bridge abutment three and a half miles south of Pittsburg, Texas on what is now called the old Gilmer Highway.

Unknown to me at the time in 2005, I bought property about a mile from where Mac Wallace died. As you approach the bridge Wallace hit, there is a steep embankment on the right as you approach the bridge.

I went to the Pittsburg library archives and looked up what the Pittsburg paper said about the accident. There was a short article with his name and not much else except a picture of the car. The picture of the car shows that the car was sideways when it hit the bridge and caved in the passenger side of the car.

I located the graveyard where Wallace is buried; it is near a small town in North East Texas. Malcolm "Mac" Wallace, the assassin of President John F. Kennedy, is buried in a quaint, church graveyard with well-kept grounds.

His grave marker notes that he had been a United States Marine and there is an American flag. I have left out the location of the graveyard on purpose; the quaint well-kept church graveyard does not need curiosity seekers tromping upon its grounds. Below is a picture I took of Mac Wallace's grave marker.

CHAPTER NINETY-EIGHT

JOSEFA JOHNSON, LBJ'S SISTER

Josefa Johnson was Mac Wallace's second known murder. Josefa was also Lyndon Johnson's sister and her killing was done on Johnson's orders. Josefa's alcoholism, life style and loose lips had become a serious liability for Johnson's political ambitions. Josefa knew too many of her brother Lyndon's secrets.

Josefa was born in 1912. She had been married three times and divorced in an era when divorces were frowned on. Josefa had a legitimate daughter, Beverly White, and an illegitimate son, Rodney, in 1948.

Josefa's alcoholism took a toll on her health and she was hospitalized several times for health reasons. Josefa was found dead in her bed Christmas morning 1961, and despite state law, there was no autopsy performed to determine cause of death. Her brother Lyndon had the J.P. simply put "died of a cerebral

The Johnson children in 1921: (l-r) Lucia, Josefa, Rebekah, Lyndon, and Sam.

hemorrhage" on her death certificate, and had her buried the next day.

Josefa was a wild child and it was rumored that she worked as a prostitute on occasion at Miss Hattie's place. Miss Hattie had whorehouses in Austin and Cuero, Texas. Cuero was not far from Victoria, Texas. It is said that Josefa worked at the Cuero place because the Miss Hattie's place in Austin was frequented by Texas legislators and many of these Texas lawmakers knew her brother Lyndon.

Josefa had worked hard in her brother Lyndon's 1948 run for the Senate. She knew all the details of the ugly truth on how Lyndon had stolen that election. Her drinking and loose lips were a constant embarrassment to Johnson and when she and her boyfriend, John

(l-r) LBJ's sister Josefa, his mother Rebekah, Lyndon and his wife, Lady Bird.

Kinser, tried to borrow money from Lyndon in 1951, Lyndon interpreted it to be an attempt at bribery and had Kinser killed. This shook up Josefa and caused her to be more careful for a while. In 1961 Lyndon Johnson was Vice President with plans to be president and Josefa had become a thorn in his side. It was not until 23 years later that we finally found out what really happened to Josefa.

Josefa

Josefa Johnson died on December 25, 1961 at 3:15 A.M. in the morning after retuning home from a Christmas party at the Vice President's ranch. There was no doctor present, the death certificate was signed by a doctor who was not there. There was no autopsy, no inquest, no examination, and she was embalmed that same day, Christmas day 1961, and buried the next day, December 26,1961.

Josefa Johnson, the Vice President of the United States' sister died, was embalmed and buried in less than 36 hours. A continuing embarrassment for Lyndon Johnson was now gone, out of the way, just another murder for Mac Wallace.

In 1984, Billy Sol Estes, who had been given immunity, was sworn in by a Grand Jury in Robertson County Texas. In that Grand Jury hearing Billy Sol told about Cliff Carter and Mac Wallace bragging about how Wallace had killed Josefa Johnson on orders from her brother, Vice President of the United States, Lyndon Johnson.

CHAPTER NINETY-NINE

HENRY MARSHALL

In the nearly 50 years since the Kennedy assassination, the death of Henry Marshall while Lyndon Johnson was Vice President has hardly ever been mentioned nor has it been connected to President Kennedy's assassination. But the fact is that Henry Marshall's death was one of the factors in President Kennedy's assassination.

Henry Marshall was found dead on June 3, 1961 on his farm in Robertson County Texas, Henry had taken his own bolt action rifle and shot himself in the side five times. It was ruled a suicide by County Sheriff Howard Stegall.

No pictures were taken of the scene, no blood samples were taken of the blood stains on his pickup truck, no fingerprints were taken from the rifle or the pickup and a new dent on the truck went unexplained.

The Sheriff had the pickup washed, Henry was buried, and the case was closed. Henry Marshall's family was devastated – you cannot point a rifle at your side, pull the trigger with your thumb, take the rifle down and use the bolt action to put another bullet in the chamber, point the rifle at your side and pull the trigger again with your thumb and repeat for a total of five shots.

The undertaker Manley Jones told the family it looked like murder, but on orders from the Sheriff, the death was listed as suicide due to self-inflicted wounds. The family offered a reward for information leading to a conviction of murder for Henry Marshall's death. For more on Henry Marshall's death read the chapter on Billie Sol Estes.

What was an important side fact in Henry Marshall's murder was that Texas Ranger Clint Peoples did not believe it was a suicide either, that Henry Marshall's death was murder. Texas Ranger Peoples did a little looking around and by chance interviewed Nolan Griffin, a service station attendant who worked near Marshall's farm.

On the day of Marshall's death, Griffin told Ranger Peoples that he had been asked by a stranger for directions to the Marshall farm. Texas Ranger Peoples had a Texas Ranger's artist draw a facial sketch of the stranger who asked directions to the Marshall farm, based on directions given by Griffin.

It took no time for Ranger Peoples to conclude that the drawing was a match for Mac Wallace, who had been convicted of killing John Kinser.

What is important to know is that the Vice President of the United States, a man named Lyndon Johnson ordered Clifton C. (Cliff) Carter, the Executive Director of the Democratic National Committee, to tell Mac Wallace to get rid of (kill) Federal Agriculture agent Henry Marshall.

Federal Agriculture agent Henry Marshall had been investigating Billie Sol Estes's cotton allotment scheme. What was raising questions for Marshall was that Estes was using leased acreage from over 100 farmers to claim payments from the government to not raise cotton, a government program that Lyndon Johnson had tipped off Billie Sol to when Johnson was a Senator. When this came to the attention of Billie Sol Estes, Billie Sol had his lawyer, John P. Dennison, meet with Henry Marshall on the 17th of January, 1961. The meeting did not go in Estes' favor. Estes' friend V.P. Lyndon Johnson was notified of the problem with Henry Marshall and the Vice President decided the best way to handle the problem was to give Henry Marshall a promotion to Washington D.C. at twice his salary and get Marshall out of Texas and Billie Sol Estes' hair. Henry Marshall did not accept the bribe and assumed Billie Sol had friends in high places in Washington.

A meeting was soon held with Billie Sol, Cliff Carter, and Vice President Lyndon Johnson. The result of the meeting was that Lyndon Johnson told Cliff Carter to tell Mac Wallace to get rid of Henry Marshall. Henry Marshall was found dead on June 3, 1961.

This was just the start of more killings and the downfall of Billie Sol Estes and his kickbacks to Lyndon Johnson. Billie was arrested in the spring of 1962, his chief accountant, George Krutilek, was found dead with a severe bruise on his head. It was ruled a suicide. Others died, Harold Orr, Coleman Wade, Howard Pratt, all committing "suicide" from carbon monoxide and the hush-hush scandal went deep into the U.S. Department of Agriculture. John Kennedy became aware of what was going on and was making plans to quietly drop Lyndon Johnson from his 1964 ticket. Billie Sol Estes told me face to face he had kicked back as much as $200,000 to Lyndon Johnson more than once. Billie Sol also told me he had to keep his mouth shut and go to prison or Lyndon Johnson would have had Mac Wallace kill him too. In November 1963 when Lyndon Johnson was in Texas with President Kennedy, Johnson was under investigation in Washington for his dealings with Bobby Baker and Billie Sol Estes. When Vice President Johnson returned to Washington D.C. he was probably facing indictment for these dealings.

LAWRENCE LOY FACTOR

It is fair to state that in all probability, Lawrence Loy Factor was the dark-skinned person seen on the sixth floor of the Texas School Book Depository by witnesses who were standing on the sidewalk in front of the Depository moments before the assassination of President John F. Kennedy.

Factor was a full-blooded Oklahoma Indian with a reputation of being an expert marksman with a rifle. All the evidence indicates that it is probable that Factor was the one shooting from the far west window of the sixth floor of the School Book Depository and it was Factor's shot that hit Governor Connally in the back near the Governors right armpit. The angles line up for this west window shot to be the shot that hit John Connally.

Lawrence Loy Factor

When Factor was finally located years later in a hospital bed and interviewed, Factor admitted he was on the sixth floor that day, but denied he pulled the trigger. He claimed he was just a back-up gunman.

Factor, a soft-spoken Chickasaw Indian from Oklahoma, had secrets, and he silently carried those secrets about the Kennedy assassination for 30 years. Factor had nothing to gain when he first told the story, he was not looking for money, he was isolated in the hospital with hepatitis, and he was a diabetic, an amputee with a wooden leg.

Factor had been bitten on the leg by a copperhead snake and when the bite never healed, he had to have his leg amputated. He may have been wrongly convicted of manslaughter of his wife Juanita; the jury had been dismissed at the first trial when they deadlocked six to six. A second trial brought the conviction.

Lawrence Loy Factor was a WW II veteran. He had a plate in his head as the result of shrapnel during the war and received disability compensation from the VA of $76.75 a month. The VA had said he must have a guardian to manage his finances. Factor was an outdoorsman, and had a reputation of being an expert marksman with a rifle.

There was one other man in hospital isolation with Factor, a young man named Mark Collom. They spent those days talking about their lives, with nothing to gain but overcoming the boredom of the endless days of hospital isolation.

Factor's story started in Bonham, Texas, the home of famed U.S. House of Representative speaker, Sam Rayburn. It was November 1961, Sam Rayburn 79, had recently died at Baylor hospital in Dallas, it was the day of his funeral and every living president was in Bonham for the funeral including President Kennedy.

Factor's wife Juanita suggested they drive down to Bonham (11 miles south of the Texas-Oklahoma line) to see if they could catch a glimpse of President Kennedy. Factor agreed to make the drive to Bonham and thought it would be a nice adventure for their children.

The funeral was a big event for the small town of Bonham Texas. I remember my father-in-law, John Hedgcoxe who was there, talking about the hundreds of people from all over north Texas who had come to Bonham to catch a glimpse of one of the former Presidents or especially Texan Vice President Lyndon Johnson or President Kennedy.

While waiting in the crowd for President Kennedy to arrive, Juanita and the kids wandered off and Factor started talking to a man who had mistaken Factor's dark skin for him being a Hispanic. The conversation led to firearms and Factor spoke of his knowledge and his marksmanship.

The stranger asked Factor many questions about his shooting abilities, wrote down Factor's rural Oklahoma address and suggested he might have a job for Factor in the future.

When Juanita returned with the children, the stranger gave Factor a $20.00 bill and told him to buy something for the children. It turned out to be a great day for the "dirt poor" Factor family; they had witnessed a famous man's funeral procession, seen President Kennedy, and a stranger had given them a $20.00 bill, an amount that was more than Factor could earn in a days work.

A little over a year later this stranger showed up at Factor's country home. The stranger was interested in Factor's shooting ability and Factor was happy to demonstrate with his 30-30 deer rifle. They walked to a clearing nearby and Factor gave a demonstration of his marksmanship with the stranger moving the target further and further away.

The stranger turned out to be Malcolm "Mac" Wallace, a friend of Lyndon Johnson. Mac was very impressed with Loy Factor's flawless accuracy with a rifle. The Indian was tickled to death that Wallace was pleased with his shooting ability.

Wallace told Factor he could make a lot of money if he was working for the right people, nothing specific was said about what kind of work, but Mac offered Factor $10,000, with $2,000 that day and the balance when the job was done. To this dirt poor Indian, it was like being offered a million dollars and he accepted the $2,000 thinking he would just wait for the specifics.

Factor was told that he must be ready to leave on short notice and it might be as long as a year before he was needed.

Loy Factor's demeanor can best be described as naïve, unsophisticated, simple minded and childlike. For the reader, let me stop here for a moment – this story that was told to Mark Collom by Factor.

Collom was told while in an isolation ward of the hospital in McAlester, Oklahoma. There has been little publicity on this story, and I have taken most of my information from my autographed copy of the book by Glen Sample and Mark Collom, *The Men On The Sixth Floor*. This book, in used condition, reached a price of $999.00 on Amazon at one time.

It is interesting to know that an investigative team was formed years later when Collom told Glen Sample about Factor and what Factor had told Mark years earlier. The team that was formed to investigate Factor's story included some of the best and most trusted researchers on the Kennedy assassination. This research team took three years to research the book.

It was not until 1993 that a serious investigation was begun into Loy Factor's story. Was he still alive? Factor was found alive in a hospital. He began to describe things that only someone who was there could describe. For instance, Factor was able to describe their escape down the stairs and out the back door of the School Book Depository to a tee, the stairs, the dock, etc. Factor said he was positioned at the far west window of the sixth floor of the School Book Depository.

One thing in the book that I do question is that Factor said two of the men he was introduced to in Dallas while waiting overnight were Jack Ruby and Lee Harvey Oswald. Common sense tells me that people planning to be involved in assassinating a President do not go around shaking hands and introducing themselves by name. I feel that he learned of those names later from news sources.

The main researchers cited in the book besides the authors were Larry Howard, R.B. Cutler and Robert Johnson. The book also mentions assistance from a host of others. This chapter I have written is dedicated to present and future historians to digest, take apart, and put back together. There is too much good evidence to not believe Loy Factor.

Back to the Story

Before Mac Wallace's car disappeared down the road, with Factor standing there clutching the $2,000, the Indian knew he had made a serious mistake. Mark interrupted Loy and asked, "He wanted you to kill somebody, didn't he Loy."

"Yeah, so he did. But they never told me until it was too late. I was stupid to go along with them, I got in too deep."

"Who was it Loy, who did he want you to kill?" As the Indian responded, Mark was so shocked his voice caught as he tried to speak.

"I never did it though, I mean, I was there, but I never did pull the trigger."

The two men looked around their hospital room and then at each other. Their voices had dropped to a near whisper.

CHAPTER ONE HUNDRED ONE

WHY JOHN F. KENNEDY?

President John F. Kennedy and his wife Jackie were loved by the public. With a year to go before the next presidential election in 1964, John Kennedy was a shoo-in to be re-elected as President of the United States.

What the public did not know was that John Kennedy was hated and despised in the Capital. John Kennedy had made too many changes too quick and upset the old guard. As an example, Kennedy had even upset the Secret Service who were there to protect the President.

Contrary to their public image the Secret Service had no respect for Kennedy.

John Kennedy, while campaigning for President in Illinois in 1960 met a brand new Secret Service agent guarding the restroom in the basement of the building where Kennedy had been speaking.

It was a terrible image, a United States Secret Service Agent guarding a toilet. This new Secret Service Agent's name was Abraham Bolden, who had been an officer in the Illinois State Police before the Secret Service. Kennedy liked him and when Kennedy became President he asked that Abraham Bolden be assigned to the White house.

Abraham Bolden was a black man, and from that point on, and behind closed doors, President Kennedy was referred to as a "nigger lover." Later, Mr. Bolden was reassigned to the Chicago Secret Service office and a few days before Kennedy was assassinated in Dallas, warnings started coming into the Chicago Secret Service Office about an attempt on President Kennedy's life.

When Abraham Bolden tried to tell the Warren Commission about these warnings, Bolden was framed, tried, found guilty and sent to prison for five years. The full story is in Abraham Bolden's book *The Echo From Dealey Plaza*. If you read Abraham's book you will find out how corrupt our government can get.

While I am at it, Secret Service personnel spoke of having a soft drink at the "The Cellar" in Fort Worth the night before Kennedy was killed in Dallas.

In my younger days I have been to The Cellar at 3 A.M., and it is not a tea room, The Cellar did not know what a soft drink was, but you could buy any alcoholic drink you wanted at 3 A.M. – it was a wide open joint. Members of the Fort Worth Fire Department stood guard over the President's Fort Worth hotel room the night before the President was assassinated, while the Secret Service partied at "The Cellar."

But then there was quite a group of folks who hated Kennedy and wanted him out of office.

Fidel Castro did not care for Kennedy. Kennedy had tried to arrange for the CIA and the Mafia to kill Castro.

The Anti-Castro Cubans had no love for Kennedy over the bungled Bay of Pigs episode. We had a cold war going on with Russia.

The CIA had become a gang of out-of-control thugs and assassins, Kennedy had on his desk; the day he was killed, paperwork to send to Congress to strip the CIA of their power.

Kennedy had done away with the Federal Reserve Bank in the summer of 1963 and that had really teed off some very heavy-duty big money.

Kennedy was going to get our advisors out of Viet Nam, that did not sit well with the military-industrial war-machine that was preparing to crank up production on war material and profits.

Kennedy was going to do away with the Oil Depletion Allowance that would cost the oil industry billions of dollars.

The Kennedy's were cracking down on the Mafia, something that had not happened before; the mob wanted Kennedy out of office or dead.

The Director of the FBI, J. Edgar Hoover, knew what was coming down and kept his mouth shut; Hoover wanted Kennedy dead, Hoover was over mandatory government retirement age and the Kennedy's were going to force Hoover to retire.

Kennedy's Vice President Lyndon Johnson hated the Kennedy's and wanted to be President so bad that he would do anything, even kill for it.

SUMMARY

O nce you understand that Lyndon Johnson and his cronies were behind the assassination of John F. Kennedy and that J. Edgar Hoover was in charge of the cover-up, the questions you have had start being answered.

The Warren Commission did not stand a chance of presenting the truth. The seven men appointed by President Johnson contributed little to finding the truth, Commission staff lawyer Wesley Liebeler probably said it best, and that was: "The seven men we know as the Warren Commission were a joke."

The staff lawyers complained that the commissioners were absent most of the time, and when a staff lawyer was taking a deposition from a witness they would, "step in for a few moments, ask a question and leave." This would blow the staff lawyer's line of questioning.

The Warren Commission had fourteen staff lawyers – to start with – hired to do the majority of witness questioning and take statements/depositions from the witnesses. When one of these staff lawyers ran into something that needed further investigation, they would go to J. Lee Rankin, their chief Counsel. Rankin would routinely turn down their request with the statement: "We are here to close doors not open new ones."

It is evident that when one of the staff lawyers stumbled onto the truth of who was behind the assassination and who was controlling the investigation, they would quit the Warren Commission. and when they quit the Commission, they were warned that whatever they had learned while serving for the Commission was considered to be lawyer-client information and could not be discussed with anyone, or they could face disbarment.

The fact that several of the Commission lawyers had quit the Commission was not made public; the lawyers that quit were still listed as staff lawyers in the Warren Report. Through the years if someone discovered something important that differed from the Warren Commission findings, not only would that person's discovery be attacked as false, but he would be attacked personally, as well. The late New Orleans District Attorney, Jim Garrison, was a good example of these attacks.

A problem is that there have been so many outlandish theories put forth in the over 2,000 books written in the last 50 years. Those thousands of books could probably be reduced to 25 reliable books. The misleading conspiracy books have been a big contributor to the personal attacks, though some are well deserved for the misinformation they contain.

That leaves the 25 or so good honest books, and yet some of these honest books also get attacked. To understand why a well-documented book can be attacked, say a book that names two of our country's most honored men as being part of a murder plot, one has to assume that some of the attackers had good intentions: They simply want our country's dirt swept under the rug.

To accept the fact that the President of the United States and the man who headed our FBI for 50 years were involved in a plot to kill another President puts our country in the same category as a "Banana Republic." But it has now been 50 years and it is time for the truth, at least what we know of it, to be told.

First, Lee Harvey Oswald was not the assassin. The story that he raced down four flights of stairs and then was seen not out-of-breath, and calmly buying a bottle of soda in the lunch room 75 seconds after the assassination was always hard to accept.

Then Barry Ernest found a School Book Depository witnesses who had been using the stairs, nullifying an assassin Oswald using the stairs. It was too simple; Oswald was actually eating his lunch in the second floor lunchroom, just like he said he was, and just like witnesses said he was.

Second, my facts come from direct conversations with Johnson insiders who have told me a consistent story over the years. And then there is that fingerprint on a box on the sixth floor.

And a "dead" United States Federal Marshall who knew the full story. Much of my references and facts come from my set of the 26-volume Warren Report that contains the peronal testimony of nearly 600 witnesses.

I also have scores of internal FBI documents that my friend Harold Weisberg sent to me after he won his Freedom of Information Act lawsuit. I have also spent hours and hours of research seeking verification of what I have been told.

That's umpteen points of verification, and then after I am through with my verification, I was handed a Russian KGB 1965 investigative report that declares Lyndon Johnson was behind the assassination of President

Kennedy. And guess what? My hours and hours of research match the Russian KGB report to a tee: Lyndon Johnson was behind the assassination of President John F. Kennedy. The public loved President Kennedy, but he appears that he stepped on some powerful toes, some big money toes, made too many changes, too quickly. President Kennedy had enemies.

The assassination of President Kennedy had to be at least two years in its planning. The heinous crime was pulled off by professionals – therehad to be many people involved. We now know that the planned assassination did have leaks, but little attention was paid to these leaks. One man even shot up a bank so he would be in jail when the killing was committed, so he would not be associated with the assassination.

The sad part is that many of the power brokers who pulled the strings with their influence on our Government, oil, banking, etc. – had no or miniaml part in the assassination, but silently cheered in their hearts and actions once President Kennedy was gone.

The public loved Jack and Jackie Kennedy, but he was making too many changes too quick to suit the big money. The hate this power and money bunch had bottled up, unknowingly helped in covering up who, and what was behind the assassination.

When someone in the power and money group stumbled onto what really happened, they simply kept silent about the truth, and used catch-phrases like: "for the good of the country," or "for the sake of the Kennedy family," so as to not seek any information beyond what the Warren Commission had officially released.

The truth has been there all the time. There have been a few good researchers and a few good authors, each in their own research being able to document a small piece of the truth. Putting the full story of the assassination together was, for me, like° working a crossword puzzle.

There are still a few pieces of the puzzle missing. They have probably been destroyed, and will never be found. When the 50th anniversary comes on November 22, 2013, I will be 77 years old and for reasons only the good Lord knows, I have been been shown information that demands I write this book. Then the public and future generations will have at least my undestanding of the Kennedy assassination.

My "public" life started by me being in Dealey Plaza *that day*, November 22, 1963. It was an accident I was even there, it was un-planned, I just happened to get stopped in traffic. Being injured during the shooting was minor, a sting on the cheek from the debris from a missed shot that had hit the street in front of me. I am proud that I spoke up six months after the assassination when it appeared the Warren Commission was about to make a total cover-up of the assassination of President Kennedy.

My Warren Commission testimony was important, it changed history. Having Harold Weisberg, the best, most dedicated and serious Kennedy assassination researcher, as my dear friend for almost 35 years was aslo very important. Harold's winning his FOIA lawsuit against the FBI and sharing the FBI documents with me was important.

Having well-meaning insiders to the assassination story step into my life unsolicited was also important. What amazes me is: I did not go looking for any of this, it all came to me and dropped into my lap. I have a thin skin, so I know I must brace myself for the dissenters and attacks once this book comes out.

There are some people, who will not accept the facts, even when it is shoved into their face. Fifty-some years ago while being interviewed on film, I was asked about my minor injury and without thinking, I motioned to my left cheek for some reason.

Actually I had been sprayed with debris on the right cheek. The point is: there are still people who want argue over which cheek I was stung on during the shooting. Then there are those that have read one, out of the many JFK assassination books, that contains one of the many theories advanced through the years, and get a mind-set that the theory presented in that book is *the* truth.

Harold Weisberg was constantly after me to write the story about the curb being altered, and I struggled to start writing about my dealings with the FBI, the Warren Commission and the tampering with the curb. My struggle was real. I tried to copy styles. That did not work.

Then Harold died, and I had promised Harold that he would be the first read the book, but now he was gone. Suddenly it happened, I started to write what I knew, it was too simple, I soon found that the truth was easy to write about, and I threw together a simple book, *Truth Withheld, Why We Will Never Know the Truth About the JFK Assassination.*

I self-published the book in 2003, and it has sold a few thousand copies and is still selling today. I took a break, the John F. Kennedy assassination had been a part of my life for over 40 years, I bought a nice place in the country, in East Texas, three miles south of Pittsburg, and I sold my home in Plano that I had owned for 30 years.

Still, after all the years that had passed, people were looking me up and coming to Texas for an interview or whatever. It seemed that I had not left the Kennedy assassination behind. Then it happened, I woke up one morning with my feet so swollen I could not put my shoes on, and I had broken out all over with what I thought was the measles.

But no, I was very sick, I had had a complete kidney failure and my body was shutting down. I was put on dialysis.

Dialysis for four hours a day, three or four days a week is not fun, the misery and pain you are surrounded with is a new way of life. I do not think I had missed a total of five days of work due to illness in my entire life. It was a constant effort to get through each four hour session without being bored to death. The health check-ups were a constant part of my life.

Once your kidney's quit on you, they are done; they are not supposed to ever work again. I was having a regular urine and blood check up on January 16, 1010 at my doctor's office and out of the blue my doctor announced "Jim, your kidneys are working again and I am taking you off dialysis."

When I recovered from the shock, he told me the odds of my recovery were over 10,000 to 1. It has now been over 3 years, I still get regular check-ups, and my doctor just shakes his head at my recovery. I am not a regular churchgoer, but I am a God-fearing man, and I do say a silent prayer for my family every so often.

I took this recovery as a signal that I am on this earth for a purpose. I did not need to guess what purpose. I knew in my heart I needed to tell the true story of the President John F. Kennedy assassination. There had been too much information dumped in my lap, and there had been too many years of the "lone nut assassin," Lee Harvey Oswald did it, end of the story.

For historians, it will not take much research to find out what a bi-polar sick man Lyndon Johnson was. I feel sorry for his daughters. I hope they do not read this book. One of his Secret Service agents probably said it best: "if he was not President, he would be locked up in a nut house."

His friend who handled the cover-up, the head of the FBI, J. Edgar Hoover, was without morals. There was also the big money and power, the men who are/were admired as pillars of society who let their power and greed sanction a murder.

They supplied the money: without asking questions to keep their lily-white hands clean. There are the known participatnts: Lyndon Johnson's attorney Edward Clark; Head of the National Democratic Party, Clifford Carter; Owner of the School Book Depository, co-founder of LTV and Malcolm Wallace's employer, David Harold Byrd; Billionaire oil man Clint Murchison Sr.; Billionaire oil man H. L. Hunt; George and Herman Root of Brown & Root, and others.

Lee Harvey Oswald was a patsy in the shooting, but may not be completely innocent of involvement. There was at least three real shooters, probably four, and maybe as many as five shooters. Two of shooters are known, Malcolm Wallace and Loy Factor; a third shooter was seen by Ed Hoffman behind the fence, and the fourth shooter could have been the third man on the sixth floor.

But the complete mechanics of the killing I will leave to others. I simply know from my direct involvement that our President was killed by very powerful people who then covered the murder up and took our country. I try here to present my story so you will understand the crime and think about what must be done.

Index